MORE SEX, BETTER ZEN, FASTER BULLETS

THE ENCYCLOPEDIA OF HONG KONG FILM

Stefan Hammond & Mike Wilkins

A Headpress Book

MORE SEX, BETTER ZEN, FASTER BULLETS

CONTENTS

	Update 2020	4
	Foreword by Jackie Chan	8
	Preface by Michelle Yeoh	9
	Thanks | In Memoriam | Dedication	11
1	**Ten That Rip**	14
2	**Dodge The Flying Witch's Head**	32
3	**Hong Kong Noir**	58
4	**Aiyah! That Had To Hurt**	76
5	**So. You think your kung fu's ... pretty good. But still. You're going to die today. Ah ha ha ha. Ah ha ha ha ha ha.**	99
6	**Bad Eggs and Naked Killers**	109
7	**Cops & Rascals**	126
8	**The Unexpected**	142
9	**Nail-Polished Fists**	155
10	**Tsui Hark**	170
11	**The Chan Canon**	184
12	**Yuen, Sammo, Yuen**	206
13	**Ringo Lam**	220
14	**The Afterburner**	232
15	**Between The Bullets: The Spiritual Cinema of John Woo**	253
16	**Creative Chaos: The Disorganized World of Wong Kar-wai**	272
17	**Hewn & Scattered**	286
18	**The Temple of Shaw**	307
	Resources	323
	Glossary	331
	Author Bios	337
	Film Review Index	340

3

MORE SEX, BETTER ZEN, FASTER BULLETS

UPDATE 2020

When *Sex and Zen & A Bullet in the Head* (*SAZ&ABITH*) was published in August 1996, it was the first English-language Hong Kong film book in a market desperate for information on these films. Paul Nerbonne of Golden Apple Books in LA said the Melrose Avenue store was selling five copies a day. The book was discussed on newsgroups, television and radio, and even the nascent Internet.

We were pleasantly surprised with the book's popularity and positive reception. Titan Books in the UK put out a separate English version with an alternate cover, and Heyne Books in Munich released a translated German version as part of the Heyne Film Bibliothek series.

There have been many moments in its 20+ years of existence that reminded the authors why they agreed to the idea in the first place. Stefan once gave a copy to Lo Mang of *Five Venoms* fame—his reaction was priceless. Mike visited the set of a Jackie Chan film and snapped a pic of Jackie holding the book.

A list of "Hex Errors" (cracked subtitles) became an email-meme, inspiring a group called Shivaree who wrote a song ("Daring Lousy Guy") using them as lyrics. A punk band in Hong Kong titled their indie album "sex and zen and a bullet in the head" and put the title on their color-Xeroxed cover.

And the fans: at conventions, book-signings, and in the lobby of the UC Theatre Berkeley, the Castro Theater in San Francisco, and Bookstar in Los Angeles. All of you were, and are, amazing.

Home video was limited to VHS tape when *SAZ&ABITH* was originally written in 1994/1995. VCDs, popular in 1996, are moribund. DVDs are still the most common optical disc format, although Blu-ray discs and streaming video are taking larger market shares.

Most importantly, subtitled Hong Kong films are no longer considered odd. The global success of Ang Lee's 2000 film *Crouching Tiger, Hidden Dragon* made subtitles and even "flying" actors acceptable on a mainstream level. For long-time fans like us, it was sweet.

Nowadays...

Hong Kong is no longer the world's third largest film industry nor is it a British colony. It's now (take a deep breath) the Hong Kong Special Administrative Region of the People's Republic of China.

Or just call it Hong Kong, or the HKSAR. The 1997 handover changed the business landscape, and an ongoing program called CEPA (the Closer Economic Partner Arrangement) ties the Hong Kong market to China's far larger economy.

But Hong Kong retained its ID card system and introduced an HKSAR passport after 1997. The former colony also kept its currency (still tightly pegged to the US dollar), border controls, and the rule of law backed by an independent judiciary.

Hong Kong hasn't become another province of the PRC. Nor are films exhibited in Hong Kong cinemas or sold on optical disc in Hong Kong shops subject to mainland China restrictions and censorship.

However, one of CEPA's phases dictated that if a film is shown on the mainland, the version shown in Hong Kong must be identical—closing a loophole that allowed films like *Infernal Affairs* (2002) to have an alternate, China-friendly ending. This means that those Hong Kong filmmakers pursuing projects without authorization from the relevant mainland authorities are far fewer than in the past. China is the world's second-largest film market now, and even Hollywood bows to Beijing's edicts.

Please note: this reboot of *SAZ&ABITH* includes copy from Stefan Hammond's "Hollywood East: Hong Kong Movies and the People Who Made Them" (published by NTC Contemporary in 2000).

Revisiting *SAZ&ABITH*

When we decided to publish it as an e-book after 20+ years, additional info was needed like a vampire-

busting sifu needs sticky rice. Of the hundreds of films we mentioned, many are now on DVD or Blu-ray with value-adds like audio commentaries, interviews, and "behind-the-scenes" footage. Regrettably, a few never transcended VHS, and are hard to find even there. The best copies of many of our favorite films are on laserdisc, and there are adherents who collect the big clunky discs and keep their disc-players in order.

We've revamped and updated the book, with plenty of material from Stefan's *Hollywood East* published in 2000. We also added the Chinese characters right next to the English titles because we can do that nowadays.

And we've stitched in some new info and anecdotes we've learned over the years. We know the core of HKFOGs (Hong Kong Film Original Gangstas) will appreciate it. Much has changed, and knowing Hong Kong film fans, we know you want more. But the core of the book remains the "Golden Age" of modern Hong Kong film from the mid-80s to the mid-90s, when cinemas were packed and film-financing in Hong Kong was freer and easier.

Technology updates

SAZ&ABITH was written in the videotape era. DVDs are the first 21st century optical-disc format, while Blu-ray discs are often the best option for home viewing. Never overlook DVDs—a well mastered DVD looks better than a poorly created Blu-ray.

We miss the cinema experience, especially at UC Theater in Berkeley. But except for some festivals and arthouse retrospectives (we'll get to those), it's all about the home experience now. That doesn't mean you can't get drag over your disbelieving friends, park them in front of your big honkin' flat-screen TV, then watch them go wide-eyed and slack-jawed. These films still provide conversion experiences.

On optical disc, there are different versions available for some films: often more than one DVD release, and of course, Blu-ray. And streaming video is increasingly becoming the favored delivery medium.

There's an overflowing squid-bucket of options out there now. We're old-school film geeks, and we like the extras found on optical discs: interviews, commentaries, alternate endings, and a choice of subtitles. A popular option is "subbed and dubbed" which allows viewers to watch a film in Chinese with English subtitles, or dial in the English-dubbed soundtrack.

And don't forget region-coding: there are multiple DVD regions and Blu-ray regions, largely based on geography.

There are other websites selling these, search around. Blu-ray players will play DVDs from all regions as well as BRs, and are useful machines. Blu-ray is the new vinyl!

The best of all worlds is a well mastered DVD or Blu-ray in the correct aspect ratio, with lots of extras, like audio commentaries, interviews, and "behind-the-scenes" footage. San Francisco-based Tai Seng released many excellent DVDs. But the UK's Hong Kong Legends releases (all Region 2 and best searched on amazon.co.uk) are well made: remastered from original prints, with commentaries and extras—sometimes hours of extras.

Some fans like the original soundtrack, while others prefer English dubbing. We like language options. With some DVDs and Blu-rays, the viewer has the option of the original soundtrack with English subtitles, or an English dub—this is the best of both worlds. While streaming may take over the videodrome, you will never find the alternate ending of *Zu* (1983) there. Nor will you hear the delight in Clarence Ford's voice as he sees long-excised snippets of his *Naked Killer* (1993) restored to the film.

As with any technology, the situation changes as more films are released in different formats. The latest advance in film-delivery—video on demand (VOD), often simply called streaming—now features more Hong Kong films, often in high-definition.

Thanks a lot you guys

At first, most thought we were loopy to write a book on these "windows on a culture half-a-world away." But we're glad we did. Thanks for sharing the ride with us.

Stefan Hammond (Hong Kong) and
Mike Wilkins (San Francisco)
January 2020

MORE SEX, BETTER ZEN, FASTER BULLETS

FOREWORD BY JACKIE CHAN (1996)

For me, making movies is about making excitement. I've made movies all over the world, but I keep returning to Hong Kong, because that's where the excitement is best. In Hong Kong films (although the local police may object), if we want to drive a motorcycle on top of a speeding train, we just do it. If we want a jeep to explode in fire and ignite the four stuntmen leaping out of it, we just do it. If we want a beautiful female police officer to sweep-kick a bad egg in the chops, we just do it. That's Hong Kong. We just do it.

... again and again. Here in this book you'll find many HK favorites; many of mine and many of yours. If you're new to HK films, this volume will open your eyes to cinematic experiences beyond your wildest dreams...and nightmares.

I'm proud that a dozen or so of my own films are here and I hope you'll be tempted to see them with your friends. Because if you have a great time watching my movies, then I'm really really happy. Because I make my movies for you. It's that simple.

Please enjoy! *Doh jeh sai*!!

Jackie Chan squares up in this screengrab from *City Hunter* (1992) and (left) 1995 signed photograph.

MORE SEX, BETTER ZEN, FASTER BULLETS

HOLLYWOOD EAST: HONG KONG MOVIES AND THE PEOPLE WHO MADE THEM BY MICHELLE YEOH (2000)

Over the course of the films I've had the pleasure of making it in Hong Kong, I have gained a sense of what we have that is unique to our corner of the film world. The particular blend of fantastic stories, gritty and realistic action—pulled together in a strikingly fast pace of production by a dedicated and talented group of artists, directors, and technical film creators—has an appeal that extends far beyond Hong Kong and Asia. Film fans around the world appreciate our finished product, even though many of them do not realize the extent to which Hong Kong films truly differ from those made elsewhere.

My education in the Asian film industry, working in Hong Kong, was a nonstop school where swirling smoke was made not by machines

MORE SEX, BETTER ZEN, FASTER BULLETS

but by men burning bundles of joss sticks in metal cans, creating a thick and aromatic atmosphere. Many of these sets were devoid of trailers, and I did my hair and make up outdoors, using a mirror propped up against a wall. Script pages were produced at the last possible moment, and stunt sequences were created with real and dangerous action, not with computers and green screens. The spontaneity gets in your blood.

There are many career highlights but I am most proud of *Yes Madam*, where I first made the transition into playing action roles, proving that a woman could be an effective action star. Stunt boys and action choreographers in Hong Kong graciously taught me this craft. Making *Supercop* with Jackie Chan was especially memorable: I got to work in Malaysia and performing some amazing stunts—such as riding a dirt bike on a moving train. *Supercop* was released in the US in 1996 and I believe that for many US audience members it was their first exposure to Hong Kong action movies.

Many of us have made the move to Hollywood, where filmmaking is a slower and more controlled process—but we have not turned our backs on Hong Kong movies. Audiences appreciate the spontaneity of the Hong Kong style, and we hope to bring about a synthesis of these two very different traditions, keeping the best of both worlds. In 1997 I appeared in *Tomorrow Never Dies* with Pierce Brosnan, and we brought Philip Kwok with his stunt boys from Hong Kong to London to choreograph a fight sequence for the movie.

By reading this book you will find out about the many people who have contributed to Hong Kong moviemaking. These are the people who are important to be in Hong Kong movie fans around the world.

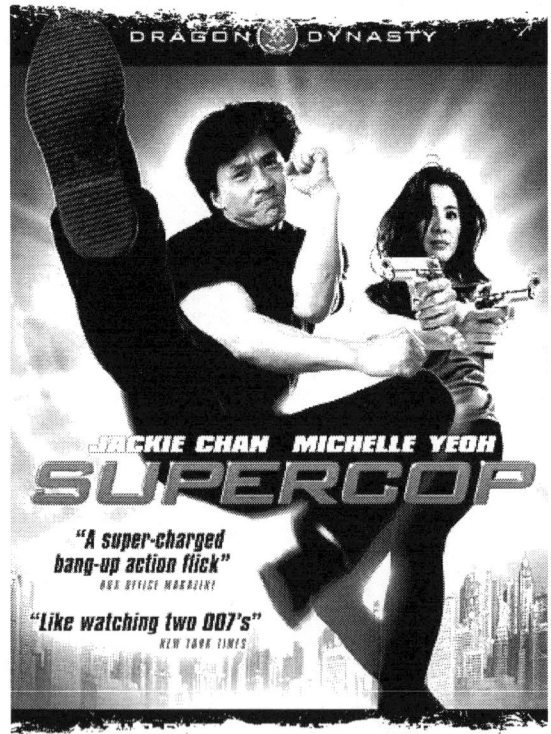

MORE SEX, BETTER ZEN, FASTER BULLETS

SPECIAL THANKS

Thank you to the following: Wade Major, whose encyclopedic knowledge of Hong Kong film and other film industries is invaluable. Andy Klein, the best film critic in Los Angeles and longtime Hong Kong film fanatic. Wade and Andy, along with arch-sifu David Chute, are all worthy ambassadors of Hong Kong film in Los Angeles. Jude Poyer, not only a diehard Hong Kong movie fan but able to explain why you put cotton wool in your ears before driving a motorcycle through stunt-glass. Jim Morton, who, when invited to a showing of *The Seventh Curse* at San Francisco's Great Star Theater in 1987, went unhesitatingly. Jim's encyclopedic knowledge of offbeat films proves invaluable time-and-again, and he's one of those fans for whom Hong Kong films are a vital part of a larger canon. Michael Bliss, who suggested a different take on John Woo's oeuvre at a surgically precise moment. His take on Woo is unique. Jeremy Hansen, who wrote a smashing Wong Kar-wai chapter and has forgiven Stefan for forcing him to watch *Ashes of Time* seven times. Tim Youngs, whose appreciation of Hong Kong films is prodigious (Tim also programs the Hong Kong section of the Udine Far East Film Festival). Helen Soo, Janie Chuck and Frank Djeng of Tai Seng Video in San Francisco, who believed in us from the very beginning. Thank also to Bernard, Jack, and the rest of the Soo family. Danielle Egan-Miller and Betsy Lancefield Lane, along with David Dunton: all literal literary geniuses who "got it" right away. Timothy Hallinan, who teaches his writing acumen as well as exercising it on multi-volume tales exploring the clotted alleys of Los Angeles and now Bangkok with his Poke Rafferty series. Richard Kadrey, longtime diehard Hong Kong film fan who named a tiki bar "The Bamboo House of Dolls" in his excellent *Sandman Slim* fiction series.

Special thanks to Richard A Akiyama, Keith Allison, Tod Booth, Terence Chang, Roberta Chin, Christopher Doyle, Sheila Duignan of Awesome Catering, Paul Fonoroff, the Hong Kong Film Archive, the Hong Kong International Film Festival, Carol Hui, Hung Ming Video Enterprise, Glenn Kay, Gigi Ko, Bruce Law, Christina Lee, Money Lo and Kimmy Shuen of Martini Films, Karen Mok, Simon Furman and David Barraclough of Titan Books, Johnnie To, Elliott Tong, Ridley Tsui, Nury Vittachi, Almen Wong, Anthony Wong, Michael Wong, Wu Chien-lien, Herman Yau.

Thanks also to: Bruce Black, David Bordwell, Carmen Bradley, Monte Cazazza, Gary Chang, John Charles, Ross Chen, Alfred Cheung, Benny Chia, Peter Coe, Bill Connolly, Colin Covert, Diane Davis, Anastasia Edwards, Joseph Fierro, Peter Flechette, Tom Gray, Richard Grosse, DE Hardy, Grady Hendrix, Titus Ho, Lars-Erik Holmquist, Ange Hwang, Kent Johnson, Tom Kagy, Keiko Kawazoe, Mark King, Edwin Kong, Kidai Kwon, Gere Ladue, Richie Lam, Mick Lasalle, Rebecca Lee, Max Leighton, TS Lo, Felix Lu, Stephen Lu, Brad Masoni, Paul Mavrides, Ron Murillo, Paul Nerbonne, Richard Norton, Ben Ng,

MORE SEX, BETTER ZEN, FASTER BULLETS

SPECIAL THANKS

Francis Ng, Hank Okazaki, Carl Parkes, Richard Petersen, William Henry Pratt, Brad Roberts, Cynthia Rothrock, Keiji Sato, Andrew Scal, Steve Schechter, Cameron Scholes, Richard A Spears, Dr Bob Smith, Douglass St Clair Smith, Lursak Thavornvanit, Steve & Joanie Tibbetts, Stanley Tong, Uncle Seven, Wendy Van Dusen, Steve Vascik, Matthew Walker, Bill Wilson, William Woo, Carrie Wong, Declan Wong, Daniel Wu, Derek Yee, Daniel Zilber, William O Zinsser.

Apologies to anyone we've forgotten as if that could possibly happen.

And a heartfelt *doh jeh* to the filmmakers of Hong Kong for all their dedication and hard work.

THIS BOOK IS DEDICATED TO...

Alex Graf

Jane Jordan-Browne

Mike Mallery

Martha Pike

Catherine Reuther

MORE SEX, BETTER ZEN, FASTER BULLETS

IN MEMORIAM

Chan Shen 詹森 (1940-1984)   Runme Shaw 邵仁枚 (1901-1985)
Chiang Sheng 江生 (1951-1991)   Barry Wong 黃炳耀 (1946-1991)
Louis Roth 魯亦詩 (1947-1994)   Jeanette Lin Tsui 林翠 (1936-1995)
Hon Yee-Sang 韓義生 (1951-1995)   Lo Wei 羅維 (1918-1996)
Li Han-hsiang 李翰祥 (1926-1996)   Haing S Ngor 吳漢 (1940-1996)
Lam Ching Ying 林正英 (1952-1997)   King Hu 胡金銓 (1931-1997)
Regina Kent 簡慧珍 (1967-1999)   Kuei Chih-hung 桂治洪 (1937-1999)
Roy Chiao 喬宏 (1927-1999)   Angela Yu Chien 于倩 (1942-2000)
Pauline Chan 陳寶蓮 (1973–2002)   Lo Lieh 羅烈 (1939-2002)
Chang Cheh 張徹 (1923-2002)   Anita Mui 梅艷芳 (1963-2003)
Leslie Cheung 張國榮 (1956-2003)   Kelvin Wong 王霄 (1962-2004)
James Wong 黃霑 (1941-2004)   Bill Tung 董驃 (1934-2006)
Kwan Hoi-san 關海山 (1925-2006)   Wong Yu 汪禹 (1955-2008)
Chen Hung-lieh 陳鴻烈 (1943-2009)   Spencer Lam 林尚義 (1934-2009)
Ho Meng-hua 何夢華 (1923-2009)   Sek Kin 石堅 (1913-2009)
Wong Tin-lam 王天林 (1928-2010)   Ricky Hui 許冠英 (1946-2011)
Austin Wai 惠天賜 (1957-2012)   Guan Shan 關山 (1933-2012)
Shirley Yu 余莎莉 (19??-2013)   Liu Chia-liang/Lau Kar-leung 劉家良 (1934-2013)
Jim Kelly 占基利 (1946-2013)   Wu Ma 午馬 (1942-2014)
Sir Run Run Shaw 邵逸夫 (1907-2014)   William Ho 何家駒 (1948-2015)
Birte Tove 碧蒂杜芙 (1945-2016)   Fung Hark-on 馮克安 (1949-2016)
Wang Hsieh 王俠 (1930-2016)   Willie Chan 陳自強 (1941-2017)
Ching Li 井莉 (1945-2017)   Phillip Ko Fei 高飛 (1949-2017)
Mona Fong 方逸華 (1934-2017)   Jin Yong, aka Louis Cha 金庸 (1924-2018)
Raymond Chow Man-wai 鄒文懷 (1927-2018)   Yueh Hua 岳華 (1942-2018)

Ringo Lam Ling-tung 林嶺東 (1955-2018)

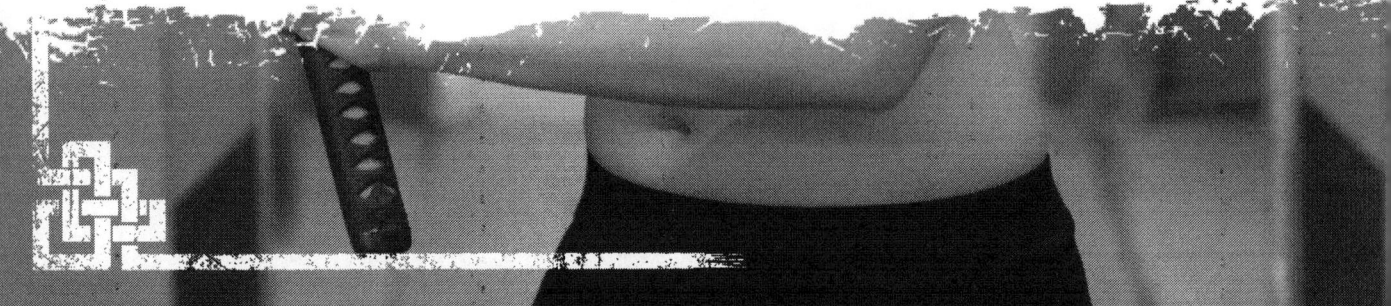

CHAPTER ONE
TEN THAT RIP

MORE SEX, BETTER ZEN, FASTER BULLETS

In keeping with our charter as a introductory guide to Hong Kong cinema, we start things off with ten films that rip. The movies in this chapter are all entertaining, well made, accessible, and great introductions to the Hong Kong film universe.

This isn't a "Ten Best" list. That particular flame war ended with the internet's "alt.asian-movies" newsgroup. (2020 NOTE: if you ever posted on this newsgroup, you qualify as an HKFOG [Hong Kong Film Original Gangsta].)

What we've done here is pick a great representative movie from some of the genres and filmmaker-specific chapters that we explore in more detail later on.

The lovely Joey Wong ponders her fate in *A Chinese Ghost Story*.

A Chinese Ghost Story (倩女幽魂)
1987 | Starring Joey Wong Jo-yin, Leslie Cheung Kwok-wing, Wu Ma, David Lam Wai, Lau Siu-ming
Directed by Tony Ching Siu-tung

Producer Tsui Hark took an ancient Chinese legend, gave it Western pacing, and created *A Chinese Ghost Story*—one of Hong Kong's breakthrough films. Elegant, earthy and unearthly, at once sympathetic yet fantastic, *ACGS* breathes flesh and nerve as it spins a love story from the midst of fantastic chaos. The female lead—drop-dead-gorgeous Joey Wong—seared her way into the hearts of male moviegoers everywhere; few who've seen this movie ever forget that face.

Good-natured scholar Ning Tsai-shen (Leslie Cheung) is the most unpopular man in any village: a traveling tax-collector making the rounds. He opts for a night at a deserted temple, but has to cross dark forests filled with wolves to reach it. Once there, he steps into the middle of an angry stare-down between the loner misfit, Swordsman Yen (Wu Ma), and Hsiao-hou (David Lam). Ning keeps the swordsmen from carving one another, but is not exactly welcomed. The misanthropic Yen warns him there are things skulking about "more scareful than a tiger."

We soon see what he means when Hsiao-hou meets a flirtatious, nubile ghostress bathing in a nearby stream and leaps lustfully upon her. A shake of her belled ankle bracelet and something unseen slithers upon him, continues down his throat and sucks out his essence, turning him into a desiccated corpse!

In the temple, Ning pricks his finger and a whole group of these desiccated blood-sniffing zombies stir to life. Hollow bones crackle as they move in unison towards the source of lifesblood. But an unaware Ning explores the source of lute and voice drifting through the window, and finds a pavilion occupied by the same nymph who lured Hsiao-hou to his doom: Nieh Hsiao-tsing (Joey Wong). She immediately attempts to seduce the tax-collector, but finds that he's different from the churls she's previously set up for drainage; despite her beauty, he tenderly and politely turns her down.

Good move. A literal concubine to Hell, Hsiao-tsing's job is targeting men for yang element absorption by her spirit-world pimp, an awful, dual-gender matron. But Hsiao-tsing gets no fulfillment from her work. She was murdered a year earlier, and is now held in bondage by the matron—who has a witching-symbiosis with the forest and sports a fifty-foot tongue, which she wraps around her enemies like a python's coils. Even worse, Hsiao-tsing is betrothed to her pimp's boss, Lord Black.

So falling in love with the human Ning would be sheer folly. But as Woody Allen once wrote, "The heart wants what it wants."

Now sweethearts, Hsiao-tsing and Ning convince the cantankerous-but-lovable Swordsman Yen that she deserves a decent reincarnation. The trio set off to recover the jar of her ashes they'll need to accomplish the job. The pissed-off matron assaults the trio with walls of tongue and other slimy effects. When these fail, she opens the portal to Hell itself and drags Hsiao-tsing down.

"Scholar! It seems we have to storm hell!" shouts Swordsman Yen as the pair descend to scrap with Lord Black and his minions.

A Chinese Ghost Story is on the Hong Kong Film Archive's list of "Best 100 Chinese Motion Pictures."

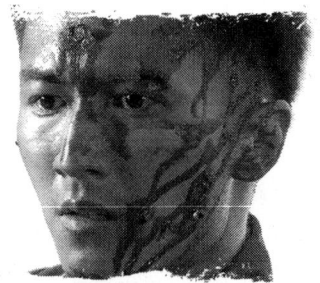

Nick Tse realizes just how bad things can get in *Beast Stalker*.

Beast Stalker (証人)

2008 | Starring Nicholas Tse Ting-fung, Nick Cheung Ka-fai, Zhang Jingchu, Dick Liu Kai-chi, Miao Pu, Derek Kwok Jing-hung, Philip Keung Hiu-man, Lau Kong
Directed by Dante Lam Chiu-yin

Since co-directing *Beast Cops* with Gordon Chan in 1998, Dante Lam continued to carve a path for himself among Hong Kong's dwindling corps of directors. The Chinese title of this film translates prosaically as Witness, but Lam vaults into our Ten That Rip chapter with a brutal drama titled "*Beast Stalker*" in English.

This is a film for a cinematic audience—buy the ticket, take the ride. the plot-line twists, sinks its fangs into itself, uncoils, then prepares to strike another part of its underbelly. It grabs your eyes as a mirror for its tangle of thorns and scars.

But you might want to read the intro of our "Hong Kong Noir" chapter before deciding to watch this one. Consider yourself warned—but if you're up for it, this is one of the better Hong Kong films of the century.

The critical fifteen-minute opening sequence begins with Sergeant Tong Fei (Nicholas Tse) meeting his plainclothes team for dim sum breakfast. Before the dumplings even cool off, Tong, a notorious hard-ass, propels his team into their day's assignment—busting a bunch of hard gangsters who bite back.

But the plan skews. While the baddies are successfully collared, his second-in-charge, Sun (Dick Liu), takes a slug in the gut. Sun waxes philosophical while he pries the lead pill out of his bulletproof vest, but the tightly wrapped Tong and career-minded Sun aren't candidates for a cop-buddy film. They're just sharp cops, fortunately, as an emergency call then buzzes their police radios: a more dangerous gangster—Cheung Yat-tung (Philip Keung) who just escaped police custody, is in their vicinity.

The undercovers chase the new bunch of crooks and—in a ferocious car chase/crash staged by Hong Kong's ace stunt coordinator Bruce Law—the fate of Sun, Tong, and just-passing-by Ann Gao (Zhang Jingchu) changes irrevocably amidst blood and asphalt.

Set-up complete, antagonist Hung King (Nick Cheung) shows his scarred face. A hard-drinking wraith self-secreted in a crumbling walk-up, he does wet work for ghoulish gang boss Chuen (Lau Kong). Chuen stops by to sip rice wine and ask Hung what he'll do for money. "Anything," Hung replies. He's not kidding.

Gao is a Hong Kong prosecutor and due in court against the homicidal Cheung Yat-tung. Chuen seeks leverage over Gao, and takes Hung up on his offer. Tong Fei, who seems to have spent his entire career developing his policing skills, must now use them even though circumstances have wrapped barbed wire around his heart. Gao too is caught in her own web of emotional agony. Just when you think things can't get worse, they do.

Beast Stalker is watchspring-tight, visually stunning, and morally shredded, with no romantic distractions and no subplots. The three main actors are given rein to fill their characters with the entire spectrum of human emotions.

Director Lam and screenwriter Jack Ng worked on-set to tweak dialogue and maintain the tension—and shot on crowded streets (sometimes without warning the citizenry that they were making a film, a guerrilla tactic that's enhanced many a Hong Kong flick). Handheld shots of ordinary Hong Kong life in grimy old-school districts (jackhammers and pile-drivers, grannies in tenement lobbies complaining about plumbing) alternate with POV shots to create a documentary feel and draw the viewer in.

Like any good noir, ordinary people are corkscrewed into situations that should break them into splinters. Action leaves its mark—characters bear physical scars. *Beast Stalker* is a hard ride, but it's worth it. Or as Sun puts it: "That's Fate. She tricks you, then she helps you There's nothing you can do."

NOTE: Zhang Jingchu was trained at the Central Academy of Arts and Drama in Beijing, where she graduated as a film director. A native Mandarin speaker, Zhang worked with a tutor to perfect her Hong Kong Cantonese—essential as her character is a senior member of Hong Kong's judiciary. She also speaks fluent English, served as spokesperson for the 13th Beijing Student Film Festival in 2006, and was named one of "Asia's Heroes" by Time Magazine in 2005.

Her character's daughter is played by a set of real-life twins: Wong Suet-Yin and Wong Sum-Yin, better known as Ling and Yee. Nicholas Tse, who says his role was exhausting as he lived within his character for the duration, credits the adorable girls with inspiration for his performance. Actors Zhang and Cheung were equally impressed with their professionalism and savvy.

Nick Cheung's portrayal of Hung King won Best Actor at: Taiwan's Golden Horse Awards, the Asia Pacific Film Festival, the Changchun Film Festival in China, the Hong Kong Film Critics Society Awards, and the Hong Kong Film Awards.

Full Contact (俠盜高飛)
1992 | Starring Chow Yun-fat, Simon Yam Tat-wah, Bonnie Fu Yuk-ching, Ann Bridgewater, Anthony Wong Chau-sang, Frankie Chin
Director by Ringo Lam

Drenched in feedback and octane, *Full Contact* revels in outrageous villains, antiheroes, and the

TEN THAT RIP

Psychopathic fashion plate Simon Yam has a thing for Chow Yun-fat—Anthony Wong looks on haplessly.

hollow rattle of brass casings hitting pavement. The film's multi-ethnic soundtrack crackles with crime glamor: psychedelic blues guitar threading together Cantorock, Yankeerock, and Thai pop. Ace director Ringo Lam cranks up all the knobs to ten in this crime-action fuelburner.

FC opens with the robbery of an antique shop in Bangkok, Thailand. The robbers are a surreal bunch: led by Judge, an openly gay impromptu magician whose colorful pocket-scarves conceal deadly weapons. Judge's accomplices are the gum-chomping harlot, Virgin (Bonnie Fu), and her muscleheaded pro-rassler-like husband, Psycho (Frankie Chin). Scarcely has this over-the-top trio terrorized the staff, shot up the local cops, and roared off with the swag (in a twitch-perfect '64 Fairlane) when the opening credits roll over a skillful funk-removing tease/strip dance by Mona (Ann Bridgewater).

Meanwhile, Mona's squeeze and fellow dance club employee, Jeff (played by Hong Kong's leading leading man, Chow Yun-fat, with a Thai-style crewcut and necklace of amulets), sets off to rescue their friend Sam (Anthony Wong) from the clutches of a local loan shark (played by longtime Ringo collaborator Nam Yin) and his henchmen. Steel rings as Jeff thumps the thugs, then zooms off with Sam riding bitch on his "Honda-Davidson" motorbike.

Discharging the sharks does not discharge the debt, so Sam arranges a joint heist with Jeff's troops and those of his cousin: Judge. But when the Jeff gang meets the Judge mob, a squabble brings out the Freudian rods. Jeff's hog-leg .45 dwarfs Judge's nickel-plated automatic, and a tense standoff ends when the cad, oozing smarm, says: "your eyes are so charming and attractive."

Judge's frustrated sexual energy is sublimated in evildoing when he's contracted by the humiliated loan shark to double-cross Jeff during the robbery. The job—hijacking an arms-laden truck on a crowded Bangkok bridge—starts with Virgin riding shotgun in Jeff's speeding car (and furiously masturbating—crime turns her on), then concludes with half-hearted betrayal Sam shooting Jeff through the chest after Judge has trapped him in a house, shot up the place, and burned it to cinders—the creep's more concerned with his hairstyle than innocent bystanders.

Jeff is left for dead with fewer friends and fewer fingers. Bruised and battered, Jeff is slowly nursed back to health by monks at a Thai temple, who are also tending a weird, bug-eyed puppy.

Meanwhile, Sam is busy rising through the criminal ranks in Hong Kong, running guns for Judge and seducing Mona (both believe Jeff was killed in the robbery). When Jeff returns to HK and contacts them, this tangled triangle struggles with their loyalties, alternately frail and tough.

Sam has to bite off his leg caught in the trap of gangster pride and help Jeff gain his revenge. They steal Judge's arm cache and hold it for ransom. Negotiations disintegrate and a "bulletcam" nightclub gunfight ensues—individual shots are tracked in flight, followed through plate-glass, hands, heads. In the finale, Jeff puts an end to Judge's incessant flirting, climbs on his iron horse and thunders off into the distance.

NOTE: There are several subtitle-versions and the more accurate ones are less fun. Characters' names change according to subtitular version: Chow's character is named "Ko Fei" but usually listed as Jeff. Bonnie Fu's over-the-top nympho-fiend thief is best named "Virgin" while Frankie Chin's pugnacious brickhead is just plain "Psycho" (he's also "Deano").

Stuntmen and every other damn thing go flying in this screengrab from John Woo's *Hard-Boiled*.

Hard-Boiled (辣手神探)

1992 | Starring Chow Yun-fat, Tony Leung Chiu-wai, Teresa Mo Shun-kwan, Anthony Wong Chau-sang, Philip Chan Yan-kin, Philip Kwok Tsui, Kwan Hoi-san
Directed by John Woo

HK cinema is a deck full of action aces, but John Woo's *Hard-Boiled* is the trump. This tale of gunrunners, double-agents and innocents-caught-in-between showcases several action sequences that suck your jaw to the floor. *Hard-Boiled* is Woo's most spectacular film—and the last one he made before transiting to Hollywood in the early 90s.

Hard-Boiled revolves around an intense, platonic relationship between two men in a violent world. Loyalty is all, superseding one's policeman or thief day-job. Either way, you pack a gun and use it when necessary.

Hard-Boiled plainclothesman Tequila (Chow Yun-fat) moonlights as a clarinet player in a neon lounge. Tequila and his drummer, fellow cop Lionheart (Bowie Lam), go for early morning dim sum in the Wyndham Teahouse, a Hong Kong landmark where customers bring along their own caged birds to sing table-side. In the large, crowded teahouse, gun smuggling mobsters hide their gats in false-bottomed birdcages. Tequila blows their cover and a trademark John Woo gun battle steeps the teeming teahouse in flying slugs and birds. As Lionheart bites it, Tequila chases crooks by sliding side-saddle down a bannister—toothpick in mouth and automatics blazing. In the kitchen, he skids across a countertop and is powdered with flour; white-faced as a ghost, he terminates the villain with a shot to the head.

As the web unfolds, we meet Tequila's apparent nemesis, Tony (played by Tony Leung Chiu-wai, often called Tony "Hard-Boiled" Leung because of his great performance). He's a flamboyant underworld killer working for the powerful Mr Hoi. His trigger skills are coveted by Hoi's gunrunning rival Johnny (Anthony Wong), who also covets Hoi's empire. Johnny's men assault Hoi's warehouse in a spectacular battle—slick, violent and beautiful—with phalanxes of motorcycles, breathtaking tracking shots and Johnny's top gunman Mad Dog (Philip Kwok) greasing row after row of Hoi's men. Loser Hoi dies stoically just as lone cop Tequila rappels down from the warehouse ceiling.

More rounds are uncapped as Tequila disassembles what remains of the assembled armies. It ends with Tony and Tequila exploring their psychic bond by pointing guns at each other's head, but the crucial chamber—for once—is empty.

Yes, Tony is also a cop, but he has gone so far undercover that routine hits mean nothing to him anymore. As the two cops gradually realize they're on the same side, they uncover Johnny's arsenal, stashed in the basement of a hospital. It's in this hospital where *Hard-Boiled* resolves itself.

The entire third act is a half-hour action sequence which dwarfs the entirety of most action movies. The battle against Johnny and his legion of "killable dogs" assumes surreal, epic proportions as patients are used as pawns and bullets fly like horizontal raindrops. Tequila and Tony battle the entire length of a hospital corridor together, step forward as elevator doors close behind them, enjoy a few moments of calm and conference, then start over on a different floor!

And, just when you think that the stakes can't get any higher, Tequila and policewoman Teresa (comedienne Teresa Mo in a Betty-and-Veronica flip wig) have to move a nursery full of babies to safety. As cops and crooks die right and left, Tequila cradles a sanguine tyke named Saliva Sammy in one arm while his free hand cradles a warm pistol. Sticking cotton balls in Sammy's ears, Tequila blasts away and prepares to escape, but accidentally catches on fire. Fortunately, the child pees and douses the fire. The underground arsenal explodes, and fireballs blow through the hospital, but the babies are saved, the bad guy croaks and the audience settles back with a loud "Whew."

NOTE: There are many releases of this film. As with other, variant films discussed in this book it'd be a good idea to check out www.dvdbeaver.com before making a purchase.

Thai poster for *Mr Vampire*.

Mr Vampire (殭屍先生)
1985 | Starring Lam Ching Ying, Chin Siu-ho, Ricky Hui, Moon Lee Choi-fung, Pauline Wong Siu-fung, Billy Lau, Huang Ha, Anthony Chan Yau, Yuen Wah
Directed by Ricky Lau

Mr Vampire is first and foremost in a long line of Chinese vampire flicks. Our bloodsucking brothers from the East do not traipse about in capes flaunting Old World charm and seductively biting necks—although they do reside in coffins and have healthy incisors. Pale and blue? Heck yes, they're dead! Are they as stiff as boards? You bet, and since they can't walk, they hop. Well, how scary can a hopping ghost in a Ming Dynasty costume be? If you find one in your face—sniffing for your breath—you'll feel your short hairs stiffen! Funny? Absolutely.

There's a fine line between horror and humor and *Mr Vampire* does everything but jump rope with it. The film also features stunning action sequences action-directed by Sammo Hung.

The film is a series of farcical vignettes involving a Taoist sifu (Lam Ching Ying) and his two well-meaning but dorkacious students: Chou and Man Choi (Chin Siu-ho and Ricky Hui). The priest gets a gig reburying wealthy Mr Yam's father, and stores the freshly dug coffin overnight.

Unfortunately, the corpse (Yuen Wah) has become cranky from twenty years of burial under poorly designed feng shui, and busts out, ignoring sacrificial black goats in favor of Yam Junior's throat. Young Yam (Huang Ha) turns blue and nasty, then goes out and kills a few locals. The Taoist is accused of the murders by the local constable (a loathsome bumpkin played with suitable bravado/cowardice by Billy Lau), but Yam's re-animated corpse proves an effective alibi! The student Man Choi is infected, and must eat, bathe in, and dance on, sticky rice to be cured of creeping ghoulification.

The most interesting subplot involves a lovelorn ghost (Pauline Wong) who appears in the forest, riding in an ectoplasmic sedan chair. Her theme song is a haunting childlike rhyme with fractured subtitular lyrics: "Her piercing look/ Shinning bright like the stars/Sure enough to make one choke/The lady ghost looks for a lover/ Who would take a bride so shady?"

Student Chou, that's who. She tempts him with wine and temporal hickeys, then fights fiercely with the Taoist master when he attempts to intervene. After tossing her head from her shoulders and sending it flying toward sifu, she eventually gives up when he points out: "you two are from different worlds."

But as one goblin is vanquished, another hops onto the scene. Vampire Yam Pere has been lurking in a rat-infested cave just waiting for the chance to return to his displaced coffin.

Mr Vampire's appeal is based on its ability to place its characters in just enough danger to straddle the humor/horror balance beam. Ghouls come in various concentrations of evil; the possessed Man Choi never becomes more than a toothy nuisance, while Master Vampire Yam takes no prisoners. Fortunately, sifu has enough Taoist tricks up his loose yellow sleeves to finally take care of everybody's business.

Mr Vampire is on the Hong Kong Film Archive's list of "Best 100 Chinese Motion Pictures."

There are several releases of this film.

Sammo's beaten but not broken as he faces fearsome Billy Chow in *Pedicab Driver*.

Pedicab Driver (群龍戲鳳)
1989 | Starring Sammo Hung Kam-bo, Nina Li Chi, Sun Yueh, Max Mok Siu-chung, Fennie Yuen Kit-ying, John Shum Kin-fun, Meng Hoi, Lowell Lo Koon-ting, Lau Kar-leung, Lam Ching Ying
Directed by Sammo Hung Kam-bo

Sammo Hung's magnificent *Pedicab Driver* is a metaphor for Sammo's career. Sammo is kung fu star Jackie Chan's big brother, and has directed or starred in some of HK's finest output, many starring his more-famous adopted sibling. *Pedicab Driver*—a wrenching love story with exquisite martial action—also remains largely undiscovered, even by HK film fanatics.

Set in 1950s Macau, *PD* centers around a quartet of working-class guys who transport people down Macau's narrow lanes in pedicabs: pedal-powered rickshaws. Their leader is the stalwart Tung (Sammo Hung), whose chums are Malted Candy (Max Mok), Rice Pudding (Meng Hoi) and Shan Cha (Lowell Lo).

Tung lives in a grotty little room next to the local bakery, where the baker, Fang (Sun Yueh) has his eye on plainly-styled-yet-stunning Ping (Nina Li). Fang's heart is in the right place, but Ping can't take him seriously as a suitor.

Undeterred, he takes her to town to pick out a jade bracelet, where she's spotted by whoremaster Yu—aka "Master Five." Yu is played with apocalyptic villainy by comedian John Shum, cast viciously against type. Master Five has slicked-back hair, gold-capped teeth, a narcissistic sense of entitlement, a motorcar and a cadre of goons in tow. The slimebag Überpimp bristles with avarice as he comes on to Ping.

Tung inserts his righteous self between the terrified woman and the odious whoremaster. Master Five, provoked, hops in his car and chases Tung's pedicab—Ping clinging precariously to the seat. Tung escapes by crashing into a gambling house, but must atone for his table-wrecking entrance by dueling with the proprietor (Lau Kar-leung).

The fight between these two masters accelerates from fists to poles. It's state-of-the-razor martial arts. Tung loses, but the casino boss is so impressed ("Fatty, I've fought with many men, but you're the only one who has scared me") that he lets them go.

Tung and Ping drift towards each other as Tung's fellow pedaller Malted Candy (Max Mok) falls for comely youngster Hsiao Tsui (Fennie Yuen). A celebratory meal at an outdoor eatery brings Shan Cha and Hsiao Tsui face-to-face in a social setting. They gaze at each other with slowly dawning horror.

Pressed for an explanation, Shan reveals Tsui's secret: she's a sex-worker he patronized her the night before. Shamed and insulted, Tsui gathers her dignity and flees the resultant brouhaha. But Ping—who's been a passive peacemaker but is now the lone woman at the table—has a few things to say.

She reminds the pedicab drivers that life's circumstances aren't equal, and that humility and compassion are more appropriate responses here than insults. "If my circumstances were different, I'd be a whore and not a baker!", she tells them (of course, Master Five's plan was precisely that). Malted Candy swallows his foolishness and makes amends.

News of Tsui's forthcoming nuptials reach Master Five, whose apoplexy reaches zenith. He dispatches goons to chop up Malted Candy and Tsui on their wedding night. When Tung arrives—too late—he looks at his diminutive friend Rice Pudding and, without a word, they go to revenge.

At Master Five's opulent gangsta mansion, Sammo must defeat scary thug Eddie Maher, and terrifying thug Billy Chow. The furious pedicab driver smashes most of the furniture as well as Chow's head. When Master Five takes that final southward elevator ride, the audience lets rip a hearty cheer.

Pedicab Driver's mix of heart-rending drama, comic touches and ferocious action make it a must-see for fans of classic Hong Kong films. It's on a par with the great Jackie Chan films of the late 80s and early 90s—thanks to Sammo's direction, his stunt team—and exquisite art direction by William Chang, who later became part of the Wong Kar-wai triumvirate. And some astute casting (if Fennie Yuen's character doesn't break your heart, check your pulse). The plethora of Hong Kong filmmakers making cameo appearances in the film speaks to the respect Sammo commanded at the time in the local industry.

NOTE: *Pedicab Driver* is (finally) available on DVD-R from Warner Brothers.

Jackie strikes a classic kung fu pose in *Police Story 3: Supercop*.

Police Story 3: Supercop
(警察故事3超級警察)
1992 | Starring Jackie Chan, Michelle Yeoh Chu-kheng, Maggie Cheung Man-yuk, Yuen Wah, Kenneth Tsang
Directed by Stanley Tong

PS3: SC presents Jackie Chan at the top of his game. As a Hong Kong cop chasing drug smugglers across Southeast Asia, his action partner is the capable (and stunning) Michelle Yeoh, whose appearance here marked a comeback from a lengthy film hiatus. Driven by a strong narrative and making the most of its striking locations, *Police Story 3: Supercop* propels the viewer with a watchspring-tight plot and Jackie Chan's trademark: an assortment of ever-escalating, heart-halting stunts.

When a pair of RHKP officers need a "supercop" to take down the heinous drug czar Chaibat, they choose the valorous Chan Ka-kui (Jackie). Telling his girlfriend May (Maggie Cheung) that he's going to Special Training Camp, he packs his bags for Guangzhou in mainland China.

Once there, he's assigned to the command of Inspector Yang from Interpol (Michelle Yeoh). Yang enlists him in a scheme to spring Chaibat's henchman Panther (Yuen Wah) from a prison labor camp; a feat he accomplishes with derring-do. Panther is impressed, and gives Jackie a job on his crook-squad, after shooting the miscreant who landed him on the work farm. Prior to sailing for HK, they pay a visit to Chen's (nonexistent) family village in Fu Shan. The undercover HK cop is desperate, but is saved by a family setup engineered by the PRC cops, who put Inspector Yang in pigtails, as Chen's kid sister! The ruse works, but a visit to a Canton restaurant ends in a ruckus, as PRC cops attack the gang with stun-guns. Yang proves her mettle by outfoxing both cops and crooks, and is taken along to HK.

Once in the lair of Chaibat (Kenneth Tsang), the undercover pair realizes just how scummy the drug gang is as bodies start to pile up: a bikinied gwailo girl who OD's, and a double-crossing associate who's forcibly drowned in Chaibat's pool. A voyage to the Thai/Cambodian border introduces them to a Khun Sa-type drug lord (Lo Lieh). The dope-lord's poppy auction loses its civility when Chaibat becomes annoyed and bashes a rival's head in with a spiky durian fruit. "Shoot if you have the nerve!" yells a combatant; everyone's nervy—and heavily armed. The scene erupts in a vicious vortex of violence as competing factions unload hollow-points by the drum-load, blasting each other to shreds. Yang, whose bulletproof vest is filled with explosives (another trick by the treacherous Chaibat), must stay out of harm's way; Chen assists with grenade attacks and by serving as an impromptu gun tripod.

Having proven themselves in battle again, Chaibat enlists the duo in a plot to bust his wife out of a Kuala Lumpur jail. But when the gang runs into May—whose job as a tour guide brings her to KL—the cop's gal pal inadvertently spills the beans. Panther and crew kidnap May and force Chen and Yang to carry out the hazardous caper, which involves springing the captive from a heavily guarded police van. Chen crashes a car filled with fake poison-gas canisters and Yang leaps on the side of the speeding van as the two factions battle over their respective hostages. The climactic battle involves stunt after hair-raising stunt as a helicopter, numerous automobiles and dirt bikes and a speeding freight train are entangled in the fray. Stunt outtakes roll under the closing credits (a Jackie Chan tradition; see Chapter 5) —the takes they didn't use are scarier than the actual stunts!

NOTE: This is the only film reviewed twice in this book: check out Andy Klein's stellar take on the film in Chapter 13 (page 197).

PTU

2003 | Starring Simon Yam Tat-wah, Lam Suet, Maggie Shiu Mei-kei, Ruby Wong Cheuk-ling, Eddy Ko Hung, Lo Hoi-pang, Wong Tin-lam
Directed by Johnnie To Kei-fung

Johnnie To's *PTU* packages all his favorite elements—cops, crooks, the porous line that divides them, and a setting that exists outside

"Into the perilous night" sums it up: Johnnie To's PTU (Milkyway Image Productions).

of conventional time and space—into one graveyard shift for Hong Kong's "Police Tactical Unit"—upper-tier cops. The PTU patrol in packs of five or six wearing sharp uniforms, boots, and berets—they maintain a public presence as part of their duties.

Director/producer Johnnie To starts in the back of a police vehicle transporting one group of PTU to their work-location—it's the graveyard shift, and commercial radio announces a police action earlier in which an officer was killed. The younger PTU members, clearly nervous, chit-chat about his fate. Mike (Simon Lam) speaks up: "He's a fellow officer. He's one of us." The newbies fall silent. Mike's second-in-command, Kat (Maggie Shiu), says nothing—she doesn't have to.

The third senior member of the squad, Lo (Lam Suet), isn't in the van, he's eyeball-to-eyeball with a bunch of triad punks in some hotpot restaurant.

He's in plainclothes, but everyone knows he's a cop. It's an uneasy gathering of different tribes sitting at plastic tables with an obsequious waiter trying to keep the peace. Then a knife comes out.

What follows showcases the surreal nature of personal violence and its aftermath. The entire film exists in the window between sunset and sunrise, or a fraction thereof. The punks scrap with Lo, who must then juggle the truth (and the evidence), to the displeasure of Inspector Leigh Cheng (Ruby Wong), who arrives on the scene with her CID unit. Lo, it seems, has gotten into serious trouble.

Kat is ready to call headquarters on the Lo situation, but Mike steps in. He says Lo has until dawn to sort out his predicament. Kat concurs—these two have the deep mutual respect enjoyed by professionals in hazardous professions.

Mike starts looking for information in the dim, smoke-choked environs of late-night Kowloonside Hong Kong, during the hours when triads have at least as much sway as any police. Calmly, Mike asserts his dominance with casually ratcheted-up violence. The realization sneaks up on the viewer: this man understands his level of peril, and knows that rising above it requires creative means of asserting alpha-dog dominance versus inexperienced punks.

Meanwhile, the seminal knifing sets serious triad hounds Bald Head (Lo Hoi-pang) and Eye Ball (Eddy Ko) on a collision course. The film expects viewers to fill in the blanks (when you see men in cages, think of who they are, why they're there, and what happened). These are hard people with hard lives doing hard business, and some scenes depict the aftermath of everyday (or exceptional) nastiness.

Appropriately, it exists in a bubble of silence alien to Hong Kong. Lam Suet (as ever) provides comic relief, but there's a method to every bit of his madness. *PTU* isn't a loud banging action films where heroes and villains fire hundreds of rounds at each other. Its slow pace and deadpan performances won't appeal to the "ten thousand bullets" fans.

That's the point. Director To likes to vary his genres, and here he's created a muted Hong Kong police procedural unlike any other film. *PTU* creates its own universe—a dark-night in a Hong Kong without crowds, a universe where startling incidents are the norm, and those with experience always have the edge. The attention-to-detail extends to the unit's serial numbers: Lo and Mike wear four-digit numbers while the younger cops have five.

NOTES: Maggie Shiu's fetching, boyish haircut under her navy blue beret isn't a fashion statement—all female PTU officers wear their hair short so no perp can execute a hair-grab.

The "diner" where the PTU takes their wee-hours lunch break is a functional sandwich/noodle/tea shop located in northern Mongkok. If you stop in, try the milk tea and peanut butter toast.

Inspector Leigh Cheng's informant, whose role in the film is to serve as punching-bag for a couple of punks in an alley, is played by director Soi Cheang.

Sex & Zen (玉蒲團之偷情寶鑑)
1991 | Starring Lawrence Ng Kai-wah, Amy Yip Chi-mei, Kent Chung Jut-si, Isabella Chow Wang, Carrie Ng Ka-Lai, Lo Lieh, Elvis Tsui Kam-kong, Rena Murakami, Mari Ayukawa
Directed by Michael Mak

Filmgoers expecting staid tantric conjoinings and ethereal advice on meditation from this film adaptation of the 17th century erotic classic "The Carnal Prayer Mat" are in for a pleasant surprise.

Erotic pageantry amid the shrimpjobs and silk sash couplings: screengrab from *Sex & Zen*.

Director Michael Mak's romping *Sex & Zen* is pure Hong Kong hijinks; loaded with both formal, flowing period piece atmosphere, and sexual shenanigans of highly improbable postures.

Mei Yang (Lawrence Ng) is a socially prominent scholar married to well-endowed heiress Yuk Heung (Amy Yip). Despite the availability of the buxotic Yip (one of HK's most notorious softcore starlets), Mei Yang is not satisfied. Peeping at the athletic ruttings of the large-and-charged silk-maker and his wife (Elvis Tsui and Japanese AV actress Mari Ayukawa), he bemoans his own less-than-enormous abilities.

With a scholar's logic, Mei Yang decides to change his lot by visiting a quack who promises to cure size-complexes through surgery. Mei Yang is sequestered in a barrel—its knothole affixed with a miniature guillotine—and submits to having his precious part replaced with that of a horse. He's locally anesthetized, the guillotine falls, and the procedure begins.

But things quickly and comically spin akimbo as the exposed scholar helplessly watches from the barrel. The horse refuses to take his anesthesia. The quack spills numbing potion all over his hands and can't grip his instruments. The quack's dog runs off with the scholar's original equipment. A thunderstorm hits—not ideal as the quack is scared of lightning.

Terrified, he flings the freshly severed horse penis into the air. The camera follows it up, twirling end-over-end, then down, where it lands—thunk!—in the agape mouth of Mei Yang's page. With time running out, the horse penis is finally rescued from the gagging page and transplanted onto Mei Yang. And it works.

This outrageous sequence, spooled out during the first reel, sets a tone which is maintained throughout, as our horny scholar—equine member aloft—successfully pursues the varied objects of his lust.

These interludes include a chastity-belt-busting session with the silkmaker's wife, who cottons quickly to Mei Yang's newfound sensitivity, and an upside-down orgy with two restaurant hostesses. Things culminate in a night-mare fantasy sequence, where Mei Yang must confront the karmic implications of his selfish and unnatural behavior, and is led away to comfort the donor horse's better half.

Meanwhile, the cuckolded silk-maker schemes a menial job at Mei Yang's court. He then evens the score with a rapacious hot-tub coupling with Amy Yip.

As an inevitable result of their wickedness, all players eventually get what's coming to them. Yip loses her social standing and ends up turning tricks in a brothel. And in the final scene, a sexually dissipated Mei Yang, resigned to life in a Buddhist monastery, meets and contritely embraces his nemesis, all lust and vengeance spent and forgotten.

Despite its cornucopia of cartoon couplings, and though some of its erotic particulars—multi-tongued licking-wheel toys, girl-girl flute manipulations, and Yip's unusual grip on her calligraphy brush—are played for laughs, *Sex & Zen* retains a high titillation quotient. The women are nubile, gorgeous and far from shy. And its high production values and deft creation of mood will impress all.

NOTE: The toes which superstarlet Amy Yip lovingly sucks (legendary Baltimore-based director John Waters calls this act a "shrimpjob") belong to cinematographer Peter Ngor Chi-kwan. Ngor gallantly served as stunt-footman.

When the film went into general release in the USA, creating boffo box office across the land, a series of three monochrome promotional shots were issued to the press. Only one—a profile of the silkmaker's wife tonguing a dangling bunch of grapes—was nudity-free, so every press review used that one. Unfortunately, the actress was misidentified as "Isabelle Chow" who plays another role in the film.

Ironically, Stefan had inadvertently glimpsed some salacious Japanese material while doing research in Tokyo, and recognized the lass as a Japanese AV starlet. By coincidence, while perusing items at a sprawling used-goods market in Tokyo's Shibuya district, he noticed her face on a VHS box—someone selling a passel of VHS tapes was passing it on. Even more astonishingly, her name was listed on the box in English.

For a mere 500 yen, Mari Ayukawa was identified and the original 1996 book corrected the error. Ayukawa spends more screentime trussed up in chains or sporting with studmuffin Elvis Tsui than working with silk, but ever since, sources have correctly identified her as a pivotal member of the ensemble cast in this particular epic.

If you're looking for a unique release of this film, get the PAL format Region 2 DVD from Hong Kong Legends. It features a lengthy essay on the film by Stefan Hammond: "A Lot of Sex, A Little Zen," unavailable elsewhere. A must for the DVD shelf of every Hong Kong film fanatic, especially those with OCD.

Thai poster for *Zu: Warriors from the Magic Mountain*.

Zu: Warriors from the Magic Mountain (新蜀山劍俠)

1983 | Starring: Adam Cheng Siu-chau, Brigitte Lin Chin-hsia, Yuen Biao, Sammo Hung Kam-bo, Moon Lee Choi-fung, Meng Hoi, Norman Tsui Siu-keung, Judy Ong, Corey Yuen Kwai, Damian Lau Chung-yan
Directed by Tsui Hark

Tsui Hark's frenetic, nutty, fantastic *Zu: Warriors from the Magic Mountain* was part of an early-80s boom in HK supernatural films. *Zu* serves as a bridge from the manic Shaw Brothers supernatural films of the same period to Hark's more-Westernized *Chinese Ghost Story* series.

Armed men clash pointlessly in one of the tenth century's numberless clan wars. A young warrior named Ti (Yuen Biao) climbs into a cave to escape the carnage, but is immediately besieged by fiendish thingies with glowing eyes. His bacon is saved by sifu Ting Yen (Adam Cheng), who attacks the monsters with a fusillade of magic swords shooting out of a scabbard slung across his back. Ti, grateful he's still in one piece, offers to become Ting's student.

The loner sifu, however, merely heads off for another evil-filled cave. But Ti wants to prove his mettle, so he joins Ting, rival sifu Hsiao, and Hsiao's student, I-Chen, to do battle with the "Evil Disciples." Who are they—this surreal troupe of hellish jokesters whose white faces are adorned with red forehead tridents?

"They're the bad guys and we are the good guys," explains I-Chen to newbie Ti, and that's all we need to know, really, as the screen detonates into an ultrakinetic, razor-edited battle featuring nets of blue electricity, huge flaming logs waved like wands, concentric circles of spinning steel death-frisbees, and twitch video game action.

Hsiao is poisoned by the Blood Monster (who is kept in check only by the eyebrows of well named guardian Long Brow), and must be taken to the Ice Fortress to be cured by the Ice Countess (Brigitte Lin Chin-hsia). In a scene of near-orgasmic—yet asexual—passion, the Ice Countess spars martially with Ting, then cures Hsiao.

But then Ting becomes possessed, turning spooky-silver in the process. Without enough energy left to effect his cure, the Ice Countess freezes everyone with an ice spell so Ti and I-Chen can go to Heaven's Blade Peak to unite the mythical Twin Swords and duel with the hideously-possessed Ting…keeping up?

Doesn't matter. *Zu* is a fantasy—Hark burning into celluloid what Georges Méliès, the father of cinematic gimcrackery, would have if he could have. But it's also about passion and loyalty and self-sacrifice and saving the Earth from certain destruction by The Forces Of Evil. Few films set so ambitious an agenda, but *Zu* manages to pull it off, largely because the thing is so visually breathtaking and Brigitte's scowl of concentration makes you damn well believe in ice spells and blasting demonic possession outta people's bodies and because Hark strung up to a hundred actors on wires in various scenes.

Zu isn't really for first-time Hong Kong blister-paced supernatural film viewers. You might want to warm up to the HK-supernatural-pace a bit. Try *A Chinese Ghost Story* or *The Bride with White Hair* first.

Zu: Warriors from the Magic Mountain is on the Hong Kong Film Archive's list of "Best 100 Chinese Motion Pictures."

NOTE: Some of the many versions of *Zu* on disc include a never-seen-before alternate ending with Yuen Biao and Moon Lee in modern dress explaining that the whole adventure was actually a complex fantasy.

The Scene

Not every HK film is a classic. Some have little to recommend them, in fact, except for one awe-inspiring bit of business: The Scene. Here are some of our favorites:

Angel Enforcers

1990 | Above-average policewomen kick-butt

film starring tougher-than-leather Sharon Yeung.

THE SCENE: An unfortunate young woman (Elaine Ngai) is put in harm's way by a psycho villain. He perches her atop a cake of ice, which rests on a heating coil. A web of taut monofilament lines is looped through the pull-rings of a dozen hand-grenades he's attached to her dress. The result?

A belief in reincarnation always helps.

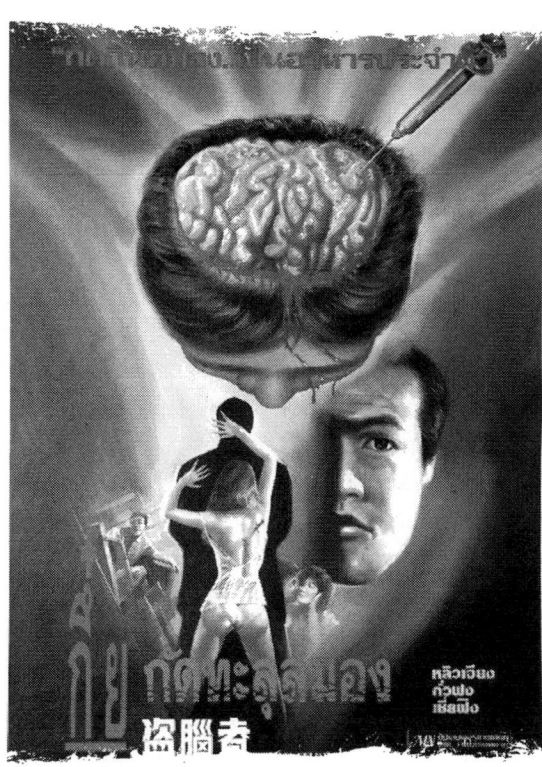

BRAAAAAAAINS! Thai poster for *Pituitary Hunter*.

Pituitary Hunter

1981 | Whole brains aren't being stolen, just the pituitary glands, which means that some good-hearted but unlicensed doctor from the mainland is pilfering pituitaries in a tragically flawed attempt to create a growth hormone potion so his dwarf son can lead a normal life.

THE SCENE: A mean nurse is the first suspect. She sneaks into the morgue, but not to thieve brains from the cadavers. Instead, she is a frustrated corpse warden who stands up a row of the stiff occupants, yells at them 'til they seem to obey her close-order-drill commands, bites one in the neck, then, cackling, knocks them over like dominoes. When police suddenly burst in on her, the nurse dies of fright.

This sets the brain thief investigation back to square one.

Escape From Brothel

1992 | Tedious melodrama about two kind-hearted HK hookers, one's criminal boyfriend from the Mainland, and the sad fate that awaits them all.

THE SCENE: Naked co-ed kung-fu! Evil Billy Chow and tattooed Sophie Crawford are starting to get it on (she's nude, he's topless), when in busts Crawford's husband and his crony. They demand money from Chow. Rather than play the badger game, he starts to thrash them.

But then Crawford's up off the bed, and with a chi-concentrating yell lands a kick to Chow's midsection. She attacks in slo-mo (like Caine in the old TV series Kung Fu) but he defends himself well, delivering a forearm shiver to her chest which reels her backward and out of the scene.

After Chow violently mops up husband and crony, Crawford returns, swinging from the top of a door frame and catching Chow around the neck with her legs. Upside down and hanging down his back, she grabs his crotch and squeezes. Chow endures long enough to fire a hold-breaking chop to her crotch. Crawford keeps fighting, but Chow subdues her, gets a gleam in his eye, and begins doing the nasty, until his pager goes off.

Holy Weapon

1993 | Dopey all-star comedy with all your favorite stars wearing Ming Dynasty costumes and being silly.

THE SCENE: Sharla Cheung Man impersonates a famous courtesan, and her beauty causes a local pervert to salivate frantically: "I beg you to eat me right now!" She transforms into a giant half-spider/half-female creature and binds him in an enormous web. Spinning a thread from her gorgeous mouth, she then binds his bodyguards and chops them to pieces with her razor-sharp legs. Then...he gets his wish.

Queen's High

1990 | Warring Hong Kong clans have too much gunpowder in their coffers.

THE SCENE: Cynthia Khan's wedding is crashed by white-suited gunmen who ventilate the wedding party. When her brother and husband-to-be shot to pieces, she goes literally ballistic with discarded nine-millimeter ordnance: slo-mo shots of psychobride in a long flowing gown—with a lovely corsage—feeding the unwanted guests hot lead.

Hex Errors

By tradition, Hong Kong films were typically subtitled in both Chinese and English in on-screen prints and on VHS. This has changed as optical discs usually offer various options for subtitles.

Translating Chinese into English isn't simple, and multiple gaffes are the inevitable result. Especially when you are translating at the breakneck pace demanded by cost-conscious HK producers. Director Tsui Hark once claimed that his feature *Peking Opera Blues* was subtitled in two days for less than US$100.

This splintering of the Queen's English adds additional—if unintended—entertainment value for those of us who don't understand the Cantoflow flying by. We've collected our favorite "hex errors," divided them into categories, and sprinkled them throughout the rest of the book.

If you are like us, some of these epithets will stick in your head, springing from long-term memory at the oddest times. Drop a cup of coffee, and out pops "Damn you, stink man" (*Caged Beauties*); when someone cuts you off in traffic, "You bastard, try this melon" (*Gunmen*); and for no good reason, "Suck the coffin mushroom now" (*The Ultimate Vampire*).

These cracked subtitles have created their own ecosystem These mutilated subtitles capture the imagination. Hundreds of these spindled chunks of language were printed in the original book, and lists were reprinted in several periodicals. Once a list of eighteen prime Hex Errors hit the Internet, it flashed its way around the world a jillion times—somebody likely forwarded it to your cyber in-box.

At one point, some joker hacked off the source-listing and added three obviously phony (overly long and unfunny) subtitles. Things got a bit frisky—in late 1998, the New York Times printed "Lost, and Gained, in the Translation", a list of purported Chinese translations of Hollywood movie titles. The "translations" came from a Web humor site called "The Top 5 List", and were fake fake fake.

Accept no substitutes! Every Hex Error in this book appeared in a Hong Kong film and is reproduced with its original punctuation and (mis)spellings intact. Genuine Hex Errors will always have the title of the film attached as a guarantee. Again, filmmakers make a greater effort nowadays, but many fans love the old-school cracked subtitles. We raise a steaming cup of tea to the folks at Discotek who offer a choice of newly translated subtitles AND "the original cracked subtitles" on their DVD release of Herman Yau's delirious masterpiece *Ebola Syndrome*.

Original punctuation, capitalization and spelling has been preserved, as has the title of the relevant film. To do otherwise would be cheating.

Hex Errors: Battle Of The Sexes

"Dammit it! You are crazy for sex!"
"Why should I be the exception?"
Lewd Lizard

"I know it, he's not an idiot, he's sexual detour"
Black Panther Warriors

"Don't shout. Balls are not broken yet."
"Yeah? My iron balls are like marshmallows now!"
Devil Cat

"He's Big Head Man, he's lousing around"
Close Escape

"Men are somehow abnormal"
Call Girl 92

"Vow, sharp looking chick"
Long Arm of the Law"

Catherine is a nasbian!"
Passionate Killing in the Dream

"You're bad. You make my busts up and down"
The Love That is Wrong

"She adulterated and cuckolds me"
Flirting

"What you need is a canned woman."
To Hell With the Devil

"I'll jelled if you ask me out"
Ghostly Love

"Got it, love machine!"
Dreaming the Reality

"I won't mind exciting sex game"
Naked Killer

"Nicked named Little-bun, also named Bitchy-bun."
It's Now or Never

"Oh, a perverted wolf is a good man too"
Master Wong vs. Master Wong

"I have piles. You won't be comfortable."
Ghostly Vixen

"I've checked, you are suffered from 'Big Penis.'"
Ghostly Vixen

"Don't do anything perverted, we are in a hurry."
Holy Weapon

Movie-painting detail from a *gyonsi* flick in Ipoh, Malaysia (Photo: Stefan Hammond, 1993).

CHAPTER TWO
DODGE THAT FLYING WITCH'S HEAD

here's two kinds of people in this world: those who like movies where the witch takes her head off and throws it at you, and those who don't. We hang in the former camp, and are pleased to report that HK boasts some of the creepiest, spookamous-jookamous flicks ever cranked out.

Inspiration is drawn from centuries of Chinese legend in which legions of hopping vampires are a common part of daily life, and whose existence is put up with as one might tolerate bad weather. Vampires are not scheming Eastern European guys in formalwear, charming the ladies and biting their innocent necks, but corpses in Ming Dynasty garb. Rigid in death, *gyonsi* ("hopping ghosts") are scary but have a cute, playful side as well.

Hopping vampires are just foot-soldiers for more powerful demons and witches. These monsters have no cute side at all, and are threats to life as we know it, using their powerful magic to transmogrify into all sorts of beclawed and squiggly red-eyed forms in their constant efforts to enslave the souls of mortals. Add Southeast Asian sorcerers with their love and death spells into the mix.

Standing in their path is the Taoist priest. Wearing yellow robes and a wedge-shaped headdress sporting the ying/yang symbol, the Taoist is forever constructing altars festooned with candles and incense sticks, mixing black ink with blood, making reams of paper charms, playing with fire, and performing laser-blast tricks with eight-sided feng shui mirrors. When the Taoist is not involved in life and death struggles with the underworld's yawning maw, he's bailing his dunderhead students out of vampire-inspired snafus.

The opening monologue often explains the rules of engagement to participants and audience alike. This helps befuddled gwailos. Not knowing what to expect next, though, is—like the first trip through a thrill ride—a positive part of the experience. Hong Kong-style spooking and howling takes full advantage of the breadth and depth of Asian ghost lore—a slithering caveful of ghoulies, gangrenous witches, and blood gluttons.

Certain horror film conventions are universal: the snarling visage lit from beneath; the malfunctioning flashlight which precedes the lightning-quick charge of the imp; the rotting monster plucking vengefully at your flesh. Other scary jolts are unique to Hong Kong: the scrumptious strumpet who morphs into a cackling butt-naked crone, and the valiant yellow-robed Taoist master with an altar of idiosyncratic demon-repellers. To jump into the ocean of Hong Kong spook-flicks means battening on ghoul plankton and dodging horrorhead sharks.

The Ghoul Rules

What fuels this juddering engine of oozing, green-lit goblins and succubi? Often, the selfsame fears and angst which plague fans of Western ghoulie flicks. Hong Kong horror manipulates old, familiar fears, and presents some new and very different ones. Hong Kong horror films have been around since the 30s, but the earliest we can find is *The Enchanted Shadow* (1960), from Shaw Brothers Studios—the four-character Chinese title is identical to Tsui Hark's 1987 film *A Chinese Ghost Story* (see page 15).

With Hong Kong's pedal-to-the-metal mix of spiritual beliefs—a brew of Confucianism, Buddhism, Taoism, animism and what-not—Hong Kong supernatural danger is diverse and fascinating. Divining your luck (or lack of it) is a never-ending pastime in Hong Kong, where feng shui experts, geomancers and shamans command hefty fees for their services.

Respecting the dead helps ensure good luck, which is why you gotta burn massive amounts of ghost paper and incense for your ancestors. Stock market gone south? Mother-in-law besotted with avarice? Boyfriend astray? Setting out food-offerings provides insurance against such calamities, or act as a salve *ex post facto*. Cooked chickens, steamed buns, oranges and hunks of roast pork are staples.

Trouble starts when young Hongkies start wisecracking and disrespecting the ancient forces of witchin' nature. Whether blockheaded vampirology students or lust-frustrated sex tourists, they invariably get the stern warning from Those Who Believe: don't diss the dark side. They laugh it off, with predictably ballistic consequences. It's kind of like the Hollywood slasher films of the eighties, where drinking/huffing/shagging teens were offed by an implacable maniac in direct proportion to their amount of sinful activity.

Ghost stories—three at a time

Oral traditions are strong in Hong Kong, and take many forms. There's the tall tale, the dirty joke and, of course, the ghost story. In Hong Kong, ghost-story films often take the form of triptychs, with a narrator introducing three terrible tales.

A stern warning for uppity Hong Kong youth is an ongoing theme of the 1990s-era *Troublesome Night* series from director Herman Yau. The first *Troublesome Night* opens with an arching overhead shot of Simon Lui in a graveyard—Master of Ceremonies for the fearful teen faithful: "Well, do you believe in ghosts?"

TN3 revolves around a group of people who work at a mortuary. They're an insular group, due to the traditional fear of anything associated with death in most Chinese societies. Fennie Yuen plays the head mortician who has problems getting a date due to her profession. She meets a studly young guy named Daviv (Michael Tse) at a bar, they fall in love and he offers to marry her. But next thing ya know, he's not returning her calls, he's being a creep, finally he blurts out that he can't stand the thought of her touching those corpses—despite his earlier protestations to the contrary. What a cad! Heartbroken, she hurls herself off a concrete building. But if you think that's the end of this tale, you haven't seen enough Hong Kong ghost flicks: just wait until he brings a hot date over a week later, anxious to show her some "Japanese VCDs"...eeek! Spooked outta his very life, as you may have guessed, by the green-lit ghost of the dead mortician. Ghosts always collect their debts.

TN4 ratchets up the stakes by plunging a bunch of lust-crazed Hong Kong stooges into the wilds of the Philippines. Nudity is added to the mix, as Filipino audiences won't bite the ticket bullet without a bit of salacious skin. Yau twists the knife by transforming yummy disrobing Filipinas into cackling topless toothless grannies at random, terrifying the other characters. The fifth installment in the *Troublesome Night* series premiered in the first few weeks of 1999, twenty months or so after the first TN film. If the Terminator film series had kept pace, we'd be seeing *Part 789: L'il Baby Terminator—War on Asteroid Pooty-poot* in cinemas now.

Pint-sized Nosferatu

European vampire traditions descend from a single parent: Bram Stoker's Dracula, a late nineteenth-century novel which introduced a seminal character of gothic menace. The creature was part dashing nobleman, part blood-draining ghoul, and was inspired by a fifteenth-century Wallachian despot—Vlad Tepes—who impaled his enemies on not-particularly-sharp wooden stakes. Western vampire dress, customs and antidotes stem from the dozens of films featuring blood slurpers.

The origins of Chinese vampire legends are more complex. It's optimal for deceased Chinese to be buried near their ancestral home, but of course, deaths sometimes occur far from home. In such cases, relatives would hire a Taoist priest to re-animate the dead person. Although stiff from rigor mortis, they could be taught to hop so that the priest could lead them (at night, unlucky otherwise) on a "corpse drive" to their home-villages for proper burial.

One useful cinematic convention is the "sifu's explanation": early on in most of these films, the wise one will explain just why the sticky rice and inked string are so important in dealing with hopping corpses (known as *gyonsi*), for the audience's benefit. There are many weapons in the Taoist arsenal for handling the undead, including coin-swords, yellow-paper charms (often set afire), sticky rice, and a handbell. Although it's never exactly clear why, child-vampires are considered cute.

A Chinese Ghost Story 2
(倩女幽魂2人間道)
1990 | Starring Leslie Cheung Kwok-wing, Joey Wong Jo-yin, Jacky Cheung Hak-yow, Michelle Reis (Lee Kar-yan), Waise Lee Chi-hung, Wu Ma, Ku Feng
Directed by Tony Ching Siu-tung

Movie-painting for *A Chinese Ghost Story 2* in Shinjuku, Tokyo (Photo: Stefan Hammond, 1990).

The sequel commences with a montage of scenes from the first *A Chinese Ghost Story* (see Chapter 1). Ning (Leslie Cheung, reprising his original character) finds himself thrown in jail in a case of mistaken identity. he's been locked up long enough to grow a long beard. However, one night his jailers bring him a rice bowl topped by a succulent soy-sauce chicken leg—unusually fine jailhouse fare. Ning eagerly sinks his teeth into the fowl, but loses his appetite when his cellmate (whose beard is even longer) tells him that the dish is known as "Headless Chicken" because one's beheading takes place the day after one is served the meal! The cellmate, Chu (Ku Feng), gives him a lucky medallion and helps him escape. Ning takes refuge in a deserted villa containing eight coffins. But after dark, when the coffins open up and their spooks come out, Ning flees.

He's set upon by the flying white-sheeted spirits, but Autumn (Jacky Cheung), a monk also taking shelter in the villa, freezes them in midair. The spirits are revealed to be fakes. They are actually a group of patriots, led by Windy (Joey Wong) and Moon (Michelle Reis), who are planning to free their father—Lord Fu—who has been unjustly taken prisoner by the Emperor's men.

Because of the medallion, the idealistic young patriots mistake Ning for the wise sage Elder Chu, who's still happily scratching on his cell walls.

Ning protests, but they interpret his remarks as wise riddles. They attach profound significance to his every word, and interpret a poem about Sian—his ghost lover from *ACGS*, Part 1—as a hint that they should intercept Lord Fu's captors at the Ten Mile Pavilion. Since Ning is smitten with Windy—his ghostly love's lookalike, played of course by Joey Wong—he too goes to the Pavilion.

Unfortunately, the place is haunted. Autumn teaches him the suspended-animation spell, but before he can show him how to break the spell, Ning accidentally freezes Autumn. He attempts to recall the correct supernatural-defrosting command, unaware that an animated ten-foot zombie is peeking over his shoulder! The frustrated Ning drags the rigid, sweating Autumn around the Pavilion as the monster freezes and defrosts with each attempt at recreating the spell.

Windy and her gang arrive, but when the towering zombie reappears, they flee. They run smack into Hu (Waise Lee), the warrior who is escorting their father back to court. Hu carves the beast up, but in the process, Windy is possessed by evil spirits, leading to some Linda Blair-like cursing and spewing. She turns into a monster, but Ning rescues her with a yang-infusing kiss (awwww...). Hu goes to enlist the aid of the High Priest to vanquish the spirits.

The High Priest turns out to be an evil impostor—he has a woman's voice, which, given HK filmic conventions, should have blown his cover already—and the source of all the dissension and chaos in the empire. His chanting voice hypnotizes everyone but Autumn, who plugs his ears and rescues the others. After a romantic interlude with Windy, Ning goes off to find Swordsman Yen (Wu Ma), the misanthropic-but-lovable monk who saved him in Part 1. Hu (who now realizes that Lord Fu is a victim of the High Priest's treachery), Autumn, Yan, and the others must destroy the evil priest, who reappears in numerous forms, including a gargantuan centipede.

After evading him through some nifty air-surfing on flying swords, Autumn and Yan are swallowed by the oversized bug. They must leave their bodies temporarily to survive; after the beast is killed, Yan rejoins his physical being, but Autumn's soul overshoots his body and shoots off into the sky. But fear not—Jacky Cheung returns in Part 3.

— Andy Klein

A Chinese Ghost Story 3
(倩女幽魂3 道道道)
1991 | Starring Tony Leung Chiu-wai, Joey Wong Jo-yin, Jacky Cheung Hak-yow, Nina Li Chi, Lau Siu-ming, Lau Shun, Tiffany Lau Yuk-ting
Directed by Tony Ching Siu-tung

The third and final installment in the Chinese Ghost Story series eschews Leslie Cheung and

his character in favor of a callow young monk named Fong (Tony Leung Chiu-wai, bald as a cue ball). Fong and his sifu (Lau Shun) are pursued by thieves who covet their golden Buddha statue. The harassed duo head for the deserted Orchid Temple, unconcerned about any lurking ghosts. After all, they're monks.

Needless to say, the temple houses its share of lovely lady ghosts. Lotus (Joey Wong) and Butterfly (Nina Li) trap the pursuing thieves and turn them over to the evil Tree Demon (the half-man/half-woman/all-evil witch with the 50-foot tongue in Part 1—played once again by Lau Siu-ming). Sluuuuuurp! Lotus then surprises Fong, who drops the Buddha into the temple's basement. The devilish cutie tries to seduce him, while he struggles to maintain his monastic vows. Despite her evil, he lets her leave.

When his master returns, he lies about losing the Buddha, then tries to search the basement in the light of day, but is scared off by snakes. Lotus returns that night; she helps him look for the Buddha, accidentally breaking it in the process. The master returns from a trip to the village; since night is approaching, he starts to seal off the temple with prayers and holy beads. Lotus is trapped, imperiled by his prayers. Moved, Fong saves her by dispersing the beads and tricking his master into leaving.

But just when you make things easy for the sexy nice ghosts, the evil ones always seem to cash in. Sans holy beads, the Tree Demon attacks. And with the protective Buddha statue broken, he's got enough stuff to trap the sifu. But thinking quickly, the resourceful holy man grows his earlobes out and—covering his eyes with the fleshy appendages—goes into suspended animation.

Fong heads into town to get the Buddha fixed. He fails, but hires the avaricious swordsman Yin (Jacky Cheung) to help rescue his sifu. Back at the temple, Lotus rescues Fong from another assault by the Tree Demon. The jealous Butterfly—whose long red fingernails can shoot out like knives—betrays Lotus to the Demon. The horrible witch threatens to marry Lotus to the Mountain Devil. Lotus escapes, but the Tree Demon binds Fong in a web of red silk and has Butterfly attempt to lasciviously suck out his yang energy. Finally, Yin and Fong's sifu unite with Lotus to wipe out the Tree Demon with their combined powers. But then they have to contend with the Mountain Devil—comprised of a glowing animated pagoda and a huge disembodied head with sharpened teeth. After vanquishing this horror, the humans emerge battered but victorious. Lotus, however, looks forward only to another shot at reincarnation.

— Andy Klein

Bio Zombie... GRARRGH!

Bio Zombie (生化壽屍)

1998 | Starring Jordan Chan Siu-chun, Sam Lee Chan-sam, Emotion Cheung Kam-ching, Wayne Lai Yiu-cheung, Angela Tong Ying-ying
Directed by Wilson Yip Wai-shun

Bam! *Bio-Zombie*'s opening credits assault the viewer from Frame One. Cruddy woodcut-looking things, reminiscent of a cheaper-than-dirt Filipino zombie classic from the sixties.

Whap! Right into the glassed-in aisles of North Point's New Town Plaza shopping arcade, where cheap fluorescent lighting makes everyone look bluish and pasty even if they're not a zombie.

A couple of punks—Woody Invincible (Jordan Chan) and Crazy Bee (Sam Lee)—strut the arcade. They are pirate video peddlers and petty thieves, but aspire to become better criminals someday. When some pencil-neck nerd complains about the lousy quality of their pirated product, they yell at him ("If you want to see clearly, go to the theatre!"), threaten him with a plastic computer-game pistol, donate a couple of porno discs and send him packing.

DODGE THAT FLYING WITCH'S HEAD

Woody Invincible and Crazy Bee, a pair of tweaked twerps nurtured in the glow of video games, children of the electric-speed McLuhan generation, spineless tough-talking dummies, become the Alpha and Omega of the known universe through a series of bizarre and horrific circumstances. While driving their triad boss' car back to the arcade, they run over some random guy. To fix him up, they pour a handy bottle of Lucozade (a soft drink) down his throat. But the innocent-looking bottle actually contains a secret Iraqi serum which turns people into hideous rotting flesh-eating bio-zombies. Thus the title.

They dump the guy in the trunk and drive to the mall. Needless to say, he busts out and starts biting people. And when you're bitten by a zombie, what happens? And to neutralize a zombie, you shoot them where?

Crazy Bee's played the right videogame, so he tells the cops where to shoot. But the zombies rip teethfirst into the spurtin' cops anyway. You can see where this is heading.

The grafting of the zombie film onto a triad-punk drama is aided by the use of inexpensively blurred and processed "zombie vision". Incidents of sloppy sentimentality produce lapses between attacks of the undead and gory live-action videogame fun. But a stream of zombie-film staples—the tough bastard who goes jelly-nellie, the emotional torment of waiting for bitten pals to turn zomb, the crucial handcuff keys falling into the insensible ghoul's mouth—ensure that the stream of entertainment continues to flow in great red gouts throughout *BZ*.

The Bride with White Hair
(白髮魔女傳)
1993 | Starring Brigitte Lin Chin-hsia, Leslie Cheung Kwok-wing, Elaine Lui Siu-ling, Francis Ng

Movie-painting of Brigitte Lin with witchy eyebrows and ice-white hair, on a cinema in Northeastern Thailand (photo: Stefan Hammond, 1993).

Chun-yu, Nam Kit Ying
Directed by Ronny Yu Yan-tai

Psychosexual drama loaded with rich visual textures and fast, furious action. Leslie Cheung plays Yi-hang, a martial arts master condemned to self-exile atop a snowy mountaintop. In flashback, his tale reveals a childhood spent learning sword technique. Young adulthood brings a mosh-pit coiff and a bright future as the heir to the Chung Yuan organization—a powerful alliance of eight clans.

But Yi-hang is not fond of the martial life, and longs for freedom from swords through flesh. A beautiful warrior (Brigitte Lin) swirls into his life. She can rip people apart with her whip, but rather than sparring, they fall into thunderbolt love—

consummating their obsession in a crystalline pool surrounded by stalactites, their deadly careers forgotten in giggling washed-innocent abandon. Yi-hang learns that his new girlfriend has no name and christens her Lien Ni-chang.

Ni-chang didn't have a name because she was raised by wolves (really), and is now sponsored in her lethal activities by a cult leader named Chi Wu-shuang. Chi is a back-to-back brother/sister Siamese twin, a creature burning with malevolent intent. The male half (Francis Ng) blisters with unrequited passion for the beautiful Ni-chang, while the female half (Elaine Lui) mocks her brother as an unlovely abomination.

Ni-chang wants out of the cult, so she can start a new life with Yi-hang, and offers herself to the male half of the monster if he/she will release her. But she can't even pretend to get excited by his slathering advances, and the female twin on his back shrieks with derision as she realizes that Ni-chang will never be her brother's in any way, misshape, or form.

As punishment, Ni-chang is forced to walk the gauntlet barefoot: jagged shards underfoot and rabid fellow cult members clubbing her besides. She survives, but the vengeful Chi Wu-shuang resorts to scorched-earth subterfuge—slaughtering the leaders of the Chung Yuan organization. This blood-letting brings him face-to-face with Yi-hang with the issue of trust (the highest virtue these less-than-savory characters can aspire to) at stake. And few things hath greater fury than Brigitte Lin scorned.

While *The Bride with White Hair* shares elements with other "legend films" like *A Chinese Ghost Story*, it's darker and more erotic than most. The film features some lovely graphic violence and fans of stage-blood-jetting-out-backlit won't be disappointed.

Ha Ching Fa isn't pleased, neither is Master of Ghost: screengrab from *Deadful Melody*.

Deadful Melody (六指琴魔)

1994 | Starring Yuen Biao, Brigitte Lin Chin-hsia, Carina Lau Kar-ling, David Lam Wai, Wu Ma, Elvis Tsui Kam-kong, Siu Wing-sang
Directed by Ng Min-kan

After Brigitte Lin gleefully stole the show as the she-male villain(ess) of *Swordsman 2*, she appeared in a succession of films as mighty witches, deadly swordswomen or cold-blooded assassins. As Lin herself put it: "I seem to fulfill some fantasy the audience has about a beautiful girl performing violent acts." In *DM* (a reworking of the Shaw Brothers 1983 film *Demon of the Lute*), she excels in another role demanding toughness and invincibility—a musical martial artist who dresses in manly garb and wields a magical stringed lyre which blasts her opponents into plumes of colored smoke.

Lin plays Snow, a character inhabited with a likable air of menace. As told in flashback, Snow's parents were slain by rival martial arts masters intent on possessing the lethal lyre. Seeking vengeance, Snow concocts an elaborate ruse to lure the killers out in the open. She hires a naive but headstrong security guard named Lun (Yuen Biao) to transport a case containing the lyre to the Mo Yee mountains.

DODGE THAT FLYING WITCH'S HEAD

Fire demands the magic lyre, as Ha Ching Fa seeks someone to rip with her whip: *Deadful Melody*.

This turn of events is perplexing and worrisome to the rival martial arts clan leaders, who are a bizarre lot. There's Master Of Ghost (David Lam), a tall and scary pale blue demon. Fire (Wu Ma) is balding, portly, and bright red. And then there's Ha Ching Fa, the Hard-Hearted Witch (Siu Wing-sang)—a comely young woman who enjoys ripping people's heads off with a whip. Master Of Ghost's twin sons are pale blue and twitter about like the Wicked Witch's flying monkeys, and the entire assemblage is something like a Clive Barker remake of *The Wizard of Oz*.

Naturally, the villains want the magic lyre, and pursue Lun with a vengeance. Snow shadows him to insure his well-being, and to see her plan to its bloody fruition. Eventually she discovers that Lun is her long lost brother whom she thought had perished with her parents.

Lun, however, remembers nothing of his tragic past, and he vows revenge against Snow when his foster father becomes a casualty of her vendetta. The two siblings finally reconcile, but their long-delayed reunion is interrupted as the evil martial arts masters rally their forces for the final showdown.

The hellbent Snow pulls back the strings of the musical instrument like a hunting bow, and fires bursts of energy which lead to some imaginative carnage. Master of Ghost watches his men blasted into smoke and body parts, but still stands as Snow takes a breather and plays a soft melody on the deadly instrument. She tells him that he's been hit internally by the 8 Magic Keys of the lyre, and his body will explode if he takes two steps forward. M of G lets loose with hearty mocking laughter, takes one step, takes a hesitant second one...BOOM!

Ha Ching Fa fares no better, as Snow's tuneful fu penetrates the Hard-Hearted Witch's inner organs and causes her to spew out a geyser of blood prior to her own detonation. Snow survives the ordeal, but she and hardheaded brother Lun part at movie's end, to pursue their separate martial goals.

Devil Fetus (魔胎)
1983 | Directed by Lau Hung-chuen
Starring Shirley Lui Sau-ling, Eddie Chen, Lu Bei-bei, Leung San, Lau Dan, Chui Mang-gwong

A quasi-phallic jade vase sold at auction possesses a young Hong Kong woman, Suk Ching (Lu Bei-bei), who buys it upon supernatural impulse. In her boudoir, the vase transforms into a monstrous humanoid she finds strangely attractive. Even though her husband Ji Cheung (Lau Dan) is away on business in Japan, her fondness for the bizarre item puzzles her extended family—including her young nephews.

When hubby returns from biz, he sees his wife in the clutches of the amorous monster, which changes back into a vase. He seizes it and smashes it to the ground, but smoke pours from it and turns his face into a throbbing blue horror. Ripping part of it off to reveal a carpet of maggots, the supernaturally cuckolded businessman leaps

MORE SEX, BETTER ZEN, FASTER BULLETS

Splittin' and a-grinnin': *Devil Fetus*.

out the window, melodramatically widowing his young bride...and we're barely ten minutes into the movie!

She barely has time to grieve before nausea's detected by her savvy sister-in-law, who deduces that Suk Ching is pregnant (demon-spawn no doubt, as her husband's been away for six months). As the now-pregnant widow lies in bed mourning, the ghostly voice of Ji Cheung is heard ("the worms are biting me so painfully"). She's then attacked by the family cat and falls down the stairs to her death.

The family brings in a Taoist priest for her funeral—spying preternaturally into her coffin, the priest spots her post-mortem bump expanding Alien-style into an imminent infant-ghoul and seals the coffin with a paper charm.

As if all this wasn't bad enough, the Taoist tells sister-in-law that both victims fall into the "half-a-dead-body" category reserved for untimely deaths, and their wooden memorial tablets must be sealed in a room within the house for 12 years before they can reincarnate. More paper charms are ceremoniously pasted on the room's door and we flash-forward a decade or so.

The nephews are now rambunctious young adults, and the older, Ken Cheung (Eddie Chen), comes home after a victorious kendo match to find cutie-pie JoJo (Shirley Lui—a "god-daughter" from Singapore), swimming in the family's backyard pool. Is the curse broken, is young love in the air, will the prosperous Cheung family escape the malevolence of the Devil Fetus?

In a pig's eye. Director Lau Hung-chuen (cinematographer on films by John Woo, Tsui Hark and Ringo Lam) trowels on myriad horror-movie tropes—cheesy synthesizer music, demonic possession, canine disembowelment, and a worm-infested birthday cake smear the screen, along with an endless parade of generic disco, bad 80s hairstyles and fashion-violations. The moral? Don't go to Japan on six-month business trips.

The Eternal Evil of Asia
(南洋十大邪術)
1995 | Starring Ellen Chan Nga-lun, Chan Ka-bong, Ben Ng Ngai-cheung, Elvis Tsui Kam-kong, Lily Chung Suk-wai, Bobby Au-Yeung, Ng Shui-ting
Directed by Cash Chin Man-kei

Bon (Chan Ka-bong) is passionately attached to his lovely fiancee May (Ellen Chan), but when his three buddies crave a laddish odyssey...what are

DODGE THAT FLYING WITCH'S HEAD

Ellen Chan realizes her path to revenge against lust-crazed Thai sorcerer Laimi in this screengrab from *The Eternal Evil of Asia*.

ya gonna do? The quartet of Hongkies set off for Thailand intent on bad behavior. They pile into a taxi headed for a mythic neon-lit hostess bar located somewhere in the middle of nowhere, cracking dopey condom jokes on the way.

The joint writhes with friendly working gals, but suddenly one lurches towards them screaming "I have AIDS!". The idiots panic and rush out of the place pursued by a stream of chopper-wielding goons. Our heroes run into a nearby forest and take shelter in a nearby hut—the residence of sorcerer Laimi (Ben Ng).

The wizard's not pleased—he's busy preparing for a duel with a rival sorcerer couple. Plus his uninvited guests are smartin' off. He warns them ("In Thailand, a wizard won't use enchantment as a joke"), and when Kong (Elvis Tsui) calls him a "dick-head," the exasperated shaman transforms the frustrated sex-tourist into a literal dick-head.

His pals laugh uproariously at Kong's new "German helmet" but there's no time for frivolity as sorcerer couple Barran and Chusie show up and immediately square off. Green explosions fill the darkened skies of rural Thailand as the witchy couple supernaturally flies through the air gettin' after it doggy-style to prime the ju-ju, then attack Laimi and wrap him in a monstrous green and gooey witch-born placenta.

Bon saves the day by impulsively dousing Laimi's opponents with enchanted powder. The grateful wizard introduces his minxotic kid sister Shui-Mei (Chin Gwan). She develops a girlish crush on Bon and persuades big brother to cook up a love hex.

But the preternatural love-bomb misfires and bewitches his three stooge-buddies instead. When Shui-Mei emerges from her daze to realize the naked truth, she goes bananas and falls on a razor-sharp fruit knife—unfortunately, fatal impalement ensues.

The numbskulls return to Hong Kong to escape the wrath of the Thai shaman, a ploy which fails miserably. Nam (Bobby Au-Yeung) is possessed, annihilates his family and nosy neighbors with a cleaver, then hurls himself out the window and is impaled on fluorescent light tubes. He returns, *American Werewolf in London*-style, to dispense advice and scare the hell out of his surviving chums, while the jagged tubes protruding from his bloody torso blink on and off.

Kent (Keith Ng) is supernaturally afflicted while at a restaurant with his girlfriend. He finishes his spaghetti, then devours his girlfriend's spaghetti. Grabs the waiter and orders "Mediterranean fried rice with vegetables." The bewitched fool then chews off portions of his fellow patrons, causing a ruckus, and finishes things up by snacking on his own left arm.

A terrified Kong seeks the help of a local Taoist, but is tricked by Laimi and given a "pin hex" which transforms him into the Hong Kong version of Pinhead from Clive Barker's *Hellraiser* films. The shaman holds Bon in spiritual bondage and demands that May satisfy his revenge-inspired lust.

Laimi pours blood extracted from seven people over his naked body and astrally projects into May's boudoir, setting up a scenario of mythic over-the-top sex between them. The Thai wizard magically strips her naked—one garment at a time. Sleazed-out sax music puffs the soundtrack as May's pouting lips succulently serenade a rigid shaft of air and expand the boundaries of thespian credulity in the process.

Moral: if you're a Hong Konger, choose your traveling companions carefully when venturing to Southeast Asia.

Mr Vampire 3 (靈幻先生)

1987 | Starring Lam Ching Ying, Richard Ng Yiu-hon, Lui Fong, Billy Lau Nam-kwong, Pauline Wong Yuk-wan, Pan Yung-sheng, Ho Kin-wai, Teddy Yip Wing-cho, Wu Ma
Directed by Ricky Lau Koon-wai

Hong Kong *gyonsi* films were popular in the mid-eighties and the *Mr Vampire* series was the most beloved of all. The *MV* films featured Lam Ching Ying as the wise, white-eyebrowed sifu and various actors as his oafish assistants. *MV3* is the best of the sequels—out of the dozens of Chinese vampire films cranked out in the mid- to late-eighties, this particular one (produced by Sammo Hung) is exemplary.

In *MV3*, Sammo stays behind the camera except for a brief cameo. The film begins with a freelance Taoist named Ming (Richard Ng) trying to earn a few taels by ridding a rich man's house of some noxious poltergeists. Ming is a charlatan, employing a pair of friendly vampires as subcontractors: adult Ta Pao (Lui Fong) and his kid brother Hsi Pao (Ho Kin-wai). The ghouls are sucked up into umbrellas (a standard method to secure the undead) and Ming is paid.

Then the real poltergeists show up on a carpet of blue-lit dry-ice fog. The rich guy built his house

Lam Ching Ying flanked by Billy Lau (left) and Pan Yung-sheng (right): screengrab from *Mr Vampire 3*.

above their family grave and its weight is pressing on the ghosts. A pitched battle ensues, and Ta Pao saves the day by extending his arms out several meters (*Nightmare on Elm Street*-style) to throttle the bad ghosts. The grateful Ming burns a pair of baby-blue shinyl-vinyl robes for the valiant duo to replace their standard Ming Dynasty vampdrag. The relationship between these dead-yet-cute ghouls and their human master is heartfelt.

But then Ming's grabbed by a group of brigands led by Captain Chiang (Billy Lau) who are convinced he's a horse thief. Chiang is about to cleave Ming's skull when sifu Uncle Nine (Lam Ching Ying, the ultimate ghostbuster, the guy who was duking it out with headless witches when you were in diapers) shows up and saves Ming's Taoist ass.

The real horse thieves appear, and they're worse than Uncle Nine and his Chiang-led gang could imagine. They're virtually unkillable and led by a shrieking Demon Girl (played by Pauline Wong Yuk-wan, not to be confused with Pauline Wong Siu-fung, the original head-tossin' witch from *Mr Vampire* [1985]). This dreadful demon's dizzying array of black magic attacks includes burping up magical maggots to heal gaping neck wounds.

Most combatants survive, but Chiang is

perplexed by the cabalistic nature of the horse rustlers. Sifu: "They sleep outdoors and drink blood/They eat venom and drink dew". Chiang: "They are no ordinary people." There you have it.

Ming is irked by Chiang and commands his blue-clad vampires to possess the Captain and make him do humiliating stunts in public. Uncle Nine figures out the game and sucks Ta Pao into a large clay pot, sealing it with a yellow-and-red Taoist charm. He then folds the child vampire over his knee and stuffs the ghoulish tyke into the same pot. The dual-ghoul pot is stored in Uncle Nine's storehouse of bottled-up demons, but Ming sneaks in and absconds with it, only to be confronted by Uncle Nine and Chiang.

Uncle Nine wants to know if Ming's manipulation of these vampires has made his life easier or harder, and Ming admits that his chicanery has made everything tougher. The clay pot is returned: "You decide yourself". Uncle Nine knows that Ming is deep-down righteous and will do the right thing: smash the pot and set the kindly blue-clad vampires free. Of course, this sifu-bonding moment leads to just that.

But the zealous Captain Chiang discovers that coating himself with tar renders him invisible to ghosts. He adds a barrel-like coat and conical hat and tries to capture Ta Pao with a magic lasso fired from a hollow gourd (Chiang's love for ghostbusting technology make him a pre-electric techno geek).

All hell breaks loose when Demon Girl suddenly appears and steals Ta Pao as well as Ming's Taoist robe. She rips the head off an iguana and guzzles the blood, then bewitches both garment and ghoul. Busting her way into Uncle Nine's stronghold (a classic arrangement of traditional Chinese buildings around an open courtyard), the banshee assaults with swarms of cockroaches and bats.

Uncle Nine and Ming counter with Taoist techniques and bamboo tubes filled with urine (apparently, the urine of a devout Taoist is a demon girl's Kryptonite). She's pierced with a coin-sword and thrown into a well, but returns. Her followers are hanged and thrown on a funeral pyre, but return. They are re-subdued, given the ol' Five Elements technique, then deep-fried in a gargantuan wok, but still return ("Bad, only medium rare!" shouts the distraught Ming).

Finally, the unified Taoists and the helpful vampires combine to knock this awful Demon Girl into hell, where she belongs. Some ghouls are pitiable and useful, and some are just pure evil. Some vampire flicks are silly fun and some give you everything you'd want in a supernatural film. *MV3*, from Sammo and his late colleague Lam Ching Ying, is one of the latter.

Red Spell Spells Red (紅鬼仔)
1983 | Starring Ken Tong Chun-yip, Poon Lai-yin, Leung Chi-hung, Hussein Abu Hassan
Directed by Titus Ho Wing-lam

RSSR's blend of sorcery and warped travelogue takes you back to the glory days of Manhattan's 42nd Street grindhouses. You can almost hear the Times Square faithful hollering for more gore or staring in dope-addled disbelief at the screen.

Creepy-crawly and aggressively weird, *Red Spell* will find no favor with hardcore PETA-philes; its scenes of pig-sticking, chicken-geeking, and scorpion attacks are rough and raw. Its Southeast Asian locations are appealing, though (as in many HK flicks), Southeast Asia is portrayed as a mighty wild and unruly place.

Stephen (Ken Tong), a director of mondo-style travelogues, takes his onscreen host/offscreen

MORE SEX, BETTER ZEN, FASTER BULLETS

Thai poster for *Red Spell Spells Red*.

girlfriend Stella (Poon Lai-yin) to Borneo. His next film will chronicle Borneo's legend of the Red Dwarf Ghost, a dwarf-sorcerer who was assassinated for his evil deeds by a quartet of righteous sorcerers and buried in a large jar. The film crew sneaks into the forbidden cave and busts open the cursed sarcophagus, which boils with red smoke. Stephen heads back to Hong Kong, while Stella and crew continue upriver to an Iban tribal village to gather more footage.

The Iban house master, Dairoma (Hussein Abu Hassan), seems affable, and the crew looks forward to "trial marriages" with the local girls, who—the portly Dairoma assures them—are free of "herres." But when the house sorcerer touches Stella's hand, he knows with electric certainty that she's got a big red birthmark on her shoulder and...well, red spell spells red.

The crew starts dying one by one. In the jungle, one gets a small cut; his spilled blood bubbles with demonic fury, animating surrounding bamboo stalks to grab, toss and pierce the poor man.

Back at the long house, a large black scorpion falls on Stella's shoulder and she flicks it off—stinger-first—into the arm of Dairoma's son Rumbang, who screams in pain. The irked housemaster immediately chops off his son's arm with a machete. Dairoma suspects that Stella carries a scorpion curse, but the sorcerer fingers local gal Satali as the curse-carrier. They prepare to sacrifice her to appease the gods, a move scotched by Mr Lau—an overseas Chinese representing a local Development Council.

When Stella passes by the town's cockfighting pit, the birds stop their fighting, and attack her as *Omen*-style music wells up. The villagers now regard Stella in a different light, especially when they realize that the now-teeming scorpions are spontaneously issuing from Stella's red birthmark. The sorcerer puts two and two together, recognizing Stella as his illegitimate granddaughter, whom he put a scorpion curse on many years ago after she was taken away to Hong Kong by her biological father. Another Pyrrhic victory from a spell-tossin' sorcerer in Southeast Asia.

Distraught, he summons a "Tibetan Lama" from Thailand. This hoodoo guru conducts an elaborate exorcism ritual which features Stella tied to a revolving water wheel—needless to say, wearing a sheer white blouse—while the sorcerer throws a powder at her made from her late mother's ground-up skull.

The Red Dwarf Ghost's spirit—which had nothing to do with the entire scorpion-curse mess—possesses Satali and she skewers Lau with just-sprouted sharp fingernails. But then the Lama steps in and puts the kibosh on the whole witchy gang.

NOTE: Stefan was introduced to director Ho by a mutual friend—Glenn Kay—at the 1997 Hong Kong Film Awards, shook his hand and said: "You must be the Titus Ho who directed *Red Spell Spells Red*."

Ho seemed thunderstruck, then affirmed that he did indeed direct the film. Later, Kay (who shared a ride with Ho after the event) explained: Ho had completely forgotten about the film. On the drive, he reveled in detailing the entire production to Kay: shooting in Indonesia, challenges and movie-tales, the actors and their personalities.

You never know when a bit of Hong Kong film lore might produce great nostalgic delight for directorial titans of witchy Southeast Asian cinematic shenanigans.

Rigor Mortis (殭屍)
2013 | Starring Chin Siu-ho, Anthony Chan Yau, Kara Hui Ying-hung, Yeung Feng, Pau Hei-ching, Lo Hoi-pang, Richard Ng Yiu-hon, Chung Fat, Billy Lau Nam-kwong
Directed by Juno Mak Chun-lung

Juno Mak's directorial debut is a unique meld of languorous, surreal horror that will shiver your vertebrae and homage to a beloved Hong Kong subgenre. The young director pays striking tribute to the *gyonsi* (hopping vampire) films, using fantastic modified vectors.

Mak cast several of the actors from the original *gyonsi* films, and none surpass lead Chin Siu-ho, one of sifu Lam Ching Ying's bumbling assistants in the seminal *Mr Vampire* (see page 20). Chin

Funnyman Richard Ng is gravely serious in Juno Mak's *Rigor Mortis*.

plays himself: now middle-aged, he takes up residence in a run-down Hong Kong apartment-building that seems a locus for odd Hong Kong characters—including Kara Hui, who won Best Supporting Actress at the Hong Kong Film Awards for her efforts—and the undead.

In an ethereal backstory, Chin's family who came to a bad end, and they haunt him. Literally. The film's opening sequence shows the tormented actor unable to tolerate a barrage of arcane death imagery, so he hangs himself from a crusty ceiling fan (director Mak used the crumbling On Wah Industrial Building as a set).

He's saved by Anthony Chan Yau (another Mister Vampire alumnus), who's an ex-Taoist priest now frying glutinous rice in a wok rather than weaponizing it against *gyonsi*. Mak's done his homework—sticky rice, inked string, Taoist charms and other lore permeates *Rigor Mortis*.

The film's template is taken from the *gyonsi* classics, but Mak's out to scare you. The vibe is modern Asian horror, complete with young-girl ghosts—co-producer Takashi Shimizu (director of *The Grudge* [2004]) helps ensure that audiences won't be sleeping easily after this one. The color palette desaturates as the grime of the On Wah Industrial Building turns to gray, then zooms up to red.

Violent moments are unexpected and unromanticized. There's no "shakycam" or other gimcrackery at work here, but low shots and overarching high angles keep viewers on edge as Chin slowly learns the secrets of this beyond-haunted building and becomes dragged into the ghostly problems created by its inhabitants (hint: there's more than one Taoist priest in residence).

It's delightful to see actors like Richard Ng, Chung Fat, and Billy Lau return in a horror film. Nina Pau Hei-ching turns in a heartfelt performance as Ng's devoted wife. But this film is Chin Siu-ho's tour de force, and his frames brim with quiet integrity and melancholy.

Mak's re-imagining of the *gyonsi* genre is a powerful Asian horror film. And to his credit, he name-checks now-departed greats Lam Ching Ying and Ricky Hui in the end credits.

The Seventh Curse
(原振俠與衛斯理)
1986 | Starring Chin Siu-ho, Maggie Cheung Man-yuk, Chow Yun-fat, Chui Sau-lai, Dick Wei, Ken Boyle, Elvis Tsui Kam-kong, Sibelle Hu Hui-ching
Directed by Nam Nai-choi

Secret lives of the HK rich and famous are explored in this splatterific yarn, which starts in the posh poolsides of Aberdeen Harbor but quickly shifts to the jungles of northern Thailand, which teem with preternatural worm tribes and fetid monster-breath. *T7C* features the characters of Dr Yuan and Wisely, a pair of cognac-sniffing adventurers created by pulp novelist Ai Hong. Dr Yuan is played by Chin Siu-ho while Wisely is given Peter Cushing pipe-puffing authority by Chow Yun-fat.

As *The Seventh Curse* opens, Dr Yuan defuses a cop/hostage drama despite the meddling of a spoiled-brat cub reporter, Tsai-hung (Maggie

Betsy comes popping out of a lake, then slices open her own breast to cure Dr Yuan in *The Seventh Curse*.

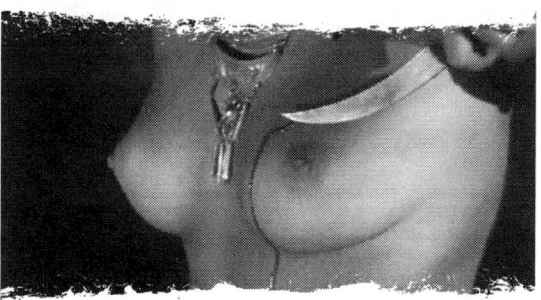

Cheung). His triumphal celebration with his gwailo girlfriend is stopped ante-coitus as Thai witch doctor Heh Lung (Dick Wei) busts into his apartment uninvited, warning Yuan that his "blood curse" is about to relapse. His final advice: "Keep away from sex." The good doctor gets after it anyway, and is rewarded with cork-popping spurts which burst from his limbs!

The proto-venereal phenomenon is explained in flashback: Dr Yuan goes to Thailand on a medical expedition and tangles with a Worm Tribe headed by Sorcerer Aquala (Elvis Tsui), a baby-grinding, cackling heathen. The tyrant silences dissenters with a flying alien-baby—a reptilian-killer-Hello Kitty-fetus—which rips into victims, then chews through their torsos.

Yuan saves the feral beauty Betsy (Chui Sau-lai) from sacrifice to "Old Ancestor"—an animated

Poster for *The Seventh Curse*.

being blown into chunks by Wisely, who arrives on the scene packing an RPG rocket launcher. Yuan heals himself by consuming the sacred grain and the two heroes return to Hong Kong to plan further adventures.

The Seventh Curse is a show-stopping midnight movie which flew under the radar of many HK fans. The film marked a possible direction for HK films (gore/fantasy/Wisely) which never really panned out. Too bad!

Aloha Little Vampire Story

1988 | A cute l'il child-vampire, Hsiu Long, grows tired of the endless feuding of Uncle Black and Uncle White (a pair of bickering vamps) and skeleton with a penchant for biting open necks and sucking out spinal cords. But Yuan is captured and receives a "blood curse": a handful of magic bullets, which he's forced to swallow, will come blasting out at regular intervals. The last bullet to go off will kill him.

The grateful Betsy slices a benign tumor from one of her ample breasts and feeds it to him, but this peculiar antidote lasts only a year. Dr Yuan must return to Thailand to retrieve sacred "grains" stored in the eyes of an enormous subterranean Buddha statue to effect a permanent cure. Yuan and Heh team up to battle the villainous Aquala; gorehound-spelunking ensues as the duo encounter Old Ancestor in his grue-drenched cave.

The skeleton transforms into a rubberized, slimy-fanged Godzilla/Alien critter which survives attacks by bullets and the now-on-our-side reptilian-killer-Hello Kitty-fetus, before

Thai poster for *Aloha Little Vampire Story* (courtesy of Putsachat Valajee).

runs away from home. Discovered by real kids pretending to be vampires, he camps out at the home of the feisty Dong Dong, who feuds with Fu, a bullying neighborhood kid. Dong Dong is scared of Hsiu Long, but when the cute little dead tyke magically heals the bruises Dong Dong got from fighting with Fu, they become friends.

Fu's uncle is an unscrupulous Taoist who's hired by a rich mobster to cure the gangster's brother, who's fallen under a rare vampiric spell. The afflicted brother wears a Victorian cloak to go with his fangs, but hangs out in trees and gibbers like a monkey. The Taoist feeds him vampire blood straight from a cold blue neck, but it's ineffective: only the blood of a thousand-year-old child-vampire will effect a cure. Of course, Hsiu Long qualifies. The human kids team up with the adult vampires to fight the evil gangsters and rescue the kidnapped kid-vamp. As absurd as can be, but despite the title, there are no Don Ho sing-alongs or parasol-topped rum-drinks.

Centipede Horror

1988 | Sensitive drama concerning a young girl and her pet centipede, Ling-Ling. Wrong! Opening credits alone are enough to give one the screaming meemies, as large, vigorous centipedes writhe toward the camera. Despite the novelty of a few reanimated chicken skeletons, this sorcerer vs. sorcerer flick is a bit on the dull side until the heroine starts heaving forth cornucopious amounts of the hideous, wiggling invertebrates!

Doctor Vampire

1991 | A Hong Kong doctor is vacationing in England when he gets bitten by a lovely vampire named Alice (Ellen Chan). He gets away, but when the British mastervamp gets a taste of his Alice-filtered blood, the gwailo bloodsucker goes

Ellen Chan's good-bad but she's not evil in *Doctor Vampire*.

bananas for it: "Don't you understand? His blood is like your Chinese ginseng!"

Back in HK, the doc finds he's lost his taste for garlic shrimp and starts going around with sunglasses and an Edwardian cloak like Nicholas Cage in *Vampire's Kiss*. His fellow MDs thoughtfully exsanguinate patients to feed him, and the kind-hearted Alice tries to cure him by reanimating a fresh corpse, which rambles around the hospital corridors with priapic intent.

The doc's meddling girlfriend and her nosy gal-pal make matters worse by bringing in a Taoist priest, whose spells cause our blanched hero to puff up with latex-bladder effects, veins a-throbbin'. And when Count Mastervamp shows up in the hospital, he's zapped with a surgical laser and pumped full of corrosive green fluid from log-sized hypodermics. This only slows him down, but he's finally defeated by the supernatural force of reanimated Chinese opera heroes.

Note: Chan's performance includes one of the most sensual bloodsucking sequences ever put on film.

Erotic Ghost Story

1990 | A tale of three sisters discovering their sensuality amid a backdrop of witches, triple-headed sex-fiends, and other erotic ephemera. Fluttering silk robes, ethereal sets and architectural hairstyles adorn the licentiousness. Alternatively silly and steamy, the film marked the debut of screen siren Amy Yip, she of sweet face and outrageous norks.

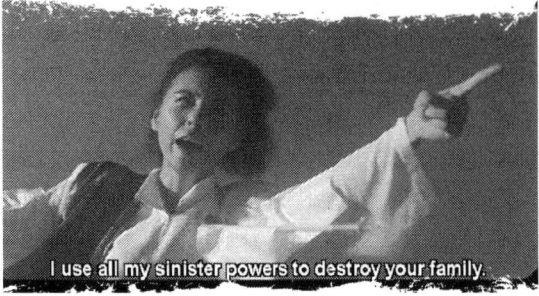

Tsui Suk Woon is annoyed: screengrab from *Evil Cat*.

Evil Cat

1987 | Veteran actor-director Liu Chia-liang (Lau Kar-leung) appears as a sorcerer whose family has been cursed by an evil cat-spirit. It returns every fifty years to wreak havoc, and has for the last four hundred. Do the math: only one more cat life to go! Mark Cheng helps Liu forever ice the feline. Stuart Ong performs creepy cat kung fu and Taiwanese sexbomb Tsui Suk Woon (*The Ghost Snatchers*) does a Terminator number, wiping out an entire cop shop with her bare claws. Blue-lit and spooky.

Hello, kitty...Mark Cheng gets sucked dry: screengrab from *Evil Cat*.

Thai poster for *The Ghost Snatchers* (courtesy of Putsachat Valajee).

The Ghost Snatchers

1986 | A new high-rise office building in Hong Kong starts experiencing problems; giant hands are reaching through the air-conditioning system and abducting people, then possessed secretaries are biting off executive's ears. An attractive female geomancer (Joyce Godenzi) is called in to diagnose and exorcise.

The problem? A legion of dead Japanese soldiers is buried beneath the foundations, and they're continuing their imperial efforts at world domination from beyond the grave. As wild as it sounds, the film is based on a true story. In the 70s, the Hong Kong Department of Public Works main building was diagnosed as suffering from

Japanese WWII ghosts. Civil servants refused to work overtime and a geomancer had to be called in to perform an exorcism.

The Ghost Snatchers includes one of Joey Wong's earlier roles, as Godenzi's assistant.

Ghostly Vixen

1990 | Vivacious Amy Yip plays Evil Girl, a ghost who must suck off 100 virgin boys to gain an eternal body. When we first meet her in a Thai bar, she finds and finishes #98. But before she can enjoy the afterglow, a rugged ghost hunter named Hui (Shing Fui On) brandishes his coin-operated sword at the vixen. She supernaturally projects into a mahjong tile bound for Hong Kong.

Cut to Hong Kong, where virgin junior executive Sau Yan (Nat Chan) just can't get laid. He takes one hooker to his apartment, but the power goes off. Trying to stay suave, Sau Yan brings out candlelight and champagne. The champagne cork pops his date in the eye, and when he tries to help, the candle sets her hair ablaze. Dousing her with the champagne, he tells her to wait in the bedroom. After drinking a sex charm, he follows her in, only to discover that the bedroom has been invaded by a pair of armed and horny robbers. Sau Yan offers them the services of his hooker, only to discover that they are gay.

He's having trouble getting laid because he's supernaturally promised to his old home-village sweetheart, a spinster-in-training named Yumy (Sandra Ng). Sau Yan wants nothing to do with the frumpy Yumy. But she's a gamer and, armed with a couple supernatural charms, heads off to the big city to get her man.

She arrives, catching Sau Yan with a second hooker's hair caught in his zipper. Pissed off, she uses the first charm to give him a leg-length penis which scares off his escort, then gets him into trouble at the next day's corporate presentation to a manufacturer of skimpy lingerie.

Disposing of ghost hunter Hui (he's a virgin, too) in a Hong Kong mental hospital, Evil Girl starts a seek-and-destroy sortie for Sau Yan, virgin boy #100.

Yumy tries to save her guy by sleeping with him, but Sau Yan can't get it up, even when Yumy holds photos of the supermodels over her face. So they must fight the Evil Girl.

Yumy dies, then comes back as a ghost and defeats the Yipster. A momentarily grateful Sau Yan marries Yumy in a ghost wedding, but after consummation, Yumy turns his dick into a flower (to keep him from straying), a spell which only she can reverse. Laughter and freeze frame.

Thai poster for *The Golden Swallow* (courtesy of Putsachat Valajee).

The Golden Swallow

1988 | A ripoff of *A Chinese Ghost Story*, but a good one. Cherie Chung plays Hell's Handmaiden, snaring souls for consumption by the scary black-eyed Old Witch who delivers wisecracks like "there's only one type of man: the edible ones." Chung falls for a cute traveling tax collector and shields him from edibility, but complications occur. Lots of beautiful photography, flying silk and extra-creepy human-freezing effects in this one.

Thai poster for *The Holy Virgin versus the Evil Dead*.

The Holy Virgin versus the Evil Dead

1991 | The moon turns red as the Moon Monster (Ken Lo) visits Hong Kong and slaughters the students of nerdy professor Donnie Yen. Scholarly attempts to defeat the Monster prove futile, as do various forms of killing him! All parties involved must take a holiday in Cambodia, where the Holy Virgin and her tribe vanquish the Lazarus-like green-eyed monster with sacred steel. Lots of martial action and witchy-nudie stuff, plus 1987's Miss Hong Kong Pauline "*Dragons Forever*" Yeung as a Cambodian sorceress.

Horoscope 2: the Woman From Hell

2000 | Casting luscious Pinky Cheung as the lead in a cheap horror film might seem foolhardy. But in *H2:TWFH*, from the marvelously named Bad Boy Film Culture Company Ltd, Cheung uses her archery skills (years before Jennifer Lawrence ever notched an arrow) to fight off an endless array of ghouls, nasty critters and reproductive nightmares.

Jess (Cheung) is married to a successful doctor, Yeung (Simon Yam). But when fellow doc Jimmy drives over for a BBQ, he's hit by a "black spell," hallucinates worms crawling over his arms, then sticks them in the blazing coals for relief. Pneumatic screen siren Senna (Sophie Ngan), the titular Woman From Hell, dances topless-save-glitter in a silver lamé miniskirt while waving long curved fingernail-extensions in a gauze-enclosed Hell altar—Senna, who naturally is Thai-Chinese, has put a "Potato Spell" on Jimmy, thus the vermin-inspired chaos.

So it goes: nonstop witchery, a warlock to oppose Senna introduced by a trusted friend, worms everywhere, hallucinatory infidelity and genuine betrayal, spells and counter-spells. And a fabulous bit of hotpot mushroom tarantula fu.

Cheung and Yam play it all straight, and when Pinky grabs her archery kit to put a stop to all the madness, you can't help but cheer the lass on.

MORE SEX, BETTER ZEN, FASTER BULLETS

Will she score a bullseye on the Woman From Hell, or is she even shooting at the right target?

Jail House Eros
aka Haunted Jail House

1991 | Women's prison. Haunted women's prison. The warden is a sadistic woman who makes with the firehose on the unfortunate inmates—including Amy Yip. Fortunately, the evil warden dies in a tragic accident. Unfortunately, she returns as a fierce ghost.

A trio of local goobers—who just want to romance the incarcerated crimekittens—pose as Taoist priests to get inside, but lack the right stuff for exorcism. So it's up to the Good Witch of the Cellblock (Loletta Lee) to whack the demon. Red-blooded males want to know how Amy Yip looks when shorn of makeup and wrapped in plain jail-dresses. Terrific!

My Neighbours Are Phantoms

1990 | Four 30s-era ghosts (two male and two female) escape from an old black & white photograph and begin to slake their thirst for human blood. First slated for slaking is the household next door—police inspector Dragon and his two sisters, Yummie and Sandy. But good female ghost Siu-Sin, whose ashes are controlled by the evil boss ghost, falls for Dragon—even before his trophy-winning performance at the annual high society Dirty Joke Contest (it's for charity)—and tries to protect his gang from the fangs of her master.

The superstitious sisters are the first to suspect all is not right with the new neighbors. Fortunately, another cop moonlights as a Taoist priest, and provides the necessary charms and holy water.

As Siu-Sin and her unwitting beau drive around in a giant paper Hell Car (see "Hell Bank Note", page 57), the sisters, with help from Dragon's ex-fiancée (played by the perky Amy Yip), holy-rope the evil female. But they must hold her tethered motionless 'til the priest/cop gets there. The angry ghost unfurls a six-foot-long tongue that attacks the only thing within reach—the straining buttons of Amy Yip's tight blouse.

In the final fight, a fleeing Dragon slows down a cemetery's uprooted tenants with a cha spell, but accidentally aims it at a mirror, and slows himself down, too. The life-or-death chase continues in frantic slo-mo. He finally must confront the mean boss ghost inside the old photo (an inspiring act of courage for someone's who's peed his pants twice already) to save Siu-Sin. He triumphs, but Siu-Sin can't follow him back to the temporal world.

Dirty jokes, blood-sucking, Amy Yip, and a doomed man/ghost love story—bring a date.

Operation Pink Squad 2

1988 | A bunch of female cops must pose as hookers in order to trap a counterfeiter. Unfortunately, their hideout is haunted by a rabid lady ghost. They chop this ghoul's head off with a shovel, which makes her really angry.

Not only does the head go flying around trying to bite people in sensitive spots, but the headless body proves a fearsome foe as well. The local Taoist is summoned to shoot down the head with an array of red-on-yellow Buddhist toy helicopters, but she uses the radical "Blood Out" technique to best him. The cops' only hope is to invoke "the Elf"—but which of the male characters possesses the prerequisite for Elfhood: their virginity?

Possessed 2

1989 | A HK cop moves his family into a flat facing a cemetery. Of course, they quickly become possessed by demons. The daughter turns on the schoolyard bully with a face full of fangs and popping red veins. The wife becomes a Suzy Wong vamp and sets out seducing weirdoes. She traipses into Central Market, finds a porky meat-cutter hacking up a huge oinker, and lures him into the back of a truck hung thick with hog carcasses. AIYAH! She transforms into a hairy monster and fries his bacon.

A jive-talkin' 1973-style fly-guy shows her his African snapshots and holds a lighter to his foot to prove his mettle; of course, he's toast. The exorcist can't get the job done because he's a really a beat cop named Dick who performs demonic duels only as a hobby. It's up to a traveling gwailo Hare Krishna to decode the demonology and bust the ghosts. Looks like the makers of this flick stayed

up all night watching *The Exorcist*, *Altered States* and *An American Werewolf in London* and ate waaaay too much ginseng.

Saviour of the Soul

1992 | Andy Lau and Anita Mui play star-crossed lovers hunted by master-criminal Silver Fox (Aaron Kwok). Fox sucks purple smoke out of test tubes and uses his "Terrible Angel" stance to possess Anita—she can only be cured by the Pet Lady (Carina Lau), a haughty sorceress living in the Pet Palace. The camera angles and art direction of this fantasy-romance are styled after Japanese anime. Lots of wirework and surreal action. Anita Mui plays a dual role as her own wisecracking sister.

Spiritual Love

1987 | Your typical love story: girl dies, boy meets girl's ghost centuries later, they fall in love, boy loses girl's ghost—it never works out. The lovers here are megastars Chow Yun-fat and Cherie Chung, but the show is stolen by Chow's vengeful, bitchy girlfriend May (portrayed with exquisite malice by Pauline Wong Siu-fung).

"Jealousing" over Cherie, May sets up a sympathy-evoking tableau for Chow to stumble upon: at midnight, she perches on a stool with her head in a noose, wearing a red dress. Dying under such circumstances turns a soul into a virulent, vengeful ghost, but this is all for show... until May's cat jumps at her and knocks her off the stool. She strangles, then returns from the dead in pissed-off mode to take a bite out of Chow. Cherie sends for reinforcements from Hades: her ferocious, feral ghost hubby, who rips May in half. Neither half goes quietly.

The Ultimate Vampire

1991 | Taoist hijinks with Lam Ching Ying and Chin Siu-ho of *Mr Vampire* fame. Watch for the "Hell Police"—four undead constables in monochromatic shinyl-vinyl garments; their muttering is only made intelligible when sifu chews on a ball of mud. Carrie Ng appears as an impudent young ghost ("You don't look 37." "I died when I was 20, and it's 17 years ago!") lusting after sifu. Be sure to stay tuned for end-credit outtakes, which demonstrate some spectacular flubs in wirework.

Thai poster for *The Ultimate Vampire*.

Ten Things We've Learned Watching Hong Kong Supernatural Films

1. Fierce ghosts and vampires can be subdued by affixing Taoist charms—written in red ink on yellow paper—to their foreheads. But the temptation to play with these immobilized ghoulies (push them, insult them, etc.) is completely irresistible and completely unadvised...

2. Because if you taunt or belittle a subdued ghoul, the chances that the charmed paper will come off—restoring the monster's lethality—is 100%.

3. Witches' heads just won't stay on. If they're not getting accidentally chopped off in battle, they're purposely being shucked with a neck-toss. In either case, witch-opponents get preoccupied with the disembodied heads, which fly around howling and trying to bite. But you can't ignore the headless body, which always hops up and gets into the fight!

4. Humans have Yang energy; the undead are Yin-heavy. Since human men have more Yang energy than human women, they are a prime target for the seductive powers of female ghosts. Whether the ghost's motives are noble or duplicitous, this kind of love never ever works out. As a Taoist priest put it in *The Golden Swallow*: "There's no love between man and ghost, Sonny."

5. Born under a bad sign? Stars crossed in your horoscope? Sorcerers and Taoist priests shrug their shoulders; they can predict your fate, but can't change it. Even if you started out as the hero of the film, if the geomancer says trouble ahead, you better stock up on incense and Hell Bank Notes, because you are done for.

6. When the exorcist asks for sticky rice, he damn well means sticky rice. Sticky rice is the active ingredient in poltergeist poultices. Regular rice is a spurious (and dangerous) substitute, often sneaked into the rice bag by dishonest salesmen because it's cheaper. The consequences can be dire.

7. The Chinese word for the number four sounds like the word for "death." So don't count on finding any Room #4's in Hong Kong hospitals, or even Room 14. On the other hand, the number eight is considered lucky, and you'll spot it everywhere, from restaurant prices to personalized license plates.

8. If your pet fish die, expect trouble.

9. Ghoul knowledge:
(a) Ghouls can't see humans, but spot them by smelling their breath. If you hold your breath, you are invisible to a vampire. But he will put his blue face about an inch from your nose and sniff furiously!

Japanese poster for *Mr Vampire 2*.

(b) The undead hop (or glide) only in straight lines along the floor. This is why Chinese temples often have a threshold you must step over, and why pawnshops have a screen directly in front of the entrance. Many a terrified human has received a reprieve when the vampire chasing them simply couldn't hop a log or high curb.

(c) Chinese zombies are Chinese first, and zombies second. They'll help repel unwanted foreigners before biting the locals.

(d) Chinese child-vampires are children first, and vampires second. Human children recognize this, befriend them, and shield them from meddling adults. In *Mr Vampire Part 2*, kids try to protect a kid-corpse by claiming that he's an illegal alien from the mainland.

10. No monster is ever really finally dead until it explodes.

Hell Bank Notes

What happens to stuff when you burn it? It goes up in smoke, right, but where does it go? The answer is that it goes to the spirit world; prayer-directed into the hands of one's departed loved ones.

With this direct pipeline, wouldn't you want to make your relatives' afterlife as comfortable as possible? You'd like to see them enjoying their time in the afterworld with a nice house, luxury automobile, servants and pots of money.

Well, here's your chance to help. Buy a wad of Hell Bank Notes and burn them ceremonially. Since the notes are legal tender only in hell, you can buy a large packet of them at your local Asian grocery for about eighty-eight Earth cents. Every Hell Bank Note is a heavy piece of change—burning denominations of less than ten or a hundred million is an insult.

But you don't have to stop with money. HK funerals often feature elaborate houses, servants and Mercedes-Benzes—all constructed of brightly-colored paper and then torched. Although the Chinese concept of "hell" is not one of fire-and-brimstone, colored-paper air-conditioning units have been spotted going up in smoke as well.

Hex Errors: Ghostly Grumbling

"My wife is human, how come she's a rabbit?"
Erotic Ghost Story-Perfect Match

"Does it suck blood, like the foreign ones?"
The Musical Vampire

"I've lost every cent gambling here in the underworld!"
The Occupant

"Now, I'd like to open your mysterious 8 sinus."
Top Bet

"Don't be afraid. Tie up that monster and it'll be allright."
The Imp

"damamed! Try to disguise a vampire to scare me?"
One Eyebrow Priest

"A ghost in the fridge!"
Black Magic With Buddha

"Is there telephone in hell?"
"No, they transmit with frequency wave."
Haunted Mansion

"You bastard, you want to have fun, don't you? You said you saw a girl in nude, and you said you saw ghost... Well, tonight, I'm sure a group of female ghosts will chain rape you."
Troublesome Night

"Crazy, this is corpse!"
The Beasts

"Crazy Corpse, kill them for me!"
Ten Brothers

CHAPTER THREE
HONG KONG NOIR

"Film Noir" is a genre normally associated with Hollywood films of the late forties and early fifties. Hollywood noir set the standard: a shadowy world of sneaky criminals, marginalized McGimps and double-crossing lovers all wrapped up together in that bleak blanket called fate.

In the decade-or-so preceding the handover, film noir spiked again and again into the Hong Kong cinemadrome. Films like Ringo Lam's excellent *City on Fire* (1987, see page 223) won awards and critical acclaim. Johnny Mak's *Long Arm of the Law* (1984) and Alfred Cheung's *On the Run* (1987) are must-sees for fans of the genre. Johnnie To has continued the tradition into this century, and Soi Cheang's near-nihilistic *Dog Bite Dog* (2006) kicks off our new HK noir chapter.

These films are brutal masterpieces, with not-happy endings. The hero often ends up feeding the worms, and if a villain holds a gun to a kid's head, there's a 50/50 chance the kid gets plugged. Skip the popcorn.

Dog Bite Dog (狗咬狗)

2006 | Starring: Edison Chen Koon-hei, Sam Lee Chan-sam, Pei Pei Wei-ying, Eddie Cheung Siu-fai, Wayne Lai Yiu-cheung, Lam Suet
Directed by Soi Cheang

The Chinese title of Soi Cheang's ode to savagery translates exactly: "dog bite(s) dog." It's a Cantonese idiom: because dogs bond together in a pack, one biting another when hunting a common enemy indicates a problem.

The rogue dog is Hong Kong undercover cop Wai (Sam Lee). He's a cynical young street punk whose fed-up supervisor hurls abuse at him. Wai's a bottom-feeder—we don't know who he

Feral: *Dog Bite Dog*.

hates more: his fellow cops, the lowlife druggie thugs he thumps for information, or himself. Lee owns the role—it's impossible to imagine another actor in the part.

Wai's supervisor, Inspector Sum (Eddie Cheung), would love to donate him to the Humane Society but must instead keep him on a leash—Wai's father was a much-respected police officer. Others in his pack tolerate him, most notably Fat Lam (Lam Suet), who tries to keep the peace.

Wai's antagonist is smuggled into Hong Kong below decks in an anonymous ship. Blazing eyes stare up from the bilge abyss as he slurps congee and dried fish from a shattered porcelain bowl. Hellbent on survival, the man lurches from the ship to a local dim sum eatery after his contact gives him a wad of cash and a pistol.

Edison Chen: haunted beyond haunted in *Dog Bite Dog*.

Clutching the bag that conceals the gat, he wolfs down several orders of dim sum, then strolls to a nearby table and shoots a woman in the head. As Pang walks out, he grabs the dead woman's freshly steamed order of shrimp dumplings and stuffs it in his mouth.

Pang's an amoral assassin from Cambodia, played with backblast intensity by Canadian-born actor Edison Chen. Pang's human-shaped, but he's barely human. His goal is to eliminate all possible threats in order to survive. Chen's performance harks back to the classic Universal Studios monster pictures of the 30s: he moves like Lon Chaney's Wolfman, but he's more like Karloff's Frankenstein Monster, an outcast whose speech is unintelligible, someone who destroys to communicate. His backstory explains why he's so brutally twisted.

The Hong Kong police are the immediate threat and *DBD* switches deftly into action mode. But don't expect slo-mo Beretta ballet romanticized Hong Kong violence here. Let's just say Pang interacts with Wai's undercover squad and then escapes.

The agile Cambodian misfit finds refuge in the middle of a trash mountain—the landfills in Hong Kong weren't big enough, so the filmmakers went to Thailand to find a suitably gargantuan pile of garbage. The character seems at home here, and finds an actual home (a corrugated tin shanty) occupied by people as marginalized as he is. There he finds Yu (Pei Pei)—he'd just as soon kill her, but she takes a shine to him. A match made in hell is better than none, so Pang takes her with him on the run.

The cops view Pang as dog-garbage and are keen to put him down. But he's spent his life being hunted—and sharpening his teeth. His goal is to make it back to Cambodia with his impromptu sweetheart in tow. To accomplish that, he needs a boat...

The finale of *Dog Bite Dog* will enthrall half its audience while the others will howl in protest. Whatever your opinion, this is what director Soi Cheang wanted to depict. The film's not about pride or police procedures. It's about the tremendous human will to survive.

Cheang says he insisted on a exceptional level of brutality, and the actors deliver. Consider yourself warned.

Dream Home (維多利亞壹號)
2010 | Starring Josie Ho Chiu-yee, Eason Chan Yik-chun, Lawrence Chou Chun-wai, Derek Tsang Kwok-cheung, Juno Mak Chun-lung, Felix Lok Ying-kwan, Norman Chu Siu-keung, Pau Hei-ching, Lo Hoi-pang, Michelle Ye Xuan
Directed by Edmond Pang Ho-cheung

Even by the standards of Category III films, and even in its slightly trimmed Hong Kong theatrical release version, *Dream Home* remains one of the most shockingly violent of Hong Kong films (so appalled, for example, were Singapore regulators that they posted a separate document on their website to explain their disallowing of the film). Most of the violence is perpetrated by a lone female killer (Cheng Lai Sheung, played by Josie Ho), whose sundry acts of carnage and cruelty include choking a condominium security guard with a plastic zip-tie device and watching as he slices his own jugular vein with a box cutter in an effort to remove it; impaling a domestic helper's head with a screwdriver, using so much force that an eyeball is pushed from its socket; suffocating a pregnant woman with a plastic bag and a vacuum cleaner; and impaling a young man with a knife while he has sexual intercourse and slicing off his penis, before tossing it onto the bed next to his sexual partner, who is herself soon to be forcibly impaled through the mouth with one of the slats from the bed.

Such stunning and over-the-top violence is rendered all the more disturbing not only because of the relatively realistic visual style with which it is presented, but also because the acts are carried out with a methodical determination and at times a suggestion of sadistic relish, and because the precise motivation for the woman's exceptional violence is initially withheld from us. The storytelling means by which this information is delayed is a complex flashback structure, which jumps around among various periods in the killer-protagonist's life as far back as her childhood—with intermittent return to present-day slasher-type activities—before leading up to scenes of a relatively recent emotional breakdown (evidently the last straw prompting the killings).

The backstory briefly hints at a certain native disposition toward willfulness and violence on the part of the protagonist in her childhood (in one scene she is chastised for beating up her younger brother when unhappy with his behavior), but it soon becomes clear that the key forces which drive her to her acts of carnage are an obsessive desire to fulfill a promise to her hard-working mother (even after the latter's death) to provide her with a nice home, and in particular to be able to have an apartment with an ocean view of the type her family once had and then lost due to the rise of modern residential developments. This leads to a single-minded fixation on acquiring one condominium apartment in particular by scrimping and saving—and when a deal almost within reach falls through (owing to the rapid rise in HK property values), she snaps and pursues a strategy of brutally murdering those in neighboring apartments to drive the prices down.

What separates *Dream Home* from more standard horror or exploitation fare is not only the care taken with its visual style and storytelling approach, but also its ostensible seriousness of purpose: From its opening titles, *Dream Home* explicitly situates its narrative in relation to Hong Kong historical and political contexts, and is thus able to position Lai Sheung's violence (as indeed the excessive gore of the film's own representational practice) as an outcropping of a warped capitalistic ethos: This carnage, the film's dark satire tells us, is the human toll of Hong Kong's modern developmental drive taken to its logical extreme. Nor is the female gender of the killer an inconsequential detail: *Dream Home* figures the conditions she is reacting to as at once capitalist and patriarchal, the desire for control over wealth and over women as part of one and the same societal affliction.

Dream Home may not succeed in articulating all of this social critique with the same clarity, but it nevertheless marks itself out as a distinctive, engaging, and singularly unsettling attempt to render political a popular cinematic form. (And in its focus on the destructive force of the Hong Kong property market, it also makes for interesting comparison with another like-minded Hong Kong horror film, Soi Cheang's 2005 *Home Sweet Home*.)

— Adam Knee

The Unceasing Path: Andy Lau stares down Tony Leung's gun barrel in *Infernal Affairs*.

Infernal Affairs (無間道)

2002 | Starring Andy Lau Tak-wah, Tony Leung Chiu-wai, Anthony Wong Chau-sang, Eric Tsang Chi-wai, Sammi Cheng Sau-man, Kelly Chen Wai-lam, Edison Chen Koon-hei, Shawn Yu Man-lok Directed by Andrew Lau Wai-keung and Alan Mak Siu-fai

Infernal Affairs is a knockout piece of film noir that follows the life paths of two very different men from their teenage years to adulthood. Lau Kin-ming (Andy Lau) is a child of the triads, and loyal to a crime boss named Hon Sam (Eric Tsang). To gain a leg up on the police, Hon enlists several of his young wannabe gangsters, including Lau, to infiltrate the Hong Kong Police Force and acts as his moles. Lau manages to rise through the ranks quickly, and is soon put in a position where he can monitor all of the police efforts to take down Hon.

Meanwhile, another young man named Chan Wing-yan (Tony Leung) really does want to be a policeman. Like Lau, his superiors are impressed with his hard work, but they've got different plans for him. They want him to infiltrate Hon's gang. To accomplish this, Chan is dishonorably kicked out of the police academy, and eventually manages to get into the good graces of Hon. From here on out the film is a tense cat-and-mouse game between Lau and Chan, with each coming to admire the other his loyalty and belief in his cause.

Eric Tsang plays the crime boss with remarkable precision. Normally Tsang stars in comedies, but like other comic actors, Tsang is at his best in serious roles. He plays the role straight, with just the right balance of charm and menace. We recognize him for the amoral reptile that he is, but we can also understand why Lau admires him.

Tony Leung is perfect as the long-suffering undercover agent Chan, who allows his devotion to justice and morality to destroy his personal life. But the film belongs to Andy Lau, who has the toughest role here. While Hon and Chan never waver from their positions, it is Lau's character that provides the films real story arc as he starts to question his values and wonder if his loyalty is misplaced. Also along for the ride is Anthony Wong, who plays Chan's superior Wong Chi Shing. He doesn't have much screen time here, but every minute of it is golden.

Infernal Affairs is a great film title—one of the best—but it's not the original title of the film. The Chinese title for the film (無間道) roughly translates along the lines of "The Unceasing Path" and refers to the lowest level of Buddhist hell. There are some pretty grotesque levels of hell in Buddhism, including being ground up and boiled alive, but these all have escape routes via reincarnation. The lowest level is the only one from which there is no escape. It is the closest equivalent in Buddhism to the Christian concept of hell.

Reportedly, the idea for the film came from co-director Alan Mak's disappointment with John Woo's *Face/Off*. Mak liked the idea of a gangster pretending to be a good cop, but wanted to find a believable way to tell that story without resorting to non-existent surgical procedures. The idea worked so well, that Mak followed it up with a prequel (*Infernal Affairs 2*), and a wraparound film that that chronicled events before and after the story in the first film (*Infernal Affairs 3*).

Infernal Affairs was submitted to the Academy of Motion Picture Arts and Sciences for Oscar consideration in the best foreign film category and was rejected. Four years later, the Academy awarded Martin Scorsese's film *The Departed* with Oscars for Best Picture, Best Director, Best Editing and Best Adapted Screenplay.

The deep irony of Scorsese—director of critically acclaimed films like *Raging Bull*, *Goodfellas*, *Casino* and *Gangs of New York*—being gilded for remaking a Hong Kong film is palpable, all the more so as *Infernal Affairs* is unquestionably the better movie. While both films move to jazzy rhythms and feature outstanding cinematography, *Infernal Affairs* offers a tighter story with more believable bad guys and a moral conflict at the end that Hollywood films rarely touch.

— Jim Morton

The First Time is the Last Time
(第一繭)
1989 | Starring: Carrie Ng Kar-lai, Andy Lau Tak-wah, Season Ma, Wang Lung-wei, Elaine Ngai Suet
Directed by Raymond Leung Pun-hei

FTITLT is a women's prison movie. But instead of the standard WIP tropes, it plays against genre and centers on female-driven drama. Women and their relationships under trying circumstance are explored, while the loser-males (fathers and boyfriends) who mess up their lives are also portrayed, adding depth, texture, and good, raw story elements.

Season Ma plays a naive moll who's playing

Carrie Ng and Andy Lau in love and in trouble, and what's the difference anyway?

being dope mule for her cheap-punk-triad boyfriend, and sentenced to six months in the slams. Her cellblock is run by "He-Man," a six-foot hellion who extorts cash and chicken wings from her fellow jailbirds. The guards use He-Man as corrupted muscle to keep the other prisoners in line.

The matronly, pregnant 5354 (inmates are numbers here) takes the "new fish" under her wing. But He-Man assaults the new inmate in the shower. In the process, though, she annoys the only inmate who scares both the guards and He-Man—"Crazy Bitch" (Carrie Ng in fine form). Crazy Bitch thumps He-Man senseless, not out of a sense of outrage but because she's annoyed at having the showering process disrupted.

Order is restored and the inmates are returned to their cells. When a grateful 7144 (our New Fish) reaches out to Crazy Bitch in friendship, she finds a burned-out shell of a woman, huddled on the cell floor chain-smoking her self-detested life away.

In flashback, we learn why Crazy Bitch (known as Winnie before her incarceration) is no fuzzy puppy. Sold to a brothel at nine by her heroin-addicted father, she drifted through a crud-injecting, pimp-dependent existence until snaring a handsome gangster/sugar daddy named Yung (Andy Lau). After a gang fight, the two consummate matters in a leaky, industrial men's room—Winnie wiping the hot blood from Yung's Kwan Ti tattoos—and fall into that desperate sort of love at which the socially marginalized excel. Yung proves his love by forcing her to kick the junk, holding her all night while she shivers and shakes from opiate withdrawal.

As Winnie's story unfolds, it becomes clear that she and 7144 share a secret of which neither is fully aware. Yung was greased by a group of hoods and Winnie extracted revenge with a pistol, blowing the killers away for taking the only thing which offered her any hope—the guy she loved. The thugs were members of the same gang to which 7144's boyfriend belongs.

When 7144's scum-sucking beau comes to visit, he tells the bewildered young thing of her new friend's past transgressions. He further convinces her to perform a jailhouse assassination on Winnie. The attempted hit—and its consequences for 7144, a wayward teen a long way from home—leads *FTITLT* to its shocking conclusion.

Gangs (童黨)
1988 | Starring Ricky Ho Pui-tung, Leung Sap-yat, Ma Hin-ting, Tse Wai-kit, Tam San-san, Wong Chung-chun, Tam Kin-shing

Directed by Lawrence Ah Mon (as Lawrence Lau Kwok-Cheong)

Gangs examines the misadventures of a bunch of unpleasant juvenile delinquents—in particular, the teenaged tribulations of "Big K." Big K (Ricky Ho) belongs to the Sun Hing gang, an innocuous-looking band who extort money from local businesses. Other members of the group include Big K's brother, Little K; a cool and amoral toughie known as Coma; and an undersized psychopath called Little Demon. The gang is under the control of a charismatic thug named Wen, who works for Uncle Sing, a local triad boss.

After a brutal fight with their rivals—in which Wen and two others are killed—the gang goes into hiding. The stress of the situation takes its toll on the fugitives, and the gang soon flies apart. Coma is captured by the police after Uncle Sing rats on him. Big K's girlfriend—Lard Cake—is kidnapped and raped by a rival gang. Coma's girlfriend Kitty becomes a whore. Little Demon is drugged and thrown into the sea.

There's little comic relief in *Gangs*, and every scene is played for its grimness. "Cruelty's the name of the game," says one gang member, while watching his buddies pour kerosene on a rat and ignite it.

Like director Lawrence Ah Mon's other underworld-peek—*Queen of Temple Street*—*Gangs* is uniquely Cantonese. The way these kids talk to each other is as important as what they say. This is the Cantonese of the streets, with its sing-song roughness and drawled word endings.

The stars of *Gangs* are not the usual, well-known assortment of HK actors. The kids in this film look like and act like real teenagers. The fight scenes are chaotic, haphazard, and refreshingly free of any martial arts pretense. The kids charge at each other, shouting and swinging pipes. They run away and taunt each other. They cover their heads and scream.

There's no ambiguity about the message of this film: winners don't join gangs.

—Jim Morton

Gunmen (天羅地網)
1988 | Starring Tony Leung Kar-fai, Adam Cheng Siu-chau, Carrie Ng Kar-lai, Elizabeth Lee Mei-fung, Waise Lee Chi-hung, Mark Cheng Hau-nam, David Lai
Directed by Kirk Wong Chi-keung

Kirk Wong's films are notable for their oblique approaches to the crime dramas. Wong is a subtler, more enigmatic director than John Woo or Tsui Hark, yet his films don't wither for lack of action. Like Ringo Lam, Wong seems more concerned with characters' relationships with each other, and sincere moments of tenderness blossom amid the carnage.

Gunmen is a period piece set in Shanghai in the turbulent 30s. Ding Chun-bee (Tony Leung) plays a Shanghai cop torn between his duties and his family—dutiful wife Chu-chiao (Carrie Ng) and young daughter Sze-Sze. Things are further complicated by the lovely urchin-turned-courtesan Mona (Elizabeth Lee), who acts as Ding's informant and Chu-chiao's counterfoil.

Ding is determined to bust an opium-smuggling syndicate operating in Shanghai, but loses face among his fellow cops when one of his tips fails to yield a collar. The cops, who dress in long fleece-lined coats with stylin' hats, get a better tip and are soon staked out outside the gang's headquarters.

Inside, Haye (Adam Cheng) is squabbling over profits with flunkies when a fracas erupts. Haye hoses his opponents with gasoline and sets them afire; they fight and shout at each other while on fire, faces clearly visible amid the flames. The cops bust in and Ding shoots Haye's boss Uncle Liang. Haye reciprocates by killing Ding's boss Captain Kiang. The cop swears revenge against the gangster as an ill wind blows the bloodstained sheet off Kiang's still-warm corpse.

Ding receives more grief in the form of a hard-ass new superintendent who's sent by French bureaucrats to root out police corruption. He becomes involved in a foot chase on Shanghai's crowded streets and is thrashed by a group of rickshaw drivers who resent the crooked beat cops. The rickshaws, though, turn out to be old army buddies Kwong, Ching and Fan (Mark Cheng, Waise Lee and David Lai)! Ding wastes no time signing them up as fellow gunmen. Things move rapidly towards their grinding, violent conclusion.

The finale of *Gunmen* is reminiscent of an epic Western. Rickshaws, huge trucks and mounted combatants clash. Everyone is shot repeatedly. Finally, the frightening Haye is terminated by Ding's cute daughter who picks up a .38 and plugs the thug.

Long Arm of the Law (省港旗兵)
1984 | Starring David Lam Wai, Wong Kin, Chan Ging, Yeung Ming
Directed by Johnny Mak Tong-hung

This seminal film, co-produced by Sammo Hung. foreshadowed the violent realism of later efforts by Ringo Lam, John Woo, and Kirk Wong. The story (based on a series of HK robberies committed by mainland Chinese) could have leapt from the pages of the South China Morning Post. The neon-flamed Christmas ambience of Hong Kong has never looked meaner.

HONG KONG NOIR

Trapped inside the Walled City of Kowloon, criminals attempt to settle an argument (screengrab: *Long Arm of the Law*).

HK crook Tung (David Lam) takes the train up to mainland China to rendezvous with his ex-army buddies. Together they plan a 48-hour junket to Hong Kong with a jewelry heist as the centerpiece. The men are attracted by the money he offers, but complain that there's not enough time to visit the massage parlors ("not even enough time for shopping!").

Trouble starts as they climb the fence separating HK from China; one of the gang is ripped apart by German Shepherds. As they case the joint prior to the job, they're intercepted by beat cops, forced to shoot it out on crowded Kowloon streets, then escape in a commandeered taxi.

Tung decides to wait three days and try the caper again. While the troops are not criminally engaged, they're busy enjoying themselves with nightclub hostesses. One of the bumpkin-punks—Rooster (Chan Ging)—latches onto a haughty strumpet, waves a wad of cash and demands satisfaction. She suggests he watch TV unless he has $10,000. "I'll give you ten, where do you want it?" yells Rooster as he pulls out his .45 automatic. Wearing a ridiculous paper foil crown on his head, he makes her crawl at gunpoint—gentlemen they are not.

The fence (Tai, boss of the Crimson Kid video arcade) is not pleased when Tung shows up without the goods, but he offers a little side employment: rubbing out a corpulent creep named Fatso. The gang executes the hit and Fatso swansongs onto the ice-skating rink at Tai Koo Shing's Cityplaza shopping mall.

But as Tung's men glimpse Fatso's handcuffs gleaming through bloody crushed ice, they realize that Tai has conned them into murdering an undercover policeman. Furious, Tung has the crime boss tied inside an automobile, douses it with gasoline, and sets it afire. As Tai screams from within the burning car, Tung has the flames extinguished and takes up the dialogue again. Tai rats him out anyway.

When the heist finally happens, it goes badly. The gang barely gets away, and when they go to fence the stuff, they confront a battalion of pissed-off cops. In the shootout, Tai is shot by both sides and Tung's man Blockhead takes a few slugs. Blockhead's only chance is an underground doctor in Kowloon's infamous Walled City—a solid city block which is off-limits to regular HK cops. But the doc's wife finks on them, and a battalion of SDU (Special Duties Unit) invade. The ensuing shootout—waged in the claustrophobic alleys of the Walled City—cements *LAOTL*'s reputation among fans of bleak HK gangster killcake.

Long Arm of the Law is on the Hong Kong Film Archive's list of "Best 100 Chinese Motion Pictures."

On the Run (亡命鴛鴦)
1988 | Starring Patricia Ha Man-jik, Yuen Biao, Chan Cheuk-yan, Lo Lieh, Charlie Chin Chiang-lin, Philip Ko Fei, Ida Chan Yuk-lin
Directed by Alfred Cheung Kin-ting

There's no better example of Hong Kong noir than the Sammo Hung-produced *On the Run. OTR* tells the story of Ah Chui (Patricia Ha), a lady assassin of surreal calm and extraordinary skill. As the film opens, the liquid-nitrogen-cool hitwoman steps into a restaurant and shoots Lo Huan (Ida Chan), a female narcotics officer in the Royal Hong Kong Police department.

Lo Huan was married to Hsiang Ming (Yuen Biao), a policeman working in the political department of the Hong Kong Police—an office similar to US Internal Affairs departments. The two were separated but Hsiang needed his wife's help to emigrate to Canada. The hit, it turns out, was paid for by the villainous Superintendent Lu (Charlie Chin)—head of the homicide department. The bullet-riddled policewoman had been having an affair with Lu, but when she threatened to blow the whistle on Lu's heroin smuggling, he had her killed.

Hsiang manages to capture the hitwoman before Lu and his men catch up with her, and discovers that he has more to fear from the police than he does from his wife's murderer. Soon, Hsiang and Ah Chui are running for their lives (along with Hsiang's adorable daughter Lin, played by Chan Cheuk-yan), while Superintendent Lu uses the full resources of the police department to track them down.

Ah Chui—with her Jackie O hairspray-hardened flip—is played to perfection by Patricia

Patricia Ha and Chan Cheuk-yan: ironic goofing around.

Ha. Ha gives an evocative, emotional performance as a character who—paradoxically—never once betrays her emotions. She also wields a Walther PPK pistol like an artist's red paintbrush.

On the Run was made at a time when fear in Hong Kong over the impending takeover of the colony by the People's Republic was at a fever pitch. The film is as much about that paranoia as anything. Even Lu's heroin smuggling is motivated by his desire to get enough money to emigrate. When Hsiang Ming first encounters his wife's killer, he does not rage at the assassin because she killed the woman he loved, he's angry because she's eliminated his means of getting out of Hong Kong!

On the Run is more than just good Hong Kong noir, it's good film noir. The film is shot in a dramatic, nihilistic style with deep shadows and strong lighting. The romance is so understated it never seems forced or unbelievable. And in spite of a tortuously complicated plot, we never lose track of what's going on or why.

— Jim Morton

Queen of Temple Street
(廟街皇后)

1990 | Starring Sylvia Chang Ai-chia, Rain Lau Yuk-tsui, Lo Lieh, Alice Lau Nga-lai, Kwan Hoi-san,

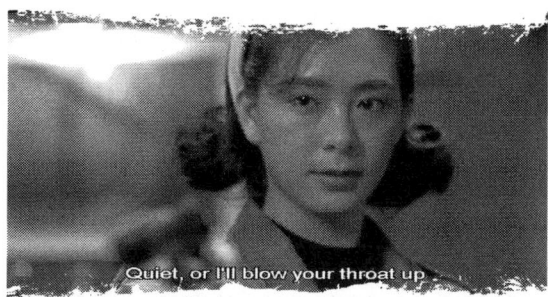
She's not kidding: *On the Run*.

HONG KONG NOIR

Poster for *Queen of Temple Street*.

Josephine Koo Mei-wah, Teresa Ha Ping
Directed by Lawrence Ah Mon

Tough love among the hard-bitten. *QOTS* focuses on a mother-daughter relationship between a middle-aged female pimp and her juvenile-deliquent-hooker daughter. Actress-director Sylvia Chang turns in her finest performance as "Big Sis" Wah, and teen phenom Rain Lau burns up the screen as the lip-curling, chain-smoking tart that sprang from her loins. The dialogue is deft and cynical, and the relationship between the two women is explored with depth and compassion.

Big Sis stands pimping near touristy Temple Street Market, muttering a mantra: "Young girls, young girls." "How many positions?" asks a potential john. "As many as there's in a coffin," replies Wah, snuffing out a cigarette butt on the grimy pavement.

Upstairs, cramped red-lit cubicles brim with murky water basins, drawers bulge with industrial-grade condoms and half-squeezed K-Y tubes. Pretty Woman this ain't as Wah works her girls—Candy, Octopussy, Big Mouth, and Swallow—through thirty tricks or so a night. Bored, aging harlots with punchcard-clock privates, they all carry dope habits, gambling addictions, and/or worthless boyfriends on their working backs.

When Wah learns that her estranged daughter Yan (Lau) is working as a nightclub hostess (several strata above the coffin-joys), she seeks her out. These two tangle hard, like gladiators circling each other seeking weak spots.

Yan's playing grown-up with Marlboros, Louis Vuitton, and gangster-daddy accessories. Mom wants to tell her that regular gynie exams are more important than designer-accessories. Wah obviously loves the little hellion, but sees an earlier version of herself, future mistakes dead ahead. As Yan brags of her fast life and taunts her mother, Wah tells of her own hard-learned lessons of street-life abrasion.

Yan isn't thrilled by her mother's company, but needs Wah's underworld connections to squelch some quick-buck nudie pix. Big Sis confronts the publishers, matter-of-factly calls in triad muscle, has heads cracked, then backs off once the negatives are returned ("a punch for any that's missing!" cries Yan, triumphant).

Wah has her hands full running the brothel and caring for two sons from a second marriage to Shu—a former cop now running a mahjong dive and gambling away the boys' allowances. When she learns that Yan has signed with an escort agency,

Wah realizes that while her young, pretty daughter is likely to follow her own wreckage-strewn path, it's fate. Fortunately, Yan is arrested—caught with a grandfatherly type at a no-tell motel—and again calls Mom to bail her out.

Reunited, Wah and her younger self scrap like terriers. Yan wants something from Mom which her nihilistic sex/money/fashion world view can never deliver: an audience with the father she never met.

Wah cannily sets it up. But when the kid finally meets her dad, failed-criminal Elvis (Lo Lieh) at his oil-smeared auto-repair shop, she deflates. "Disappointing, isn't it? Daddy didn't turn out like Paul Newman," consoles Wah as Yan cries a river of salt on the ride home. QOTS closes with the two reaching a grudging, yet honest respect. Perhaps fate isn't bulletproof after all.

NOTE: Rain Lau's incendiary performance earned her the Best New Performer prize at the Hong Kong Film Awards.

The Stool Pigeon (線人)

2010 | Starring Nicholas Tse Ting-fung, Nick Cheung Ka-fai, Kwai Lun-mei, Dick Liu Kai-chi, Miao Pu, Philip Keung Hiu-man, Lu Yi, Lau Kong
Directed by Dante Lam Chiu-yin

Dante Lam's sort-of-sequel to his magnificent *Beast Stalker* (see page 16) lacks the cross-plotting of the original, but doesn't let up on either irony or intensity. *TSP* reunites actors Nicholas Tse and Nick Cheung, along with many cast-members from the original *Beast*. Lam flips roles for Tse and Cheung—the Chinese title translates as "Informer": Tse's character.

Fresh out of jail with no hope and little prospects, shaven-headed Ghost Junior (Tse)

Korean flyer with Nicks Tse and Cheung, and the transcendent Kwai Lun-mei.

knows his sister (Sherman Chung) is paying off their late father's triad debt one trick at a time in grime-smeared hourly hotel rooms. He tries to free her by force, but all he gets for his sibling-piety is a nasty kicking on a mean deserted Kowloon Street.

Inspector Don Lee (Cheung) needs inside information, and he already has enough dirt on Ghost. Fate, ever the trickster, forces the freshly sprung punk to turn stool pigeon for Inspector Lee. He even gets a salary from the Hong Kong Police, but Ghost needs big bonuses, and fast.

Bureaucratically-minded Lee gets him into the illicit street-racing scene. Ghost's hard-revving and drifting skills at a Fast-and-Furious-style street race earn him a gig with thugs Barbarian

(Lu Yi) and Tai Ping (Philip Keung).

Barbarian's gang are a typical bunch of thugs, save his gal Dee (played with malicious/delicious malice by Taiwanese actress Kwai Lun-mei). Ghost and Dee have some history, as explicated during a drunken hotpot meal on a Kowloon street. But it's not until Ghost has to outrun the cops during an impromptu roadblock (the film burns just enough rubber to satisfy any gearhead) that she gives him the TV Eye—fans may recognize the lovely actress as the facially tattooed Tartar princess from Tsui Hark's *Flying Swords of Dragon Gate* (2013). Barbarian's got another gal on the side anyway.

Inspector Lee's got a couple of backstories, but the important one concerns his previous informant, whose cover was blown due to Lee's eagerness to call in a bust, and who suffered a horrendous chopping as a result. The violence in *TSP* is loud and painful—it erupts in bursts throughout the film. It's a hard film about hard lives wrapped in a heist procedural (the caper itself seems based on the dramatic 90s jewel store robberies perpetrated by Yip Kai-foon and his cohorts). Lam juggles a lot in his story (scripted by Jack Ng) but the edge never lets up throughout *TSP*'s 113-minute running time. Tse's heartfelt yet ruthless performance earned him the Best Actor prize at the Hong Kong Film Awards.

It's the aftermath that squeezes the characters in a gargantuan vice as they turn on each other and things get bloodier. And bloodier. Dee proves her mettle, but as Inspector Lee well knows, stool pigeons aren't the swiftest or luckiest of birds.

Taxi Hunter (的士判官)
1993 | Starring Anthony Wong Chau-sang, Yu Rong Guang, Ng Man-tat, Athena Chu-yan
Directed by Herman Yau Lai-to

A Hong Konger walks past a Kowloonside wall plastered with posters for Herman Yau's *Taxi Hunter* (Photo: Stefan Hammond, 1993).

In the 1950s, American International Pictures was notorious for the dizzying rapidity with which they brought topical themes into the theaters and drive-ins of America. Let a Russkie satellite blast into space, and three weeks later the kids would be heavy-pettin' in the balcony during Rock 'n' Roll Sputnik. Was AIP celebrating the sweet transience of AmeriPopCulture in those proverbial Good Ol' Days? Creating reams of rich cinematic mulch to assist creatively bankrupt future generations? Nah, just trying to make a buck.

During its glory years, the Hong Kong film industry hold fast to the AIP exploitation model: milk a newsworthy topic for box office cream. In 1993, HK taxi-drivers came under fire for all sorts of rude behavior: levying illegal surcharges in bad weather, refusing to take people short distances, etc. A sizable groundswell of ill-will spiked up. Almost immediately, *Taxi Hunter* banged into the theaters, featuring Anthony Wong as a meek-mannered businessman bedeviled by those horrid hacks.

Wong (visually styled like Michael Douglas in *Falling Down*) puts up with cabbie abuse and corruption until the Hong Kong taxidrivin' mob causes the death of his pregnant wife (Athena Chu). Crestfallen, Wong starts hitting the San Miguel beer hard, and eventually turns into a vigilante, taking out taxi drivers (whose transgressions range from rape to rudeness) with his "Barnetor" nine-millimeter automatic. As he treads gingerly between meek accountant and crack-brain taxi-vigilante, Wong does a sendup of Robert DeNiro in *Taxi Driver*, and explains to buddy Ng Man-tat that his serial-killings are okay because "I only kill those blacksheeps!" No sympathy allowed for *Taxi Hunter*'s cabbies, who exude sneering greed and arrogance—the lone honest driver in the bunch, however, always gets a big hand from Hong Kong audiences!

The Big Heat (城市特警)

1988 | Starring Waise Lee Chi-hung, Philip Kwok Choi, Matthew Wong Hin-mung, Lo King Wah, Paul Chu Kong, Stuart Ong, Joey Wong Jo-yin, Betty Mak Chui-han
Directed by Andrew Kam and Johnnie To Kei-fung

A wild ride through the soulless world of gotta-get-out-before-'97 HK criminals. This film is visually rich, well-cast, and exceptionally brutal. For openers, the first scene depicts a power drill boring through the center of a human hand.

The hand-drilling, though, is just a dream. John Wong (Waise Lee) is a cop who's suffering from some sort of Police-Special Repetitive Stress Injury—his right hand freezes on him during gunfights. Squeezing off too many rounds? His doctor suggests retirement, but when his partner Skinny Tse is torched in Malaysia, he puts everything on hold, including his forthcoming marriage to Maggie (Betty Mak), until he cracks the case.

Wong and his men inspect the evidence: Tse's crispy corpse, a shipping schedule, and a series of blackmail-bait photos showing the wealthy

Joey Wong and Matthew Wong ponder the rat-maze they inhabit in *The Big Heat*.

and powerful Mr Ho (Stuart Ong) in the sweaty embraces of a male hustler. Wong's men find that they are under surveillance themselves (Lun (Matthew Wong) comments: "I thought only cops tailed people, how come we're being tailed?"). Compatriot Kam (Philip Kwok) goes to question the hustler; too late, as the punk is in the process of being executed. When Wong and Lun confront the tailing creeps, weapons are unholstered and the screen ignites in a furious chase which ends with one of the miscreants splattered across passing autos on various freeway levels.

The cops pose as blackmailers to force Ho to divulge the name of his crime boss. Ho slashes his wrists in anguish, but Wong chases him to the hospital and browbeats him into giving up Ching Han (Paul Chu), a scurrilous Malaysian who forced Ho to smuggle a mysterious substance in milk-powder cans. The hospital is crawling with Han's assassins, and a shootout drags nurse Ada (Joey Wong) into the fray and marks the end of Ho.

Ching Han, sensing he's been found out, meets with Wong's group and slips them a wad of banknotes, which the cops toss gleefully in the air. When Wong has his fiancée Maggie analyze the stuff found in the milk-powder cans (it turns out to be raw coca), Han has her killed as well. The scoundrel then transfers a large sum of money into Wong's account, which causes him to be brought up on corruption charges. Han just wants to get rich and get the hell out of Hong Kong, working in tandem with the Russian villain Mr Molotov (!) to smuggle contraband.

Naturally, Han's comeuppance comes in ultraviolent fashion, as his car is pancaked by a commandeered garbage truck. But his death doesn't end matters. A turncoat cop—who'd helped Han smuggle—appears as Wong is lying bloodied on the ground and points a shotgun at him. Our hero's hand has frozen up on him again; what to do? Thinking quickly, he hooks Maggie's neckchain around the trigger and fires a shot directly into the pumpgun's magazine. The remaining shotgun shells explode and pepper the rogue cop like a cartoon character.

Rouge (胭脂扣)
1988 | Starring Leslie Cheung Kwok-wing, Anita Mui Yim-fong, Alex Man Chi-leung, Emily Chu Bo-yee, Irene Wan Pik-ha
Directed by Stanley Kwan Kam-pang

Rouge begins in 1934, a Romeo and Juliet tale of two lovers from different worlds. The man, Chen-Pang (Leslie Cheung), is the son of a rich landowner and stands to inherit his family's fortune. The woman, Fleur (Anita Mui), is a courtesan at a high-brow brothel. When Chen-Pang's parents turn down the couple's request to marry, the lovers decide to commit suicide together rather than live apart.

Suddenly the scene changes, and it's 1987. Fleur has returned from hell to find Chen-Pang, and find out why he did not join her in the netherworld.

Anita Mui and Leslie Cheung in *Rouge*.

It's important to note here that "hell" in Hong Kong films rarely conforms to the Western concept of the word; it's merely a misty afterlife without the joyous connotations of heaven.

Fleur meets a yuppie named Yuan Ting (Kenny Bee) who works at the newspaper where she places an ad to find Chen-Pang. When Fleur follows Yuan Ting home, he believes that she is merely crazy. Once he realizes that she is dead—and once he overcomes his initial fright—Yuan offers to let her stay at his apartment until after the ad appears in the newspaper. Over the course of the film—through a series of flashbacks—we learn the details of the love affair between Fleur and Chen-Pang.

A sadness over what Hong Kong has become pervades *Rouge*. there's a subtle anti-commercialism here, lamenting the effects of Western civilization on Hong Kong. Shots of the Chinese theaters and markets from Fleur's time dissolve into shots of the Seven-Elevens and shopping malls that have replaced them. Fleur looks at the Coca-Cola that Yuan offers her with a mixture of curiosity and disdain.

Rouge moves at a languorous pace, with a haunting, sad mood uninterrupted by shock, gore, or slapstick.

Rouge is on the Hong Kong Film Archive's list of "Best 100 Chinese Motion Pictures."

— Jim Morton

Bury Me High

1990 | Feng shui freaks will rejoice at this action film which celebrates the geographical divination abilities of protagonist and antagonist. Wisely (Chin Ka-lok) is an LA computer hacker with powers of geomancy and an IQ of 200. He must travel to Indochina to sort out some ancestral burial problems (which are causing his inoperable brain tumor, naturally).

Yuen Wah has the plum role as an Indochinese military leader who uses geomancy to create a despotic dystopia. LA businesswoman Moon Lee and Indochine Sibelle Hu model stunning evening wear at social functions, but change into more sensible outfits to kick butt. Lots of sound and fury, plenty of tanks, land mines, heavy artillery, and other war surplus, and evil Yuen Wah has a Blofeld-style hydraulic feng shui divination diorama which rises out of the floor at the touch of a secret button.

Call Girl 92

1992 | One of those amazing, female-centric films Hong Kong cranked out regularly. Veronica Yip, Carrie Ng, and Cecilia Yip are nightclub hostesses willing to go for "midnight snacks" with customers for a fee. Some jerk brings his nerdy wife (Sharla Cheung Man) in for a drink so he can show off. One of his friends comments: "your wife is more obedient than my dog." Wrong! When he serves her with divorce papers, she takes up school chum Carrie Ng on the offer of a hostess job. She's shy with the customers, preferring the caresses of Carrie. As entertaining as all this is, the show is stolen by Cecilia Yip, who plays her "alkie hooker" like a genuine raging, outta-control gin-disposal unit—rather than the romanticized tipplers so often found in films.

Japanese actress Yuko Aoki plays a Thai woman who brings all kinds of trouble to Hong Kong. (Photo of *Flirting* lobby card at the lobby of the Great Star Theater, San Francisco by Stefan Hammond, 1988).

Flirting

1988 | Steamy Kowloon is the backdrop to this eccentric, erotic love story. Director Lee Tai Hang constantly thrusts his characters into close, sticky proximity, and the humid look of summertime Hong Kong is guaranteed to make you crank up your air-conditioner.

A puerile hothead, Tsai (Alex Man), grows weary of contracting the clap at Mongkok "yellow boxes" and goes to Thailand to purchase a bride. He returns to his sweatbox-flat (and its panoramic views of the Kai Tak airport runway) with his new "locally-born Overseas Chinese" bride, played by gorgeous Japanese ingenue Yuko Aoki.

His lifelong buddy Hsi also shares the flat, and becomes sexually obsessed with the couple, boring a peephole in the paper-thin walls. The trapped bride gravitates towards Hsi—not because he's such a great guy, but because Tsai is such a beer-swilling, philandering jerk. No one is innocent, and it all ends in unsurprising tragic splendor, leaving the characters to work out their "desire issues" in the next lifetime.

Her Vengeance

1988 | The terrific Pauline Wong Siu-fung stars

HONG KONG NOIR

Thai poster for *Her Vengeance*—misspelled as HERVENGENT.

in the HK remake of the "can-you-take-this?" vengeance classic *I Spit on Your Grave*. Wong works at a Macau nightclub and an on-the-job dispute with unruly poltroons leads to assault and rape in a blue-lit graveyard. The scumbags leave her with a virulent, untreatable case of VD and an elaborate revenge scheme involving Lam Ching Ying, who plays the wheelchair-bound owner of Wanchai's San Francisco Club. The splatter finale is spectacular; Wong and Lam fight the miscreants with crossbows, noose contraptions, dangling nets of fishhooks, sharpened plumbing pipes, and a wokful of boiling oil. Directed by Nam Nai-choi (*The Seventh Curse, Story of Ricky*).

The Incorruptible

1993 | Ray Lui, a 1950s undercover triad-buster, and his spouse take on mobsters both on the streets and within the ranks of his own police department. Waise Lee is wondrously sleazy as a by-the-book gangster and Carrie Ng is even better as his sultry, opera-gloved, torch-singer moll. Simon Yam also appears as a turncoat triad member. Stolid and solid period piece; Hong Kong's answer to *The Untouchables*.

Tiger Cage

1990 | Jacky Cheung and Donnie Yen are cops busting dope-slinging thugs in typical two-fisted Hong Kong fashion. In a departure from her usual comedy roles, Carol "Do Do" Cheng plays a policewoman whose fiancé was murdered by the joy-powder merchants.

When Donnie finds that fellow cop Ng Man-tat is on the payroll of the local drug-dealers, he becomes enraged and bursts a bag of cocaine in Ng's face, powdering it white. Police supervisor Simon Yam arrives on the scene, but he's dirty too, and Donnie's blood sprays across the whitened face of the disgraced (but alive) Ng. When Jacky finally unravels the mess, the fur and bullets fly. A dark, violent tale of double-crosses, loyalty and revenge—directed by Yuen Woo-ping.

Women's Prison

1988 | Patricia Ha (the ultracool hitwoman from *On the Run*) looks marvelous in her wedding dress. But hubby-to-be Simon Yam is in hock to the loansharks, and her nuptials are disrupted when she ends up bludgeoning one with a plaster statue. An assault conviction brings six months in an odious women's "bird cage" and the festivities kick off with a handcuffing to tuff gal Carol "Do Do" Cheng. Do Do has a running feud with the hideous

MORE SEX, BETTER ZEN, FASTER BULLETS

Thai poster for *Women's Prison*.

"Fatty" over who gets to run this particular joint… you can see where this is going.

Hex Errors: Civics

More fractured English subtitles from your favorite Hong Kong movies. (See page 30 for a full explanation.)

"Today we're here to purge…a bourgeois slut who only cares for immoral sex and hedonism. She stole a pair of basketball shoes from the Fatherland."
Reincarnation of Golden Lotus

"What? Is this rebellion?"
"It is. Kill!"
Descendant of the Sun

"You damned intellectual, kneel down"
Red and Black

"HK will soon be China's, and you bedding a Soviet"
On The Run

"They took me as anti-revolutionist and punished me, and I was stink for 3 years."
The Nocturnal Demon

"Go sue the England."
The Big Heat

"Hi Chekov, losing up. This is America."
Black Cat 2: Assassination of President Yeltsin

"You're our enemy by using perfume"
Red and Black

"This is not Taiwan. This is Hong Kong! How can you go around hitting people on the head all the time?"
Night Caller

"We are nearly blown up in pieces."
"You deserve that. It's because you're civil servants."
Princess Madam

CHAPTER FOUR
AIYAH! THAT HAD TO HURT...
by Jude Poyer

"What the hell are you doing? Don't waste my time if you're scared!" "Sorry. I don't want to jump out of frame," replies the hesitant stuntwoman. "Are you out of your mind?" barks the action director. "Roll camera!" Ah Kam peers down from the concrete overpass to the freeway meters beneath her. It's taken enough courage for her to stand precariously on the ledge, but now she must dive from it onto a truck passing below. "Action!"

In the film *Ah Kam*, the stuntwoman lands successfully. In real life, the leap sent actress Michelle Yeoh to the hospital.

For every film student who's drawn to Hong Kong cinema by the twisting narratives and visuals of Wong Kar-wai's pictures, for every curious couple who've watched *Sex & Zen* to marvel at Amy Yip's curvy antics, there's ten other Hong Kong movie devotees who became converts when they discovered the meaning of "Action" with a capital A.

Hollywood satisfies the insatiable international hunger for bullets and body blows by churning out buddy-cop flicks, big-stomping robot flicks, and endless superhero conglomerates. But for all the high-tech explosions, computer generated thrills, and glossy stylization, no "high concept actioner" can compete with the underlying reality of an action scene in a Hong Kong movie.

Now, the film itself might stink. Its poor excuse for a plot may be as recycled as the note paper it was jotted down on. We may not care whether the characters live or die but we know that the actors playing them (and the stuntmen doubling for them and being clobbered by them), went through hell to bring us our ninety minutes of escapism.

How do these action stars (and starlets) keep their teeth when getting kicked in the jaw? How come Jackie Chan and his team didn't slice their arteries demolishing every pane of glass in the shopping mall of *Police Story*'s manic final reel? Why didn't Yuen Biao break both legs cartwheeling off a burning building in *Shanghai Express*? How can Tony Ching Siu-tung make a motorcycle somersault its way across the screen in *The Heroic Trio*? And how the hell do they make those shirt-tearing bullet hole effects where blood bursts forth like an oil well?

The power and skill of Hong Kong stuntwork

In Jackie Chan's *Project A*, we see Jackie summon all of his rapidly depleting strength to hold on to the hand of an enormous clock on a tall clock tower. The camera, positioned directly above him, shows the star and then a drop of about 40 feet to the ground below.

There's no green screen, no airbag to cushion

Yes, he's doing it for real: Jackie clings on in this screengrab from *Project A*.

him should he fall—all that stands between Jackie and the packed earth below are a couple of flimsy window-awnings. For a dreadful interval he battles to hold on, then the last of his strength leaves his arms, and so he loses his grip, and falls.

In *Shanghai Express*, Yuen Biao's only possible escape from a burning building is down. We watch him drag a rug from a washing line and lay it over the blazing edge of the building's roof. He stands on the rug, pauses for a split second, then nimbly cartwheels down to earth! Anyone whose watched one of those "Hollywood's Greatest Stunts" shows knows how a high fall should be done: with a stuntman falling through the bottom of the frame and onto an unseen safety-rig, followed by

Striped cloth awnings below: *Project A*.

a separate shot of the actor making the remaining few feet to touchdown. But in *Shanghai Express*, the camera follows Yuen Biao—the lead actor—all the way down to the ground, where he dusts himself off and delivers a line of dialogue.

The list of eye-popping moments in Hong Kong action scenes is virtually endless. Whether it's the slow-motion spectacle of Sammo Hung punching Australian martial arts actor Richard Norton square in the jaw in *Twinkle Twinkle Lucky Stars*, or in *Pantyhose Hero*, a speeding auto sweeping the burly Sammo off his feet, into the windscreen (which he smashes) and back onto the road, all in one spine-splintering shot, no words on a printed page can do justice to the spectacle of Hong Kong's stunt masters at work. Once witnessed though, on video or (better still) cinema screen, you'll be fascinated by what's emerged from Hong Kong action movies, particularly in the last two decades. We'll endure the nonsensical plots and cranky subtitles because these scenes of cinematic carnage and chaos are downright mesmerizing—and often appear to have been downright life-threatening to their participants.

But is what we see really that hazardous? Are the men and women who seemingly put their lives on the line in these films relying on their own guts and fate alone? Yes and no. For example, it's true that Michelle Yeoh learned how to ride a motorbike for the scene in *Supercop* where she rides one onto the top of a moving train. It's also true that Yeoh's bike was lowered onto the train from cables attached front and rear. Audiences accept that in the world of celluloid Jet Li can really do those "no shadow kicks", and many swallow the real-world hype of press agents. It's often difficult to separate myth from reality, so don't believe everything you hear about Hong Kong stuntwork in books, documentaries, interviews and on the Internet.

Michelle Yeoh rips it in mid-air: *Supercop*.

"Your skill is your safety"

For almost as long as films have been made in Hong Kong, people have been fighting in them—according to the Hong Kong Film Archive, the first Hong Kong martial arts film was 1938's *Fong Sai Yuk: Battle in the Boxing Ring*. The source of these films is the territory's rich heritage and affection for martial novels and the different regional forms of Chinese opera (both of which placed an importance on physical action), as well as genuine styles of kung fu: Chinese martial arts.

Sifu Yam Yu-tin (who worked in the mainland as well as Hong Kong) was the first action choreographer of Chinese cinema. In addition to staging the fights for many black and white films of the time, Yam also directed films and oversaw the martial art training of his daughter Yam Yin. The popular fictional tales of Wong Fei-hong were adapted for the screen by director Wu Pang from the late 40s, and Ms Yam often played the female lead.

But Wu soon found that unlike Ms Yam, regular actors couldn't perform the fight scenes—a main attraction of the series. Wu hired some genuine kung fu practitioners to work on the films on account of their direct teacher-student lineage to Wong Fei-hong. He hoped their proficiency would bring some level of authenticity to the action of an otherwise fantastic set of tales. To find the remaining fight performers—Hong Kong's first stuntmen—the film makers looked to the opera schools.

Opera training

In Chinese opera, the theatrical tradition of China, performances consist not only of storytelling and singing, but also elaborate fight sequences and displays of acrobatic skill. Expertise requires years of rigorous, almost-sadistic, training.

Stuntman turned action director Tony Leung Siu-hung recalls his childhood Cantonese opera training, under his father Leung Ban: "He used to make me hold a handstand position, with my feet touching the wall, while an incense stick burned away completely—forty-five minutes to an hour! If you tried to get down too early, 'BOOM!'—you'd get hit. For the splits, I'd sit with my back against the wall with one leg attached to a bamboo stick, and the other attached to a rope which he would tighten, pulling my legs towards the wall. I used to cry!" Many kung fu films (starring former opera students) contain torturous training scenes showing how their characters achieve such a high level of physical skill.

While Hong Kong films were in their infancy, so too were their action scenes unsophisticated. As more and more younger opera players began to enter the scene, things began to change. Fights evolved from loosely choreographed movements executed in long static takes (with minimal camera movement) into something more cinematically refined. By the late sixties there were four opera schools in Hong Kong. Three were for part-time students—kids who would head there after school for several hours' practice, followed by a nighttime performance for the paying public. One institute, run by Sifu Yuen, was for girls and boys who lived, trained, ate and slept on the premises five days a week, for a contract period up to seven years. Parents were paid a monthly sum by the money-minded master who, in return, pocketed the profits from their children's appearances on stage and in motion pictures.

Alex Law's 1988 film *Painted Faces* depicts life at Yuen's school, and focuses on a group of the most gifted students, the Seven Little Fortunes. Law's film is not an attempt to accurately represent the school, its performers and the times and circumstances in which they found themselves at the close of the sixties. The film shows the 7LF turning to film stuntwork as opera's popularity in the colony declined—though Chinese opera retains a degree of popularity in the HKSAR. The stars of the stage, having graduated from the academies, were attracted by the rapidly growing kung fu film industry. It was more lucrative than their stage work, and stuntwork was a vocation in which their hard-earned physical wizardry could be put to use.

An introduction to the industry was easy to come by for a gifted opera player, since the films' fight choreographers tended to be opera masters. The schools had become surrogate families for the performers, and besides, nepotism is perennial in the motion picture industry. But gifted martial artists, gymnasts and even trampolinists

AIYAH! THAT HAD TO HURT...

found that they too could earn their keep being slaughtered by invincible heroes or standing in for somersaulting, sword-wielding heroines.

"Master!!!!"

A fortunate stuntman might find himself serving as apprentice to an action director. The stuntman would learn the "trade" of action-direction by performing and assisting with numerous fights and stunts over the course of many productions. If he was good, he might gain the status of assistant action director, where his job is to demonstrate exactly what the coordinator wants of the stuntmen performing an action. The assistant is also relied upon to provide the action director with new ideas for choreography. Naturally, many stuntmen eventually tire of seeing someone else rejecting their ideas (or worse, taking credit for their ingenuity), and aspire to be action directors themselves.

Tony Leung Siu-hung spent several years as one of Tony Ching Siu-tung's assistant choreographers, but parted ways with Ching when he felt he had enough ideas of his own worth filming and receiving credit for. Not all sifu/student relationships are so businesslike—they can be more flexible, with the assistant gaining more responsibility on smaller-budgeted films, then returning to assist his master on a large-scale film when needed.

Stuntman-turned-director Ridley Tsui is one of the last generation of opera students. Tsui, a stuntman from the age of twelve, followed sifu Lau Ka-wing, acting as his assistant on films like *Tiger on the Beat 2*. His tie to Lau wasn't exclusive though. Following an introduction to Sammo Hung from Lau, Ridley worked as a member of Hung's stunt team and even choreographed and doubled Sammo in the Lau-directed *Skinny Tiger*

Screengrab-montage of Conan Lee's stunt-gone-wrong.

MORE SEX, BETTER ZEN, FASTER BULLETS

& *Fatty Dragon*. But up until the late-eighties, stuntmen tended to stick to their designated teams—on Jackie's self-directed films, he uses his JC Stunt Team, while on the ones Sammo directs, it's his boys who take the knocks. It wasn't until the formation of the Hong Kong Stuntman Association in 1994 (see "Club Mad," page 96) that things became less restricted.

Aiyah!

It was Ridley's job to demonstrate to actor Conan Lee how a stunt should be performed in *Tiger on the Beat 2*. This was no simple fall. Pursuing a pickpocket (played by Tsui) on a busy pedestrian overpass, Conan's character takes a running leap over the side-fence towards a lamppost, intending to slide down it to street level. Before he would allow the actor (who rejected the idea of being doubled) to attempt it, director Lau Kar-leung had Tsui and his other assistant demonstrate the stunt. Take One—pickpocket Ridley jumped off the overpass, landing safely on the back of a passing goods vehicle. Then Conan made his leap.

What followed is ingrained in the memories of all those present: Lee clears the fence and falls towards the lamppost below. He grabs it but instantly loses his grip. His body twists in the air as it spirals downwards thirty feet below. There's no airbag, box-rig, or mattresses—nothing but Hong Kong asphalt. "Everybody was shocked," remembers Ridley. "How did it happen?"

Amazingly, Conan didn't break a single bone. He did however, spend a considerable amount of time in hospital and filming slid to a halt. Did letting his leading actor perform such a hazardous stunt constitute gross irresponsibility on Lau's part? Ridley Tsui believes not. "He's an actor. He didn't have to do that [stunt], but [Conan was] like: 'I want to be Jackie Chan!'" In Tsui's eyes, Lee would have been better served by following Lau's direction and the assistants' examples. Rather than grabbing the lamppost and slide down fireman-style, Conan "grabbed the wrong part. He tried to grab the horizontal arm that holds the light, like a gymnast. You can't hold it! [The way we showed him], you can use your arms, your whole body, not just your hands."

Lau wasn't very happy with Lee's boldness, but rather than re-shoot the stunt, producers included the botched jump into the film's final cut! "He was bleeding from the mouth," recalls Ridley. "He's so lucky he didn't die."

Death did occur during the filming of Sammo Hung's *Licence to Steal*, which features a protracted action scene in a building site. At one point, two pole-wielding gangster thugs pursue comedian Richard Ng and are about to catch him when two planks of wood spring up from a workman's pit in the ground. The cronies run straight into them and fly violently back. To the viewer it looks like a simple stunt, but the stuntmen were not completely relying on their own agility. Each was wearing a harness attached to a wire fed through a slit in the back of his jacket. The wire trailed back several feet, where it ran through a pulley at ground-level. Behind the pulley stood members of the stunt team who yanked on the wire, hurling the stuntmen backwards.

It took the combined strength of four men to pull back each stunt-performer. The force of their tug, and a misjudged angling of the pulley, meant that one of them (to the left of the screen) was jerked back violently into the ground. Not onto his padded back, but instead, the back of his skull. However, despite misinformation to the contrary, a stuntman's death is a far-from-typical Hong Kong action movie set occurrence—this particular fatality is the only stunt-related one in recent memory.

AIYAH! THAT HAD TO HURT...

Full flame contact

Accidents, though, aren't rare in the Hong Kong movie world where time is money and productions are in limited supply of both. Stunt performers the world over know that bruises and cuts are de rigeur, and most seasoned pros have the odd horror story to tell. Needless to say, Hong Kong stuntmen are no exception.

Ridley Tsui lists his ankles, back, nose and jaw as vocation-battered body parts. But his worst experience was no fracture or sprain. Ridley was part of a team of stuntmen assembled in Thailand by Lau Ka-wing for Ringo Lam's dark crime thriller *Full Contact*. In the film, Chow Yun-fat's character takes cover from gunfire by diving through the open kitchen windows of a riverside house. A rocket is fired through the same window, and the whole place is instantly ablaze.

Chow Yun-fat is one of Hong Kong's tallest leading men and since six-foot Ridley was the only tall member of Lau's team, the job of doubling Chow fell to him. Tsui positioned himself on the floor, facing away from the windows. On action, fire tore through the house and scorched Tsui's exposed right shoulder. As directed, he bolted out of the house and out of frame, but not exactly intact. "My shoulder was like a banana: yellow, with the skin all peeling down. Chow Yun-fat threw a bucket of water over it, but the pain was too much and I dived into the (nearby) river."

Several factors limited Tsui's ability to protect himself during the stunt. As his upper body was covered only by a leather waistcoat and tight t-shirt with rolled-up sleeves, Ridley's arms and shoulders were exposed to the oncoming flames (the heat alone could cause injury even with no contact). His costume did not allow for him any protective fire-resistant clothing (like a Formula-1 driver wears) underneath.

Another factor was Ringo Lam's auteur approach to filmmaking. In most instances, Hong Kong action directors enjoy high autonomy when filming action scenes. The action director is usually given control of choreographing the physical movement of the performers and rigging whatever special equipment might be required, and also the positioning of the camera and sometimes even the editing of the finished scene. Because of this free-hand approach, the Hollywood work of Hong Kong action directors rarely resembles the home-grown product.

Ringo Lam is one of the few Hong Kong directors who hire stunt coordinators to rig and execute his vision for a scene. Lam usually tells the action director what he wants to see, what he doesn't like, and what he wants changed and also maintains strong control over the camera and editing process. Lam's vision for the burning-house scene in *Full Contact* dictated that the kitchen go up in flames in the same shot as Chow's character gets up and out. In instances where the action director has control, he is freer to devise safer ways to bring the script to life. It's evident in *Full Contact* that the stunt team was well aware that the shot was hazardous—all the other "actors" are dummies!

Where's your tool?

Just as foam dummies often substitute for the

bodies of actors, Hong Kong stunt makers employ a variety of different devices to make their action scenes both safer and more spectacular. Some of these props are as old as action cinema itself and have remained pretty much unchanged since those early days.

New devices, or new ways of utilizing old ones, are constantly dreamed up by the innovative minds of competitive choreographers. The minds that create these tools (and stuntmen bold enough to work with them) leave spellbound audiences asking "How the hell did they pull that off?"

Taking a knock

Although their films contain the occasional neck-risking stunt, most Hong Kong stunt performers and directors pay considerable attention to safety. But since Hong Kong action films can't compete with Hollywood flicks on scale, budget, or built-in hype, they must have a unique selling point. Often, this hook is stunts of the kind that American filmmakers could never dream of executing, for fear of accidents, death, rocketing insurance premiums and litigation. Due to time and money pressures though, Hong Kong filmmakers can't take the same amount of time in preparing and executing those stunts as Western filmmakers would.

Unlike a major studio film from Hollywood, which is often guaranteed global distribution through cinema chains and video labels, most Hong Kong films rely on international distributors acquiring the territorial rights for a movie to make money. Distribution throughout Asia is essential if a production is to be profitable. Distributors (and their audiences) from Thailand, Malaysia, Indonesia and the Philippines want as much bang as they can get for their buck. It's often not the Jackie Chan/Jet Li/Chow Yun-fat flicks but the

Ignore the outsized gat and check the sleeve—Cynthia Rothrock's arm is padded against an impending strike.

Hong Kong movies featuring less-exalted names that contain the craziest stunts—the ones that had to hurt.

Hong Kong filmmakers aren't crazy though, and as much attention to safety is given as time and budget will allow, as long as it's not at the expense of the action's excitement factor. Any actor or stuntman about to engage in a bout of fisticuffs will be padded-up. Slipping a cotton and foam pad over a forearm and under a jacket sleeve is quick, and enables the wearer to block an oncoming kick, punch or club without fear of serious bruising.

The audience also gets to see contact being made between the strike and block. Similarly, if a performer is to receive a kick to the torso, he likely be padded under his costume.

The Western tradition is to use false perspective to give the impression of a hit. Hong Kong fight scenes often favor camera angles which clearly capture the impact of a strike. While most fight performers have sufficient enough control to enable their blows to touch but not injure (pulling punches), some techniques call for padding.

There's a scene in Dragons Forever (see page 207) where Sammo Hung is held by gangsters and villain Benny Urquidez plants a running sidekick in his chest. Benny "The Jet" is a real-life undefeated kickboxing champion, an immensely powerful fighter who used to yell "The power of Jesus is in my hands!" as his opponents crumpled unconscious. Needless to say, Sammo (also the film's director) sensibly opts to wear a large protective pad over his sizable abdomen. Watching the scene, it looks like Sammo's reaction to the kick, and that of the stuntmen meant to hold him up, is genuine!

The kinds of pads worn in stuntwork vary from the elastic cotton-and-foam variety worn in semi-contact karate tournaments to harder ones like hockey or rollerblading pads worn over the elbows and knees. For really serious falls or reactions, moto-cross rider padding is used—back and chest protectors made of hard, articulated plastic. Sometimes these will be worn over the karate pads—the soft pads absorb the impact, the hard pads protect the bones.

Fight scenes have become bolder as films have moved away from the "stripped to the waist" kung fu duels of yesteryear. At one point in Jackie Chan's fight in the pachinko amusement parlor in *Thunderbolt*, the doors of a steam bath open and out rush several near-naked, tattooed attackers—mostly Hong Kong stuntmen playing Japanese yakuza. Note that those who receive the hardest punishment from Chan (thrown violently to the floor or onto one of those "test your strength" metal striking points intended for mallets) are the ones who put on jackets before fighting! While he's dealing with this bunch, one assailant clad only in his underwear (stuntman For-Sing Mars) grabs Chan from the front. Then Japanese actor Ken Sawada proceeds to clobber Chan's back with a metal chair. Look closely, and the outline of Jackie's back-pad is visible through his loose fitting jacket.

To further enhance the effect of hard contact between combatants and object, "Power Powder" (a better name for talcum powder) is sometimes used. For example: before a kick, powder is sprinkled on the target area of the person to be kicked and on the shoe of the kicker—creating a shower of dust on impact. Likewise, the floor may be sprinkled with powder prior to a fall. Although unrealistic (where does it come from?), it is surprisingly effective: the finales of such films as *OUATIC 2*, *Eastern Condors*, *The Iceman Cometh* and *Tiger Cage 2* bear this out.

It's easy to imagine a heavily padded actor enduring re-takes of a kick to the chest, but what about those head shots, where an expertly placed right-hook sends sweat flying from the face of a screen-star? We've seen Jackie Chan getting booted in the cheek in *Project A* Part 2, Sammo Hung delivering a jump-roundhouse kick to some guy's head in *Lucky Stars Go Places*, and Yuen Biao planting a tornado kick on the jaw of Melvin Wong's double at the end of *Righting Wrongs*. All of these had to hurt! There are some measures that can be taken to lessen the damage of such blows, though. A mouthguard (the kind worn for MMA or rugby) or a mouthful of cotton wool helps an actor keep his teeth. Recently, action directors favor shooting punches thrown at slower-than-real speed, which make contact with faces yet inflict almost no damage. This already slow action is then shown in slow-motion: The viewer's mind subconsciously accepts that the slow-motion strike and impact occurred in real(istic) time.

Close ups of kicks to the face are less problematic. Usually a stuntman will put his arm through a trouser-leg, put a sock and shoe over his hand, and then give a light slap to his screen-opponent's face. If the shoe has some Power Powder sprinkled on it prior to shooting, the "kick" can appear even more punishing.

Wired for action

Wires and mini-trampolines often lend actors superhuman skill. Mini-tramps aid stuntmen in aerial kicks and acrobatic maneuvers. They're popular in the fantasy genre—whenever masked swordsmen somersault over low angle cameras, it's likely they've leaped off a mini-tramp. In contemporary action films, mini-tramps are used to project stuntmen into the air as if thrown by explosions, a primitive (but safer) alternative to the air-rams used in Western stuntwork, which use compressed-air pistons to catapult the stuntmen. In Hong Kong films, the stuntman will run towards the off-camera tramp, jump on it, and go airborne as the effects crew triggers the explosion behind him.

The use of wires in Hong Kong films is an art form in itself, making the gravity-defying shenanigans of such films as *Swordsman 2* and *Zu: Warriors from the Magic Mountain* possible. Cloak-clad eunuchs take to the sky to dispatch a dazzling array of darts at a noble horseman, an Ice Queen glides along the heads of her assembled courtiers before assuming her throne, or (as in 1998's *Storm Riders*) a pair of dueling warriors spiral down hundreds of feet towards a crashing waterfall, their combat set against a breathtaking Buddha statue carved from the surrounding cliff face.

Wirework is also in (less obvious) evidence in modern day films. Steel cables (thin enough to be largely undetectable on screen, but strong enough to support the weight of a person) perform a dual purpose in present day films. As in the swordplay and fantasy flicks, they are sometimes used to enhance the physical skill of the performers' leaping and kicking, but they also perform a vital safety function. Most viewers know there's more than just martial skill in evidence as Jet Li bounces his way across the evil White Lotus Cult's temple (in *OUATIC 2*), unleashing flurries of kicks. But not all Hong Kong film aficionados are aware of the degree to which "wirework" was also used in non-period films of the 80s and 90s.

A wire-rig works by using a pulley system to make an actor or stuntman travel upwards and/or backwards. Beneath his costume, the performer wears a harness around waist and thighs or waist and shoulders. The wire leads from this harness, passes through a hole in the costume, and leads to a pulley attached to the set or studio ceiling. If the scene is being filmed outdoors, the pulley is attached to scaffolding or the arm of a mobile crane. The wire runs through the pulley and back down to the stunt team, who hold a rope attached to the wire—the combined strength of the team pulling on the rope lifts the performer up off the ground. If the ascent is intended to be more forceful, the stuntmen holding the rope may stand on a ladder. When they jump off the ladder down to the ground a few feet below, their combined body weight will jerk the harness-wearer off his feet.

In *Thunderbolt*, car mechanic Ah For (Jackie Chan) is visited by gangsters intent on bribery and a long-haired goon produces a wad of cash. Cut to a wide shot and Ah For front-kicks the money from the thug's hand with his right leg, then delivers a jumping left-leg, right-leg combination of two more front kicks. The three kicks are basic ones and wouldn't pose a problem for any Hong Kong stuntman, but a wire is being used here to make the technique appear more powerful. If the stuntman performing a jumping kick doesn't have to expend energy to gain height, he can deliver the kicks with more power and more dramatic impact.

To the viewer, the three kicks appear skillful but not fantastic or unrealistic. That's because action director Sammo Hung knows that when working in the modern day genre, audiences won't accept the degree of wire lift they would in a fantasy flick. Likewise in *Who Am I?*, when Jackie (his hands cuffed behind his back) springs off the floor onto his feet, leaps through his cuffed hands so that they are in front of him, then delivers a jump-roundhouse kick to a spy's head—all in one continuous shot—the wire lends lifts to his leaps, making him appear superphysical, not superhuman.

In Hong Kong films, most actions using wires will have the performer attached to a single wire. With just one cable, the stuntman can coordinate his ascent (the job of the team pulling the wire), with his body rotation by using his shoulder muscles to generate spin. This is how the spiraling/corkscrewing affect of swordplay films is achieved. More than one cable would get hopelessly tangled.

Double wires are worn at either hip if the stuntman is to perform a somersaulting motion. Yuen Biao's backflip kicks to the jaw of his foe in *Iceman Cometh*'s final reel are examples of these "double-acro" wire rigs. If his body is to spend more time horizontal than vertical, the stuntman may find that double wires aid balance. In the scene in *Hard-Boiled* where Anthony Wong's gang shoots up a rival's warehouse, we see Mad Dog (Philip Kwok) slide in on his bike and spray a bunch of suited triads with Uzi lead. One of the mobsters is shown in slow motion, flying horizontally over a desk and into some boxes. Yes, he's wired: one cable between the shoulder blades and one near the spine.

One reason why Hong Kong filmmakers seldom use more than one wire on a person is for fear of them being visible in the completed film, as they are for brief instances. Because of visibility problems, wires used in Hong Kong productions are thinner than the cables used in Hollywood. Stateside, actors and actresses can perform an action with two or more strong, thick cables to perform an action which are later "painted out" with sophisticated, expensive computer editing equipment. In Hong Kong, a popular wire used for flying effects is just 1.5 mm in diameter, but it can easily support a "flying" performer.

Wires also act as safety tools. In *City Hunter*, Jackie Chan leaps over a balcony onto a model dolphin suspended by a cable from the ceiling. He then swings on it, firing happily away with his machine gun. In the end credits of the film though, we see an outtake where Jackie does lose his grip. But the prudent Mr Chan was wearing a harness, with a wire running through his sleeve which was attached to the prosthetic porpoise. With wires running through jacket-sleeves, stars and stuntmen alike can cling onto buildings, helicopters and vehicles for long periods without fear. They know they won't fall, because they're bolted-in tight.

Just as wires lift people up, they can help them descend safely as well. For a good example of wires aiding a fall, look to *Royal Warriors* and Michael Wong's sacrificial dive to save lady-love Michelle Yeoh. We see Wong, who's hanging over the side of a building by a rope around his ankle, untie himself. Cut to a medium shot showing Wong falling out of frame. We are then treated to wide shots from low-angle (emphasizing the height of the building) and see Wong's double falling on a wire. Because it's in slow motion, the descent does not appear staggered—rather, it's extremely dramatic, especially when cross-cut with shots of onlooker Michelle's reaction. For the last portion of the fall, a drop through a glass canopy, we actually see a separate fall altogether. Here the stuntman is bereft of wires to slow him down.

Michael Wong's double plummeting... see the wire?

Boxing clever

Of course, when jumping off buildings without the aid of wires, something has to cushion the impact. In the West, airbags are used for high falls, but falls from heights requiring an airbag are a rare occurrence in Hong Kong films. What do Hong Kong's stuntmen choose to take a dive into? Cardboard boxes. It's not as unsophisticated or as unsafe as it may first seem. The world record, set by a Czech stuntman, for the highest fall into a (cardboard) box-rig, was from 200 feet.

Here's how Yuen Biao did that spectacular fall to earth in *Shanghai Express*: After cartwheeling off the burning building, he's seen dropping all the way to the ground, not out of frame or onto cushioning. How did he avoid injury in this unprecedented stunt? He's falling into a "dug out": a trench in the ground into which a box-rig has been placed. When the rig is covered over by sand and straw, it's camouflaged level with the ground and largely undetectable. "That (rig) was just one box deep, with one layer of foam mattresses covering the boxes" recalls Biao (a ready supply of foam mattresses are always on hand during action filming, to cover box-rigs, or for stuntmen to rehearse low falls). Biao is still proud of his cartwheel into stunt history and rightly so. When describing the safety precautions taken for the stunt, he's quick to add, "At that time, I'm the only one in Hong Kong who would do it!"

Box-rigs aren't always 100% efficient. In the UK, the top layer of boxes will have their upward-facing corners cut off (to avoid gouging the stuntman upon impact). Care will be taken to make sure that all the boxes are tightly packed together. The latter of these two time-taking measures that might have spared Michelle Yeoh her hospital stay following that jump from the bridge in *Ah Kam*, an Ann Hui film on a (fictional) stuntwoman's experiences. After stuntwoman Ah Kam fails to jump on the first take, the action director (played by Sammo Hung) gives her a helpful push for the second. In the final release print we see her sail onto the back of the moving truck. Michelle's on a wire but her leap is a swan dive, and on a single wire it's hard to maintain a horizontal position. As she falls, her body pivots upright. Another shot—a low angle—was to capture Michelle (sans wire) swan-diving off the bridge and out of frame onto a box-rig. The boxes weren't packed together tightly enough and instead of absorbing the force of her landing, they shifted apart. Just as the single wire was against her, so was the position of Michelle's body for the stunt: Landing on the front leaves the spine especially vulnerable. Yeoh was lucky to escape serious injury this time.

Another bad landing, this time on the 1987 smash fighting femmes flick *Angel*, put one stuntman in a wheelchair and his coordinator Tony Leung Siu-hung, in court. The stunt required that two stuntmen perform a twenty-five foot fall onto a box rig. Leung was confident in the stunt's safety, enough to choose his own brother as one of the stuntmen: "This stunt's actually very simple for every stuntguy, especially for the injured guy (who was doubling for the actor). He was my assistant, very professional and experienced. He permanently injured his backbone because he did the wrong landing: he landed on his bottom, not his back." Leung found himself in court since the production company that had hired them for *Angel* had dissolved (a common practice in Hong Kong which allows producers to avoid any financial responsibility after shooting has ended). "There's a regulation for those bankrupt companies that all damages they owe can be refunded by the government. The stuntman wanted money from both the government and me. We went through the civil court. My lawyer advised me in advance that if I lost I'd have to pay HK$5,000,000. I'd [already] spent over HK$250,000 just for lawyers. Finally the government paid [in line] with their bankrupt company regulation."

Discouraged from spending more trying to get his costs refunded, Leung (a devout Buddhist) accepted this unfortunate turn of events as part of his karma. The silver lining was that the accident and its ensuing litigation was one factor that made him an active participant in establishing the Hong Kong Stuntman Association. The mishap, which had left one stuntman paralyzed, could hardly be blamed on Leung. "I'm very concerned about safety." The accidents on *Angel* and *Ah Kam* have to be seen in context: two injuries for the hundreds of times box-rigs have been used in Hong Kong films.

A pane in the glass

Wires, boxes, and pads are the responsibility of the stunt team, but there are other instances where the team must work in conjunction with the film's effects crew. If a stuntman is to be torched, exploded, riddled with machine gun fire or sent crashing through a window, then he has to have faith not only in his coordinator, but also

Sugar smacks: Jackie face-plants in *Police Story*.

whoever is responsible for handling the various props which facilitate the stunt.

Princess Diana once demonstrated to the world the safety of a sugar-glass bottle by smashing one over her spouse's head at a James Bond exhibition. But sugar isn't always the answer, and not all the glass used in stunt sequences is phony. Sometimes budget-conscious film makers use bottles molded from thin wax. But in Hong Kong, if an actor or stuntman is to smash into a picture frame or cabinet, the chances are though, that it'll be made from sugar.

That's how Jackie Chan's stunt team keeps their arteries intact at the end of *Police Story*. Sugar-glass is safe enough that actress Brigitte Lin was hurled through the odd store display too, rather than a stunt double. But sugar-glass sheets aren't cheap, and sometimes (especially for actions involving large window panes), real glass is used. Of course you don't crash straight through: The effects department attach an explosive charge to the pane of glass, and the charge is triggered an instant before the performer hits it. The glass (the reinforced kind used for car windscreens) shatters into thousands of tiny fragments. "Charged glass", though relatively safe, can inflict small cuts. Few action directors expect actors to work with it: a small cut to the face isn't a serious health risk but could cause major continuity problems. Stuntmen can travel through charged glass without too much worry. Naturally, if he's traveling through it face-forward, a stuntman will close his eyes and try to shield his face with his arms. He may also put cotton wool in his ears to prevent any small fragments getting trapped there. All should be safe, so long as the effects man doesn't detonate the charge too late!

A stuntman charges through charged glass in *Crime Story*.

It's generally easy to distinguish between sugar-glass and real (charged) glass. If it's genuine, the glass will have a mosaic appearance to it just prior to it being broken, because the charge has been detonated. Sugar-glass, ironically, breaks into real-looking shards when smashed. In *Task Force*, a bold raid on a triad hangout is executed by a stunt double crashing through the locked front doors, which are solid glass. The doors are charged, so when they break, they shatter, and the stuntman can safely roll over the debris without sustaining serious cuts. By contrast, the display cases that Yuen Biao and Yuen Wah send each other into at the end of *Iceman Cometh* are made from sugar-glass—that's why they look so real!

Going with a bang

How do filmmakers create the illusion of bullet-hits tearing through clothing and flesh? Through ingenious devices known as "squibs". In Hollywood

Squibs: on-body mini-explosions.

films, look back to James Caan's assassination in *The Godfather* or the bloody battles of Sam Peckinpah to see the kind of devotion to the squib that suffused marvelously politically incorrect Hong Kong cinema in the 80s/90s.

Squibs are small plastic packets (condoms can be used) filled with fake blood—a mixture of food coloring, for redness, and cough syrup, for texture—and linked to an explosive charge. They are most commonly placed under or in the lining of clothing. When detonated, the explosion tears through the material and glorious red goo gushes forth. In Hong Kong, squibs are just part and parcel of creating a gunfight scene. Single-squib rigs are quick to prepare. Usually these are detonated by the effects crew and it's the job of the actor or stuntman wearing the squib to react as if shot, in time with its detonation. For the simplest single-squib rigs, the explosive charge is attached to a pair of electrical wires trailing down the trouser leg of the performer. The one squib is to be set off in a given take, the crewman may be exploded by touching the wires to a battery's terminals, causing a short circuit.

If the performer is wearing multiple squibs, the wires usually lead to a detonating board, where they're set off in a preset sequence. The performer knows the sequence, and can jerk his or her body appropriately. That's how the effect

AIYAH! THAT HAD TO HURT...

Whoopsie: someone's wire is showing in *Hard-Boiled*.

of several bullets hitting the chest, stomach and arms of a person can be achieved in a single shot.

Both camera crew and performer must take care not to make the trailing wires visible. During Chow Yun-fat's warehouse raid in *Hard-Boiled*, there's a memorable moment just after Tony (Tony Leung Chiu-wai) has told Johnny (Anthony Wong) to leave. Tony, armed with two handguns, comes from behind a car to face Chow. One gangster in a light jacket and dark pants is in front of Tony—he's ready to shoot Chow but gets blasted in the chest by Chow's pump-action shotgun. In the shot which established this unfortunate triad just seconds earlier, the camera (following Tony) tilts low enough for us to see a large group of wires trailing out of his left trouser leg. Thankfully though, the action, camera-movement and editing in the scene is so fast and furious that such oversights tend to pass undetected.

Squibs are, on the whole, safe. As with any action tool though, there are safety measures which lessen the chance for mishaps. With multiple squibs or powerful single squibs, closing the eyes keeps them clear of any nasty flying (fake) blood. If the squibs are on the chest, one's arms should be kept clear—one *Thunderbolt* actor's bicep was badly scarred by the flames of his exploding squibs. Accidents involving squibs are rare, but stuntmen tend to do the most squib work since they're not expected to waste as much time as actors with "NG's" ("No Good" takes) or pre-detonation nerves. Actress Shu Qi was reportedly in tears when Tony Ching Siu-tung required she be rigged with multiple squibs in *The Blacksheep Affair*.

Some action directors don't hesitate before attaching squibs to the heads of actors and stuntmen (see Yuen Wah's slo-mo demise in *On the Run*, or Theresa Lee paying the price for indecision in *Extreme Crisis*). But care should be taken that the squibs aren't too heavily charged.

Ouch!

Karel Wong Chi-yeung was eager to please on the set of the 1989 Ocean Shores production *The Last Duel*. Having won a much-coveted television acting contract with TVB, the 22 year old hoped that he could create an equally impressive impact in his big screen debut. He was therefore willing to perform whatever hazardous actions stunt director Lau Chi-hon (*The Killer*) required from him without using a double. When the time came to film his character's justly grisly demise, Lau decided that Wong should take a bullet through the head. Two squibs (loaded with ample stage blood) were attached to the back of the actor's head on either side. The camera was "overcranked" (so that the image—giving the impression of the bullet tearing through Wong's skull, and his reaction—could be shown in slow motion), and began to roll. "Action!"

"It felt like two baseball bats smashing the sides of my head," recalls Karel. "I was weak, I was deaf—I mean I thought they'd deafened me. It wasn't 'til three hours later that I started to hear again."

Wong is careful not to lay any blame on Lau.

"Often, it's not the stunt director's fault. It's the effects' guys that you've got to be careful of. Maybe for an explosion they are afraid to "NG" and be told off for not using enough explosives, so they overcharge the bomb." After this experience, Wong became more cautious about what he'd agree to perform without the aid of a stunt double. "Back then I was young, so I would say 'Yes! Yes! Yes!' to whatever they asked. I was young and new [to the film business] and wanted to make a good impression."

In Hong Kong, an actor (unless already established as a box office draw) cannot afford to be unaccommodating. If he's perceived as "trouble," producers know they'll have no difficulty finding a willing replacement. Yet even little-known actors have it easier than stuntmen who (as individuals) are largely anonymous to the moviegoing public. Ridley Tsui explains: "If they ask you [a stuntman], 'Can you do this?', you don't have time to think about it. Just say 'Yes'. If you say 'No' someone will replace you and you'll lose your chance." Unfortunately, if a stuntman backs out of a stunt, he runs a serious risk of never being employed again. While Hong Kong stuntmen are as competitive as any group of peers, most undertake hazardous work less for glory and respect than for a pragmatic desire to be regarded as employable by stunt coordinators.

Bruce Law: he's the firestarter

One stuntman brave enough to turn down a job is Bruce Law. A former Taekwando champion and motorbike enthusiast, Law spent much of his youth speeding around the streets of the New Territories in not-quite-legal races. Law's introduction to the film business came in 1985 when stunt riders were needed for a chase scene in Sammo Hung's *Heart of the Dragon*. Several stunt jobs later, Bruce was asked to be the stunt coordinator on a film.

The honeymoon period ended when Law balked at producers telling him he had to hurry preparations for a speedboat crash-scene. "The last time that a scene like that was tried, the stuntmen were injured. So I planned how it should be done safely and the producers said it was too timely and expensive. They asked me to change it and I said 'No.' They kicked me out and got someone else."

For any other stunt coordinator, the dismissal would have badly marred his career, but Bruce had found himself a niche in the world of action filmmaking. The industry had realized that for stunts involving moving vehicles, fire and explosions, Law was the man for the job. Parenthetically, when the speedboat sequence was attempted without his tutelage, all the stuntmen got hurt.

AIYAH! THAT HAD TO HURT...

Bruce Law modeling a stunt-harness in the back of his production truck (Photo: Stefan Hammond, 1998).

An avid follower of Western stunt technology, Law has educated himself in Hollywood's latest and safest methods of onscreen destruction. Directors such as Tony Ching Siu-tung and John Woo started counting on his expertise beginning in the late-eighties. It was Law who masterminded Michelle Yeoh's riding-a-motorbike-onto-a-moving-train-roof sequence for *Supercop*, and he even doubled the actress for some of the more hazardous shots. "For one shot, I asked to have ten thousand cardboard boxes alongside the train for me to land in. On the day [on location in Kuala Lumpur], they told me that they only had five thousand. When I did the jump, I missed the boxes." Despite a hard landing, Law would not allow himself to be confined to his Malaysian hospital bed: "I wanted to try jet skiing, and you can't do it in Hong Kong. So I had to do it while I was there, even though my back was painful!"

Law (unlike many other Hong Kong stunt coordinators) likes to leave nothing to chance, and his intricately designed car-rigs and explosive devices are often tested days prior to filming. Law is keen for actors to safely perform their own stunt sequences if possible. How did he convince Stephen Chiau to have his arms set ablaze in *The King of Comedy*? Law led by example: "I just stood there, with my arms on fire, for over a minute while chatting with him. I said 'Do you trust me?' and he was ready to do it."

To execute safe body burns, Bruce uses flammable liquids or glues which burn with a cold (yellow) flame, while emitting minimal smoke to limit the risk of harmful inhalation. The performer wears fireproof clothing under their costume, and protective gels over the exposed skin and hair to prevent singeing and blistering. For explosion effects, Law likes using propane gas flames which are controllable, allowing actors to work outside the (predetermined) distance of the flames' reach. That's how Jackie Chan can jump out of the window of an exploding hut (in *Supercop*) and be closely followed by tongues of flame, without being exposed to serious risk of burning. "Of course, I had him wear a fire-suit anyway. You cannot injure a star!"

Law's company, "Stunts Unlimited", is located in the New Territories' town of Yuen Long, not far from the Chinese border. Several cargo containers house his stunt equipment and welding gear, and it's also here that Law parks his personal collection of police vehicles and trucks specially rigged to accommodate camera crews. "A guy from the States came here. He's got thirty years' experience with the fire department there, and he regulates all the LA stunt workshops. He

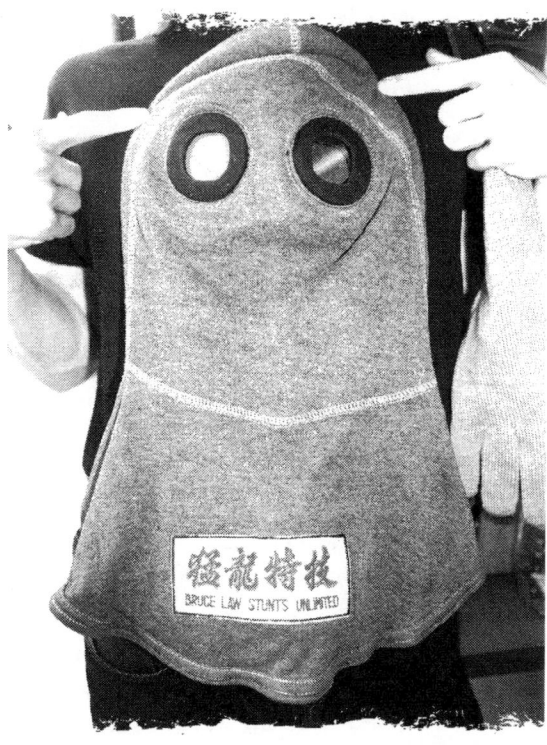

A Bruce Law Stunts Unlimited fire-hood (Photo: Stefan Hammond, 1998).

said mine's as safe and as well maintained as any US outfit, if not better," boasts Bruce, whose Hollywood inspired professionalism seems somewhat out of place in the maverick Hong Kong movie scene. His safe approach keeps him and his stunt crew busy.

"Where's your permit?"

In early 1997, an assistant propsman was killed by shrapnel from an exploding car on the location of *Downtown Torpedoes*. While the press and police criticized the film makers for not clearing the set of all personnel not integral to the stunt, the film community retorted by saying that if permits were granted for such explosions, time could be taken to carry out such safety measures. Although Law didn't oversee that explosion, he knows all too well that in Hong Kong, rather than have a permit request denied, it's easier to just film and hope the police don't interfere until the footage is in the can. Amazingly, according to Law, that's how the car and motorbike chases for *Thunderbolt* and *Full Throttle* were achieved. The death on *Downtown Torpedoes*, however, led Law to demonstrate to government officials the safety of his explosive equipment, in the hope that a system of regulating stunt facilities might be introduced, leading to permits being made available to those demonstrating responsible techniques.

1998 saw the release of *Extreme Crisis*, Law's directorial debut. Although even Law himself is quick to remark on the shortcomings of its' script, the film showcased his approach to stuntwork. In shooting the film, Law used sophisticated Hollywood stunt gadgets and digitally removed all visible trace of them using computer editing. Crash-mats, wires and air rams mysteriously disappeared while the stunts they facilitated remained.

In one scene, filmed under strict secrecy in the wee hours in Hong Kong's Central district, an explosion sends several parked cars into the air, where they corkscrew a full 360 degrees before landing. Bruce managed to avoid a run-in with officers of the law, but on returning home after that thirty-hour shift, he found a photo of the acrobatic vehicles adorning the front page of the Oriental Daily News. "Later that morning, the police called me down to the station for a chat."

Another highlight of the film is a scene in which several SDU officers are ignited by a Japanese terrorist's flame-thrower. Law's stuntmen are engulfed in flame yet simultaneously react to squibs and keep firing their machine guns. "Dangerous?" remarks the man with over 200 films under his belt, "Not at all!" Naturally, Bruce Law is selective when it comes to choosing who will execute his stunt sequences: "I want stuntmen who are smart and clear-headed, not crazy. Those crazy guys will kill themselves."

Acting in peril

It's a widely perpetuated myth that all actors in Hong Kong do all their own stunts. It is true though, that they are expected to perform more hazardous work than their counterparts elsewhere. Often, if a role in a film is particularly action-oriented, rather than casting an actor (who will either have to be exposed to possible dangers, or doubled extensively), a stuntman will play the part. When Anthony Wong torches his mahjong buddy in the opening scene of *The Untold Story*, the audience can see that the guy getting toasted is the same chap who was earlier spouting colorful abuse at Wong. That's because he's played by a stuntman—James Ha—also the film's stunt coordinator. Likewise, when a bunch of opium dealers are set alight in Kirk Wong's *Gunmen*, they are all played by stuntmen. Actors can't be so easily trusted to hit their marks and deliver their lines correctly while ablaze.

Finding the face that fits

If a movie features terrorists, gangsters, robbers or hitmen, there's a good chance they'll be played by stuntmen, especially the characters required to kill (or be killed) rather than speak. For example, the disloyal triad boy getting a pounding from Roy Cheung in the opening scene of *Young & Dangerous 3* is stuntman Jack Wong.

The casting process in Hong Kong is not as arduous as in other countries. Stuntmen rarely attend castings—the action director hires them based on his familiarity with them and their relative merits. When they do attend castings, it's to see whether they are suitable to play more substantial character parts, or if they must convincingly pass off as a certain nationality or type of person. In the summer of 1997, casting personnel visited Hong Kong Stuntman Association rehearsals for a handover spectacle, in order to find action men who could pass for Korean terrorists in the movie *Option Zero*.

Some unimaginative casting finds Bruce Law playing a car mechanic in *Thunderbolt*, a motorbike racer in *Full Throttle* and an SDU chief in *Extreme Crisis*. Stuntman/assistant action director Chan Man-ching plays a dreadlocked assassin for his mentor Tung Wai in *Downtown Torpedoes* while almost a decade earlier he dueled with Moon Lee for Stanley Tong in *Angel 2*. "I was too baby faced then!" says Chan, but what action director wants, action director gets.

It's not unusual for a stuntman to be cast in a major role in one film, only to return to regular stuntwork in the next, as did Benny Ko—the superkicking deaf mute in *Police Story 2* who also had minor stunt roles in *Twin Dragons* and *Thunderbolt*. Some lucky stuntmen do find steady acting work later in their careers. Veteran kung fu movie villain Li Hoi San is now a contract player for TVB, regularly appearing in their soap operas. Former top stuntman Chin Ka-lok's acting was criticized in reviews for films like *Operation Scorpio*, which attempted to make an action star out of him. Just as his body was tiring of taking knocks though, he showed impressive dramatic sensitivity in a major role in Derek Yee's *Full Throttle*. By the time he played a romantic, non-action part in the female-driven drama Intimates, he'd proved that he no longer needed to kick and flip to be worth watching.

Future kicks

It's ironic that Hong Kong action directors now enjoy

unprecedented status and demand in Hollywood, while in Hong Kong the stuntmen's legacy risks extinction. Even if the Hong Kong film industry does manage to overcome its current rapid decline, action-Hong Kong style may not, and diminishing box office returns aren't alone to blame.

The Chinese opera schools are extinct in the former colony, so that fertile pool of talent has dried up. Aspiring young stuntmen keen to break into the business are few, and ready jobs are similarly rare. In status-conscious Hong Kong society, many parents discourage their children from pursuing careers in the entertainment industry, which they regard as insecure and even disreputable. Many Hong Kong youngsters can easily earn as much in less strenuous fields like retail and banking. Even if the kind of training that Jackie Chan, Tony Leung Siu-hung and Ridley Tsui underwent was readily available today, it's unlikely that many of today's Internet-weaned Hong Kongers would be willing to endure it.

The new blood entering the action film industry in recent times tends to be wushu athletes from mainland China or Western martial artists keen to get their mugs on Eastern screens, sometimes perceived as a stepping stone to Hollywood careers. These days though, they are seldom given the opportunity to show off their skills. There was a time when an agile villain could make a hero of the kung fu fighting lead actor, but nowadays, the villain would likely demonstrate that the lead is more at home in the recording studio than in any gymnasium. Clever choreographers can make popstar-actors appear capable combatants, but this requires that their opponents restrain themselves and eschew their full repertoire of moves.

Perhaps Hong Kong action films, like the gallant swordsmen and swordswomen they used to portray in abundance, can narrowly avoid plummeting into oblivion and return to their heroic, mythic status of old. Perhaps there's hope.

The annual dinner of the Performing Artists' Guild of Hong Kong, held towards the end of 1998, saw Jackie Chan telling members of the Hong Kong Stuntman Association how he hoped to make things better. The action icon, enjoying his greatest success ever with *Rush Hour*, had made time to assume a post on the Association's board and helped devise a Stuntman Diploma Training Course for 1999. The course—aimed at interested youngsters—is designed to teach prospective stuntmen various skills related to the job such as kicking, gymnastics, trampoline work, and fight scenes. The course's creators (and thousands of Hong Kong action film lovers worldwide) hope that this scheme will provide a new generation of stuntmen for tomorrow's action directors to put through their paces—and wow audiences with—in years to come.

Ballerina dangle

A total disregard for human life sometimes appears to be the hallmark of a good Hong Kong action director. Based on one infamous scene in *Fatal Termination*, a 1990 femme-fightin' flick starring Moon Lee, director Philip Ko Fei seems to fit the bill. Moreover, he seems a prime candidate for an injunction forbidding him from working with children, for in this movie he appears to put the life of a sweet little infant girl on the line.

The scene is a favorite among Western fans of Hong Kong action as it typifies the films' blatant disregard for all that Hollywood codes hold sacred. Moon Lee's cute young daughter (played by Chan Cheuk-yan from *On The Run*) is dressed for ballet class. Unfortunately, no sooner has she parted with Mom than she's kidnapped

AIYAH! THAT HAD TO HURT...

Moon Lee asks a simple question but no one's listening: the infamous stunt from *Fatal Termination*.

by smirking crims. The baddies' car speeds past the girl. From the back seat, a demented hairy gwailo—think: Chewbacca on crack—reaches out of the window and picks up the child by her hair!

The vehicle takes off at speed and races down busy streets with Moon's speeding-away daughter held inches above the asphalt. Multiple camera angles clearly show the little girl, dressed in a pink ballerina outfit, hanging inches off the speeding asphalt, legs flailing.

"The critics wrote, "Those film makers are crazy! How can they treat a little kid like that?" remembers Ridley Tsui, who was working under Philip Ko for that film. "But they didn't know that we set things up very safely." Of course it wasn't a human arm holding the little girl, but a metal bar "wearing" a jacket-sleeve. The bar was securely attached to a sturdy metal cage inside the car, like the ones fitted inside racing cars. The little girl was wearing a wire harness, with a strong metal wire trailing up her back and onto the metal, and the wire is concealed by the tuft of the girl's hair in the "hand" of the bar. Locked into place, she was as snug as the proverbial bug in the rug.

The girl's parents were on hand to oversee the execution of the sequence. Tsui adds: "Of course she was OK. The little girl was very relaxed, just pretending to be crying when we needed her to." In between fake sniffles, she's vigorously clawing at her tormentor's eyes. This ferocious pint-sized cutie has been awarded the special Toughest Tiny Ballerina in a Hong Kong Film Award in perpetuity.

Club Mad

This chapter avoids the terms "stunt person" or "stuntwoman" not to avoid political correctness, but because the Hong Kong Stuntman Association only has two women members (one is former Shaw Bros queen Yeung Ching-ching and the other is named Li Fai). If a slightly built starlet needs doubling, more often than not, a slender stuntman will do the job.

The HKSA was established in 1994 to help unify stunt performers from different groups and to protect their interests (examining issues like insurance and production companies covering medical costs for those injured). Unlike the entertainment industries of the UK or USA, Hong Kong has very little union regulation. While (in theory) anyone can undertake stuntwork in Hong Kong, the HKSA attempts to grant membership solely to competent professionals. Potential members must be approved by a number of established action directors, and once accepted, agree to work only under pay and conditions set by the association.

While its membership once numbered close to 300, the current figure almost halved. In addition to its two women, the HKSA also boasts four gwailos and one Japanese member. Key HKSA figures include action directors Tony Leung Siu-hung, Ridley Tsui, Steven Tung Wai (*Hitman*), Yuen Bing (*Lifeline*) and Jackie Chan, whose *Drunken Master 2* helped raise funds for the association.

Seven Little Stunt Nuggets

Not all great films, but, for various reasons, of "stunt interest."

Painted Faces

1988 | Alex Law's moving dramatization of life for the Seven Little Fortunes of Sifu Jim Yuen's Opera school. We see little Jackie ("Big Nose"), Sammo and Biao shed tears of pain at the hand of their master's beastly training and beatings. We shed tears of our own at the extent of the bond of brotherhood between the sifu (portrayed by Sammo Hung) and his Opera buddy-turned-stuntman (the performance of the late Lam Ching Ying's career): a man who's endured one stunt too many.

Counter Attack aka *The Chinese Stuntman*

1981 | An unsuspecting insurance investigator lands himself a career as a Hong Kong movie fall guy. Worth watching not only to see "Bruce Li" (real name Ho Chung-tao) in a role in which he doesn't exploit his namesake, but also for the props used in action sequences of different genres, as Ho fights his way through period costume dramas and contemporary (seventies) cop flicks. Rumor has it that the plot device of gangsters rigging stunt equipment to cause "accidents" is based on fact. True to life or not, you're sure to wince when Ho dives onto a mattress, only to discover someone's planted metal spikes in it!

Runaway Blues

1989 | Starring Andy Lau, in one of his signature "rebel without a cause" roles, what sets this gangster film apart is its crazy stunts, handled by veteran Blackie Ko. In one shot, a guy slides down the side of a moving bus, onto the road, and into the pathway of a rush of oncoming traffic. With just inches to spare, his legs narrowly avoid being mangled by one car's wheels. Another scene sees an unfortunate gangster set on fire. Why this burn differs from other fire stunts is that this human torch is tied up, and only wearing a pair of shorts!

No Regret No Return

1993 | There's little new in terms of plotting in this medium-budgeted hitman caper starring Max Mok, but there's plenty to recommend. Stuntman-turned-director Ridley Tsui delivers a terrific action film, especially remarkable as he was just 26 when he made it. Tsui not only directs, stunt coordinates and co-stars, but also performs some ace stunts, including using an ambulance roof to break his fall as he jumps from a second story window ledge! The best stunt though (guaranteed to have you reaching for the rewind button in disbelief) comes near the film's start, when Mok's double, speeding on the back of a motorbike, is plowed into by a car.

Extreme Crisis

1998 | While Ridley Tsui draws upon his acrobatic and martial arts skills to design and execute his action scenes, Bruce Law's action is influenced by his pioneering (for Hong Kong) use of technological stunt apparatus, as well as his willingness to study Hollywood "Making of..." documentaries. Law's first film as director is an ambitious Asian reworking of *Die Hard* and *The Rock*, which packs in enough explosive action set-pieces to distract the viewer from the script's shortcomings. Lorries explode, Rolls Royces flip in the air, Shu Qi negotiates an out-of-control car (despite the actress not owning a driver's license), Theresa Lee falls from studio scaffolding and Julian Cheung goes airborne. It's no wonder Law calls his company "Stunts Unlimited."

AIYAH! THAT HAD TO HURT...

Michelle Yeoh smashes through stunt-glass in *Yes Madam* (1985).

reputation for demanding on-schedule wraps to avoid paying stuntmen overtime. Former Hong Kong Stuntman Association chairman Steven Tung Wai even puts in a cameo appearance as a possessive sports car owner.

Ah Kam
1996 | Although incorrectly referred to as *Ah Kam: Story of a Stuntwoman*, the misnomer's a pretty accurate one. Sadly the schizophrenic end product can't decide whether it's a serious, true-to-life drama, or an action film. This is partly because shooting ground to a halt when lead actress Michelle Yeoh was hospitalized performing a fall. Footage showing the aftermath of the accident is included in the closing credits, and generates more pathos than the preceding ninety minutes of film. Worth seeing though, for its portrayal of the loyalty (both good and bad) which exists in the Hong Kong stunt circle, and the notions of hierarchy and brotherhood found there. Sammo Hung is appropriately cast as the patriarchal stunt coordinator, and real stuntmen play members of his team.

Jackie Chan: My Stunts
Jackie Chan, the stuntman success story, talks, leaps and punches his way through the history and development of fight and stunt sequences, displaying many of the tricks of the trade as he revisits locations from his movies to show how he pulled off some of his most famous work. In addition to the new video footage of the camera-friendly Chan, this fully sanctioned one-of-a-kind documentary uses furiously edited montages of the actual film-fights to good effect, bringing the man's words to life. Just don't expect Jackie to reveal all of his stunt secrets. He's far too smart to do that!

Nightlife Hero
1994 | Another Max Mok starrer, distinctive if only because the supporting cast is largely made up of stuntmen. Of course this means that plenty of characters get to fight, fall, and roll over car hoods. There are industry in-jokes: one scene alludes to action director Tony Ching Siu-tung's alleged

CHAPTER FIVE
SO. YOU THINK YOUR KUNG FU'S... PRETTY GOOD. BUT STILL. YOU'RE GOING TO DIE TODAY. AH HA HA HA. AH HA HA HA HA HA.

SO, YOU THINK YOUR KUNG FU'S... PRETTY GOOD.

Shaolin Masters of Savage, Violent Death. Flying pigtails, acrobatic fighting, punches and kicks that sound like bashed rotten cabbages. Badly...dubbed dialogue with odd, pauses. These cinematic images of Chinese martial arts and kung fu Iron Fisted their way into seventies' Pop Culture.

These films are electric versions of martial arts tales which have been told and retold for centuries. Scholar John Minford, in the foreword to his translation of Louis Cha's *The Deer and the Cauldron*, summed things up:

"Bruce and Jackie are just the tip of the iceberg. Their films are only a tiny fraction of the vast kung fu film industry, and that industry itself is only one of the most recent growths of a much older tradition of Chinese storytelling that goes back well over a thousand years. Since at least the tenth century crowds have gathered in Chinese teahouses, marketplaces and parks, to hear stories told of the great heroes of their past, often to the accompaniment of a drum and a musical instrument."

Louis Cha (also known as Jin Yong) is a modern-day novelist who writes epic martial arts novels. His books have served as blueprints for many Hong Kong films, including *Swordsman 2* (1992), Jeff Lau's *The Eagle Shooting Heroes* and Wong Kar-wai's *Ashes of Time* (both 1994), among others. Cha's popularity attests to the staying-power of martial arts as a creative force. It's no less important as a film genre—before Hong Kong films came into vogue in the nineties, most non-native fans of the movies were martial arts students attracted by the stances on display.

Martial arts is a broad category which encompasses traditional Chinese performing arts as well as the pugilistic stuff. Singing, dancing, punching—all revolve around timing. It's no coincidence that many of Hong Kong's action heroines like Michelle Yeoh, Cynthia Khan, Kara Hui Ying-hung and Moon Lee were ballet-trained prior to stepping in front of the camera, and many action heroes had Peking opera or acrobatic training.

But what of kung fu flicks in the Western film markets of the seventies? Kung fu punched its way into American pop consciousness with a film originally called King Boxer, but re-titled *Five*

There's a flick where they cloned Bruce Lee and here they are: *The Clones of Bruce Lee*.

MORE SEX, BETTER ZEN, FASTER BULLETS

Fingers of Death for the Led-Zep-on-the-8-track drive-in-movie crowd of 1973. The plot of *FFOD* was none too taxing—nerd gets oppressed by bad guys, learns deadly kung fu skills, comes back and knocks the snot out of them—but the fanciful fisticuffs, killer kicks, and jumping-to-the-rafters thrilled and impressed audiences. A hilarious sidelight was the dubbing: inane dialogue, absurd music, and thwack-a-sonic sound effects. "How could anything so coolly violent have such a doofus soundtrack?" mused guys lounging in their Buick Electra 225s with their dates, swilling Boone's Farm wine and honking their horns at every skewering and butt-kicking.

FFOD ignited the kung fu craze in America, pre-dating the usual landmarks: kung fu the TV series, the Top 40 hit "Kung Fu Fighting", and everybody's main man: Bruce Lee (see "Kung Fu Theater, or the obligatory Bruce Lee piece," page 103). An enormous amount of wild kung fu product continues to be popular with people who like to stay up all night watching *The Clones of Bruce Lee* or *Wolf Devil Woman*.

The grindhouses of urban America—faded movie palaces found in districts like New York's 42nd Street ("The Deuce") and San Francisco's Market Street—pumped out triple-bills of badly dubbed chopsocky to mobs of urban denizens. As far as the grindhouse faithful (an audience raised on ghoulies, roughies and kinkies) was concerned, the over-the-top hyperaction and maniacal bloodletting of the kung fu flicks were sheer delight. Their concern wasn't the flawless execution of a Wing Chun form but the number of wings broken and legs splintered.

Kung fu films were notorious for killing people in particularly hideous and novel ways. This was part of the thrill, and made them a natural inclusion on a grindhouse triple-bill—sandwiched

between a head-busting Italian zombie film and a blaxploitation wonder with wicka-wicka guitar shootouts between leather-clad urban warriors sporting beachball-sized afros.

The grindhouses featured sticky rivers of spilled soda pop studded with flattened nuggets of popcorn, distorted urbopop burbling from cassette-blasters, shouts of patrons threatening the blaster-owners with death, the aroma of noxious weeds consecrated by fire to the God of Stupefaction, drunken denizens yelling wisecracks at the screen or muttering or snoring, aisles filled with salesmen murmuring "smoke, smoke, smoke" and a guy in a wheelchair rolling up and down the aisle yelling: "Tony! Tony! Where the hell you at, Tony?" It was a glorious time.

Urban audiences appreciated kung fu in their own (often vocal) way. In London, kung fu films

seeing guys walking around his neighborhood decked out head to foot in kung fu garb, from the black slippers/white socks combo to the Mandarin collars. What an image!

Nowhere in America was kung fu more warmly embraced than in the urban black moviegoing community. Black action films—popularly known as "blaxploitation"—often featured kung fu as a thematic element or plot spine. Black martial arts stars like Jim Kelly and Fred "The Hammer" Williamson emerged, and black-oriented action films like *Black Belt Jones*, *Way of the Black Dragon* and *TNT Jackson* were chock-a-block with mythic kicks and monosyllabic yodeling. Some even included location shooting in Hong Kong—

played at the Scala, a notorious rockin' funhouse near King's Cross Station. When combatants squared off in fighting stances, shouts of "Shapes! Shapes!" came from the crowd: appreciation for the geometric patterns of robed bodies. An absurd leap or wire effect would be greeted with "Lies!", but a well-executed maneuver would draw the accolade "Wicked lies!". Black fans took the tube up from Brixton to join in the fun, likely feeling more kinship with the Chinese guys fighting onscreen than with fellow UK citizens prancing during Opening Day at Ascot.

Many US cities supported a thriving kung fu moviegoing population. A few cinemas on The Deuce specialized in it, dodging other grindhouse staples like mondo documentaries, softcore pornies and zombie massacres. Actor Wesley Snipes has spoken of growing up in the Bronx and

Watch out Mister, here comes the Twister! The Human Tor-nay-duh!!!

Jim Kelly brought his afro and polyester flares to the then-Crown Colony for *The Tattoo Connection* (1974). Rudy Ray Moore (America's greatest black comedian) performed a side-splitting parody of Bruce Lee's kick-yo'-ass stances and vocal excesses in *The Human Tornado* (1975).

Many of these films remain beloved by people nourished in the sickly blue glow of late-night television ("Black Belt Theater presents...") or in the grindhouses. Jimmy Wang Yu's one-armed swordsman was a limb-challenged death machine who spawned many a sequel, and the flying guillotine was also popular (this was a death-frisbee attached to a chain which would transform into a head-slicing cakebox when thrown with malice). The differing styles of martial arts were the subject of much serious banter among the martial arts students. Those Bronx badasses were more interested in working Shaolin-Buick-Kickbutt moves into their street-fighting routines.

Some of these films achieved a special patina through the unique English-language dubbing they enjoyed/were subjected to (see "Ya bastard, you must be tired of living!" page 108).

Kung Fu Theater, or the obligatory Bruce Lee piece

Flowing robes and topknot hairstyles. Plot? Characters? Combat! Combat accompanied by sound effects collages of fresh fish slapped on concrete and bare-derrière gym-towel snaps. Poorly dubbed into English, a never-changing stable of hammy voice-overs delivered dialogue like "Chan, you're too arrogant, see? So we're going to have to chop off your wife's arms." (*The Crippled Avengers*).

Film critic David Chute refers to them as "But Still" movies after the oft-used phrase which helps sync English dialogue to longer-duration

Bruce Lee will come back from the grave to kick your ass!

Chinese mouth movements: "But still, you killed my master. I'm going to have to use my Berserk Piglet style on you." We called them "Right Then" movies, for the same reason. For the past twenty-five years, "Right Then" movies have been the purvey of insomniac TV addicts and inner-city kids catching a double-feature at the local grindhouse.

Chopsockies—the generic term for these types of motion pictures—are ripe for satire, and have been parodied by American comedians since their stateside introduction in the early seventies. Whether in *Kentucky Fried Movie* (1973) or *Wayne's World 2* (1993), the jokes are the same. Chopsockies have become a part of the Pop Culture lexicon, helped along by spinoffs like the kung fu TV series and Carl Douglas' 1974 Top 40 hit "Kung Fu Fighting."

Right then, we should point out that there are more than a few gems among the thousands of gutbucket chopsocky flicks cranked out in the seventies. And the name that leaps to mind—somersaulting over a banquet table in the process—is Bruce Lee.

"Live fast, die young, and leave a good-looking corpse."
(Apocryphal Hell's Angels motto)

What Elvis Presley was to American rock 'n' roll, Bruce Lee was to celluloid kung fu. Bruce got his start on the American small screen, playing sidekick Kato in *The Green Hornet*. He was subsequently discovered by Golden Harvest boss Raymond Chow, and his first film—*The Big Boss*—was a smash hit. Although Lee made only a handful of films (including *Fist of Fury*, *Enter the Dragon*, and *Game of Death*), he possessed a charisma and sexuality which defined a proud underdog masculinity. His angular, intense face and astounding physique were legendary in Hollywood as well as HK, and his fame helped launch the film careers of Americans like Chuck Norris and Jim Kelly. Moreover, Lee's warmup-suit/gradient-sunglasses look acquired a certain celebrity chic.

It was only after Bruce's death in 1973—at age 33—that he became a cottage industry. Bruce Lee imitators like Bruce Li, Bruce Le and Dragon Lee came boiling out of the woodwork as producers frantically milked the legend. Betty Ting Pei—the woman who was with Bruce when he died—starred as herself in a fictional sexploiter she also wrote called *Bruce Lee: His Last Days, His Last Nights*.

Lee's slice of the Hong Kong movie verbiage pie is wildly out of proportion to his brief career span. He was an intensely talented martial artist as well as screen dynamite, and he knew it. His ascendance shifted the focus of martial arts films from the fight to the fighter.

For many fans, Lee's buffed-yet-emaciated physique (sunken cheeks, veins throbbin' along his cord-tight biceps and delts) was the thriller. For others, the exhilaration of Bruce's lightning moves as he mopped the room with bad-guy sweat was the kung fu zenith. Then there were the "duck-calls" Lee let loose as he did his thing—somewhere between a turkey gobble and a war-whoop.

His signature behavior was that of reluctant hero: righteous and loathe to fight, but always kicking every ass in sight when left with no other path to justice. The scene in *Fist of Fury* (1974) where he kicks apart that signboard reading "No Dogs or Chinese" is a classic.

Despite Lee's athletic grace and ripped physique, he was never overtly sensuous in his films. His female co-stars were treated like one of the guys—there to be rescued, not wooed. But the Bruce sex appeal boiled beneath the surface as—topless—he showed a gaggle of villains just who was alpha male. As longtime martial arts film fan Karen Tarapata put it: "In a time of talky films and sensitive heroes, Bruce was a shot of pure animal energy, rebellion with something to back it up."

Although Bruce was a star in Hong Kong movies and a guest star on TV shows from Green Hornet to Ironside, Hollywood success came only in his last film—*Enter the Dragon*. As an expert from the Shaolin Temple, Bruce infiltrates the fortress island of the evil "Han" (Sek Kin), a drug dealer and babe-enslaver. In this, his last film (discounting the cobbled-together *Game of Death*), Lee transforms himself into a feral Christ simulacrum: dripping stigmata inflicted by his

MORE SEX, BETTER ZEN, FASTER BULLETS

Polish poster for *Enter the Dragon*.

Through his fame, Bruce Lee represents the Hong Kong movie industry for many fans. But as talented as he was, as deserving of his myths as he is, Bruce Lee is not the be-all and end-all of the Hong Kong's martial arts genre. There are filmmakers every bit as vital among his contemporaries. Directors and stars like Sammo Hung, Lau Kar-leung, Lam Ching Ying, Alexander Fu Sheng—all these guys have portfolios of hard-made world-class martial arts films that will light up the viewer like a pinball machine.

As for Little Dragon, his wired, win-at-any-cost attitude assures that he's still trashing legions of the unrighteous. Hope those angel wings don't cramp his style.

From no-shadow kicks to electric-shadow kicks: the true history of Wong Fei-hong *by Karen Tarapata*

Jet Li leaps from ladder to ladder in a dockside warehouse, a blur of speed, dodging deadly blows from dozens of attackers. The audience sits spellbound. "WAAAAHH!," they manage to breath as he springs up to the rafters, whirls around, and sweeps back down upon his adversaries.

The film is Tsui Hark's *Once Upon A Time In China*. And Jet Li is the star. But make no mistake, the audience hasn't come to the "electric shadows" (a literal translation of the Chinese characters

opponent's Dr No death-claws as the camera zooms repeatedly into his contorted face, the trademark battle-whoops cranked to the max.

But there was a lot more to Lee Siu-lung ("Small Dragon Lee"—Bruce's Chinese name) than painted-on blood stripes in the hall of mirrors. Lee was obsessed with self-improvement and physical mastery, and the energy he put on film raised the expectations of action movie fans worldwide. The screaming face and sinewy fist icons have passed into the pop culture lexicon, and premature extinction brought him that first class ticket to the souvenir shop, just as it did to celeb death-mask icons like Marilyn, Elvis, Hendrix, and James "Little Bastard" Dean.

Jet Li as Wong Fei-hong in *Once Upon A Time In China 2*.

SO, YOU THINK YOUR KUNG FU'S... PRETTY GOOD.

Master martial artist Lau Ka-leung in *Drunken Master 2*.

for the word "films") to see Jet Li. They've come to see the character he portrays, the legendary Wong Fei-hong. For more than forty years, no individual has dominated the history, ethics and culture of Chinese martial arts more than Wong Fei-hong.

Think of him kind of like Wyatt Earp. Both were real people who achieved fame as kick-asses during periods of change and upheaval: Earp during the last days of the Wild West, and Fei-hong in the fading light of the Chinese Empire. And both were mythologized well past their actual deeds—first by tabloid writers, then by screenwriters.

But the legend of Wong Fei-hong has a much more direct connection to the cinematic world, as well as to the political climate of today, than the legend of Wyatt Earp could ever have. Wong Fei-hong is much, much more than a revenge-maddened mayhem-wreaker or high-jumping hero. he's the spirit of kung fu in the real world, a scholar-fighter steeped in restraint and respect, battling the forces which oppress the Chinese everyman.

The real Wong Fei-hong lived from 1847 to 1924. Wong was a master of such kung fu as the no shadow kick, drunken boxing, hong ("flower") fist, and the lion dance. He learned his skills from his father Wong Kei-ying, who was one of the Ten Fighting Tigers of Kwantung. In fact, there's an unbroken lineage of sifus and students from the founding of the Southern Shaolin Temple to many of Hong Kong film's current kung fu stars.

One of Wong Fei-hong's favorite students was Lam Sai Wing, a heavyset pork vendor known as "The Magnificent Butcher." Lam went on to teach his own students, and his favorite pupil, Liu Chan, moved to Hong Kong and got work in the movies.

After WWII, the Hong Kong movie industry found itself in need of fresh material, and turned to the popular pulp novels and newspaper serializations, which were filled with tales of Wong Fei-hong. In 1949, Liu Chan found himself playing "The Magnificent Butcher" in the first WFH film, opposite Kwan Tak-hing as Wong Fei-hong.

Many other WFH films followed over the next two decades: 99 in total, all starring Kwan and most relying on a stable of actors (called Wong's Troupe) which included Liu Chan's sons. Two of them, Liu Chia-liang and Liu Chia-yung, went on to successful careers,.

Liu Chia-liang (aka Lau Kar-leung) directed his own films about Wong Fei-hong beginning in the 70s. The Liu-directed *Drunken Master 2* (1994) starred Jackie Chan as WFH, but few appreciate that it's Liu himself fighting with Chan on a train track, underneath a train, and that they, the audience, are watching a direct link to China's martial arts past.

WFH movies petered out in the mid-1980s, as modern-day hitmen dominated the big screen, with criminal carnage outselling costume drama. When Tsui Hark made a new WFH movie (*Once Upon A Time in China*) in 1991, no one predicted its phenomenal success. Cinematic emphasis on legendary kung fu shifted to Fong Sai-yuk, then later to Ip Man, but Wong Fei-hong and his heroic, anti-colonial exploits, remain a favorite among lovers of classic Hong Kong kung fu.

Chick Flicks: Shaw Brothers Kung Fu Films *by Karen Tarapata*

Long before Calvin Klein uncovered the marketing muscle of underdressed men, movie moguls Run Run and Runme Shaw uncovered an interesting fact: bare chests sell seats. The shirtless stars of Shaw Brothers kung fu epics filled movie palaces around the world. Men may have come for the mayhem, but the ladies came to see the boys.

These Hong Kong "chopsockies" of the late seventies and early eighties delivered some of the most eye-blistering male beauty ever tossed on screen. Month after month, year after year, the Shaws sold prime quality beefcake in a kaleidoscopic selection of sizes, shapes and personalities. The boys were buff; the look was lush, colorful and sensuous; the stories simple variations of the classic heroes' tale of feuds, revenge and redemption.

No other movie company got it so right. The Shaws knew how to pick them, how to dress them and how to film them. The effect was devastating. The Shaw Studios movie machine brought female fans whole coveys of stars possessing physical beauty, martial precision and animal energy.

Picture one of these kung fu heroes. A finely-muscled torso rises from soft white harem pants. His waist is wrapped with a broad silk sash. From the waist up he's exposed iron, from the waist down...concealed silk.

Subtle androgyny was the key to their red-hot appeal. Chinese clothes look oddly feminine to the Western eye. An open vest cinched over a hairless chest. A gold-wrapped top knot or ponytail. A long gown flicked aside before a fight. What made these stars so enticing were the boundaries they crossed. It's light-years from the Hollywood aesthetic of more brawn and bigger guns.

The effect is pure fantasy. A death blow delivered with a little black slipper in a fresh white sock. These boys have total animal presence, but they're clean; they don't smell. They have virtually no body hair, just impossibly thick, shiny braids to swing around their necks before they begin the carnage.

And the fights. Those unending, unrealistic fight scenes were the foreplay, main event and afterglow of these films. Extended kung fu fights let us see these magnificent boys kicking, leaping and rolling on the floor. Every fight leading to the final showdown leaves the hero with fewer clothes. Those fighting heroes climbed the walls and so did the women watching. The combination of beauty and sensual violence was sexy without sex, violent yet unthreatening. Here are a few tips:

Ten top Shaw throbs
Ti Lung
Alexander Fu Sheng
Chen Kuan-tai
Chi Kuan-chun
Lo Mang
Sun Chien
Chiang Sheng
Lu Feng
David Chiang
Philip Kwok Tsui

Ten to make your socks roll up and down
Five Venoms: Five foxy fighters. The Snake's demise is worth the whole trip.
Crippled Avengers: The showdown with the rings is the one to watch.

Avenging Eagle: Ti Lung and Alexander Fu Sheng, well dressed. 'Nuff said.
Heroes Two: Fu Sheng fights for righteousness while removing his clothes.
36th Chamber of Shaolin: The debut of Gordon Liu's bald head.
Dirty Ho: Long gowns flicked aside before fights.
Opium and the Kung-fu Master: Ti Lung tragic and appealing.
Martial Club: Wang Lung-wei gets to be a good guy.
Five Shaolin Masters: Exotic weapons and all.
The Water Margin: Ti Lung and the boys in some of the best long form fights.

Ya bastard, you must be tired of living!

Viewers of kung fu classics from the seventies and eighties warmly recall the hilarious dubbing which graced the English-language versions of such films. Insomniac viewers of kung fu Theater can doubtless recall dozens. Here's our Top Ten List:

10. "Anyone... who happens to make a mistake... must be prepared... to die 'cause I pay generously."
The Angry Guest

9. "Chan, you're too arrogant, see? So we're going to have to chop off your wife's arms."
Crippled Avengers

8. Kara Hui, tweaked with fury when she discovers that a stooge has tried to hide the Yang Family Golden Sword, threatens him with its sharpened blade: "Hold it! Where did you get the Golden Sword?"
Hapless stooge: "I forget."
Eight Diagram Pole Fighter

7. "With people like you, I always start by fighting!"
Dirty Ho

6. "My brand of kung fu is not for revenge. It's for universal peace."

"Hmph! That's a stupid kung fu!"
Return to the 36th Chamber

5. "But still...Teacher will be real mad."
Shaolin Challenges Ninja

4. "So you're the Four Kings, huh? Well you're no "four-king" good!"
Invincible Shaolin Superfighters

3. "Dammit! Beaten by a woman! And a bean-curd seller at that!"
Five Superfighters

2. "Look, there are two gorillas coming our way! And they know kung fu!!"
The Shaolin Invincibles

And the Number One dubbed kung fu line:
1. "Poison Clan rocks the world!"
Five Deadly Venoms

You are bastard! Bad eggs!

CHAPTER SIX
BAD EGGS AND NAKED KILLERS

"The dizzy joy in moviemaking, the uninhibited emotionalism, and the compulsive slapstick physicality of these Hong Kong pictures is exhilarating—even the bloodiest fight sequences feel like explosions of high spirits. The giddy, silly, headlong elements of Hong Kong cinema should be embraced, not resisted. No matter how cinematically jaded you may be feeling, these films are potent enough to reawaken the most moribund affection for the medium—and if they can't, you're probably a lost cause."

— David Chute, film critic

Hong Kong filmmakers are less inhibited than their Western counterparts. The creativity-stifling rules and regs laid down by political correctitians and self-appointed moral guardians inhibit scripts of would-be blockbusters—rewrite-by-committee is preferred lest concepts, words or images offend one pressure group or another.

Not so in Hong Kong, where productions are like buzzing mosquitoes—ultra-light on budget, stingers at the ready. The biggest industry-

Massive painted movie hoarding for *Erotic Nights*, Jordan Road, Hong Kong (Photo: Stefan Hammond, 1989).

change is of course the mainland China film market, now the world's second-largest.

To pass China's censorship laws, certain plot elements (often the very elements that made Hong Kong films famous in the first place) are proscribed. Most Hong Kong films featured in this book wouldn't be allowed screenings north of the border. One infamous incident: the "mainland ending" for Andrew Lau's *Infernal Affairs* (2002), which essentially whitewashed the film—and was, ironically, offered as an "extra" on a DVD release.

But China isn't the only entity to pressure Hong Kong filmmakers. In 1998, a leering cheapie originally titled *Mr Viagra* was set to hit Hong Kong screens...until a certain pharmaceutical conglom got wind of the project. The magic blue pill is known as Wai gor (literally, "Brother Wai") in Cantonese, so the English name was changed to *Mr Wai-Gor*, and all images of trapezoidal blue pharmaceutical products were meticulously inked out of promotional material with big black Magic Markers. The flick features creambomb Angie Cheung as a sex-starved widow, perky Pinky Cheung as a "PR Girl" and Anthony Wong in a dual role as both an outsized spermatozoon and a porn star who can't stiffen unless he spies on his wife doing housework.

Fortunately, Hong Kong's cinematic gurus have been tweaking the noses of the censorious for decades.

Outrageous hats

Naked Killer is a sort-of-famous film which mutated into a Pop Culture Virus whirling its way around the world. Made on a shoestring budget by producer Wong Jing and flamboyant director Clarence Fok, the film grafts a star-crossed love story onto a saga of feuding deadly hitwomen. *NK*'s combination of high-gloss kink, fashionable headgear, over-the-top action, hysterical violence, comminuted subtitles ("The reproductive organ was bursted by bullet") and Carrie Ng's hellcat performance as lascivious Sapphic hitwoman Princess drove Western audiences wild.

Many English-language Hong Kong movie books reproduced one of Chingmy Yau's *Naked Killer* publicity poses—draped in a bandoleer of full metal jacketed ammunition with leather shorts, thigh-high leather boots and an enormous gun. Few, however, made the elliptical connection with Chu Yuan's 1972 film *Ai Nu* ("Love Slave"). The beautifully lensed film stars Lily Ho as a Ming Dynasty peasant girl sold to a famous brothel—she charms the lesbian brothel-owner (a devastating first-ever performance by Betty Pei Ti) into teaching her fantastic martial arts skills and wrecks...everything. Fok was entranced by *Ai Nu*, which is the genesis for *Naked Killer*.

Naked Killer (赤裸羔羊)
1993 | Starring Chingmy Yau Suk-ching, Carrie Ng Kar-lai, Simon Yam Tat-wah, Madoka Sugawara, Kelly, Ken Lo Hwei-kong
Directed by Clarence Fok Yiu-leung (Clarence Ford)

MORE SEX, BETTER ZEN, FASTER BULLETS

This flick arches its back and spits at you for ninety minutes. Stylish, erotic, and entertaining as hell, it's the story of anti-heroine Kitty (Chingmy Yau), a woman who really, really hates girlfriend-bullying cads. In fact, she grabs a pair of scissors and stabs one in the crotch (and he's her hairdresser, no less). As he screams "I lost one ball of mine!" she makes good her escape, only to be followed by police officer Tinam (Simon Yam). But his attempt to collar Kitty fails because Tinam vomits whenever he pulls his gun.

Plot shards pile up as Kitty first toys with the copper, then beds him, then falls for him—a bad career move for both. As Kitty explains it: "I'm a professional killer and you're a cop...we have conflicts in our jobs."

Kitty's killer instinct is being developed by her mentor Sister Cindy (Kelly), Hong Kong's Svengali of man-hating hitwomen. After much training, the pair takes a commission in Tokyo, which requires nightclub dancing prior to creep decapitation by dual-femme garrote.

Kitty's growing affection for Tinam not only softens her edge, but also arouses the jealous ire of Princess (Carrie Ng)—a lethal lesbian assassin with the hots for our heroine. Princess—once trained by Sister Cindy, but now operating as an independent contractor—enjoys tossing her male victims across the room before blasting their privates to shreds with a silenced automatic. She's consumed with lust for Kitty that her own muffinbutt protégé, Baby, (vanilla-bean Japanese cutie Madoka Sugawara) cannot satisfy. This naturally brings Princess into conflict with her former teacher.

Carrie Ng plays Princess with cigar-chompin' Harley-humpin' focus. Combat is in the nostalgic format of 1960s secret agent films and TV shows (especially Hong Kong's *Rose Noire*): poisoned lipstick, flying ropes and darts, masquerade-ball masks and black Spandex jumpsuits.

Screengrab from *Naked Killer*'s credit-sequence—Carrie Ng in foreground.

NOTE: Top-shelf HK actresses usually refuse to shed blouse, whether the script calls for it or not, because they know that doing "Category III" (nudie) work puts them in a different category, and the stigma is nigh impossible to overcome. This helps explain that while there are the naked and killers in *Naked Killer*, the killers are not always naked. The lengths some killers went to to disguise their nakedness is a silly and disappointing sidelight to this silly but definitely not disappointing movie.

The best place to enjoy *NK* is at a theatrical venue like your local college film series or at a repertory house like San Francisco's charming Roxie Theater, soundtrack boom-booming and crowd a-howling over the way-loopy subtitles.

UK-based Hong Kong Legends has released the definitive version of *Naked Killer*—on Region 2 DVD. This single-disc package restores the cuts made by Hong Kong censors, including expository scenes that streamline the plot-line. On the audio commentary (by director Fok and Hong Kong film expert Jude Poyer, Clarence repeatedly exclaims "It's back!" when formerly deleted shots appear). *Naked Killer* finally makes sense in this essential DVD release.

Painting on the Newport Theater on Hong Kong's Jordan Road—stars Chingmy Yau and Carrie Ng embrace awkwardly as censorious grey paint hints that more will be revealed (Photo: Stefan Hammond, 1992).

Her Name is Cat (豹妹)

1998 | Starring Almen Wong Pui-ha, Michael Wong Man-tak, Chong Wing, Ben Lam Kwok-Bun, Noelle Tzik King-man

Directed by Clarence Fok Yiu-leung (Clarence Ford)

The guys who ran American International Pictures in the sixties—James Nicholson and Samuel Z Arkoff—had a marvelous scheme for project development. They'd mock up a poster for a hypothetical movie and show it to investors. If they got a good reaction, then they'd make the movie. "Sell the sizzle, not the steak" is something these guys understood without a platoon of marketing consultants whispering in their ear.

The poster for *Her Name Is Cat* is something these twin masters of film promotion would have appreciated. The central image—Almen Wong striding the landscape fresh from a tussle, all lips and stare and scratches and shining plastic cladding and a big blue hog's leg—stops people in their tracks. Sizzle.

The film is more about imagery than coherence or character development, but its snappy action sequences are naturals for dance-floor wall-video use. Almen Wong as Cat exudes power, bringing the Cantonese title ("Panther Girl") to life. She's a ruthless titan from Northern China who works as a hired assassin for manly Sister Shin (Chong Wing).

Cat's upbringing was harsh, and with a horror of food shortages, she stocks up on instant noodles. All this Panther Girl will eat is noodles, sometimes even the ones from the local greasy chopstick with "luncheon pork"—a greasy pig emulsion which makes SPAM look like filet mignon. This supplies her nutritional needs for sweaty workout sessions and coke-dusted triad rubouts.

Michael Wong co-stars as police officer John Cannon. He's a cop, and as she's a professional assassin, they have conflicts in their career paths. He's getting divorced and his daughter is cute, so Cat stalks him. She becomes obsessed with Cannon and breaks into his flat to smoke his cigars, write funny notes, cuff him to the four-poster, and bite down on a big leather belt.

There's suggested kink at every opportunity: blasted water suggesting golden showers, superblack cat burglar slinkwear, even over-the-top piped-in roaring panther sound effects when the heroine attacking someone sexually or homicidally. In this flick, there's little difference.

Almen Wong's not afraid to kiss death in *Her Name is Cat* (courtesy of Fitto Movie Group).

MORE SEX, BETTER ZEN, FASTER BULLETS

When *Her Name is Cat* came out, they made an action figure of Cat in sniper-disguise. Here's Almen Wong modeling it (Photo: Stefan Hammond, 1998).

Panther Girl gets to kill a bunch of people, stomp her female adversary (a too-brief appearance by Noelle Tzik), bust through a wall, waste a politician with a badass black sniper rifle, experience torture at the hands of the Hong Kong police, ride the MTR to Park 'N Shop, and rescue her pet chicken Grandpa.

Sex & Zen redux

The original *Sex & Zen* (1991) blasted into US cinemas a few years after its Hong Kong release, startling and delighting exhibitors and punters alike. The film's soft-core shenanigans were packaged in Ming Dynasty gauze, a layer of removal which allowed Caucasian audiences to vicariously enjoy outrageous sexual situations. Few films would dare to lop off their central protagonist's precious part and replace it with that of a horse, yet *S&Z* accomplishes this in the first reel. Another big plus was the breathy presence of Amy Yip, a sweet-faced starlet of Russ Meyerian proportions. Yip's notorious norks (one hundred per cent free of silicone, she proclaimed to all who would listen) made for a fab frontispiece, but the success of *S&Z* was largely due to its high production values and impressive costuming. As global audiences discovered to their delight, nothing is shed as sweetly as a flowing sheet of silk.

Sex & Zen 2 (1996) featured Loletta Lee, who shed the demure image she'd cultivated in films like *Shanghai Blues* and a newcomer named Shu Qi. An attempt was made to top the amazing-transplant gag of Part One: a penile Swiss Army knife bristling with attachments is grafted onto the protagonist. This sounds funnier than it is—even diehard Shu Qi fans prefer *Viva Erotica* (also 1996). The warm heathen touch of the *S&Z* formula returns fully in the third installment.

Sex & Zen 3 (玉蒲團3官人我要)

1998 | Starring Jane Chung Chun, Karen Yeung Ka-ling, Tung Yee, Elvis Tsui Kam-kong, Timothy Zao, Wong Pan, Noelle Tzik King-man, Tim Shaw
Directed by Aman Chang

Gorgeous women in fantastic sexual predicaments, costumed-stylings with dance and music and shaven-headed superstud Elvis Tsui guzzling mystic potions while shouting "I've taken philtre! I can last an hour!". *S&Z3*'s softcore shenanigans include gauzy dance numbers and an array of stunning starlets. The production values and cinematography are at odds with the absurd sex and lurid situations—how such a garishly entertaining flick could be cranked out on such a

BAD EGGS AND NAKED KILLERS

Susan and Chinyun become buddies forever in *Sex & Zen 3*.

narrow budget, using centuries-old Chinese texts as inspiration, is another Hong Kong mystery.

Virtuous Susan (Karen Yeung) is a pouty and strapping young lass, but her parents are cabbage-poor, and career opportunities in rural China are limited. So they peddle her to Fragrance House, the most famous brothel in the region, for 40 taels of gold. Though Susan is apprehensive, she has company: Chinyun (Jane Chung) and Fanny (Tung Yee). As the title slate appears, the three young women are perched doggy-style on a series of wooden benches for inspection by the mistress of Fragrance House, Tall Kau (Noelle Tzik).

Tall Kau is the sexual equivalent of the martial arts sifu: assessing the girls carefully in a scene which produces a rapid-fire plethora of shredded subtitles, and outlining training techniques which will enhance their earnings potential as practitioners of the carnal arts ("make men die on bed"). The scheming and competitive Fanny gets the thumbs-up from the brothel mistress: "I guarantee you'll become a famous prostitute." Fanny is delighted.

Alas, poor Chinyun suffers from an "iron vagina", and is worried that she cannot produce sufficient income for Fragrance House. Tall Kau reassures her by promising to teach her "special blow-job skills." Susan is inexplicably compared to a labyrinth, and even more inexplicably, this is regarded as an asset.

All three nascent working girls are directed to carve a wooden phallus to familiarize themselves with the tools of the trade—Tall Kau's manservant Hark (Tim Shaw) serves as model for this absurd exercise. Though the trio are supposed to preserve their virginity for auction, Fanny can't resist the obvious charms of Hark. Caught trysting, the couple is subjected to punishment. Fanny has a series of butterflies tattooed on her lower back, while Hark is gelded.

Meanwhile, Susan is gagging on wood. Chinyun sympathizes with her and her plight. She cuddles up with buxom Susan and tells her: "We're buddies forever." The two women bond. They bond all over the bearskin rug.

Summertime is high season at Fragrance House, with visiting businessmen and scholars journeying to the capital as customers. Horse trader and pervert-with-a-heart-of-gold Lui Tan (Elvis Tsui at his scenery-chewing best) drops by, as does scholar Chu Chi Ang (Tim Zao) and his servant Hwang Lien (Wong Pan).

Sir Lui befriends the young scholar and they hoist cups of wine together before the showpiece "Best Girl Contest". Susan bests her rivals with

Tall Kau assures a delighted Fanny of her career goals: *Sex & Zen 3*.

a shuddering onanistic performance, and the horse trader offers top tael for her cherry, only to cede *droit de seigneur* to his newfound drinking chum. The scholar protests that such a gift is too generous, so Lui offers to let him pay 8,000 taels towards the fee, and graciously selects the runner-up, Fanny, to satisfy his own lust.

The scholar and the virgin whore engage in athletic vanilla pursuits while Mister Horse Trader and his tattooed companion go for the tutti frutti. Lui swills down an aphrodisiac as Fanny demonstrates her "Hot-Cold Eighteen Hell" oral technique. An improvement on the everyday "Fire and Ice Stance" (alternating mouthfuls of ice cubes and hot tea), Fanny's variation incorporates mouthfuls of freshly chewed raw chilies. Lui is so impressed that he buys her out as his concubine.

Meanwhile, scholar Chu falls hopelessly in love with innocent Susan. His exam forgotten, he squanders his allowance by hanging around Fragrance House eating melon and "drowning in sex." Poverty-stricken, he's not much use to Tall Kau, who's seen plenty of these young whelps before, and kicks his useless butt out. Chu must hightail it to the woods and learn the 13 Virgin Tricks before his fortunes start to change.

The 13VTs are taught by a forest-dwelling sexual wizard named Hung Chi, and consist of outrageous sexual positioning with shouted titles for the various nipple-pinging stunts ("Frog popping across a river! Lighting a lamb [sic] at bedside!"). Hung Chi, energetically coupling with his four lithe wives to instruct Chu in these mystic sex techniques, is played by veteran actor Lo Mang. Those who recall Lo Mang as "Toad" in the Shaw Brothers' *Five Venoms* (1978) will get an extra thrill from Virgin Trick number eleven: "Toad climbs the stone!"

When Chu must return to save Susan from the evil Fanny, who schemes to implicate her in a murderous plot, those 13 Virgin Tricks come in very handy. A little torture, a bit of revenge, comeuppance all 'round...a great date movie.

Erotic Ghost Story 2
(聊齋艷譚續集五通神)
1991 | Starring Charine Chan Ka-ling, Anthony Wong Chau-sang, Kwok Yiu-wah, Sayuri Ichijo, Noelle Tzik King-man, Amy Yip (cameo)
Directed by Peter Ngor Chi-kwan

More stylish and weird than its predecessor, *EGS2* features Anthony Wong as Wu Tung, who runs around his cave in whiteface wearing little more than big plastic shoulder-boards, growling a lot, like a refugee from a KISS-revival band. He's growling because he's an underground demon. He's growling so that the village above him gets the hint: have a monthly lottery among its young ladies (to choose a playmate for him), or he'll put the hurt on everyone. But who knows why his demon concubine (Ichijo Sayuri) dances around naked, dripping molten wax from a candle into her mouth?

The village seems resigned to the system, and has their naked sorceress chant over each month's lithe tithe, who is oiled up, put on a sedan

chair, and then left in the woods at the mouth of Wu Tung's cave, where she's transported beneath to party.

In between sacrifices, village life is pretty much normal, and lovely Yu-yin (Charine Chan) falls in love with grinning beefcake fisherman Shan-kan (Kwok Yiu-wah). But wouldn't you know it, her number comes up, and she's gone with the draft. Shan-kan is one of her sedan chair bearers, but when he sees that she's smuggled along a knife to fight with, he decides to help out with his big double-bitted battle axe.

Mr Big Demon gets wounded in the fight, and must retreat down to his fortress of solitude, where, naked, he locks himself up to his neck in a giant spikey ball—evil's reducing cabinet. Back in town, Yu-yin and Shan-kan are given a hero's welcome.

The demon's concubine wants revenge, and appears on earth where she finds Shan-kan's friends, a lusty rural couple. The concubine seduces the wife, while the husband sits in front of a cluster of bananas, smoking a cigar. Then the trio get after it on a precarious jungle-gym made of bamboo poles as goofy disco-reggae plays and Lawrence Welk bubbles float. The demon wench kills the husband, then takes the wife back to the Pit.

Back underground, the demon is feeling better and to celebrate, fornicates with the wife, magically cleaving her across the torso. While he sexually enjoys the lower half, the upper half complains about a lack of satisfaction.

The concubine's not through tormenting the village, and sends a plague of storm and madness, forcing Shan-kan, Yu-yin and Shan-kan's Frazetta-model sister (Noelle Tzik) to take it on the lam. They seek the wisdom of a dwarf monk, but the demon and his concubine catch up with them. The dwarf monk turns himself into a fiery bolide, but is no match for his opponent.

Fortunately, Yu-yin is a dead ringer for the demon's lost love of long ago, Hsiao-yen. In fact, Hsiao-yen's essence was put into Yu-yin's pregnant mother, so the resemblance is more causal than casual. That old devil moons for Yu-yin, and prevents his jealous concubine from killing her. He does take Shan-kan back to the cave, and encase his naked body in a block of ice positioned so he has to watch Wu Tang get it on with half of his friend's wife.

Yu-yin and Shan-kan's sister sneak in to effect a rescue. As Yu-yin melts the block of ice by pressing her naked body against it, Shan-kan's sister fights with Mr Big D. The two combatants then plunge into a stalagmite pool and have fierce underwater sex. Shan-kan is released, and chops

Why still standing there?

off the demon's phallic tail, which spews green slime from the stump.

Finally, Yu-yin's birthmark is activated by sex, and Hsiao-yen appears from it in ghostly matte. Hsiao-yen's spirit joins with Wu Tung and they perish together in purple flames.

There's a lot of good nudity in *EGS2*, a lot of sex, a lot of supernatural hoo-ha, colorful sets, and spinning dwarf monks. Note: Amy Yip appears only briefly, and under a shapeless robe as a Buddhist nun!

Sex and the Emperor
1994 | Starring Yvonne Yung Hung, Leung Si-ho, Sung Boon-Chung, Stuart Ong, Kingdom Yuen King-tan, Julie Lee
Directed by Sherman Wong Jing-Wa

This yin/yang deal is more than just the cool twirly symbol on the touristy stuff. It diagrams the duality of the universe—harmony and balance and all that. Too much yin is no good but that doesn't mean you get to overload on the yang stuff.

Yang is considered "male essence", which is why female ghostresses are always sniffing after it; they are yin-laden and perennially seek balance. However, those who voluntarily cede their male essence can gain power in a spiritual dimension. The custom of trimming the clockweights from young boys seems barbarous as seen from a twentieth-century perspective...well, it is barbarous, but it certainly cuts down on any surfeit of yang. The castrati were often ushered into the inner circle of the Imperial Court and given opportunities denied the betesticled. Cold comfort perhaps.

Sex and the Emperor attempts to answer the historically important question: in the land of the eunuchs, is the one-testicled man king? Oh, no it doesn't; this movie is pure sleaze from Minute One, flashing its celluloid panties at ya, utterly shameless.

Li Lianying (Leung Si-ho) has a date with the "Castration Master", but Li's father once saved the Master's life, so the gelder agrees to surreptitiously preserve one of the family jewels. Li's ability to sport a woodie proves popular in the imperial palace, where the boy-emperor Tongzhi (Sung Boon-Chung) is attended by eunuchs and a bevy of chambermaids. Imperial intrigue? Not really; this film eschews historical analysis for heaps of gratuitous sex and torture, horsewhippings, mindless cruelty and pervy situations, amid pageantry and costumes that will delight the *Sex & Zen* crowd.

When the defiled-innocent Guilian (played by Yvonne Yung) is sold to the brothel, she's treated to a demonstration of the "Eight Semi-devil" sexual skills by the brothel's headmistress, Hongyi (Julie Lee). With much shouting, arm styling and great gouts of chi energy blasting out of every orifice, Hongyi puts on a display of sexual martial arts skill guaranteed to ban her from most video rental shops yet draw applause from the kung fu students in the audience. Dressed in a diaphanous Qing Dynasty nightie and knee-high white cloth booties, she instructs her students with exultant shouts ("Throw!" "Sift!" "Rub!"

Boy-emperor Tongzhi gets the royal treatment in *Sex and the Emperor*.

"Wrench!" "Swing!") while zealously swinging her pelvis for emphasis. She juggles a huge clay pot with her feet ("Double Slut Foot!") and hurls it in the air, then uses her bare bottom to scoot a series of blank sheets of paper into a huge rectangle.

Her canvas prepared, Hongyi takes an unusual nether grip on a gargantuan calligraphy brush and flows black ink over the paper, tracing characters with savage concentration. Reading out the resultant lustful ditty, she fires the inky brush into the face of a servant and caps the stunt by squeezing dry a half-meter stick of sugarcane without using her hands. As absurd as the circumstances are, Lee performs it all straight-faced, with the dignity of a white-eyebrowed sifu in hard demonstration mode.

Robotrix (女機械人)

1991 | Starring Amy Yip, David Wu, Chikako Aoyama, Hui Hsiao-dan, Billy Chow, Kwai Ching
Directed by Jamie Luk Kin-ming

In this entertaining, nonsensical flick, topheavy androidettes battle a robotic villain with a penchant for carnal mayhem. *Robotrix* is a T&A flick—supposedly titanium and aluminum, but bearing a strong resemblance to old fashioned pneumatic exuberance.

An oil sheik stages a robot competition in Hong Kong to garner competitive bids on his plan to build a "Robot Legion." Will-triumphant androids from Germany descend from the ceiling and strut their stuff. When an American scientist challenges the German product, the Teutonic titanium titan (Mark King) is pitted against the American entry. The Krautbot smashes the Yankbot's brain-wiring and it goes berserk, attacking the crowd. But waiting in the wings is Eve R27, the product of lovely Japanese engineer Dr Sara (Hui Hsiao-dan) and her assistant, the fetching Anna (Amy Yip). Eve—who looks like Maria from *Metropolis* and has mad martial skills like a Mighty Morphin' Power Ranger—chains up the runaway robot as the crowd cheers.

But there's bad news for the sheik, who learns that his son has been kidnapped. The kidnappers delivered a videotape to the Hong Kong cops, which include Chou (David Wu) and the voluptuous Selina (Chikako Aoyama).

On tape: mad scientist Ryuichi Yamamoto commits *seppuku*, then transfers his consciousness into a powerful android (Billy Chow). He wants to convince the sheik to build an evil Robot Legion. This psychobot spends his time using a Freudian power drill on the kidnappee,

Robotrix: robocore has never looked so good.

MORE SEX, BETTER ZEN, FASTER BULLETS

Chikako Aoyama tries to convince David Wu that robot sex can be fun in *Robotrix*.

or running around HK in Billy-Idol-drag and murdering hookers. Transfer cracked-shell, evil-egghead brains into killer androids and stuff like this is going to happen.

The not-so-bright cops get the bright idea to use Anna as a prostitute-decoy to trap Yamamoto. Anna (who, naturally, is an android herself) is keen on the idea as she's curious about human sexuality. They pour the pneumatic CyberYip into a red minidress, and set up a hidden camera in her brothel room.

Voyeuristic video glimpses of her passion cause a hairy cop named Puppy (Kwai Ching) to experience nosebleeds! He excuses himself, then puts on an absurd disguise and returns as a customer. The ruse fails, but soon there's a line around the block and they have to abandon the operation.

The cops then put Informer Hui on Yamamoto's trail. Hui's killed, but the scientists remove his eyeballs, hook them up to their robotic supercomputer and view the dead man's last image. The eyeballs finger the sheik's bodyguards as stooges for Yamamoto, who kills them anyway. Finally, the Yipster traps the manmade monster in a junkyard, tosses him (via electromagnet) into a car-crusher and terminates him.

Naked Soldier (赤裸戰士)

2012 | Starring Jennifer Tse Ting-ting, Sammo Hung Kam-bo, Andy On Chi-kit, Ellen Chan Nga-lun, Philip Ng Wan-lung, Ankie Beilke, Lena Lam Kai-ling, Anthony Wong Chau-sang, Timmy Hung Tin-ming Directed by Marco Mak Chi-sin

We have "popcorn movies" in the West, and "shredded-squid flicks" from Hong Kong. With the latter, you park your brain in neutral and chew squid snacks while watching the eye-candy stream.

The premier sweet here is Phoenix (Jennifer Tse). As a youngster, she was stolen by the evil Madam Rose (Ellen Chan, in her mid-40s when she made this and looking fabulous) and trained to become, what else, a lethal assassin destined for fab fashion and homicidal assignments. As an adult, she's all that and a university student too.

Her father, Lung Chi-keung, (Sammo Hung)

BAD EGGS AND NAKED KILLERS

Philip Ng and Jennifer Tse get ready for some shootin' in this screengrab from *Naked Soldier*.

80s Hong Kong stars reunite: Sammo's not impressed by Ellen Chan's Beretta: *Naked Soldier*.

was the only survivor of the initial raid in which his daughter was purloined and his whole family wiped out. So he's not a fan of Madam Rose and her sleek hitwomen squad, which includes Selina (German actress Ankie Beilke) and Ivy (Lena Lam). But Sammo still has the gravitas and martial arts skills to pull off numerous fight scenes—it helps to have Corey Yuen Kwai and Yuen Tak as action directors.

As the original *Ai Nu* DNA becomes further diluted, we have more slick action, actors on wires, and none of the soldiers get particularly naked. This is the sort of film you spin when it's raining all day on a weekend, and all that's in the cupboard is a bag of shredded-cephalopod and maybe some instant noodles.

NOTE: Timmy Hung, who plays Pete in the film, is an accomplished actor and also the eldest son of Sammo Hung.

Naked Weapon (赤裸特工)
2002 | Starring: Maggie Q, Daniel Wu Yin-cho, Anya, Jewel Li Fei, Cheng Pei-pei, Almen Wong Pui-ha
Directed by Tony Ching Siu-Tung

This flick proffers well lensed eye-candy, fierce chickfighting (even if sometimes it's bewigged stuntboys), exotic locales and other bling. But it illustrates two points: (1) why films like this never made a splash in the international market, (2) why Hollywood filmmakers could so easily borrow elements of "Hong Kong-style" to work into their own films.

Shot entirely in English, *NW* features slick action sequences and stars Maggie "Q" Quigley, Anya, and Jewel Lee as a trio of ace-assainatrixes nurtured and trained by the amoral Madame M (Almen Wong). Maggie and Anya have some tender femme-bonding moments, and male lead Daniel Wu (playing a CIA agent) forms a liaison with Maggie's character, despite their career conflicts.

Naked Weapon never made much of a splash because Hong Kong filmmakers all-too-often think that a film in English—especially with native speakers like Quigley and Wu—has some sort of magic touch. If the film fails to have a defineable plot or characters with depth, well...it's in English! We've got beautiful Asian women fighting each other! Nope, it doesn't work—and *NW*'s vile and gratuitous gang-rape scene will slam potential buyers' briefcases shut.

With the femme-battles, it's all about "the

MORE SEX, BETTER ZEN, FASTER BULLETS

Anya and Maggie Q bond in *Naked Weapon*.

Jewel Li and Anya square off with machetes in *Naked Weapon*.

optics" which gives us cool images to publish, but also allows Hollywood to gleefully swipe elements developed in Hong Kong for their own efforts—vacuous or not. Nowadays, streaming services offer up screenfuls of tuff-chick action flicks, and this is just another thumbnail on that particular screen.

And there's a third point here: despite its flaws, *Naked Weapon* is Maggie Q's best Hong Kong effort (in *Model from Hell* (1999), she had to run around with a rubber head glued to her shoulder). She went on to star in feature films and toplined her own TV series—ironically, based on Luc Besson's *La Femme Nikita* which spawned a Hong Kong remake (*Black Cat*, with Jade Leung).

Quigley's potential was noted and leveraged, giving her a sustainable career. So too co-star Daniel Wu, who now boasts a lengthy career in movies and television. But not from *Naked Weapon*.

This may not be the best film for a soapbox-rant. We praise its style with not-so-faint damnation for its substance or lack thereof. The film's a slick entry in the "Naked Whatever" canon that originated with *Ai Nu* back in the early 70s, and might be more amusing than *Sharknado 9* or whatever.

Queen of the Buxotics

Her career lasted only a few years, with a few dozen films under her sash. But Amy Yip (aka Yip Chi-mei) was a va-va-voom Hong Kong film sensation in the early 90s. Director Russ Meyer would have loved Amy. Diminutive and sweet-faced, Yip's prime assets were (mostly) on view in such classics as *Erotic Ghost Story* (1990), *Ghostly Vixen* (1990), and of course: *Sex & Zen* (1991).

Despite her obvious charms, Yip, while not the world's greatest actress, could flick her trademark "OMG!" shocked expression on cue, and even whip out a bit of cinematic kung fu. Most importantly, she would tolerate any sort of celluloid nonsense a director lucky enough to point a lens at The Yipster could devise.

Contemplate her output during a single year—1991—to grasp what this dame went through—before marrying some rich guy and retiring sometime in the mid-90s. Set the Wayback Machine to 1991...

Hopping vampires are still popular, so Amy hopped into *Vampire Kids* (1991), then appeared as a gangster moll in *To Be Number One* (1991).

Yip's toplined the Sherman Wong-directed *Queen of the Underworld* (1991). This, gentlemen,

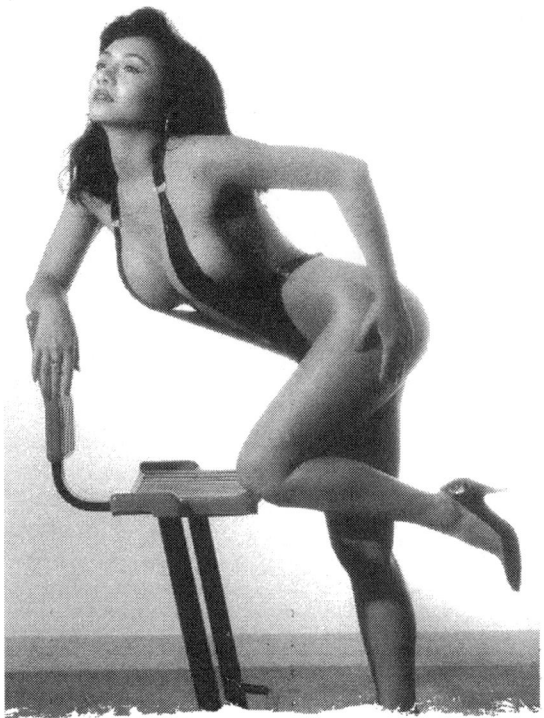

is her only lead role: as Helena Wong Ha—shove this concept into your fevered brain: Amy Yip as the top gangster over three crime-and-boob-filled decades, strutting around in cheongsams, with a cigarette holder, like a BOSS.

She then tossed on a blonde wig and picked up some *Easy Money* (1991) playing lingerie-clad "Susie Yip" before lensing *Sex & Zen* (1991).

She then did a cameo as a character called "Death Rays" in Shing Fui-on's only lead role: *The Blue Jean Monster* (1991)—starring the late actor nicknamed "Big Sillyhead." After that was *Robotrix* (1991), still a favorite among Hong Kong cult film afflictionados.

Having exhausted all other permutations of her name, the filmmakers who made *The Great Pretenders* (1991) simply called her character Yip Mei Mei. The indefatigable actress with the dreamy face and great big overbite ended the year with a cameo in *Erotic Ghost Story 2* (1991). Yip Chi-mei retired from acting in 1992.

The Z-list: A few Hong Kong films that very stink.

If you take a liking to Hong Kong films—and we hope that you do—sooner or later you will be fooled. Sooner or later you will run across a movie with a video box, poster or title that's just says, "I'm great." But it will not be great. It will suck. It's happened to everyone. It's happened to us. It'll happen to you. Here are some tempting examples to avoid:

The Avenging Quartet

1992 | Take one look at the poster—four potent action heroines holding down bad motorscooters and holding up sleek weaponry. But *TAQ* is a melodrama, with Moon Lee and Cynthia Khan gooning inexplicably over nerdo painter Waise Lee. Yukari Oshima and Michiko Nishiwaki appear only peripherally as villainesses, and a dorky cop mooning over Moon gets far more screen time. Action is tame and sporadic.

Laboratory of the Devil

1992 | The sequel to the highly-disturbing

With these four, did the director even call "ACTION!"?? The Avenging Quartet.

Man Behind the Sun, a dramatic presentation of experiments in germ warfare conducted by Japanese troops in occupied Manchuria towards the end of WWII. But while *MBTS* balanced the horror by maintaining a sense of purpose and reason, *LOTD* has no such compunctions. Based around a ho-hum love story between a Japanese officer and the kimono-clad gal he left behind, *LOTD* uses the gruesome details merely as an excuse to make a movie.

Malevolent Mate

1994 | The cartoon poster depicts a pair of skeletonized arms (with batter-fried hands) perched on a Japanese sushi plate, against a backdrop of flames and under a blood-spattered half-visage with off-staring eyes. Lobby cards of Bonnie Fu (the slutty thief from *Full Contact*) in full creep-on mode look good. But the film is an uninspired ripoff of *The Untold Story*, and its aimless brutality is truly brutal. Here, the cops beat their suspect and torture her with electricity to obtain a confession. But that's not all—they torment the suspect's daughter by setting fire to her teddy bear.

Crocodile Evil

1986 | The video box cover art is tempting, but...we have yet to see a subtitled version, and there are far too many scenes devoid of crocodiles or evil.

Trust Me U Die

1999 | This torporous, disjointed tale starts with Mark Cheng as a sicko doctor, then switches over to Simon Yam as another sicko doctor, then sort of runs around like a mangy street cur chasing its ratty tail. Some inspired bits of business with always-good Sam Lee, but this production's main

Thai poster for *Crocodile Evil*.

claim to fame was tarnishing the rep of co-star Joey Tan, aka Miss Malaysia Chinatown 1997-98 (also featured as January cover girl in Penthouse Magazine's Hong Kong edition). The pageant's organizer said these actions violated a three-year exclusive management contract and were "calculated to bring discredit, disrepute, ridicule and contempt on herself and the promoter." If only they had brought some life to *TMUD* as well.

PR Girls

1998 | Certain films are so astonishingly bad that they roar up in agonized triumph, going straight over the top into a new dimension of wildly entertaining super-bad filmdom as they provide new realms of jaw-dropping fun.

PR Girls is not one of them.

Hong Kong X File

1998 | A wiseacre wiseguy named Horny Keung wiggles his shaven dragon-tattooed head around as he works black magic with purloined pubes from his staff, psychically transforming them into shameless hornbags. And kung fu guy Chin Ka-lok (*Drunken Master 2*, *The Legend of Wisely*) is sure to whip wicked moves on some baddies! Sounds like great entertainment, a Friday-night bag-of-cuttlefish-and-a-sixpack kind of flick, right?

Ix-nay.

Black Magic With Buddha

1983 | Horror flick about a Hongkie who smuggles a bleeding, breathing, disembodied brain from Indonesia. Sounds good, but this cheapie veers from ghoulie-lunacy into a $1.98 Hollywood snooze-o-rama. One keeps watching, hoping for something, anything…gratuitous nudity, witchy subtitles, exploding vermin…until one just gives up and…EJECT.

Hong Kong Showgirls

1996 | The opportunity for overripe parody looms large and luscious. Some toothsome starlet (preferably a dropout from the Miss Hong Kong competition) on an overacting jag, stripping off at every opportunity, mispronouncing designer brand names, boning moronic stallions of the entertainment industry, tangling claws with bitchy rivals. A gaggle of hopping child vampires replacing the garlic-scarfing chimps of Verhoeven's unjustly maligned, twisted comedy. One would think that the industry to whom exploitation is a warm fuzzy selling point would take the Showgirls ball, run gleefully into the end zone, and spike that orb into a blizzard of seedy shards.

Not even close.

Hong Kong Showgirls fumbles along for ninety minutes, never sure what it wants to be or indeed, if it is still running through the projector. Protagonist and antagonist (Veronica Yip and cleavage-impaired Diana Pang) eschew leotard-peeling in favor of amateurish dance routines—Pang can do the splits, a stunt the filmmakers seem fixated upon. The other one either can't, or won't do the splits, but *Hong Kong Showgirls* doesn't suffer from this. It suffers from everything else—ghost effects include a smoke machine and a 99¢ Woolworth's skull-on-a-stick popping up from a bathroom stall.

Hex Errors: Naked Wolfen Lust

"You know I always like little-snaking women."
The Fruit is Swelling

"He'll go on practicing 'Iron Scrotum'"
Sex & Zen 2

"I want 4 lustful instruments."
A Chinese Torture Chamber Story

"I must let you try heaven tortures"
Erotic Ghost Story-Perfect Match

"If you mean tits, left or right?"
Ten Brothers

"I am now going to whore in the coffee shop."
Troublesome Night 4

"You erotic collected so many 'lewd' photos, what for?"
On Fire

"Bastard, you shouldn't shout so loudly for visiting hookers!"
Our Neighbor Detective

"Sex den, it's great!"
The Occupant

MORE SEX, BETTER ZEN, FASTER BULLETS

"You're a horny monk? Want to look? Pay money"
Erotic Ghost Story-Perfect Match

"Sorry, honey. I took $1,200 from your wallet for this hooker."
Task Force

"That bastard, to him sex is always more important than friends."
Stooges in Tokyo

"You are sending your husband lunch and sex, right?"
A Chinese Torture Chamber Story

"People say one part of his body is as long as that of a horse. Of course that part is not the face."
Sex & Zen 3

"Yeah, me evil and you flirty. we're two of kind. Must I reveal the monkey affairs between you and Fatty?"
The Fruit is Swelling

"Kidding? Say 'Big tits baby', 'Lustful bitch' etc? And 'Japanese girl VS Machine Monster'."
Sexy and Dangerous

Lambs that slaughter: *Naked Weapon* (2002).

CHAPTER SEVEN

COPS AND RASCALS

Gangsters and motion pictures go together like garlic and squid. Gangster iconography—gunplay, dames, payoffs, rubouts, and vice smorgasbords—provides natural plot elements, and colorful underworld characters are cinematic perennials. Actors like James Cagney and Edward G Robinson owe their careers to real-world thugs like Al Capone. Wiseguys on film span the decades from *Scarface* (1932) to *Scarface* (1983) and on into the nineties and our present century.

Don't be fooled by cinematic stereotyping: the vast majority of Asians aren't tattooed thugs with gold chains, toothsome molls, and murder on their minds. But the few that are make primo camera fodder.

Businessmen at heart, triads (ethnic-Chinese gangster organizations with worldwide tentacles) rarely engage in the wholesale bloodshed which characterizes many wiseguy tribes. Hong Kong turf wars are never as anarchic as the kinetic carnage of Juaréz, Monrovia, or Chicago. Cinematic rumbles with platoons of chopper-swinging youths look groovy onscreen, and wiseguy glory makes for a great script, but unstructured violence plays hell with real-world profits. The term "rascal," often used to label triad members, clues viewers in: Hong Kong gangsters aren't a direct analog to their counterparts elsewhere.

Triads in the Hong Kong film industry

In the early nineties, triad interference in the industry was so vexing that Hong Kong film stars—including Jackie Chan—took to the streets in a major protest in the summer of 1992. But triads are mostly interested in quick profits, and as Hong Kong film profits have declined sharply over the years, so has triad interest.

This is not to suggest that wiseguys have abandoned the Hong Kong film industry—they remain on both sides of the camera. But most Hong Kong triads are lower-key than the "rock stars": the bright lights who fade quickly. These baddest-of-the-bad find their luminary careers enhanced by endings featuring imprisonment or (better yet) violent death. And then the cameras roll.

Biopics and bombs

Macau is a former Portuguese colony noted for fine food, exquisite architecture and a profitable gambling industry. In April 1998, Judicial Police director Antonio Marques Baptista (a Portuguese citizen—Macau was under Portuguese administration until its 1999 handover to China) was out jogging with his dog. As they approached his automobile, the dog, which was trained to sniff explosives, pulled a U-turn and ran the hell away from the vehicle. Baptista followed suit.

The vehicle then exploded, hurling debris in a ten-meter radius. The dog, a golden retriever, presumably kept running—it was never seen again.

Baptista called in a territory-wide sweep for reputed triad boss Wan Kuok-koi ("Broken Tooth Koi"). That night, the cop nabbed the Hawaiian-shirted kingpin in the restaurant of Macau's famous Lisboa Hotel. The arrest—on charges of attempted murder, drug trafficking, employing illegal immigrants and using phony identity documents—prevented Broken Tooth from attending a film premiere.

Starring Simon Yam, as a gangster, in an US$2 million production financed by the flamboyant Broken Tooth. According to Wikipedia: "In the autumn of 1997, Wan approached [a] Hong Kong movie producer...to produce a film based on his life. The result was the 1998 movie *Casino* starring

Simon Yam as Giant, a triad boss living the high life in the Macau underworld. Wan agreed to extensive research meetings to make the film as accurate as possible, as well as using his influence [in] Macau to help the crew film."

His arrest co-starred the photogenic Baptista—an intense-looking fellow with a bristling beard. But Broken Tooth's televised performance in the police van, nonchalantly chewing a piece of gum as his eyes darted for the cameras and he thrust out his jaw upstaged the cop. Broken Tooth was born to play a gangster. The weird thing is, he was a gangster—Wikipedia again: "In November 1999, in a landmark trial, he was convicted and jailed, along with eight associates including his brother Wan Kuok-hung. Wan was sentenced to 15 years in prison...later reduced to 13 years and 10 months."

Broken Tooth was released from prison on December 1, 2012. It's said that he spent his time (in a specially built wing of Macau's Coloane prison designed to prevent him from communicating with the outside world) learning English. Although various media outlets predicted gangster mayhem upon his release, Wan re-integrated into civilian life and is said to be living quietly in Macau.

The *Casino* saga received its most ironic twist when, just after its cinematic release in 1998, triad members wearing white gloves and armed with metal pipes smashed up three Mongkok shops selling pirated VCD copies of the film.

Spend big

Casino wasn't the only film in which Yam portrayed a triad kingpin. A few months later, he portrayed Cheung Tze-keung, an even more notorious gangster known as "Big Spender." Another Cheung epic, *Big Spender*, starring Ray Lui, hit screens in early '99.

As these films were allegedly bankrolled by the wealthy gangsters they portray, it's unsurprising that they depict wiseguys as heroic, absurdity be damned. In *Operation Billionaires* (1998), from the wonderfully named Good Fellas Production Company, Yam as Big Spender treats his subordinates to lavish meals and abundantly be-hostessed karaoke sessions. An unintentionally hilarious opening scene shows Big Spender single-handedly helping a little old lady to cross the street.

The crook kidnaps the son of an Hong Kong property tycoon, but as he carefully explains to the distraught tycoon, both he and the businessman are just trying to earn a living, and thus much alike. He befriends a tough-yet-righteous goon named "Cyclone" (modeled on real-life Cheung henchman Yip Kai-foon), who is shot in the back by duplicitous minions of the law.

The reality wasn't some gangsta's paradise. The real-life Cheung preferred stealing from the rich and giving to himself. Cheung was subsequently arrested on the mainland, extradition to Hong Kong impossible due to a lack of evidence (the wealthy victims never reported the kidnappings to Hong Kong law enforcement). The trial wasn't a drawn-out affair—Cheung was convicted of firearms smuggling and robbery in a Guangzhou court, fined 662 million yuan

MORE SEX, BETTER ZEN, FASTER BULLETS

(about 80 million US dollars, in cash), stripped of his political rights, then taken out and shot. As Hong Kong doesn't have capital punishment, and Cheung was an Hong Kong resident, the case caused controversy. Still, public sympathy for Cheung on either side of the border wasn't much in evidence.

Yip Kai-foon was indeed shot by police, but the cops didn't fire from behind. They were in front of him and dodging his bullets. Yip, who has his own biopic (*King Of Robbery* [1996], starring, yes, Simon Yam), had a reputation for enjoying gun battles with the police, especially with his trademark AK-47—which has appeared in a number of gangster films, often wielded by a character reminiscent of Kai-foon.

With real-life cases like these, it's no wonder that Hong Kong produces such excellent crime films. The interplay between cops and rascals—who both offer incense to the same red-faced deity, Kwan Ti—is explored for your entertainment in the following films.

9413

1998 | Starring Francis Ng Chun-yu, Amanda Lee Wai-man, Fredric Mao Chun-fai, Christine Ng
Directed by Francis Ng Chun-yu

In spoken Cantonese, this quartet of numbers sounds like "nine chances to die, one chance to live." Actor Francis Ng makes his directorial debut with *9413*, shot on a budget of HK$3 million. That's about US$400,000, which wouldn't pay the catering bills on most Hollywood pictures. Writer/director Herman Yau served as cinematographer on Ng's project, and the cooperative effort is laudable—*9413* is one hell of a film.

Ng plays an eccentric cop named Ko Chin-man, better known as Smash-Head—a stubborn guy

Francis gets nasty in *9413*.

who batters through obstacles forehead-first. Ng's character is a Hong Kong take on the relentless nihilist—Takeshi Kitano's dangerous gendarme in *Violent Cop* (1989) or a hell-bent Peckinpah desperado (think Warren Oates). Violence is what Smash-Head's best at: threatening a witness, smashing up a bar, or screaming at his superior Kar (Fredric Mao).

Most Hongkongers pretend that we aren't living on a mountain of garbage, but Smash-Head screams in horror at the stinking polyfoam reality of Hong Kong's throwaway culture, and he's just as dirty. The loose-cannon cop desperately seeks the smearing caresses of marijuana, alcohol, and violence. His drugbunny partygal Mandy (Amanda Lee) enjoys slipping dope into his mouth with her tongue, hoping it'll calm him down. But the chemical seductive mix fails him—his romantic excursions fall apart when he discovers she's wearing environmentally incorrect plastic slippers, or his bloodstream wins and he passes out.

The excesses are tolerated—his superior knows Ko has no scruples when it comes to dirty work. Kar hands him a stolen service revolver to pass on to a loathsome Vietnamese gangster for some bad business. But Smash-Head notices the unlucky serial number—9413—the revolver of his ex-partner Fatty Chuen, who was killed by the very same gun. Ko loses his cool and beats the Viet's head against the asphalt until lifesblood literally flows into Victoria Harbour.

Ko seeks redemption from an angelic therapist, Carmen Leung (Christine Ng), who becomes enraptured with him. But Smash-Head's failure to deliver the stolen gat leaves Kar fuming and furious. One chance in nine…slim odds.

Yau's camera crisply grips the urbanscape of Hong Kong as well as the confines of TST's Amoeba club, where much of the film is set. Rather than sickly Cantopop interludes, industrial synth music mixes with pile-drivers on the soundtrack—the perfect complement to this unique cop noir drama.

Beast Cops (野獸刑警)

1998 | Starring Anthony Wong Chau-sang, Michael Wong Man-tak, Sam Lee Chan-sam, Patrick Tam Yiu-man, Roy Cheung Yiu-yeung, Kathy Chow Hoi-mei
Directed by Gordon Chan and Dante Lam

Beast Cops is a challenging police drama. Chan (who co-wrote, produced and co-directed the film) describes it as a comedy.

Which it is. Its comedic opening features up-the-spine screech of a glass-cutter crushing a narrow path through the title-credit, melded with gliding bleary video of Kowloon neon. It's a comedy which spirals into savage unromanticized violence lubricated by corruption and lust for power. It's a comedy about the beasts coiled up in men.

The beastliest of the film's cops is Tung (Anthony Wong), who knows how to get along. When we first see him, he's gambling in an illicit casino. Tung's in so far with the triads that he serves as casino dealer when he feels like it.

"Triads are a joke": *Beast Cops*.

His fellow cops include Cheung (Michael Wong), a straight-arrow toughie who's been transferred into the district. Wong reprises his role as no-nonsense cop from *Final Option* (1994) and *First Option* (1996). Cheung drives a Humvee, smokes hefty cigars, and rents a spare room to always-broke Tung. Another cop-roomate is goofy-haired Sam (Sam Lee), a skin-and-bones chick-magnet whose duties include in-depth interviews of local massage parlor girls.

The casino's manager, Fai (Roy Cheung) hires a mainland killer to ice a rival mobster. The hit goes well, but during the getaway, Fai accidentally squishes the hired assassin with his car. He has to flee Hong Kong until things cool down, but his moll Yo Yo (Kathy Chow), the mama-san at his hostess nightclub, isn't. So the gangster lets his little head do his big-head thinking, grabs an understudy—a doxy named Suzy—and splits.

Fai's sudden "vacation" generates a power-shift. The gang boss, Father Tai (Arthur Wong), has his career goals sorted: to eat egg-custard tarts daily and make sure venerated kingpin "Grandpa" gets his monthly stipend. But there's a problem: triad middle-manager Marvin has ambitions in this dangerous new vacuum. "Custard" Tai offers promotion to anyone who can solve the problem.

Up steps young turk Ted (Patrick Tam), who

But these guys aren't laughing: *Beast Cops*.

deals with Marvin by shooting him repeatedly. Next thing you know, Ted is scarfing egg tarts with big boss Tai. But the lad also wants Alphonse's woman—who's now dating Cheung the cop. Ted doesn't take rejection well. He starts forcing Yo Yo's girls to push ecstasy in the club, and when she objects: "Alphonse never allowed..." SLAP! The sharp crack of the young punk's slap outlines the new-school universe of profits-before-everything, versus the old-school give-and-take of cops like Tung and gangsters like Fai and Custard Tai.

Beast Cops culminates in an extended end-battle. Tung, stoked to the gills on imported beer and imported pills, dueling with triad punks in a cage-like under-construction garage-casino with surf music and animal howls as soundtrack. Ted and Tung fire handguns at each other, progress to choppers, then sharpened steel pipes and fluorescent light tubes, then roll around on a carpet of smashed glass trying to slice each other. The brutality redeems Tung for his moral ambiguity, though whether it restores the old-school structure is debatable.

Beast Cops spins gleefully into the details of its characters and paints them in toughness and frailty. Problems in communication and problems with women (often one and the same when it comes to men) are explicated realistically—Chan used input from the actors to craft realistic dialogue. *Beast Cops* was the opening film at the 22nd Hong Kong Film Festival, and won Best Picture, Best Director(s), Best Screenplay and Best Actor for Anthony Wong at the Hong Kong Film Awards.

Big Bullet (衝鋒隊—怒火街頭)

1996 | Starring Lau Ching-wan, Jordan Chan Siu-chun, Francis Ng Chun-yu, Yu Rong Guang, Anthony Wong Chau-sang, Berg Ng Ting-yip, Theresa Lee Yee-hung, Spencer Lam Seung-yi, Cheung Tat-ming
Directed by Benny Chan Muk-sing

Big Bullet barges straight in—RHKP office Bill (Lau Ching-wan) in mid-shootout. It's a hostage drama and it goes wrong. His later testimony before an investigatory tribunal fingers scummy superior Inspector Guan (Berg Ng) as the culprit.

Close pal Inspector Yang (Francis Ng) suggests Li transfer from the Serious Crimes Unit to the less-raucous Emergency Unit. But when Li shares a cop-shop elevator ride with a cuffed-and-escorted badass named Professor (mainland actor Yu Rong Guang), the two hotheads glare at each other. The mainland perp starts singing a delicate and traditional Beijing opera refrain: "Now I'm locked up/But still I'm tough...it's Mandarin, you should learn it", he taunts the Hongkie cop. Bill spits the lines back in Cantonese, then slugs the handcuffed crook in the gut. The stares get better.

Right onto the street where Professor is released from custody by his confederate Bird (Anthony Wong), who punches out his escorts with a 12-gauge pump. Professor was busted by Interpol, who took his nine million in cash as evidence, and now he wants it back.

Lau Ching-wan with 12-gauge intent in *Big Bullet*.

Bird visits a cafe to interview Richard (William Tuen), an Interpol cop, about the matter. Yang and Li are on the scene and tension clicks up as opponents circle 'round. Richard's girl Sandra isn't taking this too well. She starts to whimper.

So Bird shoots her through the head with a large-bore automatic pistol. Confined warfare ensues. Principals are tracked throughout the fury, and most survive. When the smoke dissipates, Bill Li is left with his crew in the Emergency Unit van, led by rigid officer-candidate Jeff (Jordan Chan), who can't handle Bill's flexible policing style. But they must get along to solve the mystery of Richard's gun hand, which was blown clean off yet somehow went missing.

Big Bullet is a swaggering and satisfying crowd pleaser. Slick production, destructive car chases, and apocalyptic gunfight sequences replete with tracking camera will impress action fans. Insightful bits of police procedural business intersperse with hard action, creating a fertile and virulent mulch, and *Big Bullet*'s eccentric villains are great fun.

Legacy of Rage (龍在江湖)

1986 | Starring Brandon Lee, Michael Wong Man-tak, Regina Kent, Michael Chan Wai-man, Meng Hoi, Kuk Fung, Shing Fui-on, Ku Feng, Bolo Yeung Sze
Directed by Ronny Yu Yan-tai

The late Brandon Lee (Bruce Lee's son) left precious little cinematic legacy. *Legacy of Rage*—made for Dickson Poon's D&B studios in 1986—displays Brandon more favorably than his Hollywood snorers: *Showdown in Little Tokyo*, *Rapid Fire* and *The Crow*. With his good looks, muscular frame and glowering, "freeze 'em" stare, one wonders what Lee might have accomplished had he been as prolific as most Hong Kong action stars.

In *Legacy of Rage*, an early effort by *Bride with White Hair* director Ronny Yu, Brandon is a working stiff holding down two jobs: junkyard crane operator and nightclub waiter. He dreams of a happy home life with his girlfriend, fellow nightclub employee May (Regina Kent).

But his inexplicable friendship with dope dealer Michael (Michael Wong) leads him to ruin. Michael lusts after May, and when Brandon turns down a lucrative drug-merchandising offer, Wong sets him up as the patsy for the murder of a rival drug lord.

Lawyers and corrupt policemen conspire to frame Brandon for manslaughter and he ends up with an eight-year sentence. Meanwhile, Michael's violent sexual advances towards May convince her to flee to the South American country of "Basil," with a benevolent sugar daddy who admires her Can-Can dancing. Brandon befriends Four-Eyes (Meng Hoi), a bespectacled fellow inmate, and burns with vengeful lust over Michael's betrayal.

Eight years pass, and Michael has devolved into a repugnant, cocaine-crazed Hong Kong godfather when he crosses Brandon's path once again. He kidnaps May and her son (Brandon's, unknown to him), and sets his thugs on the

MORE SEX, BETTER ZEN, FASTER BULLETS

Brandon Lee takes aim in *Legacy of Rage*.

elderly sugar daddy, turning him into worm food. Brandon escapes the hit by evading his pursuers in a chicken coop, and the feathers really fly when he assaults Michael's fortified gangster hideout with his old prison buddy Four-Eyes, whose gunrunning business provides the necessary hardware.

Brandon's screen presence, and his chemistry with Michael Wong, makes us wish they had had the chance to team up as heroes just once. The final gun battle—clearly influenced by Brian DePalma's *Scarface*—is humorously apocalyptic, but Brandon's duels with veteran heavy Shing Fui-on and Michael Wong are taut and gory. The bittersweet ending reunites Brandon with his son—unfortunately, the real Lee legacy was not so generous.

Shing Fui-on fires his concealed gat in *Legacy of Rage*.

The Log (三個受傷的警察)
1996 | Starring Michael Wong Man-tak, Kent Cheng Jut-si, Jerry Lamb Hiu-fung, Cher Yeung Suet-yee, Stephen Fung Tak-lun, Fredric Mao Chun-fai
Directed by Derek Chiu Sung-kei

Police work is often described as years of boredom interspersed with seconds of sheer terror. In recent years, cop flicks on both sides of the Pacific have given us more perspective into the lives of the people involved. In many cases this has led to more complete characters and better films.

The Chinese title of *The Log*—"Three Wounded Cops"—makes sense. The three cops are a diverse lot. Dixon (Michael Wong) is a hardass inspector who prefers speaking English to Cantonese. Jerry (Jerry Lamb) is a young street cop who identifies more with triad punks than with his fellow officers. Then there's Gump (Kent Cheng), a balding shlumpo who's been around forever and knows he'll never get promoted. Cheng, who shaved part of his head for the role, won Best Actor at the Hong Kong Film Awards for his masterful performance.

The three unlucky cops have their fates written in lead. Dixon goes heatedly into a hostage situation, kills both kidnapper and kidnappee, and is thrown in jail. Jerry confronts some rascals making trouble in a teashop and accidentally blows one's brains out. The punky cop is forced to visit the morgue and, saddened by the pain of death, seems to mature overnight, his streetwise veneer now tarnished by remorse.

As for Gump, he's the non-aligned, the negotiator, the guy who brings warring factions together and makes everyone get along. But his workaholic tendencies drive his wife to seek comfort from another (his supervisor, Koo).

Three unlucky policemen: *The Log*.

The horns of the cuckold bore holes in his brain. Something snaps, and he invades the senior officers' traditional New Year's Eve celebration—the rear-echelon types decked out in ice cream suits—with red-rage thoughts on his mind and a .38 snub in his pudgy hand.

Though his wife still loves him, though his son wants to be a cop, though he's played by the book all through his undistinguished/unblemished career, Gump is the unluckiest policeman of all.

Tiger on Beat (老虎出更)
1988 | Starring Chow Yun-fat, Conan Lee, Nina Li Chi, Gordon Lau, Norman Tsui Siu-keung, Shirley Ng Ling, James Wong, Ti Lung, Phillip Ko Fei, Shing Fui-on, David Chiang Da-wei
Directed by Lau Kar-leung

Veteran HK actor/director Liu Chia-liang made *Tiger on Beat* as Chow Yun-fat was achieving fame for his roles in crime dramas like *A Better Tomorrow* and *City on Fire*. Francis Li—Chow's character in TOB—is introduced with a hard-rocking theme song by HK power diva Maria Cordero. The polar opposite of his twin-Beretta/high-fashion slayin' persona in *ABT*, he's decked out in a ridiculous leather visor, driving a gussied-up Renault Le Car; a clueless Chow Yun-fat wannabe.

After waking up foot-cuffed to a nubile (Elaine Ngai), Francis escapes to one of Hong Kong's plastic fast-fooderies and gobbles a spraypainted-to-the-plate ham-and-eggs breakfast (chased with a tumblerful of Rocky-style raw eggs, slugged down in one stomach-churning take). But some lunkhead robs the place with a pistol and takes Francis hostage—cramming the gun in his gob. Fellow undercover Michael Cho (played by buffed Conan Lee) rescues him, but not before Francis has pissed his pants in terror and passed out on the floor.

Back at the cop shop, his supervisor (James Wong) assigns Francis a new partner: Michael. The pair begin work on a dope-smuggling case: Norman Tsui Siu-keung and his gang of creepy bad guys smuggle poppy powder in hollow surfboards.

Peppy aerobics instructor Marydonna (Nina

Chow Yun-fat eats blued steel in *Tiger on Beat*.

MORE SEX, BETTER ZEN, FASTER BULLETS

Thai poster for *Tiger on Beat*.

Li) gets roped into carrying dope for her bad-egg brother. The brother expires due to his nefarious activities, inspiring Marydonna to spill the beans. Francis and Michael bust the big dope deal, but despite a hair-raising car chase scene (with stuntmen clinging to the hoods of flying subcompacts), the baddies escape. They vengefully kidnap Francis's sister Mimi (Shirley Ng), who must be rescued from a warehouse full of heavily armed thugs.

In battle, Chow's character improvises effective weapons from dime-store items (including an around-the-corner shotgun). Despite Chow's heroics, it's the balletic martial arts fight between ultrabad guy Gordon Lau and Conan Lee which provides the kicker.

Did we mention that it's performed with chainsaws? And not those puny weekend-warrior cord-o'-wood-for-the-fireplace jobs, but big honkin' heavy-timber wood/flesh rippers. The combatants go at it sparkin' and spewin' blue smoke as they run around the warehouse trying to dismember one another. This gory Armageddon-duet consistently scores on Top Ten End-Battle Lists among HK film aficionados.

NOTE: This film is often called "Tiger on the Beat" which may be grammatically correct but isn't as snappy.

To Live and Die in Tsimshatsui
(新邊緣人)
1994 | Starring Jacky Cheung Hok-yau, Tony Leung Ka-fai, Chan Kwok-bong, Wu Chien-lien, Gigi Lai Chi, Roy Cheung Yiu-yeung, Kwong Wah, Frankie Ng Chi-hung, Xiong Xin-xin, Baat Leung-gum
Directed by Andrew Lau Wai-keung

"Sometimes, I don't know who am I. A human or a ghost. If I am a human, how can I betray my friend? Or if I am a ghost. But I am a policeman", muses Jacky Cheung in *TLADIT*, directed by Andrew Lau. In many ways the film is a blueprint for Lau's more famous undercover-cop film *Infernal Affairs* (see page 62).

Cheung stars as Crazy Lik, a deep-cover cop. He endures the gangster life because he craves promotion from his superior, Officer Suen (Kwong Wah). But as his triad sponsor Brother Tai (Roy Cheung) reminds him: "Money is easy to get, but lives are easy to lose."

Lik is trapped in the classic undercover conundrum. After a triad-meet goes wrong, Suen reminds him: "In the Royal Police Force, you're only an ordinary cop. In the Triad Society, you're

Jacky Cheung tormented: To Live and Die in Tsimshatsui.

only a traitor."

His straight life is splintering, and when his galpal Moon (Gigi Lai) invites him to her mom's birthday banquet, Lik challenges Suen to a drinking game which descends into hurled insults and fisticuffs. He consoles himself by hanging out with triad buddies Bong (Chan Ka-bong) and Fai (Tony Leung Ka-fai).

Moon ditches him for Suen, but Brother Tai's sister, tough triad babe Ah Bo (Wu Chien-lien) has her eye on him. Orphaned at eight, Bo only knows Tai's life of gangsterism—her mainland-accented Cantonese is loaded with foul language (the film isn't Category III, so some phrases are bleeped out). Lik and Bo are the most emotionally vulnerable people in the film, and share an understanding they can't express. Their subplot is rich and enlivened by classy Wu spouting Cantoslang with an imitation tough-guy accent.

All this camaraderie is spoiled by the brutality of Tai's rival, crime chieftain Father Man (Frankie Ng). The gaggle of cough-syrup-chugging punks trailing Father Man like adoring ducklings are stereotypical triad kiddies. A pair are summarily culled after a botched hit, and as their blood splashes on spooled-out flypaper hanging from the ceiling of their Mongkok squat, it seems that Father Man doesn't buy into comic-book gangster glorification. The triad teenyboppers stick with the mad gangsta though, and get to some nasty business later in the film.

The Tsimshatsui district isn't big enough for both Man and Tai, and Crazy Lik's pals start going down. The stage is set for a big gun battle with a bunch of really dangerous guys (check Xiong Xin-xin's wacked-out performance as "Bald Rascal"). *TLADIT*'s characters suffer rather than just bleed, ensuring the film plays well in the pantheon of copper/rascal operettas.

Trivisa (樹大招風)

2016 | Starring Richie Ren Xian-qi, Gordon Lam Ka-tung, Jordan Chan Siu-chun, Phillip Keung Hiu-man, Tommy Wong Kwong-leung, Lam Suet, Yueh Hua, Frankie Ng Chi-hung
Directed by Jevons Au Man-kit, Frank Hui Hok-man, Vicky Wong Wai-kit

During the 2017 Hong Kong Film Awards, where *Trivisa* won the award for Best Picture, the program's feed to China was cut. Mainland officials are depicted as corrupt buffoons in the film—a fictional tale depicting the exploits of three notorious 1990s Hong Kong gangsters: "Big Spender" Cheung Tze-keung, AK-47 aficionado Yip Kai-foon, and Kwai Ching-hung.

Trivisa's production was unusual: producer Johnnie To gave three young Hong Kong directors (Jevons Au, Frank Hui, and Vicky Wong) the chance to make one of the three stories each, then the footage was edited together into a single film. It's part homage, part fantasy, and while it might seem odd to romanticize thugs, there's an edge of nostalgia in Hong Kong that expresses itself here. These gangsters may have been evil, but they lived large lives during a pre-handover

MORE SEX, BETTER ZEN, FASTER BULLETS

Richie Ren demonstrates Yip Kai-foon's notorious AK-47 pose on the set of *Trivisa* (inset: photo of the late Yip Kai-foon).

era when their exploits were shown on flickering TVB broadcasts in homes across Hong Kong. They cared little for societal norms, and still make great film characters.

The most flamboyant is "Big Spender" Cheung, played loud and large by Jordan Chan. Cheung as interpreted by Chan prefers loud suits in colors like purple and orange, puffs huge cigars, and prefers over-the-top crime concepts. The film's central premise is explicated on a remote island, as Cheung's henchmen torture some poor slob to extract some gangster info. Cheung fiddles with a cheap radio, trying to tune in a broadcast by the "Four Kings" of Cantopop, who are singing in a concert together. His lieutenant says he can't tell what song is playing—Cheung retorts that it doesn't matter, as anything the Four Kings do is automatically good.

Brainstorm. Waving his cigar, Cheung tells the lieutenant to contact Yip Kai-foon and Kwai Ching-hung so they can become the "Three Kings of Crime." Why? "Because any crime we commit will be good!" says Cheung. Thus goes gangster logic and so the quest to unite this trio of famed Hong Kong n'er-do-wells begins. But as in real life, the fate of the gangsters is not kind.

Ten Best Moments of *Goo Wat Jai*

Goo WHAT?! Translating this term from Cantonese is inappropriate, as this phenomenon is an only-in-Hong Kong thing. You could call them "triad kids" but that's not descriptive enough.

The GWJ genre originated in a series of comic books influenced by Japanese manga: stylized dramas featuring steroid-muscled tattooed opponents who violently vie for power and impossibly cantilevered molls. These comic fantasies play well among disaffected urban bumpkins in Hong Kong's densely populated environs. The Cantonese phrase *goo wat jai* is best compared to a Japanese term for their yakuza equivalents: *chimpira* (little pricks).

Why were these films so popular in the mid-90s? Blame it on Cantopop—the bland poptones prevalent throughout southern China. With no defined musical alternatives, GWJ films became the louder/harder/faster anthem for Hong Kong's disaffected youth. Not coincidentally, their soundtracks often bristle with hard-edged tunes.

The seminal GWJ film is Andrew Lau's *Young and Dangerous* (1995). Mister *Y&D* himself is a pop singer originally known as Noodle Cheng, who became Ekin Cheng (he was "Dior Cheng" for a while). Cheng sports a big fake dragon tattoo and plays a teen triad leader whose adventures form the core of the *Y&D* franchise.

Ekin Cheng (right) negotiates some gangsta biz: *Young and Dangerous 3*.

GWJ shenanigans raised concern from sociologists about the glorification of gangster lifestyles presented to Hong Kong's impressionable youth. Things came to a monstrous head in early 1999 when a group of youths received lengthy prison sentences for the execution of a fellow teen. The victim had been first tortured, then dispatched, in a manner depicted in the GWJ comic *Teddy Boy*. It wasn't a nice way to go. Such incidents are rare, but the comics are popular.

GWJ protocol dictates lots of melodramatic double-crossing and perilous romance. Macho posturing, scowls and disdain for social norms prevail. Male-bonding quotient: sports-bar level. The look-and-feel is pop-metal: hair worn long or cropped-and-colored, black leather or skimpy minis, cigarettes and preening. A staple of these films is the cleaver melee, where combatants flail furiously en masse, chopping at their opponents with machete-like weapons known as "choppers" or "melon knives". The myriad *Y&D* sequels and spin-offs exploit these elements to the extreme.

An interesting sidelight to these films is the inventive use of curses and insults—alas, few manage adequate translation from the original Cantonese. The context of these films also fails to travel well—just as viewers in Asia are confused by the urban Americanisms of "gangsta" films like *Boyz N the Hood*, so too are Western viewers puzzled by the patchwork quilt of Hong Kong concrete squalor, lousy education, and triad traditions displayed in the GWJ films. As spectacle, these films have their adherents, though few over the age of fifteen are going to glean any heroic vibes.

Here's a series of GWJ moments to cherish:

10. Billy Tang's *Sexy and Dangerous* (1996) refreshingly transposes *goo wat jai* to *goo wat lui* (triad girls). The gang is led by tuff chick Marble (Loletta Lee) and butane-snorting butt-kicking moppet Van (Karen Mok), stylin' from her pixie haircut to her goofy Doc Martens, as first lieutenant. Marble has eyes for long-haired pretty-boy Brother One (Michael Tong), but is also desired by loser George (Francis Ng at his dopiest), who advertises his low triad rank of "49 Boy" by wearing a T-shirt with the number emblazoned on it. Marble's smooth and glamorous underworld life is complicated by the homicidal Lurcher (Ben Ng) and his partner in hatred and revenge, Aids (Lily Chung—yes, the name of the character is Aids). Lurcher and Aids don't like...anybody.

A furious girlie fight erupts when Aids and a bunch of her murderous followers invade a sauna. Van, nursing a hangover, is marinating her spiraling snake tattoo in a gigantic hot tub as towel-wrapped cuties display their tats for the camera. Choppers unpeel. Van comes whirling out of the tub and assaults them with the blade she'd been hiding under the water. She kicks a bar of soap under the foot of one, slices the others, then goes off to help Marble struggle with AIDS.

9. Roy Cheung's edgy performance as Brother Crow in *Y&D3*. He's just weird enough to remind

Roy Cheung addresses a flunky (played by stuntman Jack Wong): *Young and Dangerous 3*.

you of people you know, but let's hope you don't know anybody quite this homicidal. Roy's been at this a long time—check him as Brother Smart in Ringo Lam's 1988 *School on Fire* (see page 277).

8. *Street Of Fury* is a violent GWJ drama made, like almost all of 'em, in 1996. Hot-head Hu (Michael Tse), the teen terror of Kowloon's grimy Lam Tin district, is on the outs with his cutie-pie girlfriend Yi (Gigi Lai). She takes up with less-pleasant triad dude Brother Beast (Ben Lam). In one scene, Hu and Yi both visit separate fortune-tellers on Temple Street, spinning their tales of romantic woe. Then they start shouting at each other over the heads of the startled soothsayers. Hu comes closer, and Yi offers him the timeless advice every pouty gangster-toy moppet gives to every young punk hell-bent on wiseguy apocalypse: "Hu, forget it, even if I part with Beast, we can't get on together again." Awwww.

7. The first *Y&D* introduced avuncular Spencer Lam as a priest. When the gang hang out in a local coffee shop, he tries to convince them that Jesus's biblical actions prove that JC's the ultimate "big brother" and they should follow him rather than earthly mobsters. Chicken (Jordan Chan), whose hair color changes from scene to scene, is contemptuous. The attempted conversion is interrupted by the arrival of Chicken's father-in-law, an imposing triad boss played by Johnny Wang Lung-wei. Bull-necked and gold-chained, the veteran Shaw Brothers actor brings the requisite gravitas, and Chicken goes chicken.

6. Shuk Fan (Karen Mok) gets a teaching job in *Y&D4*—she's not really a triad, just kind of triad-friendly and fond of Chicken (Jordan Chan).

But she gets thrown straight into Band Five: during the 90s, this classification was for the lowest-ranked students in the Hong Kong school system and thus the best candidates for triad recruitment. As one of Shuk Fan's students points out: "We are the sacrificed ones under the Hong Kong existing education system. We are the trash, rubbish, dirts." Much as in real life, they are also big fans of GWJ.

5. Jordan Chan's sprawling tribal neck tattoo in Herman Yau's *War of the Underworld* (1996). Any Mongkok kid wild enough to sport something like this in the 90s would likely have been kicked out of the gang.

4. A couple of interesting GWJ films are *Once Upon A Time In Triad Society* (*OUATITS*, pronounce it as you like) and its sort-of sequel: *OUATITS2*. The

films star Francis Ng and have an odd appealing quality—Ng's triad middle-manager is the polar opposite of sexy pop star Ekin Cheng.

OUATITS2 features a big gang showdown which is set up to allow the youths to breathe hard and go home talking tough, but gets touched off by accident and turns into tragic carnage. One furious moment emerges triumphant—Roy Cheung as Dinosaur, chopper in hand, spin-kicks his way into the lobby of the Newport cinema on Jordan Road. The spacious and open lobby of the cinema serves briefly as cinematic triad-punk-warfare arena as Dinosaur chops at his enemies under a poster from fellow GWJ film *War of the Underworld*. Art imitates life, and life chops art.

3. **1997's** *Y&D4* staged an absurd debate between the two candidates for the branch leader of Tuen Mun. With all members of the Hung Hing triad seated in Tuen Mun Town Hall listening attentively, Chicken and Barbarian (each with his own microphone and podium) start dissing each other's credentials. "Barbarian, since the death of your boss Dinosaur, Tuen Mun has become a mess", accuses Chicken. This gangster-sponsored exercise in democracy is terminated by a big gang fight.

2. Director Billy Tang populates his GWJ films with interesting characters and a paucity of metal/cleaver "rhetoric." *Street Angels* (1996) revolves around Tung Yen (Chingmy Yau), a street-tough lady bound to wiseguy beau Walkie Pi (Simon Yam). Supporting characters include Valerie Chow as Tung's nemesis Karen—Canadian-born Chow became a Revlon covergirl under the name "Rachel Shane." Elvis Tsui chews some scenery as lustful Brother Moro, and Maria Cordero (Hong Kong's best female singer: a powerful Filipina diva) belts out a Cantotune live.

But SA's most intriguing character is Ming Ming—Shu Qi, in one of her earlier film roles. Shu plays a cheerful teenage hooker Tung Yen recruited from a low-level Mongkok brothel. Shu Qi's performance is delightful—in her inaugural scene, she greets a morbidly obese patron with a cheery "Hey Fatty, can you see your dick while pissing?", and complains of repetitive-stress-injury symptoms from giving too many handjobs.

Walkie Pi betrays Tung Yen, so good-hearted Ming Ming duplicitously dolls up in a kimono to serve him dinner in a private room at a Japanese restaurant. She flatters his male ego, and drops the kimono. Walkie strips off his gaudy gangster garb, showing big dragon/tiger tattoos. "Don't you fear I'll melt you?", he asks, and sniffs her neck like an animal.

The resultant sequence is a skillful blend of passion and danger. When Walkie has Ming Ming up against the wall all sweaty and pink, she whips out the killing spike hidden in the hairpin. He nonchalantly pinions her homicidal hand, finishes, grins triumphantly, tosses her around the room, then grabs a delicate Japanese pottery bowl heaping with super-hot green wasabi paste. Walkie Pi is not a nice man.

1. Karen Mok's character Shuk Fan debuts in *Y&D3*. She's rollerblading in Causeway Bay and accidentally slips under Chicken's car. He steps out to see if she's OK, and she pops up spewing blasphemous curses in a spotless, dead-sexy British accent (that's Mok's real voice, by the way). Then, in mid-curse, she switches to Cantonese, delighting the boys. Chicken draws himself up and gets in her face with a vile Cantorhyme as Pou Pee (Jerry Lamb) gesticulates in mime behind him.

Shuk Fan stares calmly, knees him in the

crotch, then head-butts him. He goes down howling and she blades off blasé as his cohorts let loose a hearty cheer.

Hex Errors: Police Confidential

"I am a police, the same with others. But I am afraid of gangster and bloodshed. Neither my supervisor nor woman like me."
Haunted Karaoke

"The famous key words of being a police, you know? A for apple polishing, B for boosting, C for careless, D for dog, E for escaping duties. If you can do all these, you will be promoted without working hard."
The Log

"Pal, cuff two bastards to the police stations."
Spike Drink Gang

"Finger, finger out the policeman"
The Imp

"Officer, what course is it?"
"It's called: hell-style suicide to transit for 1997. Pension-guaranteed, dying-for-sure special training course."
Bodyguards of the Last Governor

"Bitch, your kicking is useless, we Hong Kong police are competent."
Bodyguards of the Last Governor

"You are paid to be a police, not for the standing comedy."
Haunted Karaoke

"I'm not Satan's daughter! I'm Inspector Chan Shou-ching from the Complaints Against Police Office."
666: Satan Returns

"We, cops, have no time for farts."
Twist

"I like criminal movies!"
People's Hero

"Officer Pun, you'd be righteous & fair."
Women On the Run

"Officer Cheung, your penis is over."
Women On the Run

Hex Errors: Wiseguy Wisdom

"Why do you like the Police, they are so boring. We gangsters are much more interesting."
Haunted Karaoke

"I know you, Tony is the nasty bad egg of Japanese triad society!"
Once Upon A Time In Triad Society

"If a rascal is trustable, even a pig will climb up a tree!"
Sexy and Dangerous

"We are progressive rascals. We are making an art film."
Mahjong Dragon

"Is this your territory?"
"Yes, this is called Street of Copyright Infringement."
Suicide

"We think highly your criminal genius"
My Lucky Stars

"And, you bastard, a triad society is a triad society."
Once Upon A Time In Triad Society

CHAPTER EIGHT
THE UNEXPECTED

MORE SEX, BETTER ZEN, FASTER BULLETS

Milkyway Image Productions—Hong Kong's most intriguing production house—was formed in 1996 by producer/director/writer Johnny To Kei-fung and scriptwriter/director Wai Ka-fai. To (pronounced "toe") started his career with TVB, the television arm of the Shaw Brothers empire, where he became close friends with Wai. To directed his first feature film in 1978 and has established himself as one of Hong Kong's premier directors in a wide variety of styles. At the 23rd Hong Kong International Film Festival in 1999, To was honored with a Director-in-Focus retrospective, while the To-directed Milkyway production *Where A Good Man Goes* made its world premiere as the festival's opening film.

Since then, To has directed over thirty feature films, been discovered by cinema fans in Europe and worldwide, smoked hundreds of cigars, and remains behind the camera. As he told Stefan in a 1998 interview: "I love to shoot films. You give me two people and one camera and I'll shoot!"

The sheer volume of To's directorial output (even by Hong Kong standards) deserves explanation. He's directed romantic comedies, a Chinese New Year feel-good period piece (*Wu Yen* [2002]), and other less weighty fare to get back to what he does best: murky noir cop-versus-crook potboilers, often set in Macau—the former Portuguese colony dotted with fading colonial architecture. No one films Macau like Johnnie To—and he returns there again and again.

During the 90s, Milkyway's leading man was Lau Ching-wan. Lau rocketed to prominence as the lead in Derek Yee's *C'est La Vie Mon Cherie* (1994), which also made a star of co-lead Anita Yuen. Lau was lauded by Derek Elley in Variety as one of the world's ten best actors in late 1997, and toplined many Milkyway films in the latter half of the decade.

After *The Mission* (1999), To assembled an ensemble cast whose synergy has carried them through many classic Milkyway noirs like *Exiled* (2006) and *Vengeance* (2009). Anthony Wong serves as leader, backed by lieutenants including Roy Cheung, Richie Ren, Gordon Lam, and loyal sergeant Lam Suet, with Simon Yam and/or Nick Cheung as friend/foe. Not all appear in each of To's crime-packed bullets-by-the-boxload films—it's mix-and-match—and Lau returns at regular intervals.

Sandwiched between the crime films are comedies like *Needing You* (2000) and *Love on a Diet* (2001), often starring the popular duo of Andy Lau and Sammi Cheng. To's upfront about helming these more commercial films (*Diet* starred Andy Lau and Sammi Cheng in fat-suits and earned more at the Hong Kong box office than Michael Bay's "Snora Snora Snora" *Pearl Harbor*) to help finance the crime films he loves. But To also uses his resources to support and nurture young filmmakers in efforts from Laurence Lau's *Spacked Out* (2000) to *Trivisa* (2016). He often produces and lets other directors take the reins.

NOTE: This is not a definitive analysis of Milkyway's oeuvre: To and Wai have created dozens of films in myriad genres, and this chapter sticks to the noir/crime features we think appeal to an international audience. If a film like *Election* (2005) seems of interest, check it out. But know in advance that the Hong Kong triad referents will pile up fast—and so forth with *Election 2* (2006) and *Election 3* (2015).

On the scene '99
The Hong Kong International Film Festival 1999:

THE UNEXPECTED

Wu Chien-lien: chilled yet packing heat in *Beyond Hypothermia*.

Beyond Hypothermia (攝氏32度)

1996 | Starring Lau Ching-wan, Wu Chien-lien, Han Jae Suk, Shirley Wong Sa-lee, Deon Cheung Chung-chi
Directed by Patrick Leung Pak-kin

Chilled assassin Shu Li (Wu Chien-lien) lives in an anonymous blue-lit world. She surrounds herself with boobytraps and gaffer-tapes 9mm pistols under her bed. The black polymer sheen of automatic weaponry is her preferred shade—and her body temperature's five degrees below normal.

Shu was raised to be a killer by Aunt Mei (Shirley Wong), a middle-aged Cambodian death-pimp who runs a Hong Kong beauty salon. Aunt Mei hires Miss Shu to travel to Southeast Asian locations and liquidate unsavory people.

The film's opening sequence shows Shu's chilled skills as she enters an icehouse, breaks a Heckler and Koch assault rifle out of an enormous ice block, then waits for her quarry (Wu spent hours at the Hong Kong Gun Club learning how to shoot for the role—she proved so adept at handling real firearms that the club offered her a permanent membership).

She shoots out a target-obscuring light, then sends a 7.62mm bullet into the head of her victim. The ejected brass casing melts its way into an ice block, dutifully cooling itself—ever the professional, she plucks it out, pockets it, and vanishes.

Redemption is warmth in the form of ex-triad trying the straight life, Long Shek (Lau Ching-wan). He's a lovable heart-o'-gold spud who runs a noodle stall in an anonymous Hong Kong alley.

Shu spots him while casing the neighborhood for potential enemies. Her child-like curiosity spurs her to try his noodles, wearing a long-hair wig as a disguise. He calls her "Siu-sin" ("Pretty

at the opening party, which that year highlighted Johnnie To as its featured local director. Actress Ruby Wong roamed stylish in an electric blue dress.

Screenwriter Wai Ka-fai, who directed the surreal gangster-drama *Too Many Ways To Be No. 1* (see page 149) stood by himself—no one recognized Wai, so it seemed appropriate to head over and say hello. Soon, Johnnie To came over to stand by his long-term collaborator Wai. Then Lau Ching-wan walked over to stand between them.

Lau, in fine fettle, clapped Wai on the shoulder. "He is the BRAINS!", said Lau in English. Then he clapped To on the shoulder with the other hand, joining these three auteurs together, "and he is the BOSS!" At that, all three laughed uproariously.

It was one of those moments that makes the hours spent in front of a computer fact-checking and writing reviews of films worthwhile. At that moment, those three guys were atop the Hong Kong film world. What's more amazing is that all three continue to make films, but if there's a "boss" among them, Lau's right: it's Johnnie To.

Mr To surrounds himself with the best talent of 21st century Hong Kong. If you appreciate the aesthetic of Sergio Leone, Martin Scorsese, John Woo, Ringo Lam, you need to check a few of this guy's films. So...here's a few Milkyway gems.

Ghost"—a pun on Wu's Cantonese name as well as Joey Wong's famous ghost character's name in *A Chinese Ghost Story*).

Hot broth and plain noodles warms her from the core. He's equally smitten, but when he turns his back, she's gone. Duty calls.

Like yin to yang, she returns, inner dialogue musing on the warming noodle broth, Long Shek trying to get her attention between noxious customers and local triad Brother Pao (Deon Cheung) demanding protection money. When killer and spud do get together, they're like a couple of teenagers. She flatters the lug by asking if he's got any other women, and he indulges in a bit of pseudo-macho hemming and hawing. Shu's response: "No problem, I'll just kill them all." He thinks it's cute but she's not kidding.

Romantic conundrum introduced, the film shifts its location to Seoul (*BH* was partly financed by Korean interests). Shu pops Mr Pok, a local crime-lord. This so enrages Pok's henchman Cheu (Korean actor Han Jae Suk), that he scorches the earth for the terminatrix. Duran Duran hairstyle and psycho snarl intact, he heads for a Korean restaurant in Hong Kong where the gangster-owners pamper the homemade kimchi and hand Cheu nickel-plated revenge weaponry.

Although both Shu and Long now want to erase their criminal pasts, fate intervenes. Regrettably, the apocalyptic end-battle is played out to the soundtrack of a sappy Korean pop song which is holed repeatedly by the on-screen intensity. But boiling action and cool performances by the leads—aided and abetted by Arthur Wong's crisp cinematography—elevate *Hypothermia*.

Exiled (放·逐)
2006 | Starring Anthony Wong Chau-sang, Francis Ng Chun-yu, Nick Cheung Ka-fai, Richie Ren Xian-qi, Josie Ho Chiu-yee, Roy Cheung Yiu-yeung, Lam Suet, Simon Yam Tat-wah, Gordon Lam Ka-tung, Eddie Cheung Siu-fai, Ronald Yan Mau-keung, Ellen Chan Nga-lun
Directed by Johnnie To Kei-fung

The chess pieces snap into place during *Exiled*'s opening sequence, which begins with a fist knocking on an anonymous door on a nondescript house in a Macau neighborhood where the architecture's Portuguese-colonial and the streets are narrow. Two pairs of gunsels door-knock in succession, inquiring about a man named Wai—Jing (Josie Ho), who answers the door, dresses like a housewife, but knows what's up. She says there's no such person. The quartet of trenchcoated men (Anthony Wong and Lam Suet, Francis Ng and Roy Cheung) wait outside, smoking cigars. They discuss their conflicted motives regarding the absent Wai, hinting at another corkscrewed Macau gangsta situation gone all kinds of wrong.

Wai (Nick Cheung) drives up in a truck full of furniture—seeing the men, he knows the prosaic life he'd dreamed of in Macau is not to be. He walks into his house and opens a drawer with a .38 revolver and loose rounds rolling about. The gunsels drift in. Wai fills his revolver one round at a time as they surround him. Shoot? Or talk it out?

Shu Li laments her fate in *Beyond Hypothermia*.

THE UNEXPECTED

Gunsels in Macau: *Exiled.*

A bit of both, as it turns out. Regardless, anyone who survives has gotta eat, so pretty soon Wai and his childhood friends (now foes, or not) cook up a fine Cantonese meal and reminisce about the old days.

There's still business to conduct, mostly for Boss Fay (Simon Yam at his slimiest), so the men relocate to a hotel which seems a haven for criminals of all stripes, including an attractive working girl (the venerable Ellen Chan, who excels in a non-speaking role). They're here to meet Jeff (Eddie Cheung) for paying jobs. Some guys need killing, for a price. A hit's arranged, but fate and coincidences run parallel until the rails twist and tangle, collisions inevitable.

Exiled features To's core actors (with the welcome addition of Cheung and a spirited performance by Ho as his determined wife) riffing and improvising on the script. Brutality and comedy merge as the characters accept that fate calls the ultimate shots.

While the ensemble cast is stellar, the central axis is Wong versus Yam—fans of To's noir efforts will enjoy watching these two tangle. There's some fine hardboiled humor in this one: as Boss Fay and Anthony Wong's character argue over who's to be served first at the in-hotel gangster-hospital, the working girl (who was busy with the doctor, played by Ronald Yan, when the wounded crooks came a-knockin') rifles the doc's cash-drawer and runs off with the profits.

NOTE: The hotel with the central courtyard, which looks as though it ought to exist in Macau's organic urbanscape, regrettably does not. It's a purpose-built set, and as adding a roof would have bumped the budget, that was omitted. Thus all the hotel scenes are shot at night.

Expect The Unexpected
(非常突然)
1998 | Starring Lau Ching-wan, Simon Yam Tat-wah, Ruby Wong Cheuk-ling, Hui Siu-hung, Raymond Wong Ho-yin, Yoyo Mung Ka-wai, Bak Ka-sin, Keiji Sato, Lam Suet
Directed by Patrick Yau Tat-chi

Main man Lau Ching-wan stars as Sam, a savvy and straight-up flatfoot. He's counterbalanced by Simon Yam as Sam's superior Ken and supporting characters like smooth Ruby Wong and anything-but Hui Siu-hung. They're a tight-knit group of cops whose fraternalism is caring and playful—more like a bunch of college kids than hard-bitten law enforcers. Romantic angles complicate when waitress Mandy (Yo Yo Mung) becomes a star-witness in a case Ken and Sam are working.

Complementing this kinder/gentler cop-flick vibe are the criminals they're after—a gang of bumbling thieves from the Mainland. These potatoheads can't do anything right. They try to rob a jewelry shop, but can't manage to smash the jewel-case glass. The brakes on the getaway car don't work. They don't even wear disguises,

Expect The Unexpected: precisely that.

leaving the Hong Kong cops shaking their heads at the surveillance tape.

More worrisome is a vicious group of local crooks. These deadly creeps thrive on rape, murder and mayhem—they even move in with their victims to prolong their dastardly fun. They're particularly fond of AK-47s, sawn-off shotguns, and grenade launchers. The police are outgunned by this mob and view them as a hateful nemesis to be hunted down and destroyed like mad dogs.

The ongoing soap operatic cop saga and the simmering apocalypse of gangster kill never homogenizes in *ETU*, making the film both sophisticated black humor and an enigmatic challenge. Pigeonholing the unpigeonholeable? All the giddy crushes-kept-secret are a waste of time; a fruitless void of fantasy when you're a cop in Hong Kong. Then the ending wraps all arguments in a shock blanket.

The creators envisioned the film taking place entirely in rain, with a sunny interval illuminating the climactic end-game. Alas, the vagaries of Hong Kong weather and the pressures of making a feature film for HK$6 million (US$780,000) created an ending framed in rain as well.

Intruder (恐怖雞)

1997 | Starring Wu Chien-lien, Wayne Lai Yiu-cheung, Moses Chan Ho, Bonnie Wong Man-wai, Yuen Bun, Yuki Lai Yuen-tung
Directed by Tsang Kan-cheung

Retribution is mercurial. Take, for example, former cabdriver Chen Chi-min (Wayne Lai). In a moment of startling lucidity, he blurts out: "I'm useless, I'm not human being, I deserve dying...I achieve nothing though I'm 30-something. I know nothing but call prostitute, I'm wasting my life, I'm selfish."

All true. Chen's a dirtbag who spends his time bargaining streetwalker fees. He's alienated every other woman in his life—his wife, his mother, his cute daughter Yin Yin (Yuki Lai).

Despite his shortcomings, the audience has little trouble working up sympathy for him: Chen is the target of a morally bankrupt woman whose predatory instincts set up horrific situations. Don't be fooled by the innocuous "slasher flick" packaging—*Intruder* is one long howl of anguish.

Wu Chien-lien plays the intruder: Yieh Siu-yan, a mainland Chinese woman whose motives are murky as the film opens. She coolly garrotes a young woman in a Shenzhen brothel, then strips the corpse of watch, cash, documentation and hair to adopt her identity. She then enters Hong Kong using the fake documents, and applies for a Hong Kong ID card (in a 1998 interview, Wu told Stefan she enjoyed the challenge of portraying the amoral, homicidal Yieh).

So gorgeous, so evil: Wu Chien-lien as the *Intruder*.

Yieh's next task is to find a suitable trick, which turns out to be the unlucky ex-cabbie. She goes home with Chen to case the place.

The next night, she drives a rented car to Streetwalker's Row, spots Chen trying to bargain with another working girl, knocks him down with the car, runs over his legs, then drives off. After he's returned from the hospital with his legs in plaster casts, she talks her way into his house with promises of further sexual adventures. Then she coldcocks him with a metal pipe and packing-tapes him to his wheelchair.

After that, it's time for some physical interrogation techniques. When Chen's mom (Bonnie Wong) comes looking for him, things get much, much, much, much, worse.

Yieh's cruelty is specific in nature, and the torment-edge never lets up in *Intruder*. Wu's performance sinks hooks in you, and even if you're not squeamish, you will be by the time this thing's over.

The Longest Nite (暗花)

1998 | Starring Lau Ching-wan, Tony Leung Chiu-wai, Maggie Siu Mei-kei, Lung Fong, Sunny Fang Kang, Ronny Ching Siu-lung, Mark Cheng Ho-nam, Wong Tin-lam, Lo Hoi-pang, Lam Suet
Directed by Patrick Yau Tat-chi

Adjectives like "spare" and "mean" limn this tense little film from Milkyway. The rare appearance of sunlight in *TLN* blasts the characters with vampire-frying intensity, but most of the action takes place during the space of one dark night, hence the title. The first minute or so of the film includes a rapid-fire salvo of factoids which set up the plot. Here's what you need to know:

In Macau, a power struggle between a pair of potent triad kingpins is on the verge of detonation. Brother Lung (Lung Fong) is on his way back to Macau and slated to arrive at midnight. His nemesis Mr K (Sunny Fang Kang) is determined to join forces with Lung—the ongoing shootout between their respective tribes is an attrition neither can afford.

Triad kingpins being practical folk, they seek a resolution to the bad-for-business whackfest. A mysterious elder, Mr Hung, is also returning to Macau to help sort things out as this idiot squabble is hurting his biz too.

A widely believed rumor has Mr K offering a 5 million dollar bounty for Lung's head. Every

Lau Ching-wan has problems in *The Longest Nite*...

...but Wong Tin-lam doesn't care.

gunsel in the Pearl River Delta makes a beeline for Macau, but tough-guy Sam (Tony Leung Chiu-wai) tracks them down methodically so he can shatter their fingers. Mr K, anxious to keep Lung alive until a deal can be struck, gave him this duty—loyal Sam has been employed by the powerful gangster for over a decade. K also warned him to especially restrain Mark, a guy renowned for more gun than brain. Mark, it turns out, is K's son. But Sam is a senior member of the Macau police force.

A mysterious drifter with a shaven, tattooed head (Lau Ching-wan in full glower) comes breezing into town and things start to happen to Sam. The presentation—high-contrast lighting, triad icons—is pure Hong Kong. But the predicament and its ratcheting tension corner the characters like rats as cruel violence saturates *The Longest Nite*.

Torture and murder are simply tools of the trade—gunshots are so muted they simply pop like stepped-on Vitasoy boxes. Everyone in this film is a goddam pawn. The ethos is best summed up by veteran actor/director Wong Tin-lam on viewing the grue-smeared corpse of a man his henchmen tortured for hours: "Eh, he lasted a long time."

Too Many Ways To Be No. 1
(一個字頭的誕生)
1997 | Starring Lau Ching-wan, Carman Lee Yeuk-tung, Francis Ng Chun-yu, Ruby Wong Cheuk-ling, Cheung Tat-ming, Elvis Tsui Kam-kong
Directed by Wai Ka-fai

Film people love to talk about films as "texts". Makes sense. Look at the proliferation of pulp in both media: self-help books and dumbed-down BDSM novels are the textual equivalent of big-crashing-robots and weenie-joke films.

Using the written language alone, it is possible to create a voice so distinctive it creates a unique dialect. James Joyce, Thomas Pynchon, Cormac McCarthy—for writers like these, the language is a sheet of soft metal they hammer into their own shapes. In making such dialects flesh, the power of the written word often outstrips the ability of cinema.

Yet Wai Ka-fai's *Too Many Ways To Be No. 1* aims for its own cinematic dialect. Like a precocious brat, it slaps and kicks at the Hong Kong gangster flicks it spoofs. Shot throughout

Throw those hands in the air! *Too Many Ways To Be No. 1*.

with wide-angle lenses that transform cramped spaces into reckless expanses, *TMWTBN1* presents its actors in superhuman fashion—looming like skyscrapers or buried as specks amid the scenery somewhere in the background.

The distorting camera is in relentless hard-party mode here. It laughs. It goes disco during a dance scene. When an angry gangster's wife starts punctuating her monologue with gunshots, the camera removes itself to a safe distance—when confronted by fistfuls of primed-to-go pistols, it hits the floor or clings to the ceiling like a bat. *TMWTBN1* has a look most directors wouldn't envisage, let alone enact.

But film language is never purely visual—without interesting characters and a tightly-woven plot, Wai and cinematographer Wong Wing-hang's vision wouldn't work. Wai wrote many of other Milkyway scripts, and *TMWTBN1*'s convoluted high-energy plot is fully loaded. Cacine Wong's Nino Rota-sweats-it-out-in-Taiwan score is sublime, and if you're down with your Hong Kong gangster-film referents, you'll get even more...but this film will spin you upside-down regardless. Expect bifurcated plot-lines and a non-linear timeline.

Lau Ching-wan stars as Kau—a triad guy who's a jinx. Everyone, especially his gang pals Matt (Francis Ng) and Bo (Cheung Tat-ming), knows he's a jinx. When things go wrong, they veer towards Kau, slap him on the back of the head, and tell him he's a jinx. Or if he's by himself when something goes wrong, yet again, he stares in disbelief at his hands, which bollix up everything they touch.

What goes wrong in his world is not the everyday lost-car-keys and computer-ate-my-homework frustrations. He's a magnet for cataclysmic error, which is frightening as he and his crew are skull-deep in hazardous criminal activities. Kau knows the danger. He just can't laugh about it, so we do his laughing for him.

Us and that camera.

Vengeance (復仇)

2009 | Starring Johnny Hallyday, Anthony Wong Chau-sang, Gordon Lam Ka-tung, Lam Suet, Simon Yam Tat-wah, Sylvie Testud, Maggie Siu Mei-kei, Stanley Fung Sui-fan
Directed by Johnnie To Kei-fung

What good is revenge if the wronged party can't remember the original crime? And who the heck is Johnny Hallyday?

In France, Hallyday is up there with Brigitte Bardot and Elvis Presley. Despite a 57-year

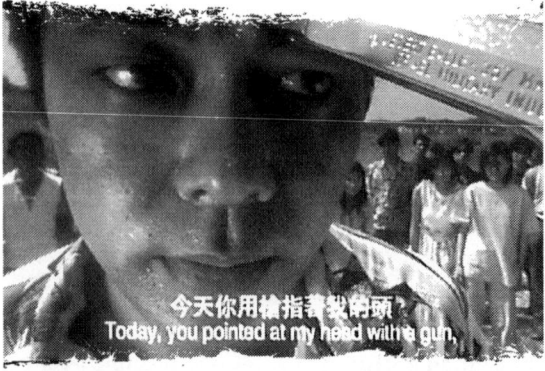
Lau Ching-wan states the obvious in *Too Many Ways To Be No. 1*.

career and 79 albums, Hallyday's "the biggest rock star you've never heard of" in the English-speaking world. He performed for a million spectators at the Eiffel Tower in 2000 and has starred in films since the early 60s. Hallyday is, as Miles Kingston wrote in The Independent: "Legendary for being legendary."

The film opens with Hallyday (playing Francis Costello: a Parisian restauranteur with an intriguing past) thrust into a dramatic situation... in Macau. He meets briefly with Inspector Wong (Maggie Siu) and, curiously, steals the police photos as he leaves. Later we see him at his hotel writing "vengeance" on every single one. Turns out Costello has a bullet lodged in his skull and doesn't know when his memory will fail him, so (like Guy Pearce's character in Memento, he writes vital information on photos).

Meanwhile, a trio of hitmen (Anthony Wong, Lam Suet and Gordon Lam) terminate the unfaithful mistress of triad boss George Fung (Simon Yam) in Costello's hotel, and he happens to be in the corridor as they exit. Inspector Wong hauls him in for a line-up, but he declines to recognize anyone. Instead, Costello follows Chu (Gordon Lam) and is confronted by the trio—he then makes them a job offer. He's got a stack of 500-euro notes, a hefty wristwatch, and offers to throw in his restaurant as well. Costello's on a mission and doesn't seem concerned about his well-being once it's done.

The gunsels accept the job, do some checking, and a bit of target practice at a rural destination presided over by Tony (Stanley Fung). Seems Costello not only makes a tasty bouillabaisse but can handle a pistol as well. The now-quartet go to Hong Kong to track down leads, only to find that this particular plot-snake bites its own tail. Caught in the loop, they return to Macau to square things up.

When Johnnie To makes a Macau-based crime

Johnny Hallyday stalks the mean streets of Macau seeking *Vengeance*.

film, he keeps his thumb on the switch. Stylized handgun-battles on narrow Macau streets, shifting loyalties, set-piece attacks punctuated by echoed guitar and percussion...*Vengeance* offers spectacle for action-film fans. Will Hallyday solve the puzzle, with Macau triads and his fading memory against him? More importantly, will vengeance offer him peace, or is there another way?

Breaking News (大事件)

2004 | Starring Nick Cheung Ka-fai, Richie Ren Xian-qi, Kelly Chan Wai-lam, Lam Suet, Simon Yam Tat-wah, Hui Siu-hung, Maggie Siu Mei-kei, Eddie Cheung Siu-fai
Directed by Johnnie To Kei-fung

To uses some of his favorite actors (Nick Cheung, Richie Ren and the incomparable Lam Suet) in this cops-chase-crooks flick. But he snaps on an unusual plot-device: the Hong Kong Police use a media-savvy officer, Rebecca Fong (played in pure ice-queen fashion by Kelly Chen), to spin the event while it's literally exploding on Hong Kongers' television screen. The crooks fight back by taking mobile-phone videos exposing the spin and uploading them to news outlets.

THE UNEXPECTED

Media-savvy policewoman Kelly Chen reveals her strategy in *Breaking News*.

Anthony Wong wants to know just what the hell you're looking at in *The Mission*.

The media-circus doesn't distract much from the central plot: how can the crooks escape? There's a wonderful scene where the bad guys, trapped in an apartment, decide to cook a meal for themselves and their hostages, then upload the mobile-phone footage. When Fong sees the broadcast, she orders a massive takeout order for both attending police and reporters. Styropod lunches are opened in front of TV cameras as cops and hacks dig in—an only-in-Hong Kong viral-media food-fight.

Breaking News is famed for its opening scene: an unbroken tracking shot that sets up the initial attempt to collar the perps. It's a seven-minute take that incorporates a lot of police business, spontaneous subterfuge, and a phenomenal amount of firepower. Tall and lovely Fong never appears on camera herself, so you just know that stylish jacket conceals a handgun...

The Mission (鎗火)
1999 | Starring Anthony Wong Chau-sang, Francis Ng Chun-yu, Jackie Lui Chung-yin, Roy Cheung Yiu-yeung, Lam Suet, Simon Yam Tat-wah, Eddy Ko Hung, Wong Tin-lam
Directed by Johnnie To Kei-fung

The Chinese title of this film translates as "gunfire" which frankly is more descriptive. There's an awful lot of posing with guns, gunfire, and assorted gun noise in this flick, which marks the transition from Milkyway's Lau Ching-wan-led films to an ensemble cast led by Anthony Wong.

The flick starts with gunmen trying to shoot Big Brother Lung (Eddy Ko). Anxious to avoid ventilation, Lung—with the help of fellow gang-boss Frank (Simon Yam)—assembles a group of men who are known pistoleros (Anthony Wong. Francis Ng, Roy Cheung, Lam Suet). There's a brief subplot featuring Lung's wife but essentially the film is one long shootout, with some stylish gunmen-choreography, a bit of double-crossing, and an exquisite performance by Ng, who plays a triad bar-owner and nine-millimeter enthusiast with just the right amount of quirks.

The film has its flaws, including a peppy synthesizer-riff theme that pops up seemingly at random. But the core group of actors went on to distinguish themselves in other To productions.

The Odd One Dies (兩個只能活一個)
1997 | Starring Takeshi Kaneshiro, Carman Lee Yeuk-tung, Bin Yue-man, Ken Choi Fung-wah, Tian

Min-zu, Lee Diy-yue, Lam Suet
Directed by Patrick Yau Tat-chi

Odd as in weird, or odd as in not-even? This is a big lovable mutt of a film, lurching at you wanting to be tickled behind the ears. *The Odd One Dies* Wong Kar-winks at you as it reels by, rewarding the viewer with rich visuals, great gags, a dynamite cha-cha score by Wong Ying-wah and a substantive subtext which skewers Hong Kong's obsession with big wads of cash.

TOOD stars Takeshi Kaneshiro as Mo: a hipster whose talon-bangs combine with fuming cig smoke to obscure his visage. Mo hires himself out as a hitman to a curry-gorging mystery man with underworld connections, gets the gig—and the down payment—then purchases a funky old car and a 1988-clunker mobile phone (image-conscious Mo strikes poses with bulky phone in-hand...cuz he's cooool). He then wrestles the curry fiend to the ground and forces the guy to produce a subcontractor for the hit.

This new would-be assassin is played by Carman Lee, an attractive actress who's allowed makeup artists to ugly her up. Looking like death at a slow boil, Lee sports a hair-nest of greasy snakes, sub-eye darkening, and a street waif/sewer rat demeanor. Her nameless character is a bundle of nerves and demands.

Mo bonds with his fellow oddball and acquiesces to her increasingly bizarre preconditions. He provides an enormous pistol for her killing work, but she insists on a backup gun, sending him to fetch it from some wastrel named Simon. Sequentially, hilariously, Simon offers marijuana, a used air-conditioner, and the sexual services of a topless waitress in lieu of a pistol. Simon has other motives.

So does the ratty one, whose incessant

Carman Lee and Takeshi Kaneshiro: *The Odd One Dies*.

demands cease once Mo starts refusing. She continues to dream of "Paradise", depicted on the tourist postcard she carries in her scrapbook alongside glamor shots of people sporting really nice haircuts. When Mo takes his friendly scissors to her snake-do, she's dissatisfied with the result and shears off his signature bangs in retribution. At gunpoint. It's that kind of movie.

Selected Johnnie To filmography

The Heroic Trio (1993) (director)
The Bare-Footed Kid (1993) (director)
Beyond Hypothermia (1996) (production)
Lifeline (1997) (director)
Intruder (1997) (production)
The Odd One Dies (1997) (production)
Too Many Ways To Be No. 1 (1997) (production)
A Hero Never Dies (1998) (director/production)
Expect the Unexpected (1998) (production)
The Longest Nite (1998) (production)
Where a Good Man Goes (1999) (director)
Running Out of Time (1999) (director)
The Mission (1999) (director)
Needing You ... (2000) (director)
Spacked Out (2000) (production)

THE UNEXPECTED

Running Out of Time 2 (2001) (director)
Fulltime Killer (2001) (director)
My Left Eye Sees Ghosts (2002) (director)
Running on Karma (2003) (director)
PTU (2003) (director)
Turn Left, Turn Right (2003) (director)
Breaking News (2004) (director)
Election (2005) (director)
Election 2 (2006) (director)
Exiled (2006) (director)
Mad Detective (2007) (director)
Vengeance (2009) (director)
Accident (2009) (production)
Life Without Principle (2011) (director)
Punished (2011) (production)
Life Without Principle (2011) (production)
Motorway (2012) (production)
Blind Detective (2013) (director)
Office (2015) (director)
Three (2016) (director)
Trivisa (2016) (production)

Hex Errors: A Pox On Thee!

"Listen. Don't shit with my Big Brother. Otherwise, I crash you penis to pieces."
To Live And Die in Tsimshatsui

"I promise to punch you less than before"
Give and Take...Oh! Shit!

"You mis-shaped my busts, beat it!"
Street Angels

"Damn you Fatty. You are in deep shit now."
Run and Kill

"Don't snap my pork!"
A Chinese Odyssey Part One: Pandora's Box

"Threatening me? I'm scared to pissing!"
Vengeance Is Mine

"Don't wet my gun by your urine."
Hero

"Try my cotton bomb."
Dragon from Shaolin

"Fat-head, you meet your Waterloo!"
The Odd One Dies

"Slighter, you asshole."
Kidnap of Wong Chak Fai

"Your boss is quite trash!"
Final Justice

"Go and snap your mother!"
Offence Storm

"You won't tell? I must beat your pubic parts."
Bodyguards of the Last Governor"

Shut your poisoned lips!"
Troublesome Night 4

"But you, you're stink"
Ghost Story "Godmother of Mongkok"

"How come there's man like you, lazy and slacken. You know nothing but ask me for money, aren't you ashamed?"
OCTB-The Floating Body

"Just take him as pork and chop!"
To Be No. 1

"You think I'll use my asshole as my brain?"
Royal Warriors

"If I don't blow your head off, I wouldn't have a sound sleep tonight."
Casino

"Pal, both your chickens and you are illegal immigrants."
Untold Story 2

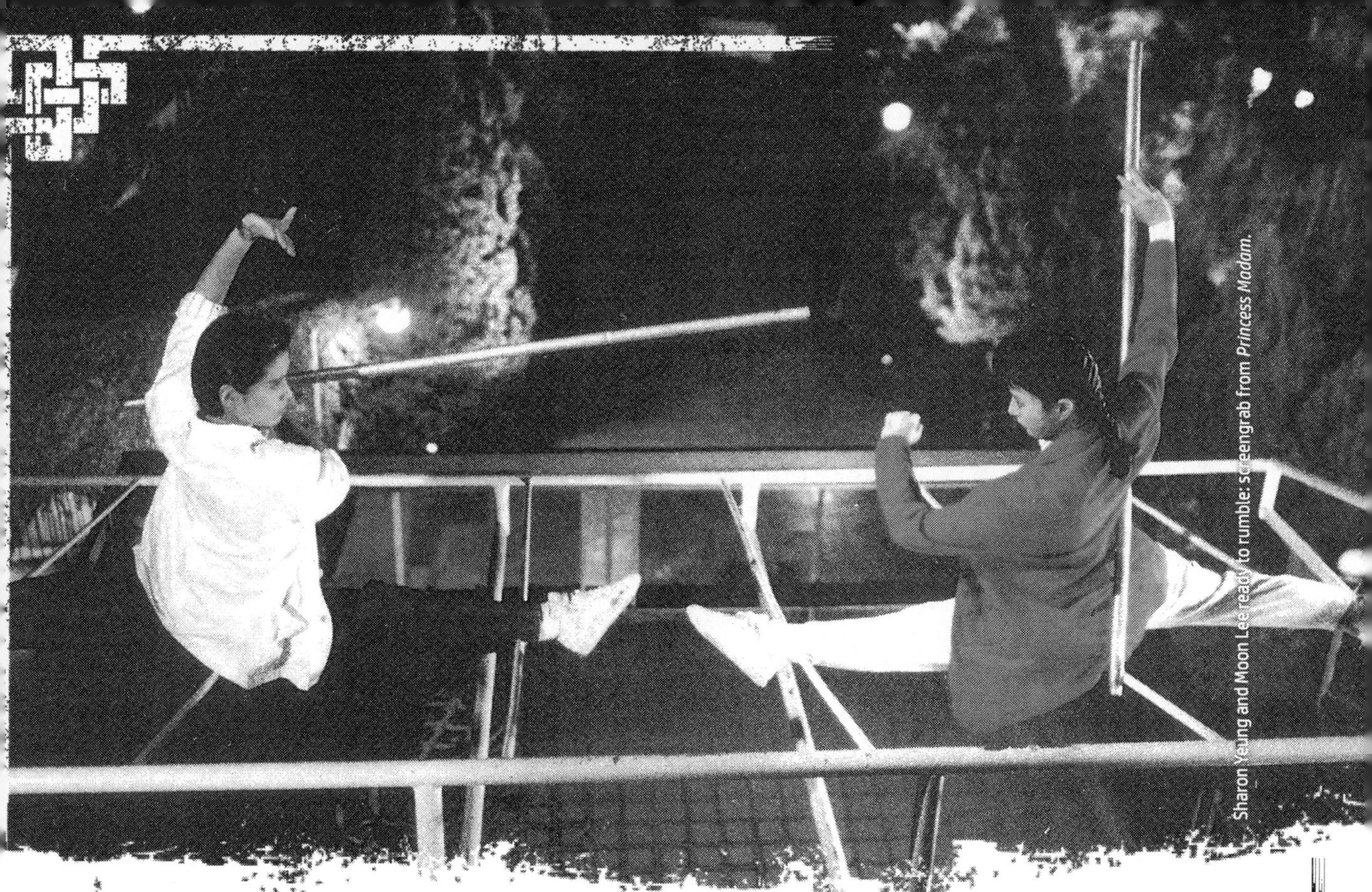

Sharon Yeung and Moon Lee ready to rumble: screengrab from Princess Madam.

CHAPTER NINE
NAIL-POLISHED FISTS

ong Kong cinema has always been a cinedrome where men and women fight as equals. Not yammering over domicile hygiene or remote control-control, but toe-to-toe you-bust-my-nose-and-I'll-bust-yours pugilism.

The first time you see this sort of cinematic fury from the fairer sex, initial disbelief quickly gives way to wide-eyed adulation. Your first gasp comes as a burly male opponent punches our heroine in the stomach—the second as she immediately lands three quick return blows on the brute, then kicks him in the head and sends him sprawling. Hong Kong fightin' femmes flicks were an opera-gloved slap to the face of 80s & 90s Hollywood machismo, where "warriors" were muscle-guys from Belgium or shaggy grim-faced blockheads.

Despite what you may have read in pictureless film journals, there's no crypto-feminist dialectic responsible for the phenomenon of female fighters in the Hong Kong cinema. China has a tradition of women warriors stretching back millennia—Sigourney Weaver said that she drew

NAIL-POLISHED FISTS

Angela Mao wants your life.

on these legends for inspiration when gearing up to fight the hideous critters in *Aliens*. The story of Princess Mulan, who disguised herself as a man to lead armies into battle, has been made into several Hong Kong films and an animated feature from Disney, with a live-action Disney film in pre-production as we go to press.

Cinematically, King Hu's *Come Drink With Me* (1966) made a sensation out of teenage actress Cheng Pei-pei and revved up the genre: Pei-pei appeared opposite Jimmy Wang Yu in Chang Cheh's blood-soaked 1968 film *Golden Swallow* (aka *The Girl with the Thunderbolt Kick*). Other efforts from the 60s/70s include *The 14 Amazons* (1972)—like the tale of Princess Mulan, it's drawn from Chinese literature. And Angela Mao tore up the screen in flicks like *Lady Whirlwind*, *Back Alley Princess*, *Thunderbolt*, and *Broken Oath*.

The stars of the 80s/90s are a diverse lot: the seminal "girls with guns" film is *Angel* (1987), directed by Teresa Woo and starring Hong Konger Moon Lee and Japanese martial sensation Yukari Oshima (Fukuoka native Oshima later moved to the Philippines where she's known as Cynthia Luster). Another Japanese actress, former powerlifter Michiko Nishiwaki found fame in Hong Kong films in the 80s, as did Malaysia's Michelle Yeoh, Taiwan's Cynthia Khan and Sibelle Hu, and a handful of gwei mui including Cynthia Rothrock, owner of five black belts in Korean and Chinese martial arts, and Sophia Crawford, who became one of the Mighty Morphin' Power Rangers.

Revenge is unrestricted by gender in Hong Kong. In films like *Princess Madam* and *Satin Steel*, women are both protagonist and antagonist while men are relegated to peripheral roles—ineffectual simps or "any moment now" pistol targets. Fury carries a designer handbag, and knocking about its bottom is a .38 snub.

A Serious Shock: Yes Madam '92
aka Death Triangle (末路狂花)
1992 | Starring Cynthia Khan, Moon Lee Choi-fung, Yukari Oshima, Waise Lee Chi-hung, Lawrence Ng, Karel Wong Chi-yeung, Ku Feng
Directed by Stanley Wing Siu

As the opening credits roll, policewomen Wan Chin (Cynthia Khan) and May (Moon Lee) practice their crimefighting techniques. They unpack nine-millimeter rounds, defuse bombs, stomp on pretend-bad-guys, and generally validate one another's feminine prowess as instructor Wilson (Lawrence Ng of *Sex & Zen* fame) looks on approvingly.

Wan Chin and Wilson—the happy cop couple—are preparing for their forthcoming nuptials.

However, Wilson's ex-girlfriend May is boiling over with jealousy. Spurned, jilted, and pissed-off, she pounds her unsuspecting sparring partner bloody during martial arts practice. Unsatisfied, she then follows Wilson into the men's locker room, screams curses at him, then knees him in the crotch.

Unaware of May's emotional toxicity, Wan Chin offers her friend a lift. But when they get to the car, they find it's in the process of being stolen by cheeky criminal, Sister Coco (Yukari Oshima). The police madams chase Coco down and bust her at gunpoint. But when she's taken to the station, Brother Boy (Waise Lee) promptly bails her out.

The two small-time crooks then head for a Houdini-like grudge match sponsored by their motorcycle gang. In an excellent piece of rumble business, Coco and some gwailo woman strip to their skivvies, shackle their ankles with heavy chain, and dive into an enormous water tank. The keys, naturally, are on the bottom—the boys shout and bet on the winner (one guess).

May discovers that Wan Chin and Wilson plan to emigrate to London, nixing any possibility of swiping her beloved from her friend's clutches. She dolls herself up in a black miniskirt and red top, and appears at his apartment to plead her case. But he's made his choice, and May goes ballistic. The diminutive, baby-faced actress slams her knee-high leather boots repeatedly into Wilson's midsection, howling "I hate others cheat me most!"

Wan Chin arrives and fires her revolver in the air, but May grabs the snub-nose from her, cuffs her to the railing, then plugs Wilson with Wan Chin's gun. Now a fugitive, her ex-fiancé's ashes in an urn, Wan Chin joins forces with Sister Coco.

This triangle moves towards their inevitable final battle in nonlinear fashion (a few expository

Philippines poster listing Oshima as "Cynthia Luster": *Death Triangle*.

scenes might have been left on the cutting-room floor), but there are plenty of opportunities for these women to work out. May's character becomes more malevolent by the frame, and then she boobytraps Coco's cute son with a backpack full of TNT. Nobody wants to see May survive, and everybody leaves the theater happy.

Black Cat (黑貓)
1990 | Starring Jade Leung, Simon Yam Tat-wah, Thomas Lam Cho-fai, Louis Roth
Directed by Stephen Shin

A remake of Luc Besson's *La Femme Nikita*, which was later remade by Hollywood as *The Assassin*, starring Bridget Fonda. Of the three, the HK version hits hardest. Newcomer Jade Leung's

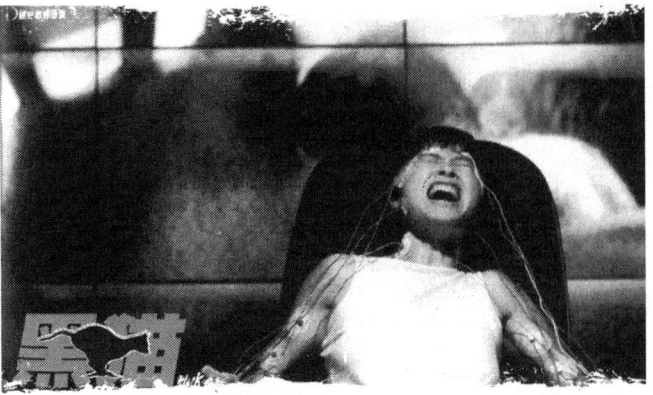

Jade Leung: wired to kill as *Black Cat*.

shuddering, animalistic performance as the Pygmalion hitlady trumps both Bridget and Anne "Nikita" Parillaud (Leung's performance won her the Best New Performer prize at the 11th Hong Kong Film Awards).

The film opens in the States, with Leung as the spitfire Catherine dispatching a few slobbering gwailos and plugging a cop for good measure. Hauled off to jail, she takes a beating from a hefty female guard and enters a state of bruised madness, grabbing the guard's nightstick and raining hell down upon her.

The cops turn a firehose on Catherine to cool her off. But she uses a bathroom break to slip her cuffs and brain a mysterious assailant with a toilet tank's top. She swipes his gun and blasts her way out of the cop shop, but is "killed" by Mystery Assailant #2.

These mystery guys are in the employ of an equally mysterious CIA-like agency headed by a suave guy named Brian (Simon Yam). Brian tells Catherine "now you're not a patient, but a dead," and proceeds to train her as a clandestine assassin. A microchip known as "Black Cat" is implanted in her head. Loads of high-tech bahooha (computerized treadmills, EKG simulations, etc) is used to turn Catherine's raw aggression into politically useful controlled lethality.

Black Cat's first hit occurs when she's ordered to kill the bride at a countryside wedding (the filmmakers never bother trying to explain why the targets need killing). She shoots the bride, the best man, then the caterer...as members of the wedding party chase after her (more Uzis here than at most weddings). Despite an intentionally ineffective getaway plan, Catherine eludes her pursuers, thus passing the last of Brian's tests.

The next assignment takes her to HK, to kill the director of the World Wildlife Fund with a mythic bullet made of ice. She pulls off this improbable stunt, but is photographed by Allen Yeung (Thomas Lam), a local bird lover. Being thorough, she goes to his house to eliminate him, but is touched by his soulful harmonica playing and falls in love with him instead.

But on a business trip to Japan, Allen insists upon prying into Catherine's affairs, and this leads to a violent confrontation with the local cops. The Japanese police are no match for Brian, who shows up to rescue Catherine and take out the meddlesome Allen. Black Cat, meanwhile, lives to kill again.

The Heroic Trio (東方三俠)

1992 | Starring Michelle Yeoh Chu-kheng, Anita Mui Yim-fong, Maggie Cheung Man-yuk, Damian Lau Chung-yan, Anthony Wong Chau-sang, Yen Shi-kwan
Directed by Johnnie To Kei-fung

The Heroic Trio features Anita Mui as a masked superheroine known as "Wonder Woman" who battles evil—when she's not playing subservient housewife to her naive husband Inspector Lau (Damian Lau). A recent wave of infant kidnappings has panicked the city, and the cops are stymied by

MORE SEX, BETTER ZEN, FASTER BULLETS

From Ghana of all places, this painting makes the stars of *The Heroic Trio* look like their waxen faces are melting.

Movie-painting of Michelle Yeoh's full-metal-bustier costume in *The Heroic Trio*, Rama Theater, Bangkok (Photo: Stefan Hammond, 1993).

the kidnapper's secret weapon: invisibility.

Wonder Woman can't nab the culprit, Ching (Michelle Yeoh). Ching's swiping those tykes under orders of a centuries-old Ming Dynasty eunuch (Yen Shi-kwan), who is trying to reclaim China's past glory by bringing forth a new Emperor via an ad hoc eugenics program. Thus, the babies.

Chat (Maggie Cheung) is a former disciple of the underground-dwelling eunuch who roars in on her motorbike ready to kick patoot. Chat's on the outs with that nasty eunuch and invades the creature's subterranean turf, setting off a wild chain of events. The trio must battle each other as well as this hideous creature to set things right.

The Heroic Trio is a delirious comic book fantasy with plenty of earthly kineticism. Action

director Tony Ching Siu-tung (*A Chinese Ghost Story*) combines sci-fi, horror and martial arts elements—he was originally listed as co-director with To, but *THT* is an ensemble effort and showcase for three ace Hong Kong actresses of the time.

In the Line of Duty 3
(皇家師姐3雌雄大盜)
1988 | Starring Cynthia Khan, Michiko Nishiwaki, Hiroshi Fujioka, Stuart Ong, Paul Chun Pui, Melvin Wong, Sandra Ng, Dick Wei
Directed by Brandy Yuen Jan-yeung and Arthur Wong Ngok-tai

After action star Michelle Yeoh made three features

NAIL-POLISHED FISTS

Cynthia Khan models a classic RHKP policewoman's uniform and .38 special in *ITLOD3*.

for D&B Films, she retired (fortunately for us, temporarily) from filmmaking. D&B then cast pixie-faced whirlwind Cynthia Khan as her replacement. With Michelle's *Royal Warriors* and *Yes, Madam!* considered the first two installments of the *ITLOD* series, Cynthia debuted at #3, with a bullet.

ITLOD3 opens with Cynthia issuing parking tickets, dressed in a sharp navy blue HK policewoman uniform. Despite a dramatic, skirt-ripping apprehension of a purse snatcher, she's stuck with her cop-bureaucrat uncle's department of bunglers: a gang of dunderheads trying to increase arrest quotas without getting hurt. The grind of HK police work bores Cynthia, who craves action.

In Japan, a couple of crooks—Nishiwaki (Michiko) and Nakamura (Stuart Ong)—are raising funds for their Japanese Red Brigade arms-gathering activities by knocking off a gala gem exhibition. They kill a few people, including a Japanese cop named Ken, whose partner (Hiroshi Fujioka) vows revenge on the ultrafashionable (dark suits and shades) crime duo. Fujioka looks like a Japanese anime character grafted onto Columbo. He resigns his commission and follows the villainous pair to HK—they're pursuing the

Action-jammed poster for *ITLOD3*.

foppish jewelry maker Yamamoto (Yueh Hua) to punish him for foisting fake gems on them in the arranged robbery.

Fujioka's task is complicated by the buttheaded cops, who handcuff him to a Volkswagen bumper while fake-gem-guy Yamamoto gets a fistful of real bullets from Michiko's Uzi. The VW bumper comes off (but the cuffs remain) as the Japanese cop pursues Nakamura to a shipyard. There they duel furiously with pick axes, lead pipes, pieces of ship, furniture, and flesh-chunkin' gaffs.

Nakamura is set afire but is bandaged by paramedics, only to be stolen directly out of the ambulance by Nishiwaki and her HK accomplice.

Nakamura then gets shot a whole bunch of times by the pursuing HK cops. He vengefully urges Michiko to extract blood, slips out of the getaway vehicle, and is promptly pulped under Cynthia's wheels.

Fortunately, revenge is unrestricted by gender in the Hong Kong cinema, as the smoldering Japanese ex-terrorist obsessively snaps the slide on her .45 automatic, murmuring "I must kill that policewoman." The result is an end-battle (conducted in industrial warehouse ambience) pitting the desperate Khan against the cucumber-cool, sledgehammer-swinging Nishiwaki—a hatred in her heart which only fire can cleanse.

In the Line of Duty 4
(皇家師姐IV直擊證人)
1989 | Starring Cynthia Khan, Donnie Yen Chi-tan, Yuen Yat Chor, Michael Wong Man-tak, Michael Woods, Lisa Chiao Chiao, Dick Liu Kai-chi, John Salvitti, Stephen Berwick
Directed by Yuen Woo Ping

The fast and furious fourth installment of the *ITLOD* series is about raw aggression, extended brawling, and fantasy-fantastic stunts. The unwitting protagonist here is a Seattle dockworker named Luk Wan Ting (played by Yuen Yat Chor). Luk has just become a resident alien after seven years of illegal status in the US and wants to live his simple existence as another hardworking overseas-Chinese-regular-guy. But like Cary Grant in *North by Northwest*, he's caught in someone else's dangerous web of deceptions.

Khan appears as a Hong Kong policewoman, helping American law enforcement officers (Yen and Wong) bust international dope dealers. Luk witnesses the bloody result of a deal-gone-bad, and is suspected of possessing a crucial

Yes the vehicle is moving: part of the ambulance sequence in *ITLOD4*.

film negative: a McGuffin that makes him a hot property for John Law and crooks alike.

Luk is collared by Donnie, but escapes from the Seattle cop shop by knocking out a protagonist and putting on his uniform. He's set upon again when returning to his apartment, and his buddy Ming (Dick Liu) is killed as Luk escapes. Trading his hard-won green card for ship's passage, Luk sadly sets off for Hong Kong—trailed by his growing entourage, who fly over on nice Cathay Pacific jets. There they pick up where they left off: hothead Donnie, cool-hearted Cynthia, and a legion of gwailo heavies scrap over Luk, who gets smashed, bashed, and occasionally shot over a negative he never had in the first place.

The *ITLOD* series is about fisticuffs and internal combustion device tarantellas, and we get plenty here. Cynthia fights while clinging to a hijacked ambulance; in the driver's seat, on the roof, hanging off the side, even pinned to the grille. Actress Khan reported repeated nightmares after filming the sequence.

Donnie Yen performs a dirt-bike jousting match with musclebound Michael Woods, using axes and shovels in place of lances—Donnie stops chasing him only when his bike comes apart in pieces. There's some goofy spoofing of Hollywood martial arts styles as well.

Magnificent Warriors (中華戰士)
1986 | Starring Michelle Yeoh Chu-kheng, Richard Ng, Derek Yee Tung-shing, Lowell Lo, Chindy Lau
Directed by David Chung Chi-man

Big budget adventure pictures like *Raiders of the Lost Ark* dominated the eighties, and this Michelle Yeoh vehicle is no exception. Like *Raiders*, it's the 1930s and the khaki-fascists are up to their usual plans of world domination. Since this is a Hong Kong movie, the bad apples are the occupying forces of Imperial Japan (the title characters translate as "Chinese Warriors").

Michelle is a barnstormer-in-a-bomber-jacket flying a biplane and supporting the Chinese resistance in a Himalayan kingdom. Michelle's cohorts are a handsome resistance leader (Derek Yee), the kingdom's ruler (Lowell Lo), and a shoehorn-faced rogue and hustler (Richard Ng). Despite leaning toward collaboration and self-interest, all eventually prove their mettle.

The Japanese villains are as cartoonish in their evildoing as our heroes are in their heroism; but no matter, we're here to watch the daredevil action. In addition to her de rigeur whip-wielding, Michelle performs rope tricks with a length of quarter-inch hemp. Jeeps, bi-planes, motorbikes, and belt-fed tommy-guns all get their bearings lubed. A huge, fiery fight culminates with four blazing stuntmen leaping out of an exploding-with-incendiaries jeep.

The thirties rough-fashion look and style of *Magnificent Warriors* is up to the *Raiders* standard, even if the film's budget wouldn't pay for Spielberg's catering. The obligatory end-battle features battlement scaling and

Wielding the whip: Michelle Yeoh stars in *Magnificent Warriors*.

catapulting (shades of *Beau Geste*), and even a John Williams-style theme which you'll be tired of by movie's end. The outfoxed Japanese slink off (to Manchuria?) and all our heroes live to fight another day.

Royal Warriors
aka *In the Line of Duty* (皇家戰士)
1986 | Starring Michelle Yeoh Chu-kheng, Michael Wong Man-tak, Hiroyuki "Henry" Sanada, Michael Chan Wai-man, David Lam Wai, Kam Hing-yin, Pai Ying
Directed by David Chung Chi-man

Another excellent D&B action vehicle for

Michelle Yeoh. A notorious Hong Kong criminal is extradited from Tokyo's Narita Airport. En route, an accomplice engineers an aircraft takeover with smuggled weapons, and the pair—Tiger (Michael Chan) and Cockerel (Kam Hing-yin)—wipe out the accompanying cops.

But a trio of undercover cops are also on the plane: Michelle, Michael Wong, and Yamamoto (Hiroyuki Sanada). They thwart the takeover, killing both crooks in the process. One blows out a plane window, but Michelle quickly stuffs him into the rectangular porthole, patching the hole and restoring cabin pressure.

Back in Hong Kong, Yamamoto is trying to patch up things with his wife and infant daughter. His workaholism has been straining domestic matters and he wants a better quality-of-life balance. Needless to say, being a cop in a Hong Kong movie (even a Japanese one), this is a bad omen.

Tiger and Cockerel have an accomplice—Raging Bull (David Lam) This brigand wasn't part of the air crew, and isn't pleased that the escape-plan was foiled and his co-conspirators killed. So he wires a bomb to the underside of Yamamoto's car.

Of course, it's Yamamoto's wife who fires up the ignition. The grief-stricken Yamamoto chases Raging Bull to a construction site, but the crook jumps on a bulldozer and starts burying our hero with gravel. Michelle arrives and kicks the bad guy off the dozer, but he escapes as she's rescuing the half-buried Yamamoto.

Vengeance on his mind, Yamamoto visits the local arms merchants and picks up a .44 magnum, then sets up a meeting with Michelle at a trendy nightclub, hoping to lure the creep. But the bad guy shows up packing an 9mm open-bolt slug-wrench and—spitting sparks and spewing chunks—shoots up the club, aerating most of the patrons. Amid the acres of broken glass,

Michelle punches the living dust outta Bandana in *Royal Warriors*.

Yamamoto gets his final-shot revenge.

But there's no shortage of crooks in this flick, and Bandana (veteran actor Pai Ying) comes out of the woodwork bent on revenge. Michael finds him out, but Bandana shoots him in both ankles, then suspends him from Energy Plaza in Tsimshatsui, twenty stories up. Michael plummets to his death, but even then he's not allowed to rest in peace—Bandana digs up his coffin and suspends it from a crane in a booby-trapped gravel quarry.

Yamamoto attacks but is neutralized rapidly. It's up to Michelle (who rides into the fray in a heavily-armored Volkswagen Bug) to slug it out with Bandana to rescue their comrade's mortal remains. Wild!

Satin Steel (重金屬)
1994 | Starring Jade Leung, Anita Lee Yuen-weh, Russell Wong, Kenneth Chan Kai-tai
Directed by Tony Leung Siu-hung

Hong Kong filmmakers are notorious for reshaping Hollywood movies, often swallowing an idea whole and spitting out something wholly different. In the case of *Satin Steel*, the movie on the carving block is Richard Donner's buddy-

NAIL-POLISHED FISTS

Jade Leung and Anita Lee: policewomen in disguise: *Satin Steel.*

buddy *Lethal Weapon*. How do you rehab that slab of ham?

Make the cops women.

The role of the unbalanced, suicidal Mel Gibson partner falls to feisty Jade Leung, who first left a trail of broken hearts and heads in *Black Cat*. Jade plays Inspector Jade Leung, whose wedding night passion is curtailed by thugs who shoot her new husband dead. Rather than sit around grieving, she opts for undercover work—Jade, it turns out, has a death wish.

She helps set up a sting operation to buy handguns, but when she flashes her cop ID, the seller panics and threatens her with a grenade. An opportunity to explode delights Jade, who obligingly pulls the pin for him. The terrified crook capitulates, earning police accolades for Jade, and a new assignment: tracking down Mr Fowler—an "American Mafia leader" selling weaponry in southeast Asia.

In Singapore, Jade teams up with Inspector Ellen Cheng (Anita Lee), whose wimpy boyfriend Paul (Kenneth Chan) constantly whines over Ellen's hazardous police job. Jade wonders what a tough cookie like Inspector Cheng is doing with such a milquetoast—Ellen says that since men are scarce in Singapore, you gotta take what you can get. The two make the best of the clingy, spineless Paul by whacking him on the head and flinging the odd cockroach in his mouth.

Efforts to capture Fowler in Singapore are fruitless, but the duo track him to Indonesia, where Jade falls for his handsome lawyer Ken (Russell Wong). Ken is forthright, and when Jade tells him that his client's as rotten as a barrel of sun-baked Borneo cuttlefish, he plans to resign. She convinces him to double-cross Fowler, and seduces him in the bargain. The chemistry between Jade and Russell is white-hot, and it's nice to see a Hong Kong action heroine so unabashedly sensual. But when she says: "Promise me you won't die before me," you know it's a promise he can't keep.

A well-choreographed fight ensues, with a bunch of creepazoid masked witch-doctors slicing hanks of hair from Jade's head as she dodges their slashing steel. The shamans are invulnerable to knives, but fortunately, Jade's packing steel. The revenge-minded policewoman pursues Fowler by grabbing onto the skid of the helicopter he's flying. And, in an only-in-Hong-Kong-stunt, you see closeups and medium-shots of Leung clinging to the skid as the helicopter flies along, dragging her through the water. Yeouch!

She Shoots Straight (皇家女將)

1990 | Starring Joyce Godenzi, Carina Lau Ka-ling, Tony Leung Kar-fai, Yuen Wah, Agnes Aurelio, Sammo Hung Kam-bo, Tang Pik-wan
Directed by Corey Yuen-kwai

SSS opens with the wedding of policewoman Mina Kao (Joyce Godenzi). Mina's husband, Tsung-pao (Tony Leung Kar-fai) is also a cop. On Mina's next assignment, she foils an attempted

MORE SEX, BETTER ZEN, FASTER BULLETS

Thai poster for *She Shoots Straight*.

abduction at a fashion show, jumping atop cars and commandeering dirt-bikes in the process. Mina's athletic bravery earns her a medal, but Tsung-pao's sister Ling is unhappy. It seems that Tsung-pao is the only male heir in his family, which carries a grave responsibility in patriarchal Chinese society. Everyone else in the family (Ling included) are policewomen, and they're concerned that Mina's success will cause the only Jack in this Jill-hierarchy to lose face.

When the law gets wind of a plot to rob the swank New World nightclub, they enlist the policewomen as undercover nightclub hostesses. Their nemesis, though, is capable and ruthless Vietnamese dissident Yuen Hua (Yuen Wah) and his gang, who cut the power and use night-vision goggles to assault the darkened nightclub. The attack is repelled by Mina and her troops, who kill one of the Viet men. The remaining gangsters flee the scene, swearing revenge on our heroines.

They get it by luring Mina, the feisty Ling and Tsung-pao to the edge of a forest, which they've prepared with Cong-style boobytraps: nets, bamboo spears, flying nooses. To their horror, Tsung-pao is pierced with a veritable forest of sharpened bamboo, and dies in front of his wife and sister. Their misery is compounded when they then must attend a celebratory banquet with the rest of the family, pretending that nothing's wrong. They choke back tears as others praise Tsung-pao and speak fondly of the future. Only when Tsung-pao's mother (Tang Pik-Wan) sees the news of his death on the television do they crumble, but, as a group, tearfully swear revenge. This melodramatic yet powerful sequence—raw with an emotion rarely seen in "feminist" cinema—lends a sharp edge to the resultant fracas.

Mina and Ling track the Vietnamese to a hideout aboard a ship and thrash them soundly with chains, machetes, and .357 magnum slugs. But the final confrontation comes when Yuen's girlfriend (Yuen Ying, played by Filipina powerlifter Agnes Aurelio) snatches him from under the cops' noses. Mina pursues them on a police motorcycle and cancels his contract, pissing off Yuen Ying, who whips off her coat and displays a physique honed by hours of ironwork.

As each has killed the other's mate, their duel is savage and unsentimental. The Vietnamese strongwoman hurls Mina sideways like a whirligig and boots her in the crotch. But Mina responds with a right hook to the jaw (repeated like Jake LaMotta's in *Raging Bull*), then kicks the muscle-queen in the chest, forcing her into submission. Mina then tosses the defeated Yuen Ying like a rag doll onto the back of the police bike and rides off.

Angel

1987 | The original GWG (Girls With Guns) flick, which helped launch the careers of Moon Lee and Yukari Oshima, not to mention inspiring about a dozen other flicks with "Angel" somewhere in the title. A straight-ahead action picture with Moon as a policewoman trying to bust pan-Asian crime syndicates. Producer/director Teresa Woo throws in plenty of fists 'n' guns, uses hunkcake Hideki Saijo (the Japanese Bryan Ferry) to good effect, and casts Yukari Oshima as a sadistic villainness.

Angel 2

1988 | Director Teresa Woo brings back Moon Lee and Elaine Lui as badass policewomen in search of a good kick. A vacation to Malaysia turns sour when Elaine falls for a local guy, Peter. Unfortunately, Peter has become a Hitler freak and is assembling a jungle paramilitary brigade for the purposes of world domination. These delicate personal matters can only be solved by the liberal application of gunpowder.

Black Cat 2: Assassination of President Yeltsin

1992 | Jade Leung reprises her role as technologically-tweaked carnage-goddess Erica—aka *Black Cat*. Tinkering with the microchip implant in her head has given her a Terminator-like visual display. She attempts to thwart the dreaded AYO (Anti-Yeltsin Organization), which is trying to kill Russia's "Fearless Liter."

When her CIA employers discover that AYO goons are shooting up with performance-enhancing radioactive isotopes, they inject the same into Erica so she can detect decay from the rotten guys. The techno-enhanced Black Cat rushes into a shopping mall and gets the wrong vibe from a grandmotherly type. She hauls out a blued-steel .44 Magnum Desert Eagle automatic and blasts the granny right between the eyes, splattering blood on a horrified mall-clown.

Performance-enhanced anti-Yeltsinite in disguise? No, a real grandmother after radiation treatment for cancer! Despite this goof, they send Black Cat to Moscow to track down those pesky Nyetskis.

Cynthia Rothrock WILL punch your lights out.

Blonde Fury

1988 | Cynthia Rothrock—Pennsylvania's most furious blonde—uncovers corruption in the HK legal system and takes it out on various creeps with a variety of weapons, including a deadly one from her own spike heel. The end-fight is great, with Rothrock battling fellow gwailo Jeff Falcon on a complex, weblike rope structure. But the real "blonde fury" in this movie is Cynthia's hair, which keeps changing length between shots.

Dreaming the Reality

1991 | Moon Lee and Yukari Oshima are raised as trained killers by the ruthless Mr Fox (Eddie Ko). Rather than forming a support group, they go on to a brilliant career in their field, until a business trip to Thailand leads to a bout of amnesia for Moon. She's adopted by the feisty, beer-chugging, cig-huffing Sister Lan (Sibelle Hu) and her brother Rocky—an ambitious young kickboxer. She recovers her memory, but in the meantime Fox has sent his henchman Scorpion to track down and eliminate his girls, whose loyalty he now doubts.

Moon and Sister Lan must make a stand against Fox and his men, booby-trapping a forest compound and blazing away with various bangsticks. They reject Fox's ruthless code and leave him crippled yet alive; the worst of all fates for a HK film villain.

Kickboxer's Tears

1993 | A Hong Kong kickboxer—Ken Lo—fails to survive a vicious match. He's avenged by his sister (Moon Lee) who seeks a rematch with Billy Chow, the boxer who killed him. Despite Chow's cheating tactic (rubbing irritating oil on his gloves), she breaks his spine, crippling him. His criminal boss smirks; the boxer was carrying on an affair with the boss' wife (Yukari Oshima). Oshima is not pleased, and demands a death match with Moon. Although this ferocious grudge duel is not the film's culmination, it's definitely the highlight of Kickboxer's Tears; Moon/Yukari freaks will not be disappointed.

Mission of Justice

1992 | Shot-in-Thailand actioner featuring Moon and Yukari busting up a drug syndicate. The jungle locations are fun, and the requisite number of kicks to the head and auto-emptied full-metal-jacket magazines aren't left out. Best of all, Carrie Ng appears as a dominant policewoman, strutting about in fetching paramilitary garb, ordering boy-cop flunkies around like the spineless worms they are.

Princess Madam

1989 | Buddy film about the adventures of two policewomen (Moon Lee and butch-styled Sharon Yeung) popping caps on bad guys. Males in this film are ineffectual pantywaists who must be protected or shot by our tough heroines.

When Moon kills the husband of villainess Michiko Nishiwaki in a botched assassination attempt, the Japanese woman stalks, seduces and torments Moon's wimpy husband. "I'm scared stiff of you!" he shouts into the phone, as he rubs the bite marks Michiko embedded in his shoulders. On the other end of the line, she smolders in front of a poster of a snarling cat, throwing darts at a photo of Moon.

Michiko kidnaps the couple and ties the policewoman—spread-eagled—five feet off the ground. Moon watches helplessly as Michiko administers more painful bites and busts liquor bottles against her husband's knees. "Do you have the guts to fight with me?" shouts Moon. "I don't have the mood," replies Nishiwaki.

Dames. Who can figure 'em? Many rounds later, justice triumphs.

Mad and bad Michiko Nishiwaki burns hot 9mm through her micro-Uzi.

Stone Age Warriors

1990 | Jungle hijinks with Nina Li, Elaine Lui, and Louis Fan (star of *The Story of Ricky*) adventuring in Indonesia. Best thing about this cracked actioner is the outtakes which roll under the closing credits. Seeing what HK directors expect their talent to undergo is scarier than any hopping-vampire picture. Watch as lovely Nina Li is first menaced by a quick and agile two-meter Komodo dragon, then dragged insensible out of a raging river! See Elaine "Angel" Lui freak out for real when covered with huge jet-black scorpions, and spit out an enormous glob of chewed-up banana mush! Eccch!

Story of a Gun

1991 | Gun-running flick with Philip Ko as the big boss and Gordon Liu as a copper trying to bust the ring, aided by gwailo policewoman Sophia Crawford. Mark Cheng and Yukari Oshima play a couple on the other side of the law—just trying to make a buck pushing blued steel. During shooting, Crawford attempted a hazardous stunt and broke her foot. Thus she was limping during subsequent action scenes, so the thoughtful filmmakers changed the script so her character is shot in the leg.

Widow Warriors

1989 | As even a casual viewer of HK films knows, turning the men into worm food just makes the women that much crankier. This is certainly the case with *Widow Warriors*. Elizabeth Lee and Tien Niu (not noted for their martial abilities) team up with Kara Hui and Michiko Nishiwaki (who are). A bleak and violent look at survival in the male-dominated triad world.

Yes Madam!

1986 | The screen debut of Michelle Yeoh, directed by Corey Yuen. *YM!*'s most memorable sequence is a large-scale fight where Yeoh and Cynthia Rothrock exchange hand-slaps before engaging in battle (at cinema-viewings, this awesome bit of business ALWAYS brings massive cheers and war-whoops). During the fight, Michelle swings upside-down and goes face-first

Michelle Yeoh shows off her pole-fighting skills in this deleted scene from *Yes Madam!*

through a pane of stunt-glass. "Before the stunt, no one wanted to talk to me," she told Stefan in a 1997 interview. "After I'd done it, all the stuntboys came up to me and said I was fabulous, really brave...turns out that type of glass, if you hit it wrong, can cut you. I didn't know!"

Yeoh went on to international fame starring opposite Pierce Brosnan as James Bond in *Tomorrow Never Dies* (1997) and toplining with Chow Yun-fat and Zhang Ziyi in Ang Lee's *Crouching Tiger, Hidden Dragon* (2000).

Hex Errors: Good Question

More fractured English subtitles from your favorite Hong Kong movies. (See page 30 for a full explanation.)

"What's a kid-corpse, grandpa?"
Hello Dracular

"You're a bad guy, where's your library card?"
Enforcing the Law

"You're a deranged snooper or what?"
Queen of Temple Street

"Gun wounds again?"
Rich and Famous

"A red moon? Why don't you say blue buttocks?"
The Holy Virgin versus the Evil Dead

"Miss, shall we make it?"
Ghostly Vixen

"Guns! You think I'm meaning puppy?"
Madam City Hunter

"You cheat ghosts to eat tofu?"
The Ultimate Vampire"

How can a bullet be breathless!?"
Saviour of the Soul

"No ripping off? How about jerking."
Queen of Temple Street

"Oh, are they chewing gums or my hearing's wrong?"
City Hunter

"Creep, bet if I'll burst your head with one shot?"
Robotrix

"Don't you feel the stink smell?"
Operation Pink Squad 2

"You circumcised me because of my cold. Now my appendix because of my headache?"
Doctor Vampire

"Can the few of you blow up the hanging coffins?"
Bury Me High

Tsui Hark and Leslie Cheung on the set of *A Better Tomorrow*, 1986.

CHAPTER TEN
TSUI HARK

Producer/director Tsui Hark (pronounced "choy hok") is one of modern Hong Kong cinema's guiding lights. Tsui was born in Vietnam and moved to HK as a teenager, but relocated to the University of Texas to study film. After graduating, he spent time in New York before returning to HK.

Zu: Warriors from the Magic Mountain (1983) was the first film to showcase the fantastic, madly paced Tsui Hark "look and feel." But when Tsui began to have creative conflicts with *Zu*'s parent company, Golden Harvest, he was inspired to create his own production company, Film Workshop. FW was designed to nurture young filmmakers and give them an outlet for expression, a task it has accomplished quite well.

After *Zu*, Tsui went on to produce John Woo's *A Better Tomorrow* (1986), and Tony Ching Siu-tung's *A Chinese Ghost Story* (1987), two of the seminal Hong Kong films of the mid-eighties. After Tsui produced Woo's *The Killer* (1989), Woo went ahead and formed his own production company. Tsui's *Once Upon A Time In China* series, which re-introduced Wong Fei-hong to modern audiences, proved popular.

Tsui, a bit of a workaholic, becomes deeply involved with everything he produces. Hark's preferred directors in the 80s/90s included Tony Ching Siu-tung and Raymond Lee.

The Blade (刀)
1995 | Starring Vincent Zhao Wen Zhou, Xiong Xin-xin, Moses Chan, Song Lei, Austin Wai Tin-chi, Valerie Chow Kar-ling
Directed by Tsui Hark

Hark himself takes the helm to remodel (not remake) Chang Cheh's 1967 classic *One-Armed Swordsman*. Chang's seminal film heralded chivalry in the face of adversity (Wang Yu gets his arm chopped off early in the flick but comes back to lop off everything from everyone who did him wrong).

Hark's film (titled by a single Chinese character which means knife/blade/sword) is about savage reprisal in a feral world where dismemberment seems part of the natural order. The martial artistic styling dovetails with Wong Kar-wai's *Ashes of Time* (1994)—it's fast, furious and often surreal. Tsui being Tsui, he stomps on the accelerator pedal any time he feels like it.

Ting On (Vincent Zhao) and Iron Head (Moses Chan) are swordsmiths at a boutique sword-making school and both these men—along with their burly colleagues—are devoted to their sifu, but suddenly the ace swordsmaker interrupts the

Movie-painting for *OUATIC 2*, Ho Chi Minh City, Viet Nam (Photo: Stefan Hammond, 1993).

Hungarian poster for *The Blade*.

Xiong Xin-xin terrifies in *The Blade*.

sweaty crew to announce he's quitting. Ting On becomes the new boss, not everyone's happy.

Antagonist Flying Dragon (Xiong Xin-xin) arrives in town to collect the bounty (if *The Blade* were a spaghetti western, this guy would be Lee Van Cleef with a Motörhead tattoo). Flying Dragon advertises his bad-assery with skin-ink that extends to his face, and no one (possibly even him) knows how many blades he's carrying. They're all sharp and he knows how to pose, but more importantly, he knows how to swordfight. He's the sort of sociopath who doesn't know or care how many men he's killed—one of them was Ting On's father.

Meanwhile, Ting On gets into a scrap with a bunch of baddies. In one of this film's intoxicating assault sequences—this one involving walls of bamboo stalks—his sword is broken and his arm is severed.

Ting On doesn't take these setbacks well. He rigs a rope to swirl from and practices attacking with the broken blade in his one remaining arm, trying and failing again and again as rain turns the ground to mud. He collapses screaming like an injured dog. He gets back up and tries again.

Persistence, revenge, and fantastic swordplay mark this as a martial arts film. But the hyperstylized bladed-weaponplay seems more like a shrapnel barrage—steel sings as it flies around the air. A cult favorite among fans of wuxia (swordplay) films.

Dragon Inn (新龍門客棧)

1992 | Starring Brigitte Lin Chin-hsia, Maggie Cheung Man-yuk, Tony Leung Kar-fai, Donnie Yen Chi-tan, Xiong Xin-xin, Lawrence Ng Kai-wah, Elvis Tsui Kam-kong
Directed By Raymond Lee Wai-man

Tony Leung Kar-fai as Chow Wai-on: *Dragon Inn*.

Dragon Inn, a clever reworking of director King Hu's 1967 film, *Dragon Gate Inn*, takes the basic premise and deepens its approach to character, while seizing on the story's opportunities for swashbuckling swordplay.

The titular hostelry is an isolated guesthouse in the middle of a vast desert. Business is brisk for the inn's crafty female owner, Jade (Maggie Cheung), who lures horny bandits up to her room with the promise of sexual favors.

But before they can even undress, they're dead meat. Not one to waste a business opportunity go to, Jade sends the warm corpses down to the basement, where her cook uses them to prepare the inn's specialty dish: "spicy meat buns."

The inn's remote locale makes it a natural rendezvous point, so government official Chow Wai-on (Tony Leung Kar-fai) and his swordswoman lover, Yau Mo-yin (Brigitte Lin, disguised as a man)

MORE SEX, BETTER ZEN, FASTER BULLETS

Desert isolation: *Dragon Inn*.

Movie-painting of Joey Wong as White Snake, on a cinema in Northeastern Thailand (photo: Stefan Hammond, 1993).

meet there. A nasty eunuch (Donnie Yen) also descends on the inn, underlings in tow, intent on wiping out Chow and Yau.

But the killers don't know what they look like. With both sides confined to the inn due to a storm, a game of cat-and-mouse ensues, with Jade ping-ponging between the two factions.

The climactic duel occurs amidst a sandstorm that nearly buries its participants, and in the end the villainous eunuch gets his comeuppance when an arm and a leg are carved to the bone: TKO!

Green Snake (青蛇)
1993 | Starring Joey Wong Jo-yin, Maggie Cheung Man-yuk, Wu Hsin-kuo, Vincent Zhao Wen Zhou
Directed by Tsui Hark

Tsui's film is based on one of China's famous legends: *Madam White Snake* (made into several films in the 1950s and 60s). It's an intriguing scenario of shape-shifting: two female snakes have achieved the power to assume human form after centuries of training, and enjoy mingling with the bipeds.

Of the two snakes who aspire to womanhood, elder sister White (Joey Wong) is the more accomplished mimic—her training lasted ten centuries. Kid sister Green (Maggie Cheung) is irrepressibly curious about humans, like a teenybopper anxious for her first date.

But Green's been practicing for only five centuries, so she tends to drop horizontal scoot around corners searching for juicy bugs. Sometimes she lacks concentration and her legs revert back to a snake's tail.

The two creatures live in a ghostly mansion on the edge of town, slithering in to observe human behavior when the mood strikes. White is devoted to the idea of living out her life as a human—she seduces, then marries, a nerdy scholar named Hsui Xien (Wu Hsin Kuo).

The inquisitive Green tags along with the couple, anxious to discover why her sister is so attracted to the idea of being human. The romance between White and Hsui Xien is mostly shown in flashy montage, depriving the voyeuristic viewer of any reptilophiliac shots of lovely Joey Wong's scaly skin or quivering rattles.

The sisters' nemesis is a self-righteous monk (Vincent Zhao) who gets bent out of shape at the idea of snakes mating with human beings. The uptight monk tries to tell the scholar that his beautiful new bride is actually a monster, but Hsui Xien's not interested.

Green spars lustfully with the pious prelate,

Joey Wong and Maggie Cheung bathe their human forms in *Green Snake*.

teasing him mercilessly. Jealously flares when—out of curiosity—Green tries to seduce White's husband, but the serpentine sisters unite to do spectacular battle with the irked monk.

Green Snake boasts a diverse musical score which incorporates everything from Hindi-inspired rockin' pop to New Age ether. The film's main drawback is a series of not-quite-there special effects at odds with the seamless fantastic landscape of film as a whole. Viewers entranced with the undulating groove of Hark's big, bad Snake won't be too bothered.

Once Upon a Time in China
(黃飛鴻)
1991 | Starring: Jet Li, Rosamund Kwan Chi-lam, Jacky Cheung Hok-yau, Yuen Biao, Kent Cheng Jut-si
Directed By Tsui Hark

Tsui Hark's *Once Upon A Time In China* was one of those rare productions that sparks latent interest in a perennial favorite, then transforms it into an instant franchise. It quickly spawned four sequels, a prequel, numerous imitations and was parodied in several comedies. Yet, *OUATIC* is not the first movie to chronicle the adventures of Wong Fei-hong—a legendary martial artist from the Ching Dynasty of the late nineteenth century. WFH was a real person whose story has become part of HK's cultural folklore.

Tsui Hark's most significant contribution was the casting of Jet Li as Wong Fei-hong. Li, a Beijing native and youthful martial artist, achieved fame in a series of early 1980s *Shaolin Temple* movies. Jet's infectious grin and dazzling martial arts skills made him an excellent choice to revive the legend. Although Jet Li has moved on to fame with a variety of other roles—including the WFH-like folk hero Fong Sai-yuk—most of his fans associate him most closely with the virtuous Wong.

OUATIC has WFH running an herbal clinic with his associates Porky (Kent Cheng) and Buck Tooth Sol (Jacky Cheung). Yuen Biao plays Wong's sidekick Leung Fu and Rosamund Kwan plays his Aunt Yee. Like all WFH movies, *OUATIC* chronicles Wong's battles with corrupt local officials and the encroaching effects of Western civilization on China.

As with its sequels, *OUATIC* is imbued with a strong anti-European sentiment. British, French and American troops have invaded China, and are portrayed as foolish, self-righteous imperialists who impose themselves, their beliefs and their technology upon the Chinese without any regard

Jet Li and Rosamund Kwan need an action-plan in *Once Upon A Time In China*.

for how it will affect their native culture.

In spite of this, there's a strong Christian theme running through the film. The one gwailo who comes to the aid of Wong and his men is an American priest. A young admirer of Wong's plays Judas by joining forces with "Iron Robe" Yim, a nearly invincible character who has sworn to defeat Wong. In a take-off on David and Goliath, Wong flicks a bullet at an evil American with his finger, striking him in the forehead and killing him.

The action is so furious that it's sometimes too fast to follow, even in slow motion. As with most martial arts films, fighting is the first order of the day. The fights scenes are always imaginative. In one, Jet Li, armed only with an umbrella, defeats a dozen opponents. He uses the umbrella in every conceivable way: tripping people with the hook, stabbing them with the point, and opening the umbrella to evade projectiles. it's like a cross between *Enter the Dragon* and *Singin' in the Rain*. The final duel between Wong and Yim has the two foes fighting atop ladders, bouncing off the walls and dodging swinging cargo flats. Of course, Wong Fei-hong emerges victorious, ready for any possible sequels.

OUATIC won Best Original Film Score, Best Action Choreography and Best Film Editing at the Hong Kong Film Awards, while Tsui Hark was awarded the Best Director prize.

Once Upon a Time in China is on the Hong Kong Film Archive's list of "Best 100 Chinese Motion Pictures."

— Jim Morton

Peking Opera Blues (刀馬旦)
1986 | Starring: Cherie Chung Chor-hung, Brigitte Lin Chin-hsia, Sally Yeh Chian-wen, Mark Cheng Ho-nam, Kenneth Tsang Kong, Wu Ma, Ku Feng
Directed by Tsui Hark

Cherie Chung and Sally Yeh in opera drag, Brigitte Lin in military getup: *Peking Opera Blues*.

For many fans, *Peking Opera Blues* was the first taste of the explosive, kinetic experience known as "new wave" Hong Kong cinema. *POB*'s combination of high flying acrobatics, excruciating torture scenes, and unabashed heroism by powerful female characters is like watching an old-school martial arts movie through a kaleidoscope.

It's 1913, and competing warlords jockey with foreign governments for power in the newly established Republic of China. Corrupt General Tun (Huang Ha) chooses to recoup his gambling losses by neglecting to pay his troops, so he's run out of town. His replacement, General Tsao (Kenneth Tsang), signs a covert document with a cabal of foreigners and secretes it in a wall-safe. Unfortunately for Tsao, his daughter Wan (Brigitte Lin) is a dedicated revolutionary who sports a manly haircut to go with her military regalia and conceals her idealism from her father.

Wan's cohorts are diverse. Pat Neil (Sally Yeh) is a backstagehand at her father's Peking Opera theater—she yearns to perform but is stymied by the tradition of men to portraying female roles. Sheung Hung (Cherie Chung) is a servant chasing after a stolen jewelry box, although her materialism gradually melts away in the heat of more substantial concerns. This trio of unlikely women unites to protect their nascent republic not only from renegade officers and sneaky foreigners, but the local officials—a gang known cryptically as the "Ticketing Office."

Throughout *POB*'s running time (best described as "120-compressed-into-90"), identities are mistaken, genders rent and bent, and the laws of gravity constantly amended. Action sequences are masterfully choreographed, but so are slapstick comedy routines, and together they create a giddy spectacle.

Swordsman 2
(笑傲江湖2東方不敗)
1992 | Starring Brigitte Lin Chin-hsia, Jet Li, Rosamund Kwan Chi-lam, Michelle Reis (Lee Kar-yan), Lau Shin, Fennie Yuen Kit-ying, Waise Lee Chi-hung
Directed by Tony Ching Siu-tung

Swordsman 2 gleefully pours a twisty plot into a sprawling, brawling spectacle of delirious swordplay. *S2*'s densely packed frames riot with exploding bodies, antagonists torn apart by whips, swords, huge bifurcated hooks, and other exotic weapons. Those with solid knowledge of Chinese history and martial arts philosophies might try to follow the breakneck plot; all others, just let 'er rip.

The opening scene finds the protagonist, "Asia the Invincible" (Brigitte Lin) wrenching the head off a powerful opponent. For a fierce, macho warrior, AtI is surprisingly feminine. Although we don't discover the details until later, it turns out that AtI has learned from the Sacred Scroll that the way to achieve supreme power is to

Lau Shin wields nasty chains in *Swordsman 2*.

supernaturally castrate oneself. To elevate his shadowy Sun Moon Sect to supreme power, he has made that oh-so-personal sacrifice; he's slowly transforming into a woman as his power increases.

We then meet the beautiful tomboy Kiddo (Michelle Reis) and the carefree drunkard Ling (Jet Li)—two martial arts students from the Wah Mountain school. The pair meet up with their fellow students (who have names like Smart Ass and Scum Bag) so they can go into seclusion as a group, retiring from martial arts. Kiddo has a crush on Ling, and tries constantly to doll herself up so he'll notice her, but she's better at handling a sword than a jar of rouge.

The hedonistic Ling thinks only of AtI's niece, Highlander girl Ying (Rosamund Kwan). Ying's father Wu (Lau Shin) is the Highlander Sect's proper leader, but he's been imprisoned by his ambitious brother-slowly-turning-into-a-sister—AtI.

While Ying and her assistant Blue Phoenix (Fennie Yuen) wait in their Highland lodge for Ling to show up, they are attacked by one of the Japanese martial arts clans hiding out in this part of China. The ninja assassins hurl live scorpions through the windows and fly in on rotating blades. Blue Phoenix plays a flute which calls forth bushel baskets of venomous snakes, but Ying's guards

MORE SEX, BETTER ZEN, FASTER BULLETS

Brigitte Lin preps her needle fu in *Swordsman 2*.

are slaughtered and Ying and Blue Phoenix are forced to flee.

Ling goes searching for besieged Ying, but finds AtI instead, bathing in a lake. Although her appearance is female, her voice hasn't changed yet, so she communicates with sweet smiles alone. She can still drink prodigiously, however, and the wine gourd she proffers causes Ling to spin hysterically out of the water with delight. He's smitten.

Ling attacks AtI's encampment singlehandedly, but is overpowered and tossed in a dungeon. Fellow inmate Wu has been rendered powerless by enormous hooks through his shoulders. Ling and Wu escape; freed of the hooks, Wu regains his strength by sucking the life force out of the jailers with his Essence Absorbing Stance.

The time in jail seems to have taken a toll on Wu, who has become obsessed with dreams of bloody revenge. AtI distracts Ling by disguising her faithful girlfriend as herself and sending her to seduce Ling in a darkened room, then slaughters all Ling's Wah Mountain brothers except Kiddo.

In the final confrontation, Ying, Kiddo, Ling, and Wu attack AtI, who, thoroughly feminized by now, fights them off with sewing-needle kung fu. The evil woman is eventually defeated by Ling, but as the film ends, Wu—now clearly over the edge—has taken up the bloody trail where AtI left off.

Swordsman 2 is on the Hong Kong Film Archive's list of "Best 100 Chinese Motion Pictures."
— Andy Klein

The Wicked City (妖獸都市)
1992 | Starring Leon Lai Ming, Jacky Cheung Hok-yau, Michelle Reis (Lee Kar-yan), Tatsuya Nakadai, Roy Cheung Yiu-yeung, Yuen Woo Ping, Carman Lee Yeuk-tung
Directed by Peter Mak Kit-tai

Another translation of Japanese anime to live action cinema, *The Wicked City* is visually abrasive sci-fi monster melodrama.

The story opens on the eve of 1997, with Hong Kong in chaos due to an influx of otherworldly immigrants who have wreaked havoc with the city's economic system and energy supply. Known as "rapters", these shapeshifting aliens have infiltrated earth's society by assuming human guise.

Beauties: Carman Lee (with pistol), Michelle Reis (without)...

...and the beast: *The Wicked City*.

The government creates an anti-rapter force to track down and eliminate the aliens. In the movie's Japan-based opening sequence, anti-rapter Taki (Leon Lai) lures a prostitute up to his hotel room and exposes her as a rapter. He then witnesses her mutate into a murderous insect woman. Taki's half-human/half-rapter partner, Ken Kai (Jacky Cheung), arrives in the nick of time to decapitate the wicked beast.

Back in Hong Kong, a powerful corporate head named Daishu (played by Japanese actor Tatsuya Nakadai) arrives for a gala birthday celebration, unaware that the anti-rapter force has caught on to his alien background and plan to expose his identity. Taki is sent to infiltrate the rapter celebration but is stopped dead in his tracks by the sight of Daishu's ravishing girlfriend Windy (Michelle Reis). Windy is a former flame whom Taki coldly abandoned years ago, rather than face the prospect of making a commitment. Meanwhile, Daishu's birthday bash turns ugly as a fellow rapter accuses him of disseminating a deadly street drug called "Happiness" which is destroying the rapter community. But Daishu is actually a pacifist seeking to foster peaceful relations with humans. It's his son Shudo (Roy Cheung) who is facilitating his own takeover plans by secretly distributing the drug.

The Wicked City cuts loose with an unending series of increasingly bizarre special effects-laden sequences. This is gaudy visual spectacle at its inventive best (and sometimes at its inanely campy worst). *TWC*'s memorably surrealistic moments include a flying killer-clock and a woman who can transform into a pinball machine, an elevator, or a motorcycle.

A Better Tomorrow 3: Love and Death in Saigon

1989 | Despite the title and the starring presence of Chow Yun-fat, this is not a John Woo film. This is a Tsui Hark-directed romantic actioner which serves as a "prequel" to the first *ABT*, depicting the adventures of Mark (Chow Yun-fat) in Vietnam. He goes to Saigon to meet his pal Mun (Tony Leung Kar-fai), who's getting out of prison. These guys fancy themselves arms dealers, but need the connections of cool-as-ice Kit (not *ABT*'s Leslie Cheung, but Anita Mui), who's got an upcoming transaction with corrupt General Bong.

A big deal turns sour and it's Kit who does the slo-mo double-fisted slug-pumping, while Mark fumbles with an M-16. Tsui—always fond of powerful and competent female characters—includes a scene of Kit teaching Mark how to shoot accurately!

Mun, Mark, and Mun's elderly father leave war-torn Saigon for HK and start a auto repair garage. Kit has fallen for Mark and follows them to HK, but things get complicated when Kit's former lover, a ruthless gangster named Ho (Tokito Saburo) takes umbrage and delivers a flower-bomb to the garage, killing Mun's father. Amid many plot twists and turns, he takes Kit back to 'Nam, forcing M&M to return to Saigon for revenge on

Movie-painting for *A Better Tomorrow 3* featuring Chow and co-star and Saburo Tokito, Shinjuku, Tokyo (Photo: Stefan Hammond, 1990).

An enormous painting advertises *The East Is Red* on the side of the Rex Theatre in Penang, Malaysia, as a street vendor prepares snacks for movie-goers. (Photo: Stefan Hammond, 1993).

Ho. But they must dodge the vicious Bong, who chases our heroes around in a tank.

The East is Red aka Swordsman 3

1993 | Supposedly the sequel to *Swordsman 2*, but mostly an opportunity to resurrect the fascinating character of "Asia the Invincible" (Brigitte Lin)—a powerful martial artist who castrated himself to attain the full mystical force of the Sacred Scroll, transforming himself into a woman in the process. Lin's multifaceted performance fuses macho swagger with feminine mystique, combining the antics of a spoiled child with the destructive force of a vengeful god.

TEIR chronicles AtI's search for her identity amidst a landscape beset by political turmoil in which Japanese and Spanish invaders do battle against Chinese warships. Nothing is quite what it seems: an armor-clad Japanese general is exposed by AtI as a midget ninja, while AtI's former lover Snow (Joey Wong) dresses in masculine garb and is herself attacked by a disguised Japanese nemesis.

During lulls in the fighting—which include a barrage of gravity-defying martial arts, as well as levitating warships, jet powered boots, lethal needles and threads, and ninjas flying through the sky like kites of prey—AtI beds down with Snow in a sensual quasi-lesbian scene (note: the actresses are both female, but as AtI is actually a male who ceded his male essence to ascend in martial arts prowess, it's actually a hetero scene…yeah, we're confused too). The sexual personae implode when the frustrated AtI batters the masochistically faithful Snow to near-death, realizing all too late that her redemption lies within the purity of Snow's unwavering love.

I Love Maria aka Roboforce

1988 | The Hero Gang, led by a ruthless cyborg called Saviour (Ben Lam) and his vicious girlfriend Maria (Sally Yeh), attempt to take over Hong Kong using a gigantic robot called Pioneer I. They are foiled by a trio of inept losers: Whiskey (Tsui Hark), Curly (John Shum), and a clumsy journalist (Tony Leung Chiu-wai). Cyborg Saviour feels that flesh is imperfect and that only machines are worthwhile since they have the potential to live forever.

To prove his love for Maria, he builds a robot version of her called Pioneer II. When that robot is destroyed, Curly—the original inventor—fixes it and sends it into battle with the monstrous

Pioneer I. Whiskey longs for the real Maria and has trouble accepting the fact that she is trying to kill him—even after an amazing outdoors chase scene, with the evil Hero Gang swinging through the trees on cables in pursuit of Whiskey, who is swinging on vines and yelling like Tarzan.

Saviour recalls the mad robot-monger Rotwang from *Metropolis*, and the Maria robot owes a nod to *Metropolis* Maria, but the film has more in common with goofy fare like *Inframan* than Fritz Lang's classic.

Once Upon A Time In China 2

1991 | *OUATIC2* is just as entertaining as its predecessor. Max Mok takes over for Yuen Biao as Wong Fey Hong's showoff sidekick Leung Fu, Rosie Kwan continues as Aunt Yee; and Jet Li returns as Wong Fei-hong. The fanatically xenophobic White Lotus Sect, led by the apparently supernatural Master Kung, is urging the local citizenry to kill all foreign devils.

At the same time, a noble revolutionary movement (led by Dr. Sun Yat-sen) has sprung up hoping to replace the Chinese empire with a republic. When Wong's entourage arrives in Canton for an East/West medical conference, Aunt Yee is injured by White Lotus adherents who spot her western garb and mistake her for a foreigner. Luckily, a kind stranger steps in to translate; he turns out to be Sun Yat-sen.

Wong wows the gwailos at the medical conference with his acupuncture technique, but the White Lotus gang attacks again, burning down the Foreign Language School and massacring the teachers. When Regional Commander Lan (Donnie Yen) refuses to shelter the now-homeless kids, Wong takes them to the British Consulate, where he joins forces with Sun Yat-Sen and his revolutionary comrade Luke (David Chiang).

Japanese poster for *Once Upon A Time In China 2*.

Eventually, Wong and Luke find themselves at the White Lotus Temple, where Wong duels with Master Kung atop a teetering array of precariously balanced chairs, and exposes him as a fraud. But it's not over yet, fight fans, there's still the villainous Lan to be dealt with!

Once Upon a Time in China 3

1992 | Tsui Hark's third Wong Fei-hong epic concentrates heavily on the martial art of lion-dancing. The notion that both East and West have to learn to adapt to each other's cultures is emphasized even more in Part 3, and the socio-political overtones are downplayed. The Empress Dowager decides to hold a Lion Dance competition to cause friction between the various foreign nationalities settling in China. Unfortunately, it causes greater strife among various Chinese factions! As Wong Fei-hong travels to Beijing (Peking) to visit his father Wong Kei-ying, dad spars with his enemy, the evil Chiu Tin Bai who is determined to take the prize.

Yee (now Wong's fiancée) meets Tomansky, a Russian who has been infatuated with her since they went to school together. He gives her one of those newfangled motion-picture cameras, making Wong furiously jealous. After he calms down, Wong does a martial arts demonstration for the camera, while Fu barks out orders through a megaphone. Later, the camera accidentally records footage that fingers Tomansky as a spy involved in a plot to assassinate the Dowager's President Li at the Lion Dance contest.

Chiu's men try to defeat Wong by pouring oil on the floor, throwing off his carefully honed balance (the bad guys are wearing cleats). Wong prevails, however, and enters the Lion Dance Competition in order to win the crown, defeat Chiu, frustrate the Russian assassination, produce more film evidence against the Russians, and lecture President Li on how his policies are dividing the country.

Naming Conventions

Nothing, and we mean nothing, caused us as many problems in cataloguing and reviewing these films as the names of the actors and actresses. Chinese names don't translate easily into English. Chinese names sound different in Cantonese than they do in Mandarin. Sometimes people change their names. It's confusing, complicated and frustrating.

Take Joey Wong Jo-yin (*A Chinese Ghost Story*, *Green Snake*, etc.) as an example. "Joey Wong"—as she's often listed—is an Anglicization of her Chinese name: Wong Jo Yin. "Wong" is the family name, which traditionally comes first, because a person's family name is considered more important than their personal name. Using the Western convention, "Wong" would appear last, while "Jo-yin" is (very roughly) her first name. So far, so good.

But we have seen this same actress also listed as Joi Wong, Wang Chu Hsien, Joey Wang, Aemy Wong, Wang Zu Xian and Wong Tso Hsien. This confusion is due to attempts to reproduce the sound of spoken Cantonese or Mandarin using English characters.

Some players adopt an English first name for just this reason. Brigitte Lin Chin-hsia is easily recognized as "Brigitte Lin" by her English-speaking fans. But we don't know why Michelle Reis is also known as Lee Kar-yan, or why Loletta Lee changed her English name to Rachel.

What we do know is that we've picked one name per person, and tried to use it throughout the book. We list the full name in a movie's credits, then use the shorter English version during the review. So please don't send e-mail saying that "Leslie Cheung Kwok-wing" should be listed as "Leslie Cheung Kuo-hweng"—we know.

Game of the Name

Gwailo Hong Kong movie fans scream with frustration at the complexity of the Chinese language. The "official" spoken language, known as Mandarin or Putonghua, is a tonal language with four distinct tones which vary the meaning of the syllables. Cantonese—or Guangdonghua—is the other major dialect, though there are hundreds more. Cantonese originated in Canton (Guangdong) Province and is the lingua franca of Hong Kong, and thus Hong Kong movies.

Cantonese has six tones that impart meaning to its rounded syllables. No, it has nine tones.

Wait a minute, more than nine. Often, native speakers can't agree on how many tones there are in Cantonese. Also, the slangier bits of spoken Cantonese can't be written down in any form. Needless to say, such an anomalous form of oral communication is learned by rote and is prone to a head-thwacking array of homonym-based puns.

The bright side to this Sisyphean task is the joy and delight of discovering tiny nuggets of meaning. A slang phrase mastered possesses much amusement value on the street. "No problem" and "I don't understand" are invaluable little weapons, as are "excuse me" and "I can't speak Cantonese".

The Art of Cursing

At one point in *Once Upon A Time in Triad Society 2*, actor Cheung Tat-ming delivers these furious lines: "Bastard, I tell you. If you stop me from seeing my wife before her death, I will cut you into 19 pieces to feed the worms under her corpse." These powerful words cause his opponent to step aside, and as Cheung passes him, he murmurs: "I don't know I can speak foul language so fluently".

Clearly, the use of Cantonese to hurl invective far surpasses any subtitle. Enjoying the wacky subtitles is our bonus, but we know the native-speaking audience is on a higher entertainment plane altogether. Our hats are off to these masters of oratory, even though we can barely guess at what they're saying.

Nomenclature

Anyone writing about Hong Kong movies in English has a problem: The names of film personnel and the titles of movies are all in Chinese. Although systems for romanizing Chinese terms exist, there are flaws. The best the writer can achieve is consistency.

For example, take the actress Wu Chien-lien. Her family name is Wu (it appears frontside). Ms Wu is from Taiwan, and the romanization is based on the Mandarin pronunciation of her name (Mandarin is widely used in Taiwan). But Wu is known to her Hong Kong fans as Ng Sin-lin, Ng (pronounced as a truncated "m" sound which can't really be reproduced on paper) being the Cantonese pronunciation. "Wu" is easier for non-Chinese speakers to deal with than "Ng", which is why a well known director named Ng Yu-sum long ago chose the name "John Woo" as his nom de filme. Are we having fun yet?

Most performers have adopted an English name, which makes things blissfully easier. But not all English names are usable or accurate. Some sources list Wu Chien-lien as "Jacqueline", but she denies any English name whatsoever, and there you have it. Many of the pivotal figures in Hong Kong film just don't have an English name

Once Upon A Time in Triad Society 2

and non-Chinese-speaking fans have to deal with it the best they can. Sometimes, life is just a beautifully lit sparkling-clean bowl of delectable cherry-red cherries and sometimes it isn't.

For the purposes of this book, English names are used wherever possible. Chinese names appear when no English name is available and when English names are confusing (there are two actors and one stunt coordinator named Tony Leung, for example). A tip for afflictionados: learn to recognize "last-name" characters—which come first when reading left-to-right. Once you can tell the Lees from the Leungs, it gets easier.

Hex Errors: Curses & Insults

More fractured English subtitles from your favorite Hong Kong movies. (See page 30 for a full explanation.)

"Noodles? Forget it! Try my fist!"
Final Victory

"Take my advice, or I'll spank you without pants."
The Seventh Curse

"Crash your tits!"
It's Now or Never

"Beat him out of recognizable shape!"
Police Story Part 2

"Damn you, stink man!"
Caged Beauties

"Well! Masturbate in hell!"
Full Contact

"Bastard, even 2 centuries in jail are too short!"
City Hunter

"Beware! Your bones are going to be disconnected."
Saviour of the Soul

DVD cover for international release: *Wicked City* (1992).

"Crazy nut, put up another nasty show?"
Iron Monkey

"Get out, you smurk"
Aloha Little Vampire Story

"You won't die in one piece"
Eastern Condors

"Damn, I'll burn you into a BBQ chicken!"
Pedicab Driver

"I'll cut your fats out, don't you believe it?"
It's Now or Never

"You bastard, try this melon!"
Gunmen

"Your dad is an iron worder, your mom sells beans."
Legend of the Liquid Sword

Jackie ready to assault the squatter village in this screengrab from Police Story.

CHAPTER ELEVEN
THE CHAN CANON

"Trying to describe a Jackie Chan film is like trying to describe a dream. Descriptions bog down in accounts of 'this happened' and 'that happened,' until you can't be sure if your mind is adding details, making logical connections in place of more elliptical ones.

"There's almost a tendency to want to file Chan's films away under the category of each picture's big stunt, if only to make his talent more comprehensible. But then another Chan film comes out, and he's at it again, somehow beyond language—too fast, too perfect and too full of nuance to be nailed down by words or memory."
— Mick LaSalle, *San Francisco Chronicle*

orn in 1954, Jackie grew up as the ward of a school for Peking Opera, where he was rigorously instructed in acrobatics. He performed publicly as a member of a school troupe called "The Seven Little Fortunes" (see chapter 16 for the film work of other 7LF members, which include Sammo Hung, Yuen Biao, Yuen Wah, and Corey Yuen—in keeping

with tradition, students would adopt the name Yuen as tribute to their sifu).

Jackie began his film career in the early 70s touted as "the new Bruce Lee," but his spirit is closer to that of silent film comedians Harold Lloyd or Buster Keaton—actors who performed hazardous stunts for a laugh. What Jackie Chan went on to create was a distinct brand of martial slapstick highlighted with film stunts of masochistic intensity.

It's comedy pushed to the point of pain. Jackie falls twenty feet and hits the ground. Jackie jumps into a bed of hot coals. Jackie hangs dangling from a flying helicopter or hot air balloon.

The stunts have turned Jackie into a one-man legend, and most of it's true. Yes, he was almost killed on the set of *Armour of God*—a stunt went wrong, Jackie was brained by a rock and went into a coma. Yes, he has a plate in his skull. Yes, superstar Maggie Cheung got seventeen stitches in her head filming *Police Story 2*. Yes, his stuntpeople threw superstar Brigitte Lin through huge panes of sugar-glass in *Police Story*.

One Jackie trademark: montages of stunt mishaps over the closing credits—you'll see him laugh over mistakes, or mug over slight injury. But when he gets this real serious look—holding a broken finger or the back of his head—and you see him bleed, you understand that for all the joking and fun of a Jackie Chan movie, this is not Industrial Light and Magic and a bunch of green screens and computerized legerdemain, but real flesh-and-bone filmmaking.

After achieving Asian fame through straightforward kung fu movies, Jackie went to Hollywood in the early eighties and cranked out some forgettable stuff before returning to Hong Kong. Chan's *Police Story* (1985) is one of the seminal Hong Kong films, redefining him and the industry at one go (it's also on the Hong Kong Film Archive's list of "Best 100 Chinese Motion Pictures"). In the mid- to late-eighties, Jackie Chan starred in, produced, and sometimes directed a handful of films which remain transcendent masterpieces of stunts, physical comedy and derring-do, often co-starring his Peking Opera schoolmates Yuen Biao, Yuen Wah, and Sammo Hung (see "Yuen, Sammo, Yuen" chapter).

At the MTV Movie Awards in 1995, at age 40, Jackie became only the third person ever presented with a Lifetime Achievement Award. Accepting the award, Chan said "I'm honored but surprised because I'm still so young. I have a long way to go yet." He's also the second ethnic Chinese actor to have a star on the Hollywood Walk of Fame, after Bruce Lee.

In 2016, Chan received an an honorary Academy Award at the Eighth Annual Governors Awards in Los Angeles. "[It's] a chance for the Academy to recognize unique achievements across an artist's whole body of work, because Jackie Chan, the man who puts the 'Chan' in 'Chan-tastic,' has worked mostly in martial arts films and action comedies, two genres that have been, for some reason, shall we say, historically underrepresented at the Oscars," said actor Tom Hanks while presenting the award. "Great acting comes in many different forms, but if you are an actor you always know it when you see it. Jackie Chan's films have been incredibly serious, sometimes gruesomely so, as well as incredibly hilarious."

This chapter covers Jackie's 1980s and 90s Hong Kong output—you won't find reviews of *Fearless Hyena* (1979) or *Rush Hour* (1998) here. You will however find reviews from some HKFOGs (David Chute, Dave Kehr, Andy Klein, Wade Major)

THE CHAN CANON

Jackie's unlikely adversaries prepare to charge in this screengrab from *Armour of God*.

sprinkled throughout. And some never-before-published photos taken by stuntman Jude Poyer on the set of *My Stunts* (1998).

For us, Jackie's bone-busting, glass-smashing, train-jumping antics of the 80s and 90s form the core of the Chan Canon.

Armour of God (龍兄虎弟)

1986 | Starring Jackie Chan, Alan Tam Wing-lun, Rosamund Kwan Chi-lam, Maria Delores Forner, Ken Boyle, Bozidar Smiljanic
Directed by Jackie Chan and Eric Tsang Chi-wai

Armour of God's main claim to fame is not its shameless appropriation of *Raiders of the Lost Ark*, nor that it's one of Jackie's highest-grossing films, or even the presence of 80s Cantopop superstar Alan Tam as Jackie's dopey sidekick. Nope, *Armour of God* is famous as the film that almost killed Jackie Chan.

A relatively innocuous stunt went awry and Jackie plummeted twenty feet to the ground, hit his head on a rock and went into a coma. But he returned to filming after a brief hospital visit.

Plate in Jackie's skull or not, *Armour of God*, which was filmed in the-then Yugoslavia, is a marvelous action-adventurer. Jackie plays a Robin Hood character named "Asian Hawk." His link with Alan Tam is explained with a schlocky Partridge Family-style rock video starring a group called "The Losers" (a play on Tam's popular 70s band "The Wynners"). One of the background singers, Laura (Rosie Kwan), comes between Jackie and Alan by dumping the former in favor of the latter. But when a group of hooded monks bust into a Paris fashion show and abduct Laura at AK-47-point, the two put their differences aside to rescue her.

The hooded figures belong to some sort of satanic Franciscan order which is determined to obtain God's Armour: an antique five-piece set which possesses special properties. They hold Laura for ransom hoping Alan and Jackie will

Hungarian poster for *Armour of God*.

deliver the three pieces they lack and bring their evil plan to fruition.

Our heroes convince wealthy European collector Count Bannon (Bozidar Smiljanic) to lend them the pieces, but they have to accept the aristocrat's beautiful daughter May (Maria Delores Forner) as their apprentice on the caper. Off roar the unlikely trio in Jackie's sportscar.

The funky monks are flushed out with a fake bag of God's Armour. Bullets rain from the battlements as Alan and Jackie fight with the friars. Despite her haughty, spoiled-rich-girl demeanor, May proves expert at providing suppressing fire—she was a European women's shooting champ.

But they're overwhelmed by a crowd of villains driving off-road vehicles and dirt-bikes, and beat a retreat in the sportscar. Wild car-and-bike stunts (choreographed by France's Remy Julien Action Team) end with a jump over a two-lane divided highway as traffic proceeds underneath them. The baddies still pursue, eventually trapping our heroes on a narrow suspension bridge. But the car transforms into a micro-racer—a sort of motorized skateboard—and they scoot out of harm's way.

Jackie and Alan then disguise themselves in robes and hitch to the hilltop monastery. They rescue Laura from the mad monks, but she's been drugged and programmed to return with hostage Alan and the armor. It's up to Jackie to rescue them, and this is where *AOG* starts to really shine.

In a fight with a hallful of monks, Jackie battles his opponents with a flaming ten-foot timber and uses long wooden tables as ramps and springboards. A face-off with the evil head monk (Ken Boyle, sporting odd eyebrows) brings out a quartet of eccentric assassins: high-heeled Amazons in slinky black dresses. A battle with these surreal opponents (in action, it's obvious that they're Jackie's stuntmen in drag) leaves Jackie on top, but he still has to dynamite his way out, with TNT strapped to his body. A leap onto a hot-air balloon completes the adventure, but stay tuned for the scary outtakes.

Armour of God 2: Operation Condor (飛鷹計劃)

1991 | Starring Jackie Chan, Carol Cheng Yu-ling, Eva Cobo Garcia, Shoko Ikeda, Aldo Sambrell
Directed by Jackie Chan

AOG's sequel came five years after the original. The film was shot in Barcelona and the Sahara Desert, and quickly went past schedule and over budget. But Jackie fans come out ahead, as many of the effects are spectacular—*AOG2:OC* eclipses the original in many respects.

Jackie plays another lost-Ark-raiding type named after a bird of prey: "Condor." As the film begins, he arouses the ire of some fierce tribesmen, and escapes by climbing into an enormous clear plastic inflatable ball and rolling down an almost-vertical hillside.

Jackie's next mission involves a trip to Spain, where he befriends a Japanese hippie-girl trinket-hawker (Shoko Ikeda). Summoned there by "the Baron," Jackie's given a UN-sponsored mission: liberate a stockpile of gold bars from a secret WWII Nazi desert base. He's also given an ornate key to the gold vault, and a partner who is an expert in desert travel, Ada (Carol Cheng).

WWII-Nazi-gold-seekers are everywhere, Jackie discovers when he goes to a locksmith to have the key checked out. As he leaves, a group of thugs accost him at gunpoint. When he escapes on a dirt-bike, a frenetic chase ensues.

Stuntmen are set up like pinball bumpers as choreographed cars and motorbikes slide around

Jackie relaxes with co-stars on the set of *Armour of God 2: Operation Condor*.

and crash through stacks of boxes—a giant-Lego village invaded by hurtling metal. Jackie finds time to save an imperiled baby in the frantic race toward the docks, where he drives off a pier, leaps off the bike and clings to a mid-air block of netted cargo as the pursuer's car fly past into the ocean.

Jackie and Ada head off to the desert, the suspected location of the gold hoard. They join forces with the Japanese hawker and her pet scorpion Ding-Dong, then fight off bandit slavers, as well as a pair of idiotic Arabs before finally locating the secret base.

But a wheelchair-bound Nazi named Adolf (Aldo Sambrell) has tracked them down, and they must fight a pitched battle against his band of mercenaries for control of the stacked gold bullion. The fight takes place in a secret underground gold dump filled with a wealth of equipment that doubles as a kung fu playground—girder jungle gyms and see-saws crawling with combatants.

The gold-sniffing mercenaries turn against Adolf and the final duel takes place in a wind tunnel, with a massive fan-turbine (controlled with wind-baffles by the now-on-our-side Adolf) blowing people around like rag dolls. What won't Jackie Chan utilize in his never-ending search for new cinematic thrills? Finally, the good guys are blown out of an air shaft by the fan and the bad guys (and gold) are simply blown up.

City Hunter (城市獵人)

1992 | Starring Jackie Chan, Joey Wong Jo-yin, Kumiko Gotoh, Chingmy Yau Suk-ching, Richard Norton, Gary Daniels, Leon Lai Ming, Ken Lo Hwei-kong, Michael Wong Man-tak
Directed by Wong Jing

There's a Japanese tilt to this fluffy, sprawling comedy, which is based on a manga featuring a rakish private eye named Ryu Saeba. Teen idol Kumiko Gotoh co-stars along with the lovely Joey Wong, who achieved fame in Japan thanks to the *Chinese Ghost Story* series.

The film recreates the comic-book style in live action, so you get ninety minutes of ridiculous sight gags and goony slapstick. Director Wong Jing is famous for his populist, goofball comedies, and *City Hunter* is similarly loaded with absurdities. Still, this is a Jackie Chan movie and action fans won't be disappointed.

The glossy opening sequence has Ryu's partner Makimura (a cameo by Michael Wong) expiring in a hail of bullets and making Ryu promise to care for his cousin Kaori. The girl grows up to become beautiful Joey Wong and the two become partners. They end up chasing after runaway teen Kiyoko (Kumiko Gotoh) aboard a luxury cruise ship bound for Japan. Also on board are a card shark with a deck of razor-edged aces (Leon Lai), sexy undercover cop Saeko (Chingmy Yau), and a passel of gwailo bandits that include Australian martial arts star Richard Norton and British wunderkind Gary Daniels.

Jackie plays the womanizing Ryu as a declawed tomcat, mugging over the occasional babe, while overtly lusting after a bowl of won ton noodles. But when the bad guys shoot the captain and take over the ship, *Die Hard*-style, Ryu's full attention turns to the crooks (who dress in natty red ninja getups).

Action is presented in a series of comic set-pieces. Ryu wanders into the ship's theater, which is showing the weird Bruce Lee versus the 7-foot 2-inch Kareem Abdul-Jabbar kung fu duel from *Game of Death*, then finds himself confronted

Movie-painting for *City Hunter* featuring Jackie and Kumiko Gotoh, Shinjuku, Tokyo (Photo: Stefan Hammond, 1992).

by an actual pair of real-life seven-foot black fighters. Taking cues from Bruce's onscreen actions, he vanquishes the giants.

In a powerfully twisted sequence, he gets thrown into a video game machine and emerges as a series of characters from Streetfighter 2. Ryu and his nemesis fight in speeded-up-and-tweaked sequences which resemble those from the video game (Jackie Chan as Kung Fu Sue spinning on her head—buff the mind's eyeball with that).

When he joins forces with Saeko, she spins around in Jackie's arms firing from twin thigh-holsters, and they finish with a brief, delirious dance routine. Finally, Ryu and Big Mac (Norton) go hand-to-hand—Mac with a couple of meter-long steel shafts that transform into sectioned whips, while Ryu duels with a pair of police batons and a pole filched from the ship's decimated decor. Triumph. Outtakes. Your ninety minutes are up. Add more coins for additional time.

Drunken Master 2 (醉拳2)
1994 | Starring Jackie Chan, Anita Mui Yim-fong, Ti Lung, Lau Kar-leung, Ho Sung-pak, Wong Yat-hwa, Ken Lo Hwei-kong
Directed by Liu Chia-liang (Lau Kar-leung)

THE CHAN CANON

Chinese martial arts manifest in many different styles. Some styles are based on the movement and nature of different wild animals, like the monkey, the crane, or the praying mantis. But one of the more eccentric techniques is based on the erratic movements of a sifu long adrift in Sot's Bay: the *Drunken Master*. The fingers hook into imaginary wine-cup supports and the face freezes with the determination of the terminally potted trying to stay upright, as the body sways violently.

Drunken Master style is highly effective, as Jackie Chan first demonstrated in 1978's *Drunken Master*. In *Drunken Master 2*, Jackie's character is folk hero Wong Fei-hong. Shaw Brothers' veteran Ti Lung (eight years older than Jackie) plays his father Wong Kei-ying while Anita Mui comically portrays his stepmother.

It's pre-WWI China, and Wong Fei-hong and his fellow student Tsao attempt to avoid paying duty by smuggling a valuable ginseng root through customs before boarding a train home. The contraband root gets switched with a valuable seal, the property of some rotten imperialist Brits. The mixup leads to a first meeting with Chinese loyalist General Fu (Lau Kar-leung) and a breathtaking spear-fight with Jackie in the cramped space under the train.

It turns out the Brits, along with a few collaborating Chinese, are smuggling curios out of the country and exploiting Chinese labor for profit besides. In round one, Fei-hong battles the evildoers and, reddened up with a smorgasbord of liquor, soundly thrashes them Drunken Style. Unfortunately, his enthusiasm (and likkered-up befuddlement) causes him to assault his own father.

Banished from the household, Fei-hong seeks solace in a bigger bottle at the local pub, where

Jackie with Ti Ling, screengrab: *Drunken Master 2*.

he becomes maudlin and ineffectual. The bruised bad guys track him down, tie him up, and leave him dangling—passed-out and naked—from the town square, with a sarcastic banner reading "King of Drunken Boxing." The disgraced Fei-hong tearfully swears off any more alcohol-fueled martial adventure benders.

But he doesn't need the booze—*DM2* provides a showcase for Jackie to demonstrate a wide range of on-the-wagon styles. A multi-level battle pits General Fu and Fei-hong against dozens of hatchet-wielding thugs. Fu spits oil on Fei-hong's buffed torso—purely for its cosmetic coolness—as the pair trash ruffians out of second floor windows and carry the day.

But when Fei-hong, white-robed and fan in hand, walks solemnly to face the turncoat BritSymps at the steel foundry, the audience is put at collective seat's edge. First, he and a second-tier toadie (Ho Sung-Pak) go at it literally hammer and tongs.

After the penultimate killer goes down in a faceful of flames, #1 Bad Dude Ah-jan (Ken Lo) leaves the on-deck circle. The tall and muscular Ah-jan—in impeccable 1913 EuroDress—raises one leg high above his head while he calmly removes his glasses. Then, still standing on one leg, he rains a barrage of kicks down with the other.

Fei-hong is backed up against an enormous bed of glowing coals, and even though you know what's coming, you still can't believe he's gonna do it. He does.

The gloves come off now and Wei-hong swigs a mouthful of industrial alcohol in order to spit fire at his adversary. He accidentally swallows the poisonous fluid, and gets a jolt of his old technique. Realizing it's do-or-die, he chug-a-lugs, enters a realm of ÜberDrunkenMaster hitherto unwitnessed, and thrashes Ah-jan into submission.

Fantasy Mission Force aka The Dragon Attack! (迷你特攻隊)

1983 | Starring Brigitte Lin Chin-hsia, Jackie Chan, Adam Cheng Siu-chau, Jimmy Wang Yu, Shin Bu Lia, Fang Jung, Sun Yueh, Chang Ling
Directed by Chu Yen Ping

Deranged and defaced Korean collage-poster for *Fantasy Mission Force*.

Fantasy Mission Force is utterly ridiculous—but never boring—in that special kind of psychotronic way. There's an admirably consistent tone of lunacy throughout: Jerry Lewis remakes *The Dirty Dozen* high on laughing gas.

Just a footnote in Jackie Chan's extraordinary career, *FMF* is notable for being the most bizarre film he ever appeared in. Chan is paired with female action great Chang Ling as a pair of bumbling thieves who intermittently weave in and out of this film's mad, mad, mad, mad narrative.

Brigitte Lin stars as Lily, the lone female member of an oddball commando squad. They've been promised big bucks by top mercenary Jimmy Wang Yu to rescue a multi-national group of generals (including "Abraham Lincoln") who've been taken hostage by the Japanese—who are in the process of invading Canada. Lily's gadabout husband, who looks like an Elvis-imitator imitator, is recruited for the squad, but she won't let him tomcat and tags along. Her weapon of choice is a slim-line bazooka, which she first uses to blow up her own home before setting out on the mission.

Our goofy band of misfit adventurers—accompanied by a soundtrack that runs from bagpipes to bluegrass to honky tonk piano in the space of a minute—are first captured by a village full of leopard skin-wearing Amazons under the command of a debonaire James Bond character (Adam Cheng). The Amazons kill Wang Yu on the fly, then humiliate our guys by making them wear sandwich boards painted with the bodies of provocative lingerie models.

Lily et al escape from, then detonate, the

Amazon village, only to spend the night in a haunted house fully stocked with cold ones. When one commando (Sun Yueh) answers the call of nature, the bathroom walls sprout rows of bloody arms, all offering him toilet paper.

We are treated to a wealth of inane costumes throughout. The crybaby commando wears a chrome-plated Prussian helmet. UN forces drill in kilts and blue tam-o-shanters. Bad guys wear Conquistador outfits.

When the fantasy mission force finally arrives at Japanese HQ, the enemy has all been slaughtered. Who's got those world leaders? Why, double-crossing Nazi Wang Yu, who faked his own death! His army of Road Warrior-style goons surf toward our force atop beswastika'ed 70s-era Detroit automobiles, firing automatic weapons as they approach.

As a sad harmonica version of "Camptown Races" plays, frantic gunfire drops our heroes one by one, until only Wang Yu and Jackie Chan remain alive. Their martial arts showdown amidst the old clunkers is good stuff (though Chan gets no help from the timid world leaders). Chan wins, gets the money, and all the Nazis and Japanese are dead. The end.

Mr Canton and Lady Rose
aka *Miracles* (奇蹟)

1990 | Starring Jackie Chan, Anita Mui Yim-fong, Richard Ng Yiu-hon, Bill Tung Biu, Gloria Yip Wan-yee, Wu Ma, Billy Lau Nam-kwong, Lo Lieh
Directed by Jackie Chan

In the mid-90s, longtime Jackie fans became disappointed by his offerings. Instead of accepting the physical limitations of his then forty-plus years, Chan seemed determined to punish himself for his fans. The stunts grew more painful and the trademark assembly of botched stunts and breakdowns at the end of his films grew longer, grislier, and harder to watch.

A grace went out of Chan's physical presentation—instead of the smoothly whirring windmill of gestures of earlier films, he seemed bent, off-centered, distracted. He showed grim determination where there once was nonchalance and joy. The stunts in films like *Supercop* (dangling from a helicopter flying over downtown Kuala Lumpur) or *Rumble in the Bronx* (being repeatedly rammed by a hovercraft) look more like tests of endurance than displays of skill. It's as if, in sensing the diminished agility and slowed reactions of middle age coming on, Chan decided that what he had to offer was the spectacle of his own suffering. The end-credit shots of Jackie being hustled off in ambulances seemed the final proof that he was willing to do anything to keep his audience's attention and preserve the loyalty of his fans.

Jackie is the great conformist among comic heroes. He's not a willed outsider like Chaplin or Keaton—who created characters poetically out of sync with their worlds—but a young man eager to fit in, to make good in a foreign environment (hence the frequent theme of Jackie as a country bumpkin freshly arrived in the big city, be it Hong Kong, New York or the Old West). He'll do whatever he can to be accepted, and it turns out that the talent most valued in his new environment is his gift for violence—a gift that, almost magically, he possesses in spite of his fundamentally gentle, boyish nature. Chan's comedy is a result of the wide gap that exists between his preternatural prowess as a martial artist and his unassuming, innocent demeanor. He's a bunny rabbit who bites like a Doberman.

As that skill diminished—even Jackie can't

defeat the ravages of time—his character was left with little but the dark underside of his talent: his ability to withstand pain. To win the hearts of the supporting characters in his films—the sweet young girls, the adoring little boys, the avuncular old men and, by extension, his huge international audience—Chan felt compelled to greater and greater risks, to absorb greater falls and more furious blows. Like Kafka's Hunger Artist, he's become the impresario of his own agony.

That it didn't have to be this way is the lesson of *Mr Canton and Lady Rose*, a 1990 film that has had even more export titles that usual for a Chan film, including *Miracles*, *Black Dragon*, *The Canton Godfather* and *Oiji*. MCALR reveals Chan as a director, actor and writer (he co-authored the script with Edward Tang) of fully integrated abilities. Basically a remake of Frank Capra's 1961 Pocketful of *Miracles* (itself a remake of Capra's 1933 *Lady for a Day*), it's a film that has received little distribution outside Asia. But in retrospect it seems the last great film of Chan's greatest period, the extraordinary eighties run that began with *Project A* and ended with *Operation Condor*.

Following the archetype, MCALR begins with Chan's character "Dragon" arriving in the Hong Kong of 1930 from somewhere deep in the hinterlands, rope-bound suitcase in hand. He impulsively buys a flower from an old lady (Gua Ah-lei), an act that sets off a chain of lucky events. Jackie's streak begins when he narrowly misses being run over by a speeding car, and ends when a dying gang leader appoints Jackie, a stranger who protected him, to be his replacement at the head of his syndicate. In a moment, Dragon's life is transformed.

This kind of miraculous, sudden success seems to have its parallel in Chan's own career: the discovery of his comic abilities in 1979's

Miracles, aka *Mr Canton and Lady Rose*.

Drunken Master instantly turned him into a star. As MCALR moves along, the parallel expands: following the advice of an older mentor, Dragon learns to play the part of the tough-guy crime chief, and is quickly accepted as boss by the gang members, but his real interests seem to lie in show-business. He turns the gang's tumble-down tea-room into a plush Art Deco nightclub, and hires singer Yang Luming (Anita Mui) to front a Busby Berkeley-style floor show.

It's Dragon's second transformation—from gangster to producer—that seems most to intrigue Chan-as-director. MCALR is itself a sumptuous, beautifully staged film that uses the widescreen format to create a distinctive sense of space, constructed around vast interior sets.

Using cranes and the Panaglide camera (one of the outtakes at the end of the film shows Chan operating the Panaglide rig himself), Chan creates a number of highly complex shot sequences—Wellesian flourishes that express nothing so much as an unbridled pleasure in the filmmaking process.

Dragon gets his second chance to create a theatrical spectacle when the aged flower seller, whose nickname is Lady Rose, learns that her long unseen daughter is coming for a visit. Rose has led the girl to believe that she is a rich widow (while actually sending every penny she earns to pay for the girl's education abroad), and doesn't want to shame her. Jackie and Anita come to the rescue, digging up a fabulous wardrobe for the old woman and installing her in a huge suite in Hong Kong's finest hotel. It's Dragon's finest act of mise-en-scene, even if the players feel obliged to drop their masks in the end.

MCALR is one of the few Chan films in which the action sequences are organically integrated into the plot. They actually advance the narrative (instead of suspending it for a martial arts interlude) by marking the stages of Dragon's development from naive outsider to assured leader. The final fight scene is an anthology piece in itself—a battle in a rope factory that turns into an aerial ballet, with the combatants flying, swinging, and catapulting through the cavernous set—but it also brings the plot to its moral climax. Instead of pummeling the rival gang chieftain who's caused all the trouble, Jackie gives him a symbolic pat on the cheek. He's put violence behind him, and is ready to move on to something new.

That "something new" is precisely the character comedy that MCALR explores in its non-action moments. As a comedian, Chan acts just as he fights, using his whole body. His lines are accompanied by a flurry of rapid hand gestures that make subtitles superfluous—every limb is in expressive movement, in a way that suggests the vigorous physical acting style of early film. There's no longer a discontinuity between the action scenes and the connective tissue that surrounds them, but a smooth relay of rhythm and sense. MCALR suggests that if the fighting were gradually to fade out, there would still be much Jackie Chan to take its place.

—Dave Kehr

My Lucky Stars (福星高照)

1985 | Starring Jackie Chan, Sammo Hung Kam-bo, Sibelle Hu Hui-ching, Michiko Nishiwaki, Richard Ng Yiu-hon, Lam Ching Ying, Eric Tsang Chi-wai, Yuen Biao, Dick Wei, Stanley Fung Sui-fan, Charlie Chin Chiang-lin
Directed by Sammo Hung Kam-bo

Shot partly in Japan, *My Lucky Stars* is primarily a comedy. It contains some remarkable action sequences, and marks the HK debut of Japanese crunch-princess Michiko Nishiwaki. Still, those who gnash their teeth at extended buddy-buddy gag sequences should be forewarned.

Jackie plays a cop known as "Skinny Monkey" in HK, but "Muscles" in Japan. He and Ricky (Yuen Biao) chase a pair of shady types out of a Japanese subway station. Pursuers and prey hop into vehicles and smush them together a bit.

Then it's off to the amusement park where ninja warriors in powder-blue suits mess with Muscles and Ricky. As Muscles is distracted by a shutterbug couple, the bad guys lure Ricky into the funhouse and kidnap him. The crook they're chasing turns out to be a "rotten apple" HK cop (Lam Ching Ying) who absconded to Japan with $100 million in contraband diamonds, and is allied with a criminal syndicate called the "Scarecrow Club."

Muscles calls his boss in HK, Inspector Tsao (Walter Tso), and requests backup. Tsao heads to the local prison, frees greasy thief Kidstuff (Sammo Hung), and gives him the job. Kidstuff rounds up his orphanage buddies: Roundhead (Eric Tsang), Rawhide (Stanley Fung), and Herb (Charlie Chin). Then, with undercover cop Miss Woo (Sibelle Hu) in tow, it's off to the land of ramen and Hello Kitty.

Once in Japan, the buddy-jokes start to pile up; the gang orders lunch by pantomime and Roundhead tries to get a sausage by surreptitiously displaying a part of his anatomy to the waiter. The bemused but polite waiter brings him a plate with…a single tiny mushroom.

This as about as funny as it gets, but Jackie starts mixing it up. He disguises himself as a huge-headed mascot and enters the amusement park's funhouse, only to find that the exhibits are genuinely lethal.

My Lucky Stars kicks into gear as Jackie fights his way through the surreal funhouse into the Scarecrow Club's headquarters. He squares off against the fierce Dick Wei as Sammo takes on some nasty joker with an eyepatch.

The money duel: Miss Woo faces off against Nishiwaki, who's wearing a kimono. She sheds the Japanese dress, displaying a brick pagoda physique which earns her a heartfelt aiyah! from the audience. Former powerlifting-champion Nishiwaki executes a few posedown moves before bruising up the HK policewoman and tossing her through a shoji screen.

Woo raises up on one elbow and says to Sammo; "She's tough," before collapsing. Sammo admires another posedown, then KO's the Japanese woman with a single punch!

Crunch-princess Michiko Nishiwaki prepares to whup ass in *My Lucky Stars*.

Police Story (警察故事)

1985 | Starring Jackie Chan, Brigitte Lin Chin-hsia, Maggie Cheung Man-yuk, Bill Tung Biu, Kenneth Tong, Chu Yuan, Charles Chao
Directed by Jackie Chan

In everyone's lifetime, there are specific instances of stimuli imprinting themselves upon the brain with napalm certainty, burrowing into conscious and subconscious simultaneous. Sometimes they're instantaneous "flashbulb" memories, sometimes sensory-interwoven slow-burn wonders: sweat and tears commingling at the birth of a child, diesel fumes and the ping of shrapnel as the helicopter plummets, the Ramones stuffing "I Don't Wanna Walk Around With You" into your earhole live in 1977. Things like that.

Certain films are famed as one-shot conversion experiences—you walk away with your Hong Kong Film Brain-Tattoo. Jackie Chan's *Police Story* (1985) qualifies. It doesn't matter how many action films you've seen—the last ten minutes of this film will put you on the damn floor.

This ability to body-slam the audience is

THE CHAN CANON

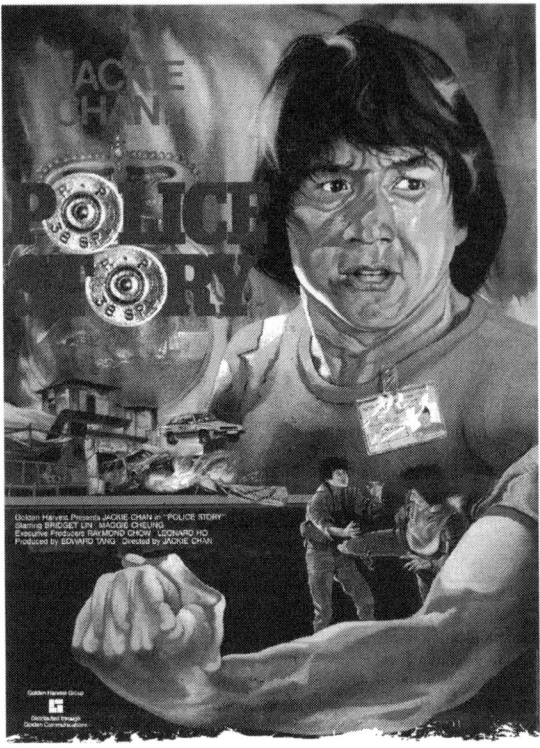

From the master of action comes more screen excitement than you've ever seen.

Police Story's trademark, but the film has much else to recommend it. This was Jackie Chan's riposte to his Hollywood flirtations of the eighties. Many of the police procedurals which helped popularize Hong Kong films around this time owe stylistic debts to *Police Story*. Chan's extensive involvement with the film include roles as director, stunt coordinator, and star.

The stunt where Jackie slides down a light pole and crashes through glass canopies is invariably included in his stunt-reel. Although it's a hell of a note, and it's repeated three times in succession, it's only one of several world-class stunts in *Police Story*. In the opening sequence, automobiles chase one another through a purpose-built squatter village, ripping corrugated tin shacks asunder and setting off explosions as they battle their way down a hillside so steep and bump-strewn that the cars are often on the verge of flipping front-over-tail into the mayhem.

Then there's the scene where JC goes asphalt-skiing from a hijacked double-decker bus careening through traffic—the stunt ends when the bus stops abruptly in front of stock-still Jackie and two stuntmen self-eject through the upper-deck windows, only to crash onto the road below. They were supposed to land on the specially padded car directly behind Jackie, but the bus didn't impart enough inertia.

And then there's the shopping mall end-battle, a nonstop bacchanal of destruction which shatters so many giant panes of stunt-glass that Jackie's stuntmen called the production "Glass Story." They throw Jackie's head through glass. They throw Brigitte Lin through glass. They drive a racing motorcycle through a huge glass case with Jackie astride it...and he's not even on its seat.

Chan plays Ka Kui, a righteous cop keen to bust rich pig scumbag gangster Chu (Chua Lam). In the opening scene—which culminates in the downhill destructo-chase—Ka Kui and his compatriots are setting up the bust. There's no corning or mugging—these guys are professionals under pressure and things are tense. As all hell breaks loose, one pisses his pants in terror. The scumbag escapes, but Jackie collars his bus single-handedly and brings him in.

But the villain gets off scot-free thanks to his slick, amoral lawyer. Injustice sets up the mechanism of revenge which winds Ka Kui up like a watch spring.

This film, true to its mid-eighties milieu, contains comedic sequences—Jackie has a series of cakes jammed in his face, Jackie scrapes poop off his shoes, Jackie juggles four phone conversations on four separate phones while rolling around in a chair. But its central theme of revenge against the corrupt forces of Hong Kong society is as raw today as it was thirty-plus years ago. And this was the second of Jackie's films to include his now-famous outtakes under the closing credits.

Police Story proved that Jackie could bring his style of martial arts wizardry to a contemporary setting and still achieve commercial and artistic success. *Police Story* won the Hong Kong Film Award for Best Picture in 1985, and spun a pair of sequels.

Police Story is on the Hong Kong Film Archive's list of "Best 100 Chinese Motion Pictures."

Police Story 3: Supercop
(警察故事3超級警察)
1992 | Starring Jackie Chan, Michelle Yeoh Chu-kheng, Maggie Cheung Man-yuk, Yuen Wah, Kenneth Tsang Kong
Directed by Stanley Tong

Jackie with prop: *Police Story 3: Supercop*.

Most Jackie films in the early nineties represented changes of pace. On the outs with Sammo and clearly concerned about the new box-office threats of Wong Jing and Stephen Chow, Jackie abandoned directing and worked with a series of different directors. The result is a strange grab-bag of flawed projects and experiments that ranged from the manic *City Hunter* (1992) to the somber *Crime Story* (1993).

Supercop (also known as *Police Story 3*) was Chan's first collaboration with director Stanley Tong. Their subsequent efforts—*Rumble in the Bronx* (1995) and *First Strike* (1996)—were clearly made with an increasing eye to the American market. For many Chan devotees, this represents a turning away from what made them love the star's work in the first place; and few would count either as among his very best. But *Supercop*—the third of Jackie's *Police Story* series about Hong Kong cop Chan Ka Kui—deserves a place on any Jackie Top Ten list.

Supercop was a change of pace from the extraordinary string of Chan films directed by either Sammo Hung or Jackie himself, from *Project A* (1983) through *Armour of God 2: Operation Condor* (1991).

While Jackie had years earlier given up on the American market, it's easy to imagine that Tong, getting his first huge break on *Supercop*, already had his eye on Hollywood. He would later fulfill that ambition with *Rumble* and, eventually, the

Sammo Hung TV series *Martial Law*. But, when one revisits the film itself, the only arguable "Americanization" is the reliance on explosions and big action at the expense of the more contained, tightly choreographed fight scenes that stud Jackie's greatest films, and the shift seems more a natural extension of the earlier *Police Story* and *Armour of God* movies than a break with tradition.

What made the film fresh was the casting of Michelle Yeoh. It is axiomatic that (in contrast to a Hong Kong industry where women are often active, ass-kicking protagonists) a female lead in a Jackie Chan film is always "the girl"—that is, someone for Jackie to rescue. Even when "the girl" is not a shrieking ninny, she is still not physically competent to survive without Jackie's intervention.

Yeoh, coming back from a career hiatus, managed to match Jackie in all areas. If she didn't actually upstage him, she came mighty close, and this is probably why Jackie hasn't had a similar female lead since. Because Yeoh and Tong were old friends—they had worked together on *Magnificent Warriors* (1986)—they conspired to make sure her stunt scenes weren't completely overshadowed by Jackie's.

According to Yeoh: "Stanley and I would hype each other up. 'Yes! Yes!' he would say. 'You're gonna be on the bike and you're gonna jump onto the train, because Jackie's going to be on the helicopter!' And I'm going, 'I wanna do the helicopter one!' And he'd say, 'Wait a minute! If you do the helicopter, what's Jackie going to do? You have to do the motorcycle!' And I'd say, 'Great! By the way, I don't know how to ride one!' 'That's OK! You'll learn that later!'"

The result was a productive sense of tension between the two stars, even though the characters they play are allies rather than opponents.

The final product (in its original Hong Kong version) is an extraordinarily paced nonstop ride. Audiences can get fidgety waiting for that first fight, which doesn't occur until nearly twenty minutes into the film. But, from then on, except for some brief, first-rate bits of comedy, there's little letup for the remaining seventy-five minutes—fight at the police academy, escape from prison, comic homecoming, restaurant fight, boat chase, scuffle at the evil druglord's house, super shootout at the criminal's convention in rural Thailand, comic confrontation with Jackie's girlfriend (Maggie Cheung), and then the final fifteen-minute capper, involving cars, vans, a helicopter, a dirt bike, and a train.

— Andy Klein

Project A (A計劃)

1983 | Starring Jackie Chan, Sammo Hung Kam-bo, Yuen Biao, Dick Wei, Winnie Wong Man-ying, Kwan Hoi-san, Wong Wai
Directed by Jackie Chan

This turn-of-the-century period piece which features three of the Seven Little Fortunes—Jackie Chan, Sammo Hung and Yuen Biao dressed up in wacky costumes—doesn't have much of a plot, but the action is furious and bruising. It also showcases Jackie's appreciation for and homage to silent film, particularly during *Project A*'s hyper bike chase scene.

Jackie, decked out in a "British Tar" ice cream suit, plays a sailor called Dragon Ma. Led by his commanding officer, Captain Chi, Jackie and the crew are preparing to set sail against the forces of Lo, a notorious pirate (played with tattooed Manchurian machismo by Dick Wei). But before shipping out, the sailors stop by the local tavern for a farewell bash, and end up brawling with

MORE SEX, BETTER ZEN, FASTER BULLETS

Thai poster for *Project A*.

an arrogant group of police led by Inspector Tzu (Yuen Biao).

Then as the crew assembles prior to departure, fire blooms in the night sky as their ships are blown up. Their fleet sunk, Dragon and his salty dogs are desalinated and turned into a police unit by Captain Chi (Kwan Hoi-san). Bad enough to be a landlubber, but the new boss is Inspector Tzu, who puts them through rigorous training exercises in their new uniforms (which include conical "mollusk" hats) before eventually patching up their differences.

First assignment: ferret out a hirsute thug who's trying to sell 100 stolen Enfield rifles to the pirate, Lo (Dick Wei). Tzu and Dragon adopt Western garb and wreck a private club trying to rein in the crook. So many stuntmen execute painful-looking floor crashes, you can almost smell the liniment.

They fail, but Dragon and fellow sailor-turned-cop Fei (Sammo) steal the rifles. Dragon is nabbed for the theft, though, and his old boss Captain Chi handcuffs him. But Dragon slips the cuffs, launching into one of the exquisitely-paced over-the-top action sequences that have cemented Jackie Chan's place in the pantheon.

Dragon takes off on a purloined bicycle. His pursuers are also on bikes, and he leads them through a rabbit warren of narrow alleys with more than their share of ladders and dutch-doors. As his attackers close in, Jackie passes a dutch door and knocks on it. The top-half of the door swings open just in time to scrape off an attacker.

Recaptured and re-cuffed, he deftly shimmies up a flagpole and leaps into a clock tower, where he uses the huge gears of the clockworks as a jungle gym in a fight with one of the arms smugglers. Hanging on to one of the clock's hands, he drops through two awnings and hits the ground headfirst. Merry bike chase, hanging from a huge clock álà Buster Keaton, and the awe-inspiring, headcrunching fall. Rewind and call in your roommates!

None of this impresses the pirates, who are bulldog determined to get those rifles. So they shanghai a shipful of foreign dignitaries and hold them for ransom. Dragon kidnaps—then impersonates—top-hatted dandy Chou (Wong Wai), the arms dealer, earning a journey to the pirates' island hideout.

And then...there's a big battle. The combined talents of Jackie, Yuen, and Sammo are used against pirate chief Lo and his forces. But once victorious, our heroes must attempt to return to the mainland by raft, and their navigational skills don't match their martial arts skills...

THE CHAN CANON

German poster for *Project A Part 2*, somewhat logically renamed "Projekt B".

Project A, Part 2 (A計劃續集)
1987 | Starring Jackie Chan, Maggie Cheung Man-yuk, David Lam Wai, Rosamund Kwan Chi-lam, Carina Lau Kar-ling, Elvis Tsui Kam-kong, Ray Lui, Bill Tung Biu
Directed by Jackie Chan

Everybody's favorite Jackie Chan movie tends to be the one they saw first. The qualities that make him irreplaceable, his earnest good humor and his unique brand of acrobatic slapstick kung fu, are present to some degree in all his films. The quality, if not the quantity, of the delight is fairly uniform. Even less successful efforts like *City Hunter* and *First Strike* have occasional eye-popping sequences.

Project A Part 2 was my introductory dose, caught first-run at the late lamented Kim Sing Theater in LA's Chinatown. I had never seen anything like it, or like him, and became an instant fan. Experience has since confirmed that *Part 2* is one of Chan's strongest self-crafted vehicles, with the action and comedy elements just about perfectly balanced. The first *Project A* (1985) may be lighter on its feet, and the handsome Kirk Wong-directed *Crime Story* (1993) is probably still the best made Jackie movie. But as a showcase for Chan at the top of his game, as both filmmaker and performer, *PA Part 2* is unbeatable.

The period setting is an asset. It's the early 1900s in the flourishing British colony of Hong Kong, and the horse-drawn carriages, the crisp sailor suits, and the pretty girls (including a dazzling young Maggie Cheung) in their flowery floor-length ball gowns, contribute to a nostalgic Gilbert and Sullivan comic opera atmosphere.

The plot recalls *The Untouchables*: The last honest cop in Hong Kong is transferred to dry land from the harbor patrol and assigned to clean up the city's most corrupt precinct. The first half-hour is a little sluggish, as a dozen opposing factions are wheeled into position. These include a pack of leering mobsters (led by David Lam), some Sun Yat-sen aligned revolutionaries (led by Rosamund Kwan), a gang of haughty imperialist spies, and a wonderful eccentric band of comic-opera Chinese pirates, imported from *PA Part 1* with their silly wigs and ill-fitting "civilian clothes" intact, who slink around en masse, brandishing matching hatchets.

Once the action starts, and the machinery begins humming along smoothly, the film becomes buoyantly airborne and remains there. Lovely set pieces include a hand-to-hand tussle inside a revolving wire drum full of drifting feathers, and an elaborate hide-and-seek sequence in an apartment crowded with grimacing spies concealed behind curtains and sofas and closet doors—a near-perfect piece of fancy-farce footwork. These scenes offer proof positive that Chan is a magnetic screen presence even when he isn't falling from a great height or kicking somebody in the head.

There's less of the latter, here, than some hard-action fans would like, and the major set-piece mega-stunt is an all-too direct lift from Jackie's idol Buster Keaton. But Mr Chan is not, finally, a hard action icon. In fact, that's the whole point. That's exactly why he's irreplaceable.

Project A Part 2 is a perfect embodiment of the lessons Jackie Chan absorbed from the great American silent comedians, when he studied them in his formative years, looking for ways to set himself apart, desperate to get out from under the shadow of Bruce Lee. He learned from Keaton and Lloyd that he could show off his skills in limb-stretching acrobatic displays while seemingly straining every nerve to avoid conflict. Like an American musical performer who seems most prodigiously gifted when he pretends to dance badly (Ray Bolger and Donald O'Conner are obvious examples), Chan is never more impressive than when he makes his triumphs appear accidental, when he ducks and dodges and winces after every blow, and still manages to lay out a dozen thugs.

Chan rarely plays vigilantes or avengers—his characters are usually earnest functionaries struggling to do the right thing, to fit in and serve the establishment. The archetypal Chan character is a reluctant master of mayhem, a well-meaning straight-arrow who doesn't know his own strength—although as a crafty performer and self-promoter, he makes damn sure that we know.

— David Chute

Twin Dragons (雙龍會)

1992 | Starring Jackie Chan, Maggie Cheung Man-yuk, Nina Li Chi, and a lot of Hong Kong film-directors
Directed by Ringo Lam Ling-Tung and Tsui Hark

Ever since Alexandre Dumas' *The Man in the Iron Mask* and Charles Dickens' *The Prince and the Pauper*, fictional forms have been glutted with variations on the "twins separated at birth" and "trading places" scenarios. Motion pictures, however, have largely ditched any serious exploitation of these themes for their broader comedic potential—human splittists have emerged as one of the cinematic farceur's most popular devices. Look no further than the Baby Boom generation's reverence for Walt Disney's *The Parent Trap* (1961, remade in 1998) to appreciate the saturation.

Jean-Claude Van Damme's separated-at-birth twin brothers entry into the genre, 1991's *Double Impact*, wasn't warmly received. Tossing martial arts into the mix seemed to further trivialize a woefully tired routine. At the time, some critic (me) wrote that "there's hardly a shared frame between the two Van Dammes that won't elicit a moan from audiences."

Given *Double Impact*'s universal dissing, it's hard to imagine any actor in his right mind wanting to revisit the idea—particularly a martial artist—if only to elude any comparisons to Van Damme. Fortunately, when it comes to filmmaking, Jackie Chan has never really been in his right mind.

Still, it took me two years to even sit down and watch the thing—fortunately, with an audience. By the time it concluded, I was hopelessly in love with what I consider one of the funnier films ever made, a comic masterpiece worthy of the silent greats whom Jackie cites as his inspirations. With time my appreciation has only increased, for in the broader context of Jackie's body of work, *Twin Dragons* is both an obvious and a not-so-obvious anomaly, an unusually multi-layered work that impresses as much for what it doesn't say as for what it does.

The twins are separated when an escaped convict (*Crime Story* director Kirk Wong) barges in on the celebrating parents (actress/director Sylvia Chang and composer James Wong) and steals one baby a hostage. When the smoke clears, the convict is recaptured but the baby has vanished, rescued by an alcoholic hooker (*Soong Sisters* director Mabel Cheung). Grief-stricken over the loss of their child, the parents flee to the USA where the one brother—Ma Yau—develops into a renowned concert pianist and conductor. His twin, meanwhile, grows up in Hong Kong under the name Bok Min, an able-bodied auto mechanic and streetwise brawler.

Twenty-eight years later, when Ma Yau (Jackie 1) returns to Hong Kong for a concert appearance, a psychic connection develops between him and Bok Min (Jackie 2), making each increasingly sensitive to the physical sensations of the other. As the connection intensifies, the long-lost brothers find themselves on a direct collision course with one another. The resulting confusion wreaks havoc with their respective girlfriends—lounge singer Barbara (Maggie Cheung) and socialite Tong Sum (Nina Li). The gangsters blackmailing Bok Min for the release of his tiny troublesome buddy Tarzan (Teddy Robin Kwan) are equally perplexed.

An all-star collaboration to raise money for the Hong Kong Film Directors Guild, *Twin Dragons* is a potpourri of giddy insider gags featuring dozens of cameos by celebrity directors (John Woo as a priest, Lau Kar-leung and Wong Jing as a feuding doctor and supernatural healer, respectively), two of whom—Tsui Hark and Ringo Lam—are credited with co-directing the film. But it's Jackie's signature that comes through most visibly—his sense of humor, irony, slapstick and impeccable action choreography indelibly engraved on every scene.

But the film also marks a courageous departure from the action film conventions that had characterized most of Jackie's prior work. Despite the blackmail subplot, *Twin Dragons* is irresistibly fluffy and buoyant, devoid of any real sense of danger or jeopardy. Rousing fights bookend the film, but its broad physical comedy, the self-conscious cleverness of its situations, and the whimsy with which Jackie breezes through his double-role belong more to the tradition of Ernst Lubitsch, whose classic comedies found their greatest joy in the creative escalation of confusion, rather than in its resolution.

Far from the hackneyed device of JCVD's doppelgangers, the psychic connection between the Jackies is a fiendishly inventive contrivance that enables Chan to entertain the most difficult kind of physical comedy—the imposition of the mechanical upon the human. Jackie so masters the deceit that the otherwise impressive action scenes pale. A nail-biting motorboat chase where Bok Min and Tarzan flee an attacking armada of gun-toting mobsters is a means to a more entertaining end as Ma Yau—seated in a restaurant miles away—frazzles and bedazzles restaurant patrons, the pulchritudinous Nina Li and himself by inexplicably swaying, bobbing and wobbling in sync with the boat's motions. By the end of the chase, Bok Min and Tarzan are safe, but Ma Yau has left the restaurant in tatters and Nina drenched in drinks. A scene in a hot tub, where Bok Min and Ma Yau must somehow convince Nina Li that she is in the bath with only one of them, will make you spit shredded squid out of your nose. The finale, set at the wondrous Automobile

Testing Facility, astonishes with Jackie's feats of agility in dodging and running over moving vehicles. But the magical moment when Bok Min—trapped in an adjacent testing chamber—saves Ma Yau from an attacker by miming the necessary moves, psychically puppeteering his twin to victory, emerges supreme.

When Bok Min and Ma Yau finally meet (at adjacent restroom urinals), the timing is so crisp, the interaction so life-like that you can't imagine a real pair of actors topping it. Elsewhere, the film manifests an almost Chaplinesque pathos, such as when Maggie Cheung's downtrodden lounge singer Barbara finds herself falling head over heels for Ma Yau, their shared love of music bonding them spiritually to each other and to the audience. Still other scenes, like Bok Min's spur-of-the-moment conducting of Ma Yau's orchestra, evoke the manic spontaneity of the Marx Brothers, eruptions of unpredictable zaniness with no narrative function, just showing the audience a good time.

And what a good time it is. For those fortunate enough to have seen the film with an roaring audience, the experience is both magical and transformational—proof positive that no genre is more universal or better served by the social dimension of filmgoing than comedy—especially when in the hands of such an able master.

Like Bok Min, Jackie was separated from his parents at a young age, raised by a surrogate and thrust into the world with little formal education. But like Ma Yau, he went on to become a world-renowned artist, beloved in every corner of the globe. In a very real sense, the two characters address the insecurities to which Jackie himself has repeatedly confessed. If his talents had gone unnoticed, if good fortune had failed to smile upon him, would he have continued to live in

Jackie, meet Jackie: screengrab from *Twin Dragons*.

meager obscurity like Bok Min? Conversely, if he had never been separated from his parents, if he had been raised without training in the martial arts, would he still have been able to succeed like Ma Yau? Whatever the confusion between the two characters in the film, it would seem but a shadow of Jackie's own confusion with respect to his fame. By his own admission, he still grapples with the price of success—the harsh, parentless upbringing—and whether or not, in the end, it was all worth it.

The romantic entanglements in *Twin Dragons* provide a resolution of sorts. After falling in love with men they believe to be from their own social classes, Maggie and Nina discover that they have actually fallen for kindred spirits from opposing classes, men whom they might never have met under normal circumstances. The greater truth, however, is that they have both fallen in love with Jackie, a realization crystallized in the film's final shot when the two brides-to-be jokingly remark that it no longer matters which brother is which.

Indeed, to his fans, it has never mattered which Jackie is which. We have always and will forever love them all.

— Wade Major

THE CHAN CANON

"Your skill is your safety": Jackie ducks under a shovel strike in *Crime Story*.

The Big Brawl
aka Battle Creek Brawl

1980 | Jackie's first Hollywood film. Directed by Robert Clouse (*Enter the Dragon*), it uses Jackie's comedic skills to good effect. Jackie plays a hard-working guy who enters a fighting competition in Battle Creek, Texas. Perky Kristine DeBell (better known for her antics in *The X-Rated Adventures of Alice in Wonderland*) chastely plays the love interest here, as Jackie scraps against a legion of guys who look like they have escaped from the World Wrestling Federation.

The Cannonball Run

1980 | Dean Martin as a drunk! Sammy Davis Junior as a priest! Farrah Fawcett's nipples poking up under her Lurex jumpsuit! In the middle of all this, you briefly get Jackie Chan as a Japanese race car driver. Directed by Burt Reynolds' former stunt coordinator, Hal Needham, who also directed the screamingly-godawful *Megaforce*.

Crime Story aka New Police Story

1993 | Kirk Wong directs a police procedural inspired by the real-life kidnapping of Hong Kong tycoon Teddy Wang. Those expecting doses of comedy will be disappointed as Jackie never cracks a smile. It's all about the action, which gets an extra dose of realism from location-shooting in the Walled City of Kowloon, which was slated for demolition anyway.

Drunken Master

1978 | Jackie plays folk hero Wong Fei-hong as a headstrong youngster who runs afoul of his father—Wong Kei-ying. Wong the Elder sentences Junior to torturous martial training under his uncle Sam the Seed. Fei-hong flees, but runs into a tough who thrashes him into submission. The chastened Wong returns to his rigorous sifu, and starts taking his training seriously this time. *Drunken Master* was popular throughout Asia, and went a long way towards turning Jackie into a star.

First Mission
aka Heart of the Dragon

1985 | Jackie stars as a cop who must care for his mentally retarded brother (Sammo Hung, who also directed). When Sammo is kidnapped by criminals to force Jackie to hand over a police informant, the screen explodes into its usual riot of martial lava.

Movie-painting for *Crime Story* (here titled *New Police Story*, Shinjuku, Tokyo (Photo: Stefan Hammond, 1993).

MORE SEX, BETTER ZEN, FASTER BULLETS

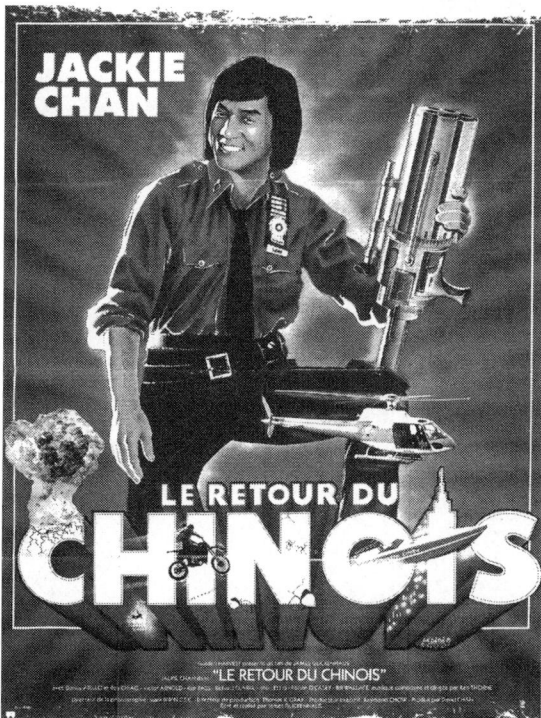

French-language poster for *The Protector*.

The Protector

1985 | If nothing else, it answers the trivia question: "Which feature film co-starred both Moon Lee and Danny Aiello?" Directed by James Glickenhaus, the film stars Jackie and Aiello as New York cops who are sent to Hong Kong to track down drug kingpin Mister Ko (Roy Chiao). There's a US version that's saltier, and a Hong Kong version geared more toward Asian audiences. After this, Jackie returned to Hong Kong and made *Police Story*.

Jackie Chan filming *Jackie Chan: My Stunts* in Hong Kong, 1998 (Photos: Jude Poyer, all rights reserved).

Sammo Hung

CHAPTER TWELVE
YUEN, SAMMO, YUEN

The exploits of Jackie Chan (see "The Chan Canon" chapter) are well known, but the cinematic efforts of his "brothers" less so. And that's a shame, as Sammo Hung and those guys surnamed Yuen created some of the best Hong Kong action films of the 1980s and early 90s.

Chan, Hung and the Yuens were raised at China Drama Academy, a Peking Opera School in Hong Kong, where martial skills were taught with arduous single-mindedness. A group of children from this school, including Chan, Corey Yuen-kwai, and the three men featured here—Yuen Biao, Sammo Hung, and Yuen Wah—toured as the "Seven Little Fortunes": an acrobatic performance troupe. All seven ended up making action movies in some capacity.

And each appear (mix and match) in the others' projects. Jackie often cast the Yuens and Sammo in his films until 1987's *Dragons Forever*, their last film as a group.

Alex Law's 1988 film *Painted Faces* depicts the singular upbringing they endured—rigorous training which turned these spiritual brothers into martial screen idols.

Sammo Hung Kam-bo

A seminal figure in the development of the modern action film, Sammo Hung has served as actor, director and/or action director on dozens of films. While Sammo's stocky build (earning him half of his nickname "Big-Brother Big") and guileless moon-face are not the usual leading man stuff, his martial arts skills are nonpareil.

Sammo also has a good touch with comedic roles, and often plays a lovable sap in ghost stories. "Sammo" comes from a popular cartoon character from his childhood: "Sam-mo" ("three hairs").

Yuen Wah

Known as the "Who was that guy!?" guy. Never top-billed, incredulous audiences want to know: who was that guy with the cigar in *Dragons Forever*? That guy with the fan in *Eastern Condors*? That Vietnamese villain with the nerdy spectacles in *She Shoots Straight*? That guy with the electric blue kung fu in *A Kid from Tibet*?

Looking like the last person you'd pick for the softball team, he's an amazingly talented martial artist who takes his opponents—and his audience—by surprise. That guy is HK cinema's number one villain, the sunken-cheeked Yuen Wah.

Yuen Wah

Yuen Biao

Yuen Biao

Yuen Biao, a junior member of the troupe, broke into film with a brash physical grace in *Dreadnaught* and *The Prodigal Son*. A cheeky chap with a grinful of crooked teeth, Yuen has played everything from hero to scalawag to bumpkin to flying-pigtail fighter. Like other members of the Seven Little Fortunes, he adopted the surname "Yuen" as tribute to their sifu Yuen Chan-yuan (Yuen Biao's first name is pronounced "byu").

Dragons Forever (飛龍猛將)
1987 | Starring Jackie Chan, Sammo Hung Kam-bo, Yuen Biao, Sally Yeh, Deanie Yip, Yuen Wah, Pauline Yeung, Shing Fui-on, Benny "The Jet" Urquidez
Directed by Sammo Hung Kam-bo

Sammo Hung is a great stunt coordinator and action director, but this 1987 Jackie Chan vehicle once again proves what a terrific comedy director he's as well. There are fights throughout the film, but—until the final fifteen-minute sequence—the main emphasis is on humor. All three leads are terrific, with Yuen Biao particularly hilarious as a verbose neurotic (his therapy scenes are great).

Yuen Wah looks an accountant, but he's a polluting industrialist, drug smuggler, AND kung fu kook in *Dragons Forever*.

Poster: *Dragons Forever*.

Lawyer Jackie Lung (Jackie Chan) has a penchant for repping dodgy clients. As the film starts, he's having lunch with a crime victim, offering her money on behalf of his client—the criminal—to drop the charges. When she refuses the money, the bad guy's henchmen interrupt the lunch and attack her. Lung rescues her, but she believes he was in on the setup. He gets his client off anyway, but, beset by guilt, decks him in the courtroom immediately afterward.

Meanwhile, another sleazy client—that guy with the cigar—polluting industrialist and drug smuggler Hua (Yuen Wah) is sued by fish hatchery owner Miss Yeh (Deanie Yip). Lung defends him, but, being an inveterate womanizer, he also puts the moves on Miss Yeh's cousin, Wen Mei-Ling (Pauline Yeung). He enlists his old buddies Fei (Sammo Hung), a smalltime crook, and Tung Te-Piao (Yuen Biao), a neurotic tech whiz, to help him spy on the two women. Unfortunately the two sidekicks can't be in the same room together without getting into a fight.

Lung keeps trying to have a romantic meal with Mei-Ling, but something always gets in his way. In one case, Fei and Te-Piao go after each other in Lung's apartment mid-date; in another, a gang of hitmen tries to polish Lung off. Two-thirds of the way through, the action slows down to let this romance develop, trading thrills for winsome courtship. Yeah, yeah, yeah.

Finally, Fei and Te-Piao break into Hua's plant and discover his big heroin refinery. Hua's men give Fei an overdose, and Te-Piao runs to gather Lung and Mei-Ling to help rescue him. And then... there's a big battle.

Lung must square off with both the twitchy, tricky Hua, who gets dumped in a vat of toxic waste, and his awesome assistant (Benny "The Jet" Urquidez). Urquidez sports a makeup job giving him a face like a shark's: pale with beady, doll-like eyes. The two launch into a fierce fistfight

Dragons Forever: bad guy Billy Chow gets the boot from Yuen Biao.

which recalls their stalwart duel in Wheels on Meals. Finally, as both are ready to collapse, Jackie pulls out the victory.

—Andy Klein

Eastern Condors (東方禿鷹)

1987 | Starring Sammo Hung Kam-bo, Yuen Biao, Yuen Wah, Lam Ching Ying, Joyce Godenzi, Haing S Ngor, Dick Wei, Billy Lau, Corey Yuen-kwai, Yuen Woo Ping, Wu Ma, Melvin Wong
Directed by Sammo Hung Kam-bo

War spectacular with an all-star cast of HK regulars and a ringer: Oscar-winner Dr Haing S Ngor (Best Supporting Actor, 1985). Action sequences are expert—all six action directors on the film (including Sammo and three guys named Yuen) appear in the film.

Lam Ching Ying is recruited to lead a *Dirty Dozen*-style suicide mission into 1976 Vietnam: A missile dump left behind by hightailing Yanks must be destroyed before it falls into the wrong hands. His squad is composed of ethnic Chinese convicts sprung from a New Jersey prison.

Parachuting behind the lines, the camo-clad mercenaries hit the ground ready for action (though one—nicknamed "Stammer"—has a particularly hard time with the ripcord-pull-count). They immediately rendezvous with three

Haing Ngor has seen it all before.

female Cambodian patriots led by Joyce Godenzi (the future Mrs Sammo). The guerilla trio are a hard-bitten, battle-seasoned lot, but is one a double-agent?

An unlikely ally is found in Yuen Biao, a local lad who peddles whiskey and cigs from a huge music-blaring motortrike, like a black-market Good Humor man. Yuen lives with his uncle, a harmless grinning simpleton (Haing Ngor). The squadron brings both along to help scout the local terrain.

They're pursued by the Viet Cong, who are led by a sanguine VC general (Wu Ma). Captured by the Cong, our heroes are confined in bamboo cages with water up their waists. In a virtual *Deer Hunter* remake, they're forced to play Russian Roulette to amuse their captors, but turn the tables and shoot their way out.

The Cong pursue them into the boobytrap-infested jungle, where the martial arts skills of Yuen Biao and Sammo save the day. Sammo quick-strips palm leaves, hurling the stems like darts into necks. Yuen tosses a coconut in the air like a soccer ball and kicks it into the noggin of an onrushing commie, braining him.

A strange commie commando commander

Former Miss Hong Kong Joyce Godenzi models the flat-black M-60 machine gun.

(Yuen Wah) starts dogging their trail. A dour paintywaist wearing silk pajamas and wire-rimmed specs, he communicates in hiccups and cools himself with a dainty folding fan as he surveys the carnage in our heroes' wake. He becomes animated when he calls in the heavy artillery on the valiant squadron, who've lost a few through attrition and are guarding a strategic bridge. Sitting in the back of a jeep, the qualmish Congster shakes his pencil-wrists in the air and hysterically screams "FIIIIIRE!" as hell pours down on the bridge-guardians.

The remaining heroes make it to the munitions dump—festooned with gleaming missiles—and set their time-bombs. But the uniformed baddies burst in and the pitched end-battle begins. After disposing of the brawny front-liners, Yuen and

Yuen Wah: "FIIIIIRE!"

Sammo's the big gun in this *Eastern Condors* poster.

Sammo face only the scrawny Mr Big.

But instead of folding like a wet noodle, the bespectacled villain explodes into eccentrically fluid, masterful kung fu! He puts up a hell of a fight, but is finally subdued, then dispatched by the old grenade-stuffed-in-mouth technique. Our heroes escape the exploding armory and live to fight another day.

Encounter of the Spooky Kind 2 (鬼咬鬼)

1990 | Starring: Sammo Hung Kam-bo, Lam Ching Ying, Mimi Kung Chi-an, Meng Hoi, Wong Man-gwan, Teddy Yip Wing-cho, Huang Ha
Directed by Sammo Hung

MORE SEX, BETTER ZEN, FASTER BULLETS

Sound advice from a purple-faced, white-haired sorcerer.

Sammo's reaction.

Sammo and his beloved are on the lam, and hole up in a haunted temple. Inside, a detestable ghoul couple molt their coffins to indulge in opium smoking and philandering with the quaking humans. Soon the four are daisy-chain bloodsucking. This is the opening dream sequence, but things don't get much better for Sammo when he wakes up.

He's the dirt-poor student of sifu Jiao (Lam Ching Ying) and hopelessly in love with the innkeeper's daughter, Chu Nai (Mimi Kung). However, the elder Chu (Teddy Yip) is unimpressed with Sammo's prosaic uprightness, catering instead to wealthy Sze (Lam Man-chung), a bejaded "toad lusting after the swan."

In a hysterical kung fu grudge match between Sze and Sammo, Sze is aided by his sorcerer (Huang Ha, a fiendish personal trainer) who bewitches a pet monkey and transfers its abilities to his client. Lurking nearby, the sorcerer has the monkey do backflips and killer kicks, which cause identical movements in Sze. Sammo's fellow student Little Hoi (Meng Hoi) comes to the rescue when he notices the subterfuge, and sics a German Shepherd on the ape.

Sammo enlists the help of a virtuous female ghost (Wong Man-gwan) in thwarting Sze, and convinces his one-track-mind sifu not to destroy her with his ghost-wrecking Taoist yo-yo. But just as EOTSK2 seems destined to cute itself out, unique spooks start getting cranked up.

Sze's sorcerer animates a Mutt and Jeff pair of zombies by stuffing them with handfuls of live cockroaches. As a terrified Sammo fights them off, their heads split open and dozens of roaches boil over his naked torso. Sammo can't stand it and his soul, butt-naked, flees his body.

The evil sorcerer captures Sammo's soul and feeds it to a piglet. Sammo's body, capable of repeating only "scared, frightened" over and over in a zombie daze, is quickly occupied by the female ghost to keep it in martial action against the sorcerer, who continues his assault with leeches and ground-skull powder.

The soul returns when the piglet is captured and Sammo does mouth-to-mouth with the pint-sized porker. But Sze subdues Chu the innkeeper with a frog-eggs charm, and sends him to chop up Sammo in the crepitorium.

All this proves too much for long-suffering sifu Jiao. He constructs a Taoist altar, then duels in warlock-space with the sorcerer, who astrally projects from his own witchin' pit—a stylish array of wacked-out furniture, red-painted cow skulls, and a big thumpin' drum. The sifu's potent

Lam Ching Ying, flanked by Sammo and Meng Hoi, blasts paper charms into supernatural flame-throwers.

spells send the warlock over the edge. Suddenly bright purple with unruly white hair, the warlock binds the loathsome Sze in a sissified outfit, then hides inkeeper Chu's antidote deep in the hapless creep's innards.

The final spooky encounter pits Sifu and his two students against the warlock, who marshals energy bolts, animated "bewitched corpses," and finally a great pair of creepy, sinuous snakefighters.

A Kid from Tibet (西藏小子)

1991 | Starring Yuen Biao, Michelle Reis (Lee Kar-yan), Yuen Wah, Nina Li Chi, Roy Chiao, Wu Ma
Directed by Yuen Biao

Yuen Biao's directorial debut opens with a shot of the historic Potala Monastery in Tibet. The camera lingers over the prayer wheels, the hall of chanting monks, and the Himalayan landscape before focusing on a crippled man painfully lurching up the Monastery's impressive 1341 hillside steps. Fortunately, when he reaches the top, the Lama on duty is Wong La (Yuen Biao), who cures Robinson's crippled leg with the cheerful flourish of a parlor magician.

Wong La has never been beyond the cloistered walls of the monastery, but is directed by the head monk to journey to Hong Kong, along with an escort, Chiu Seng-neng (Michelle Reis). His job is to transport the cap of the magical Babu Gold Bottle, which was used to repel the evil "Black Section" many years ago, and reunite it with the bottle itself.

However, the HK Lama in charge of the bottle has been waylaid by rogue priest Yuen Wah and his evil witch sister (Nina Li). Yuen is a titanic villain—that guy with the electric blue kung fu who can shout his way through plate-glass windows. His evil goal—to install "Blackism" as the national religion of Tibet—inspires him to impersonate the Lama and trick the good guys into handing over the reunited relic.

Meanwhile, Wong La is tossed unprepared into HK's pace and techno-ambience. Trenchcoated villainess Nina Li coaxes Wong La into her hot red Porsche and rips into HK traffic. Her driving technique literally scares the pee out of him.

At a deserted construction site, Nina tries to seduce the bottle cap from Wong. She whips off her trenchcoat to reveal spandex kink-glory: black satin with steel accents. Yuen's eyes bug out, but he resists her considerable charms.

Unmasked ("you've shown your cloven feet!") and angry, she pulls out her bull's pizzle and uses both whip and spells. An animated pile of 55-gallon oil drums loosen Yuen's grip and the cap falls on a live electrical grid. Nina grabs for it anyway—frying her hand—then escapes in a wall of flame.

Wong returns to Chiu Seng-neng's modern HK apartment, for a series of rube-in-the-city gags, some of which (like building a fire on the floor instead of turning on the heat) fall flat. As an exasperated Seng-neng says, "This is not supernatural power, but super-stupid power."

Finally, Wong arrives at his pre-arranged rendevous with the bottle Lama, unsuspecting a trap. When the deception is realized, it sets the stage for a final Yuen Biao/Yuen Wah showdown—two gifted martial artists flailing upon one another with fists, feet, spiritual boxing, and a pair of large and unusual swords.

Painted Faces (七小福)
1988 | Starring Sammo Hung Kam-bo, Lam Ching Ying, Cheng Pei-pei
Directed by Alex Law

A gentle mother walks her seven-year-old son to his new school. There the boy signs on for ten years, and will never go home again. The school's master will keep any money the boy earns and if the boy is killed while in the school, it's just too bad. This isn't Charles Dicken's London, it's the Peking Opera School in the Hong Kong of the 1950s.

Painted Faces is based on the early lives of Jackie Chan (here called "Big Nose"), Sammo Hung, and Yuen Biao, and their troupe called the "Seven Little Fortunes." Sammo Hung himself stars as his real-life teacher, Master Yuen Chan-yuan. Master Yuen trains these dirt-poor kids in kung-fu, acting and opera in exchange for the money made at their performances. The students learn their acrobatic acting skills under iron rule, twelve to fifteen hours a day, with a constant threat of being beaten by the master and by each other.

The kids' first performance is a disaster. Big Nose catches a pair of pants on his spear and carries them on stage. Sammo flips right off the stage into the audience. Another falls asleep, misses his cue and the show is over.

Thai poster for *Painted Faces*.

The Master is furious. Not just at the bad timing, but because they didn't look out for each other. These kids, who biological families couldn't support them, now belong to a group as close-knit as any combat patrol, where each member is responsible to and for his "brothers."

"It takes three years to train a scholar and ten years to train an actor," Master Yu tells the tailor who shares the building with them. But the tailor is not impressed. He wants his son, a mousy kid in glasses, to be a professional.

The tailor has a point. As hard as the Fortunes train, and as skilled as they become, times are getting harder for them. Hong Kong is modernizing. It's now the sixties, and the introduction of motion pictures changes the audience's tastes.

Teen stars of traditional stage, the boys still want to listen to The Beatles. They meet some girls through a Cantonese opera troupe (led by the elegant Cheng Pei-pei), but the girls are more impressed by the tailor's son, who plays the guitar.

When the theater where they perform becomes a strip show, the boys audition for extra roles at the movie studio. No-talent directors and smarmy assistants mistreat Opera alums already in the biz, but Master Yuen feels that it's the only chance he can give them. Some Fortunes are chosen and the rest rejected, and their solidarity is shattered.

Painted Faces features no kung fu fights, no sex, or guns—just a group of acrobatic baldhead kids and their Master. *Painted Faces* is about change and pain and shared experience beyond friendship. it's also about the culture and foment that shaped the creators of current Hong Kong movies.

— KA Tarapata

NOTE: According to Wikipedia: "Despite some of the more brutal exercises and physical punishments shown in *Painted Faces*, [Sammo] Hung and the rest of the Seven Little Fortunes consider the film a toned-down version of their actual experiences."

Peacock King (孔雀王子)

1988 | Starring Yuen Biao, Hiroshi Makami, Pauline Wong Siu-fung, Gloria Yip, Narumi Yasuda, Eddie Ko, Gordon Lau
Directed by Nam Nai-choi

Man's depravity has undermined justice, again, and the Four Holes to Hell are opening up. It's up to a pair of hardened Buddhist youngsters to repel the "Unholy Trinity"—Hell King, Hell's

Peacock King poster.

Agent, and the cute-yet-destructive Hell Virgin.

Peacock King opens at an archaelogical dig in Nepal, where the first hell-hole busts open. Rushing to the surface are Ashura the Hell Virgin (Gloria Yip) and Hell's Agent: Witch Raga (spidery-do'ed Pauline Wong). Ashura's eyes turn into mirrored orbs as she hurls fireballs.

This, along with disasters in China and Bangladesh, foretells of future destruction. So Tibetan sifu Ku Fong sends his pupil Peacock (Yuen Biao) to intercept Ashura and calm the waters. At Japan's Koyasan monastery, another sifu similarly directs Lucky Fruit (Hiroshi Makami). Both holy men head for the second hell-hole, which has opened inside Toyko's fashionable Odakyu department store.

En route, Peacock gets distracted while walking past a discarded burger container on the sidewalk. As the bemused monk looks on, a gaggle of cute l'il stop-motion-animated creodonts vacate the styrofoam pod. One hides up the pants leg of a passing salaryman, while another is eaten by a passing dog.

Lucky Fruit gets there first, but skeptical Miss Okada (Narumi Yasuda) is too busy setting up Odakyu's next in-store exhibition—a bunch of huge dinosaur models—to be bothered by his warnings. Then the voodoo starts, and the dinos get into the act.

A huge claw bursts into the ladies dressing room. Just as it seems poised to rip Lucky Fruit and Miss Okada to Jurassaic shreds, Peacock comes whirling in right through the offending appendage. Peacock leaps atop the rogue reptile, riding it like a bucking bronco, while Lucky Fruit attacks with spinning steel and explodes the mutants. Miss Okada is a believer.

Third hell-hole: Hong Kong. Hell Virgin Ashura turns up at an amusement park and—bored—speeds up all the rides, causing people to come flying off. Peacock scolds her, but promises to keep her amused, recognizing the child within. Witch Raga is not so kind; she drags Ashura to a sewer hideout and vengefully upbraids her, while snacking on fresh flesh plucked from a hapless, screaming victim.

The two monks (trailed by tabloid photographers) track down Raga, but she transforms into a biomechanoid monster with a vertical, multi-toothed set of jaws. Setting the silver-eyed Ashura on the monks, she eats a few startled paparazzi and gallops off.

Ashura is subdued, but has suffered serious internal injuries. The monks take her to Tibet for the sifu cure. There, Peacock and Lucky Fruit learn that they're separated-at-birth twins with unique horoscopes, who must use their yang power to stop Hell King. Lucky Fruit's sifu also arrives, as does Kubira (Gordon Lau), a freelance assassin. They've come for the opening of the fourth and final hole.

(Cue lighting) The sun is eclipsed. Ladies and gentlemen, Hell King is coming. His opening act, the biomechamonsterwitch, drops by the monastery to chomp a monk or two before our heroes can decapitate her. Hell King is a fanged giant who looks like he clomped out of a Ray Harryhausen Sinbad movie. He balls up Kubira into a disposable wad, but Peacock and Lucky Fruit combine their yang powers and triumph. Hell King goes down and the earth survives so that man's depravity can continue unchecked.

Righting Wrongs
aka *Above The Law* (執法先鋒)
1986 | Starring Yuen Biao, Cynthia Rothrock, Melvin Wong, Peter Cunningham, Karen Shepherd, Wu Ma, Fan Siu-wong
Directed by Corey Yuen-kwai

Righting Wrongs is a bleaker version of the Hollywood's *The Star Chamber*. Fortunately, the courtroom scenes are kept to a minimum and action prevails. Directed by another of the Seven Little Fortunes—Corey Yuen—the film is a skill showcase for Yuen Biao and American martial artiste Cynthia "*Blonde Fury*" Rothrock.

Biao plays a frustrated Hong Kong prosecutor whose caseload is complicated when scumbag defendants blow up the apartments of his witnesses' families. These guys play so dirty that even the judge privately recommends vigilante-style execution for the creeps. Biao

Yuen Biao and Rothrock share equal billing in this poster for *Above The Law* (*Righting Wrongs*).

takes the hint, cat-burgles into a bad guy's office and strangles him.

Rothrock plays an HK detective called Shih Li-Yi (go figure), who we meet as she emerges victorious in a mahjong parlor fracas. She performs a great bit of martial schtick by hand- and foot-cuffing four guys together using only a chair and one pair of cuffs. Tough as nails, she tells her underlings: "Book them for attempted murder, dope-pushing, assaulting, kidnapping and [slapping one] they look disgusting!"

Meanwhile, Biao is assaulted by underworld thugs in a hair-raising scene in a parking garage. He jumps on top of a moving car and, as it hurtles toward another vehicle, rolls down the hood, falling just under crashing front ends.

Undaunted, he sets out to finish another scofflaw, but turncoat cop Melvin Wong just beats him to it. Rothrock catches Biao with the stiff, and after a tussle, he handcuffs her to a balcony and escapes. The juris-imprudent judge provides Biao an alibi, but Rothrock is bulldog-determined to muzzle the loose cannon.

Wong starts executing anyone, good or bad, who might have found out about his bad-egg ways. After murdering a fellow officer, Wong earns a heartfelt hiss from the audience when he duplicitously comforts the deceased's sobbing father.

Bodies are piling up when icy gwailo assassin Karen Shepherd tangles with Rothrock. In the movie's best fight scene (coupla tuff babes flailing with feet, fists, and fashion accessories), the two go up and down bamboo scaffolding and escalators with the graceful intensity that only HK films can achieve.

Vigilante Biao finally fingers the renegade cop, but as Wong points out, "We're both killer." No man is above the law, as *Righting Wrongs* surprise finale illustrates—but only after we choke on our hearts as Biao dangles at several thousand feet from an airplane-slung rope!

Wheels on Meals (快餐車)
1984 | Starring Jackie Chan, Sammo Hung Kam-bo, Yuen Biao, Maria Delores Forner, Benny "The Jet" Urquidez, Richard Ng Yiu-hon, John Shum Kin-fun, Herb Edelman
Directed by Sammo Hung Kam-bo

Shot in Barcelona, Wheels on Meals features Jackie Chan and Yuen Biao as Thomas and David, a pair of expatriate Chinese entrepreneurs. They serve fried rice and burgers out of a tricked-out yellow van known as "Everybody's Kitchen" ("cocina para todos!"). That's more Spanish than you'll need to enjoy this action-comedy, in which everybody speaks fluent fist, and cars and skateboards fly.

Sammo Hung is Moby, a hardworking guy who takes over a private eye business because his boss (a cameo by Herb Edelman) is fleeing Alfonso the loan shark. Moby's first client is a mysterious stranger who hires him to locate the grown child of a woman named "Gloria." Gloria is dating David's father, who's in the loony bin but "getting better." Her child is Sylvia (former Miss Spain Maria Delores Forner), who David and Thomas immediately dub "Princess."

But Sylvia is involved in the unregal career of pay-for-play. Our heroes—ga-ga over this gwai mui courtesan—hide her from an irate client she's grifted. She repays them by stealing their money. Unfazed, David and Thomas play Pygmalion and Sylvia promises to turn over a new leaf. The unlikely trio goes to work pushing spring rolls and soft drinks.

When well-dressed nasties appear and kidnap their waitress, the wheeler-mealers jump in their van and chase after them. The extended chase sequence features some spectacular rolling crashes and culminates in another one of those heart-in-the-throat Jackie Chan moments: the van flies over traffic—and into a truckload of fruit boxes. Fortunately, the stuntmen lazily perched atop the boxes are quick to leap off.

Turns out that Sylvia's the illegitimate daughter of a nobleman. She stands to inherit plenty of pesetas, and her evil uncle Mondale is out to put her away. David and Thomas join forces with Moby and the trio storms a medieval castle to spring Sylvia from Mondale's clutches.

The endgame includes an extended one-on-

Jackie, Sammo and Yuen Biao with fencing foils while Gaudi's cathedral towers loom in the background: Wheels on Meals.

one match between Jackie and American martial artist Benny Urquidez. The action is so furious that one of Urquidez' kicks extinguishes an entire candelabra without toppling it over. When Benny topples over himself, Jackie delivers a kick which stands him back upright.

Yet, right in the middle of this bruising punch-up, Jackie decides to "treat it as a training session," and slumps on a chair to take a breather. He repeatedly gets up, strikes a pose, then relaxes—shifting between nonchalance and taut-bowstring readiness as Benny broils with impatience. Unfortunately, no outtakes accompany the closing credits.

Selected filmography of Yuen, Sammo and Yuen

Enter the Fat Dragon (1979)
Directed by Sammo Hung

Encounters of the Spooky Kind (1980)
Starring Sammo Hung, action Direction by Sammo and Yuen Biao

The Dead and the Deadly (1982)
Starring and action direction by Sammo Hung

Prodigal Son (1983)
Directed by Sammo Hung

Zu: Warriors of the Magic Mountain (1983)
Starring Yuen Biao and Sammo

Millionaire's Express (1986) aka *Shanghai Express*
Directed by Sammo Hung. Starring Sammo, Yuen Biao and Yuen Wah

Spooky Spooky (1986)
Directed by Sammo Hung

On The Run (1987)
Starring Yuen Biao and Yuen Wah

Painted Faces (1988)
Starring Sammo Hung

Portrait of a Nymph (1988)
Starring Yuen Biao

Skinny Tiger and Fatty Dragon (1990)
Starring Sammo Hung

The Iceman Cometh (1991)
Starring Yuen Biao and Yuen Wah

Slickers vs Killers (1992)
Directed by and starring Sammo Hung

Sword Stained with Royal Blood (1993)
Starring Yuen Biao

Kickboxer (1993) aka *Ghost Foot 7*
Starring Yuen Biao and Yuen Wah, action direction by Yuen Biao

Hex Errors: Google Mistranslate

More fractured English subtitles from your favorite Hong Kong movies. (See page 30 for a full explanation.)

"What a big fucken mess!"
Remains of a Woman

"Very simple, open the coffin, and suck the air from the vampire leader"
The Ultimate Vampire

"Chick, where's Turkey?"
Angel Terminators

"Action begins!"
Killer Angels

"You make me want to pee too"
The Holy Virgin versus the Evil Dead

"Annoying, I fight!"
Possessed 2

"OK! Your giranddaughter gonna die"
Transmigration Romance

"this is tiger penis! Hold it"
It's Now or Never

"You bitch, 1-1/2 inches to make five feet"
School On Fire

"What kind of world it is! Shoe the goose!"
Prison On Fire 2

"Are you done yet, you one-eyed trouser snake."
Once A Thief

MORE SEX, BETTER ZEN, FASTER BULLETS

"I"ve chopped him to dead"
My Better Half

"Pin me to death with the needle now"
Red and Black

"I"ll become a puppy if I were telling you a lie"
Devil Cat

"Chicken's blood and Virgin's urine?"
One Eyebrow Priest

"Your gun is awful!"
Saviour of the Soul

"You bastard, thank you for the donation!"
Iron Monkey

"trashed by both men and women?"
Gunmen

"Can you not to kill him?"
Black Cat

"I hate intruders or people"
Armour of God

"Vampire, order now, vampire"
Kickboxer's Tears

"You're finished for sure, dregs"
Pedicab Driver

"don't get trouble not belonging to you"
Dreaming the Reality

"You are asked to be gentle, not bitchy."
Holy Weapon

"You suffered a serious fumble, you'd be under observation"
Black Cat 2: Assassination of President Yeltsin

From top: Yuen Wah—that guy with the cigar, Pat Ha and Yuen Biao in *On The Run* (page 66), and the mighty Sammo Hung.

City on Fire: It's not that cold and he's not shopping.

CHAPTER THIRTEEN
RINGO LAM

Director Ringo Lam Lin-tung began his career with Hong Kong Television in the mid-70s, where he first met the rising star Chow Yun-fat. Lam then went to Canada to study film at York University in Toronto. After returning to Hong Kong, his career began to soar with the breakthrough *City on Fire*, for which he was awarded Best Director at the 1987 HK Film Awards.

Ringo Lam is best known for his street-real portraits of Hong Kong, where cops and crooks co-mingle. In stories set on both sides of prison bars, he explores the intricacies of the near-feudal loyalties that exist between his characters. He first dealt with this theme in *City on Fire*, the first installment in Lam's "Fire" series, which continued with 1987's *Prison on Fire* and 1988's *School on Fire*. Lam's 1992 over-the-top crime drama *Full Contact* (see page 17) is a crowd-pleaser that externalizes the action amid some wacky villains, but retains the trademark Ringo grit.

Lam's marque actor of choice is Chow Yun-fat, whose charm, power and versatility grace Lam's

Ringo Lam on set, 1980s.

Check if there's a hole...

...in my underpants?

No! I saw a vomiting crab.

Bonnie Fu pervs on Chow Yun-fat in *Full Contact* (page 17).

best work (Chow won Best Actor for *City on Fire*). His staple villain is the the lantern-jawed Roy Cheung, while griddle-faced Tommy Wong is often cast as the "second cop" or the "not-so-bad triad villain." For *Full Alert* (1997), Lam cast Lau Ching-wan as a stress-bent cop with Francis Ng as arch-villain in a taut thriller as psychological as it is kinetic.

Tomorrow, when you're about to shoot...

Francis Ng taunts Lau Ching-wan in a jailhouse call.

More than any other HK director, Lam has realistically dramatized the activities of the triads, while undercutting their celluloid glamorization. Still, you do get to see a lot of cool-looking triad tattoos.

Ringo Lam's film soundtracks are head-and-shoulders above the HK norm. Listen for the end-of-Empire bagpipe codas of *School on Fire*

Rotting tattooed arms as lawn ornaments: *Burning Paradise*.

And the fine print on the contract: *Burning Paradise*.

or the Cantorocking themes of Filipina diva Maria Cordero (*City on Fire*). Best of the lot is the wall of sound Lam constructs for *Full Contact*—a perfect complement to that film's visual mayhem.

Burning Paradise (火燒紅蓮寺)

1994 | Starring Willie Chi Tin-sang, Carman Lee Yeuk-tung, Wong Kam-kong, Maggie Lam Chuen, John Ching Tung
Directed by Ringo Lam

Ringo Lam's only period martial arts movie boasts Tsui Hark as producer. The film stars Willie Chi as Chinese folk hero Fong Sai-yuk. It's set in the Ching Dynasty, when rebellious Shaolin monks and students were being hunted down by the Manchurian government—a plot-line used by plenty of old-school kung fu flicks.

BP opens with Fong and his sifu pursued through the desert by a squadron of Manchu soldiers. The leader, Crimson (John Ching) has a metal pole-weapon that can slice a man's (or horse's) head off when hurled. Flying Guillotine 2.0?

The pair rush into a primitive hut occupied by a prostitute named Tou Tou (Carman Lee), but the place is overrun by surrounding Manchu soldiers, Fong's sifu is slain by Crimson, and the two remaining captives are transported to the hellish Red Lotus Temple.

The grim temple houses an underground prison where Shaolin students are caged and used as slave labor. The boss of this hellhole is Kung (Wong Kam-kong), a powerful, morally bankrupt but well dressed Manchu. "I want to enjoy life, even if it's inhuman," he muses as he cradles the head of a woman he's decapitated with his bare hands.

Lam sets most of the action inside the temple's darkened confines, where lethal booby traps abound and rotting bodies pile up knee-high. Time is marked by the decaying flesh of a buried corpse's exposed arms—perhaps the "burning paradise" is simply a grimmer version of a prison on fire.

Still, this is a martial arts movie, and there's no

The Red Lotus Temple welcome-mat: *Burning Paradise*.

shortage of guys on wires, guys on fire, and other wild action. The finale finds Fong and his buddy Hung Hei-kun (Yeung Sing) facing off against Kung, who uses his "Unlimited Stance" to fire deadly paint-drops like bullets.

City on Fire (龍虎風雲)
1987 | Starring Chow Yun-fat, Danny Lee Sau-yin, Carrie Ng Kar-lai, Sun Yueh, Roy Cheung Yiu-yeung
Directed by Ringo Lam

City On Fire opens with classic noir sax blowing solo over the crowded, murky streets of Kowloon. An undercover cop (Elvis Tsui) is knifed in an outdoor market and left to die. Hangdog Inspector Lau (Sun Yeuh) surveys the chalk-outlined scene, then sends for a new undercover cop: Ko Chow (Chow Yun-fat).

Chow's in a local nightclub trying to patch up a spat with his spitfire girlfriend, Hung (Carrie Ng). A flurry of cops rush in and drag him out in handcuffs for the meeting with Lau—his boss. Despite being a cop, Chow's loyalties run to both sides of the legal ledger. He shies from Lau's request to infiltrate the criminal gang that iced the first undercover officer: "I fulfill my duties? But I betray friends!"

Lee Fu (Danny Lee) and his men are in the process of robbing the Forever Jewelry store when several beat cops who were chasing street

City on Fire: Chow and Carrie Ng frolic in the shower.

City on Fire: Danny Lee: friend or foe?

hawkers stumble onto the scene. Despite violent bickering among his masked crew, Fu refuses to abandon anybody and tags a few back-up cops who get in his way as he leads his men out in a downpour of lead.

The post-heist street is strewn with the charred husks of police cars as Inspector Lau's command is relieved by John (Roy Cheung), a stuffed-shirt RHKP officer who appears on the scene. Loyalty clearly runs deeper in the ranks of the mobsters, as a hooched-up Inspector Lau explains later to Chow (while puking into a toilet): "Those who should die don't, those [who] shouldn't, do."

Chow takes the undercover assignment and infiltrates Fu's operation by funneling handguns to the gangster. But he soon finds himself in trouble with John's men, who are convinced that Chow is dealing in arms. Meanwhile, he's having a hell of a time explaining to Hung why he can't commit to marriage just now. While John and Lau argue over whether or not to use him as a pawn, Chow is accepted as a partner in the gang's next robbery.

As his bond with Fu deepens, Chow discovers that Hung (who has fled the country with a wealthy Canadian guy) is waiting for him in San Francisco.

But the yawning chasm of the heist awaits him. It goes down, then goes wrong, and Chow takes a slug in the breadbasket while protecting Fu. The crooks motor to their hideout—underscored in surreal fashion by a schlocky version of "Joy to the World." But as the cops close in, Fu's boss suspects that the bleeding Chow is working undercover.

Shouts and accusations are exchanged. Guns are pointed at one another's heads. Denouement, as cop/criminal covers are blown, then blown away in a storm of copper-jacketed slugs from without and within the gangster hideout.

City on Fire garnered additional attention when Quentin Tarantino's *Reservoir Dogs* was released in 1992 and invoked comparisons with the earlier Ringo Lam film. While elements of *City on Fire* were worked into the fabric of *Reservoir Dogs*, we're talking apples and oranges here. What's more important is that both films are excellent modern crime dramas which explore the complex dynamic of cops who have gone so deep undercover that their loyalties twist.

Of more importance: the film was nominated for ten Hong Kong Film Awards. Chow and Lam walked away with the Best Actor and Best Director statues.

City on Fire is on the Hong Kong Film Archive's list of "Best 100 Chinese Motion Pictures."

Full Alert (高度戒備)

1997 | Starring Lau Ching-wan, Francis Ng Chun-yu, Amanda Lee Wai-man, Monica Chan Fat-yung, Chin Ka-lok
Directed by Ringo Lam

In 1996, Lam shot *Maximum Risk* with Jean-Claude Van Damme and Natasha Henstridge, but was forced to reshoot a "happy ending", which didn't make him happy. Ringo then returned to Hong Kong to make *Full Alert*.

Full Alert: road hazard ahead.

The film's has autobiographical touches— Inspector Pao (Lau Ching-wan) is a perfectionist workaholic cop-in-charge whose impatient rages mirror those of Lam himself (Ringo's sometimes known as the "Dark-faced God" for his intensity on film sets). Pao can barely contain his fury at officials of a hide-bound Hong Kong institution, whose intransigence impedes vital details of his job—symbolic of Lam's rage against Hong Kong officials who refused to issue filming permits for Hong Kong streets.

Vulnerable yet Kevlar-tough Pao is Ringo's antacid-gobbling, stress-fueled doppelganger. Focused Mak Kwan (Francis Ng) was a civil engineer until he was jailed for peddling construction explosives. He served his time, but now that he's got a record, no contractor will

Mak Kwan (Francis Ng) has advice for a reflective Pao.

Full Alert: road hazard in full effect.

hire him. Now nihilistic and criminally minded, he intends to use his engineering (and scuba) skills to pull a serious heist to fund exodus from Hong Kong with his girlfriend Chung (Amanda Lee).

Plot puzzle pieces float in like the muted choral touches of Peter Kam's evocative score. Pao realizes that he and Mak are much alike, and begins to doubt his verve for command. "My gun is getting heavier and heavier," he tells his loving, long-suffering wife.

Full Alert delivers on the action front—Lam puts Pao and colleagues inside unmarked cars pursuing a speeding Benz full of armed baddies... right along Hong Kong's famous double-decker tram-route. The honking autos weave between the tram cars—Pao's fellow cop Bill (Chin Ka-lok at his best) screams: "They're all nuts!"

Ringo said much the same of his stunt crew during filming—nobody warned the tram drivers in advance, they just let it rip. As for the film's explosion which rains flaming debris in a crowded Kowloonside district, well, no one got hurt.

People get perforated in *FA*, but the real violence lurks in the psyches of those doing the killing. This is the big taboo for action filmmakers: many such films feature an orgy of high-velocity slaughter followed by wisecracks from the victorious shooters—this one explores the destruction to the shooters' souls.

Full Alert won Best Film and Best Actor (for Lau) at the Hong Kong Film Critics Society Awards.

Prison on Fire (監獄風雲)
1987 | Starring Chow Yun-fat, Tony Leung Kar-fai, Roy Cheung Yiu-yeung, Tommy Wong Kwong-leung, Nam Yin, Victor Hon Kwan
Directed by Ringo Lam

Prison stories are often told from the perspective of the "new fish," an innocent who is tossed into a hellhole filled with bullying, predatory gangs but protected by a sympathetic "old hand." What sets Ringo Lam's *Prison on Fire* apart is its austere look and the gritty scripting by first-time-screenwriter Nam Yin, who seems to have some (shall we say) inside knowledge of the subject. Coming on the heels of his triumph in *A Better Tomorrow*, *POF* helped cement Chow Yun-fat's reputation and the film did gangbusters at the box office.

Advertising designer Lo Ka Yiu (Tony Leung Kar-fai) harasses some punks trying to rip off his father's shop and accidentally pushes one into the path of an oncoming bus. Three years for manslaughter.

Our new fish has his belongings bagged, his hair buzzed, and his orifices plumbed by a fierce-looking Sikh doctor. Assigned to the infirmary, he soon meets the wiseacre Ching (Chow Yun-fat),

Inspector Pao has no chill in *Full Alert*.

Prison on Fire: the incarcerated complain.

a positive-thinker who knows how to work the prison rules and tweak the people-in-charge just far enough. Yiu looks like a gangly, somewhat retarded schoolboy in prison drag. He's driven to tears by the bullying of the prison's non-Sikh doctor, and forced to scrub the communal toilet. While he's there, Ching arrives to answer an urgent call, and ends up delivering some badly-needed advice to the weeping, despairing Yiu. Chow's pontificating on the pot is funny enough, but he finishes both dump and lecture with a sprightly: "Take care, there's a better tomorrow!"

Ching is in Yiu's corner, but a dust-up in the prison yard reveals the dark undercurrents of penal power systems. Baddie #1, a psycho named Madly (Shing Fui-on) is punched out of the

Prison on Fire: Chow Yun-fat, behind bars but not broken.

picture, leaving a struggle between unpleasant Mick (Nam Yin), not-so-bad Bill (Tommy Wong) and downright evil prison official Scarface (Roy Cheung). Mick and Scarface are in cahoots, and conspire against the upright, naive Yiu for their own ends.

After Yiu's girlfriend deserts HK in favor of overseas study, he stands up to Mick in the prison laundry. The resulting fight leaves him at the edge of mad despair, with a two-foot triangular chunk of broken glass gripped tightly in his bleeding hand. Mick is transferred as a result of the violence, and time passes in relative calm.

The lull implodes a few months later, when Mick is locked back in with the terrified Yiu. A prisoner fast calls for solidarity, but when it's broken, various triad factions are pitted against each other. The fracas evolves into a death-struggle between Mick and Ching. When Scarface tries to break it up, Ching goes animal-wild and thrashes him soundly, biting his ear off in the process! Yiu gets sprung on time, while Ching goes smilingly back in stir, awaiting his "better tomorrow."

Prison on Fire 2 (監獄風雲2逃犯)

1987 | Starring Chow Yun-fat, Wan Yeung Ming, Elvis Tsui Kam-kong, Tommy Wong Kwong-leung, Yu Li, Victor Hon Kwan
Directed by Ringo Lam

With the success of 1987's *Prison on Fire*, a sequel was a shoo-in. Chow Yun-fat reprises his role as wiseacre inmate Ah Ching—lampooning prison authority, scrawling motivational messages on the underside of prison stools, and even re-enacting his infamous pontificating-during-a-poo scene!

As in the original, upright folks in a Hong

Kong prison are trapped between rival factions and a sadistic, power-mad warden. In POF2, the usual local triads face another gang: a contingent of inmates from mainland China who loathe the "Hongkies." The mainland Chinese are kept in a separate cell—away from the HK contingent.

The leader of the mainlanders is a decent enough fellow named Big Dragon (Elvis Tsui). But he runs afoul of Warden Zau (Wan Yeung Ming), who is fond of breaking the limbs of would-be escapees; a sideline business in the joint is betting on how long fugitives will remain free, or on which limbs will be ruptured upon recapture. Zau cares little for the HK/mainland schism; he's an equal-opportunity sadist.

Zau uses the cover of a minor riot to smash Big Dragon's knee with a club, then humiliates Ching and denies him leave to visit his ailing son, who's been placed in an orphanage. Ching has to escape just so he can pay the tyke a visit! He surrenders and returns to the slammer.

The villainous official gets his toadie "Skull" to stab Ching in the shower but it's the tattooed "Snake" who tastes the shiv instead. Zau fingers Big Dragon for the murder, but the mainlander crashes a dump truck through the prison fence and leaps from a cliff into the sea. Ching joins him in the leap to freedom and the duo slog through the wilderness surrounding the prison, looking for a way out. They're reduced to eating snakes, and a bunch of little green apples, which prompt the aforementioned execretory soliloquy.

Dragon convinces Ching to grab his son and flee to the mainland, but they're soon recaptured. Seeking revenge, Warden Zau and Skull toss Ching into the communal cell with the vengeful mainlanders. And then...there's a big battle.

No one remains unbloodied, but Ching emerges in a patchable state, which is more than

Faces of the leads: screengrab from *School on Fire*.

can be said for Zau! The warden goes loco and attacks his own subordinates before taking a toothbrush-shank in the eye from Ah Ching and expiring. Ching survives to beam over improving report cards from his son and dream of an unbarred future. With no POF3 on the horizon, perhaps he made it.

School on Fire (學校風雲)

1988 | Starring Fennie Yuen Kit-ying, Sarah Lee Lai-yui, Damian Lau Chun-yan, Roy Cheung Yiu-yeung, Lam Ching Ying, Victor Hon Kwan, Tommy Wong Kwong-leung, Terrence Fok
Directed by Ringo Lam

Lam's final installment in the "Fire" series—*School on Fire*—is the darkest and goriest of the lot. As in the previous installments, innocents are placed in harm's way. This time, though, it seems as though no escape or redemption is possible. It's Ringo's comment on the Hong Kong school system as he experienced it and as raw a polemic as you will find in cinema.

The setting is a middle school in crowded Kowloon, overlooking the Kai Tak airport runway. No stereotypical brainy Asian students here—our

School books burn as Chu panics: *School on Fire*.

cast of characters are n'er-do-wells and wanna-get-bys trapped in a web of triad-sponsored violence, drugs, and prostitution. Schoolgirl Chu Yuen-fong (Fennie Yuen) is inseparable from her best bud, Sandy Kwok (Sarah Lee, who won Best Supporting Actress at the Hong Kong Film Awards for her performance), a nihilistic flunking-out teenybopper whose most precious possession is her call-girl pager.

When Chu sees a fellow student jumped by triad thugs, then killed by a passing van, she's warned against identifying the attackers by classmate George Chow, a triad-world bottom-feeder. Her father seeks the assistance of his old triad boss Sing, who's opposed by young turk Brother Smart (Roy Cheung at his villainous peak).

In this predatory world, the police are a nuisance. But Chu's teacher Wan (Damian Lau) and plainclothes cop Hoi (Lam Ching Ying) talk her into testifying. When Brother Smart finds out about it, he literally scares the pants off the terrified schoolgirl, forcing her to strip to her skivvies as his goons jeer.

Brother Smart then obliges her to recompense the HK$30,000 lawyer's fee for the assassin's defense. Paying off this debt—by renting her tender young body—sets Chu on the wrong path, a road that leads her and those around her (including her beau, incorrigible punk Little Scar—played by Terrence Fok) to ruination. And yes, at one point a closeup of one of the school's PA speakers announces: "Attention students, the school is on fire."

Set among cheap noodle shacks, concrete block flats bristling with television antennae and crowded, cramped classrooms, *School on Fire* looks and feels as bleak as its story. Cops and triads—opposing forces who both make offerings to Kwan Ti, the red-faced God of War—seem to follow predestined patterns of mutually-assured destruction. HK's schools can't be this bad, but the relentless dirge of *School On Fire* makes you wonder.

2020 UPDATE: This film's release on DVD is welcome—it remains a bleak-yet-insightful look into street-real Hong Kong of decades past, with intense performances by Lau, Lam, Cheung, and especially Yuen as the suffering innocent and Lee as the hellbent hellcat. A couple of notes (as told to Stefan by Ringo Lam over cups of tea and shrimp dumplings):

The Taiwanese version of *SOF* had all scenes in a school-setting censored out. According to Lam, this version runs 65 minutes.

School on Fire was released in August 1988, just before the Category III (see page 304) rating system had been implemented. Once Cat III became an option, Lam sought to restore the cuts he'd had to make to *SOF*'s initial release to pass the censors. Hong Kong's educational system is something Lam cares about passionately, and he wanted to create a director's cut of the film for re-release as a Cat III film.

Imagine Ringo's reaction when he went to the studio, who told him they'd thrown out the footage he was forced to remove from his film. Hong Kong's throwaway culture has been long criticized, but this is perhaps its most egregious example.

Wild Search (伴我闖天涯)
1990 | Starring Chow Yun-fat, Cherie Chung Chor-hung, Paul Chun Pui, Roy Cheung Yiu-yeung, Tommy Wong Kwong-leung, Ku Feng
Directed by Ringo Lam

Those expecting a rollicking bulletfest a la *Full Contact* from this Ringo Lam/Chow Yun-fat collaboration will be disappointed. But it's still a good example of Lam's prime strength as a director: developing strong characters and exploring their often surprising relationships. *Wild Search* is a crime-action film starring Chow as a hard-bitten RHKP officer, but it's also a romantic drama which sets its believable characters in a framework of powerful criminals opposed by hardworking cops.

Chow Yun-fat—whose character is named "Mew Mew" (go figure)—is slugging hooch out of a hip-bottle while he waits for an informant to arrive. The snitch puts him onto an arms deal taking place in a vacant apartment; a pair of gat-peddlers named Elaine and Bullet are doing business with some Japanese gangsters. Chow and company bust in and Elaine is killed in the shootout, leaving behind her button-cute daughter Ka-Ka.

Chow and fellow cop Tommy Wong look up Elaine's address and set off to look for clues. They end up deep in the countrified New Territories: the northern part of Hong Kong where people live in an agrarian manner, closer to Chinese village life than the chrome-and-steel breakneck pace of central HK. Lee's address is a simple farmhouse occupied by her sister Cher (Cherie Chung) and her

Cherie Chung, Chow Yun-fat seek a peaceful life for little Ka-Ka in *Wild Search*.

grumpy old dad (Ku Feng).

Mew Mew enlists Cher's help in tracing the trail of arms, which leads to Ka-Ka's natural father, Hung (Paul Chun). The man is a horrible, cokeheaded gangster—who's also a pillar of society. Mew Mew, never short on nerve, pays a visit to Hung at his office and requests a meeting with him and Cher to discuss Ka-Ka's future. Hung sends a flunky instead with a check for HK$100,000.

Insulted, Mew Mew crashes a high-society function with Cher in tow and pressures Hung for a cool million to support the illegitimate fruits of the scumbag's love labor. Hung's goombahs jump Mew Mew in the carpark, where the paparazzi photograph the aftermath: a bloody Mew Mew hauling Hung out of his white Rolls Royce at gunpoint. The ensuing scandal threatens to drive Mew Mew out of the police force.

As the personal histories of Mew Mew and Cher (obviously, they're made for each other) are slowly revealed, crusty old Grandpa also starts softening his attitude toward the illegitimate Ka-Ka. The only fly in the ointment is the vengeful Vietnamese villain Bullet (played with square-jawed greasy psychosis by Roy Cheung), who just can't stop chasing that cop. But fear not, this film is not School on Fire. Happy ending ahoy.

Show biz siblings

Ever wonder why David Chiang (Shaw Brothers star often paired with Ti Lung), veteran actor Paul Chun Pui and actor/director Derek Yee all look somewhat alike, yet not quite brothers? The robust, handsome trio who've all had decades-long careers in film and television dramas, are all half-brothers.

Patrick Tse, who's still a Hong Kong celebrity, was in his prime in the 1960s. One of Tse's starring roles was in Patrick Lung Kong's *Story of a Discharged Prisoner* (1967), which served as inspiration for John Woo's *A Better Tomorrow* (1986). Tse's son, Nicholas Tse, has a singing career but also has an impressive film career, including the transcendent *Beast Stalker* (2008). And sister of Nicholas/daughter of Patrick Jennifer Tse is not only a model, but starred in *Naked Soldier* (2012).

Veteran Shaws actor Fan Mei-sheng continued his career, usually playing burly heavies with facial hair. Fan went clean-shaven and opted for a crewcut as the villainous deputy prison warden in 1992's *Story of Ricky*. In his introductory scene, he's stabbing his prosthetic claw in a bloody beefsteak as the titular character (played by Louis Fan Siu-wong) is frog-marched in for a chat. Fan unhooks his claw from the meat and stabs it into Ricky's hand to show just who's in charge. Both actors are surnamed Fan...yes, that's a real-life father and son acting duo.

Hex Errors: Philosophy & Wisdom

More fractured English subtitles from your favorite Hong Kong movies. (See page 30 for a full explanation.)

"What is a soul?"
"It's just a toilet paper."
To Hell with the Devil

"What is it that drills your nerves? MONEY!"
The Last Message

"The human sense is nonsense."
"But human blood is superb."
The Golden Swallow

"The fart of God."
"What does it mean?"
"With a remarkable sound."
The Informer

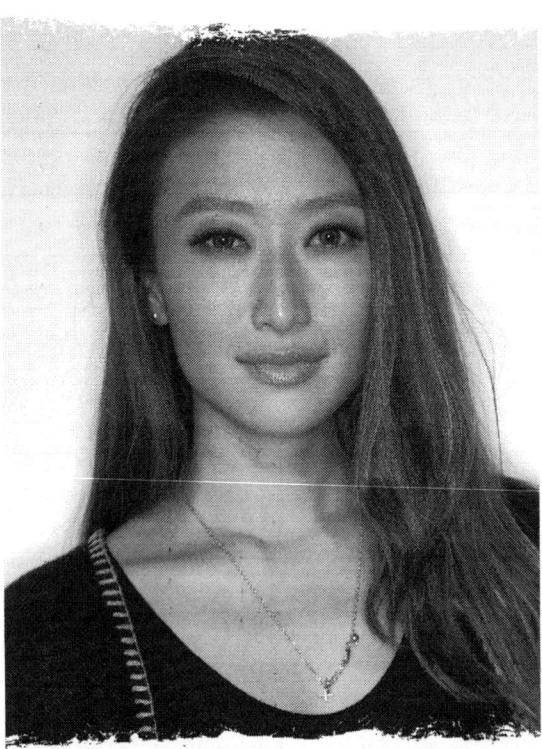

Jennifer Tse looking, well, errrr... fabulous.

MORE SEX, BETTER ZEN, FASTER BULLETS

Ringo Lam Ling-tung 林嶺東 (1955–2018). Irascible, opinionated, workaholic, lauded, respected, and never forgotten.

"Very simple, open the coffin, and suck the air from the vampire leader"
The Ultimate Vampire

"Cheat him with false leg raise"
Kickboxer's Tears

"Not any nuts will admit they are nuts!"
Naked Killer

"The bullets inside are very hot. Why do I feel so cold?"
Lethal Panther

"A toad is no match for a swan"
Robotrix

"My world is to companion with calabash till drunk"
Shaolin Drunkard

"Man! Why beat! Take it easy"
The Nocturnal Demon

"Don't get trouble not belonging to you"
Dreaming the Reality

"Bastard, an inch longer, an inch stronger"
Fong Sai Yuk

"I'm not... I'm!"
My Neighbours are Phantoms

"When the tree falls, the monkeys run."
Fantasy Mission Force

"The dying men are bored."
The Assassin

Jet Li as another Chinese folk hero: Fong Sai Yuk.

CHAPTER FOURTEEN
THE AFTERBURNER
by Wade Major

To fans of Hong Kong films like *Once Upon A Time In China* (*OUATIC*), *Fong Sai Yuk*, *Fist of Legend*, and *My Father is a Hero*, Jet Li seems a born action star. His physical dexterity, matinee idol smile, stunning martial abilities, boyish charms and seething intensity seem such a natural part of Hong Kong cinema, that it's hard to believe his success was once anything but assured.

Born in Beijing in 1963, Li Lian-jie—his Mandarin birth name—began his martial arts career at age 8 when he was sent to the Beijing Amateur Sports School to receive instruction in wushu—a regimen that mixes a variety of Chinese martial styles, including traditional weaponry training. With the help of his coach, Wu Bin, Jet's prodigious talents were realized at the tender age of eleven, when he earned the national title of All-Around Champion. It was a title which he would continue to hold for the next five years.

Had he been born in Hong Kong, a career in martial arts films would have been the obvious next step. Transitioning to martial arts movies on the mainland, however, was a stroke of remarkable luck and timing. By 1980, encouraged by the success of Hong Kong productions in the region, Chinese authorities finally decided to try their hand at the genre. Enlisting China's most famous wushu champion was a no-brainer.

In 1982, the strategy paid off with the release of *Shaolin Temple*. While the movie followed the basic plot (a young man seeks to learn the skills of the Shaolin fighting arts to avenge his father's death), it had two unique selling points: It was shot on location at the *Shaolin Temple* itself—and it starred Jet Li.

Despite lacking the dynamic stylistic flourishes of a Hong Kong production, *Shaolin Temple* enjoyed widespread success throughout the continent. Sadly, it was a shallow success—a noteworthy last gasp of a dying genre. By the time of the film's release, Hong Kong filmmakers were already embarking on a new path, pursuing what would become known as the bravest period of their cinematic history.

The New Wave washes clean

For decades, Hong Kong cinema had been ruled by mythical hero films and grittier, straightforward kung fu films. With the arrival of a new, more sophisticated breed of filmmakers, all of that abruptly changed. Seminal figures like Tsui Hark, John Woo, Jackie Chan, Chow Yun-fat and Ringo Lam were the most recognizable personalities of a 1980s "New Wave" that earned the industry artistic recognition across the globe. The poor dubbing and far-fetched fights long associated with the colony's earlier movies had been

displaced by a seductive cocktail of explosive action, death-defying stunts and stylish visuals that surpassed even the most expensive Hollywood productions. But Hong Kong's new auteurs were not simply borrowing a Hollywood formula—they were improving upon it and exporting it back to America and Europe where a fan base was growing with cult-like fervor. Gangster films and the stunt-oriented action films pioneered by Jackie Chan were fast eclipsing traditional fare like *Shaolin Temple*.

Two unsuccessful *Shaolin Temple* sequels proved the trend, and Jet's celebrity began to fade as fast as it had soared. Adjusting to new genres proved equally frustrating. A debut directorial effort entitled—*Born to Defence*—and the obscure action/comedy *Dragon Fight* likewise

failed to revive his popularity. As the 1980s drew to a close, it seemed as though only a miracle could put Jet back on top.

Then, in 1991 that miracle arrived. Its name was Tsui Hark.

Once Upon A Time with Tsui Hark

Tsui Hark's reputation as a hit-maker mogul and popular taste-maker in Hong Kong can roughly be compared to that of Steven Spielberg in Hollywood. As a producer, writer, director and occasional actor, the Vietnamese-born/US-educated Tsui has conquered nearly every genre imaginable and driven the industry's defining trends for the better part of two decades. As a central figure in the move away from traditional films in the early 1980s with his company Film Workshop, it seems ironic that he would become equally central to their revival in the late 1980s. Nonetheless, his 1987 production, *A Chinese Ghost Story*, directed by Ching Siu-tung, did precisely that. An unabashedly old-fashioned mythical hero film at a time when the genre was supposed to have been dead, *A Chinese Ghost Story* was a runaway hit, suggesting for the first time that the "New Wave" might be reaching a saturation point.

Indeed, to longtime observers, a revival of traditional fare seemed not only predictable, but imminent. Life in Hong Kong had long been characterized as a delicate balancing act between Eastern and Western influences, particularly in the cinema. By the late 1980s, the balance had swung noticeably Westward, priming audiences for yet another turnaround.

There was more to the success of *Once Upon A Time In China*, however, than just the revival of a genre. Tsui Hark also revived the legend of Wong Fei-hong, one of the most revered figures in Chinese history, already the subject of dozens of films since the 1940s. A turn-of-the-century hero renowned for his abilities as both a martial artist and a herbalist/physician, Wong's defense of Chinese culture against Western encroachment, while opposing internal political corruption,

MORE SEX, BETTER ZEN, FASTER BULLETS

New mold: Jet Li in *Once Upon A Time In China*.

continues to be seen as an atypical manifestation of Confucian values in a practical, modern setting. Wong Fei-hong was not only an emblem of what all Chinese aspired to be, but a modern example that such an ideal was attainable. With such headline issues as Chinese reunification and the perceived intrusion of Western sensibilities increasingly on people's minds, Tsui sensed that the time was right for Wong's return.

OUATIC's story finds Wong Fei-hong caught in a historic tug-of-war for the fortunes of Hong Kong—forced to battle greedy imperialist forces from England, France and the USA, as well as corrupt local officials and anyone else who placed their own interest above that of China. But without a suitable actor in the part, Wong simply would not have resonance for audiences. For most fans, Wong Fei-hong would forever be synonymous with the great Kwan Tak-hing, who played the part in more than 50 films during the 50s and 60s. And then there was Jackie Chan's immortal turn as an impetuous, youthful Wong in 1978's *Drunken Master*. Any actor seeking the part would not only face comparisons to the real Wong, but also to a pair of Hong Kong film legends.

Jettin' in

In view of these hurdles, the casting of Jet Li must have seemed foolhardy. Nine years after *Shaolin Temple*, he was still a one-hit wonder. Nor could Tsui plead ignorance, for he and Jet had already worked together on the unreleased 1988 immigrant-out-of-water tale *The Master* (finally released in 1992).

In the event, Jet was perfectly cast as Wong Fei-hong. His *Shaolin Temple* rep dated him back to a time before gangsters, gunfights and car chases conquered Hong Kong screens. And as a mainlander, his perceived ties to China's pure cultural heritage were stronger than those of his Hong Kong- and Taiwan-born colleagues. Jet was the nexus where Hong Kong's cinematic and historic pasts converged, a true son of the motherland who, like Wong Fei-hong, had weathered a period of Western cultural bombardment and emerged untarnished. When he reappeared as Wong in *OUATIC*, it was as if audiences were rediscovering two heroes from the past, spiritually joined in one movie.

To fully appreciate the magnitude of the film's impact on Hong Kong filmgoers of the time, one need look no further than the pre-credit prologue. A shipboard Dragon Dance—attended by Wong— is interrupted by a rifle assault from a nearby

French vessel. The French soldiers have mistaken firecrackers for attacking gunfire and responded accordingly. Ordinarily, audiences would expect a rousing fight to ensue, with Wong the victor. Instead, Jet Li's Wong steps in and finishes the celebration in style, ignoring the foreign interruption as though it had never happened. The movies had supplied plenty of martial heroes in the past, but none so courageous or dignified in their defense of Chinese culture as this new Wong Fei-hong. In the span of only a few minutes, Jet Li and Tsui Hark had redefined Wong Fei-hong for a new generation.

So smartly conceived was the film that it seemed to have something for everyone—first-rate production values, keen writing, breathtaking choreography, an army of popular supporting cast-members (Kent Cheng, Jacky Cheung, Rosamund Kwan, Yuen Biao), and a catchy theme song. Most importantly, the movie showcased Jet's acting and fighting skills to a far greater degree than any of his previous films. The package was irresistible.

Perhaps the most important aspect of the film's success, though, is the chemistry of the collaboration. It is a truism of filmmaking that good directors are as crucial to the creation of stars as the innate talents of the stars themselves. Though Jet was clearly no diamond in the rough when Tsui selected him for the role, neither was he the polished gem that Tsui would make of him. In the end, it took a director of Tsui's insight and sensitivity to isolate and magnify Jet's filmic strengths.

Whether by coincidence or design, Tsui conceived his new Wong Fei-hong as a cross between Hong Kong's two greatest action stars. Like Bruce Lee, he would be an unrepentant hero, courageous and forthright, exhibiting no fear in the face of a challenge. Like Jackie Chan, he would be a people's hero, easily accessible and not so obviously heroic. His enemies would find him easy to underestimate, making his eventual triumph all the more satisfying for the audience. Here, too, Jet's own experience seemed to mirror that of his character. For years, his gentle, boyish features had overshadowed his obvious physical abilities, making it hard to compete with more chiseled actors in the mold of the archetypal hero.

Such a contradiction, however, was precisely what Tsui needed to make his Wong dramatically viable; a boy who could become a man at the drop of a hat, a healer who could be a ferocious fighter, a figure who seemed to harmonize peace and violence. The advantages to the approach are clear in the film's famous finale—a dazzling dockside showdown between Wong and rival Iron Fist Yim. Fighting on precariously balanced ladders and swinging cargo flats, the two men engage in an epic battle made even more striking by the contrast between the two characters. While the grizzled, sweaty Yim grunts and growls, Wong remains composed and serene, suggesting that one need not become like one's enemies to defeat them.

One directs, the other just jets

Stylistically, the marriage between Tsui's visual sensibilities and Jet's physical skills proved even more formidable, establishing a recipe for staging action that most of Jet's subsequent directors—including Corey Yuen and Yuen Woo-ping—have endeavored to emulate. It was an approach that owed as much to the hyperactive supernatural films of yesteryear as to straightforward kung fu films. Tsui's natural instincts had always leaned in this direction, as evidenced by his landmark 1983 film *Zu: Warriors from the Magic Mountain*. And while there would obviously be no place for sorcery, ghosts or flying people in a historical piece like *OUATIC*, other motifs and techniques could be adapted to help breathe life into an otherwise familiar genre.

It is generally taken for granted by Hong Kong movie fans that the use of wide-angle lenses, extreme angles, rapid editing, exaggerated camera movement and wirework so prevalent in supernatural hero films are as much cinematic trickery as stylistic imprimaturs, devices used to create the impression that characters possessed abilities far beyond those of mere mortals. Consequently, their use in *OUATIC* suggests careful planning on Tsui's part, a conscious attempt to marry style and narrative so as to dispel any suspicion that Jet's skills might really be less remarkable than they appeared.

In the film's tamer first half, the major action sequences are straightforward and unostentatious, relying more on realistic choreography and workmanlike editing than wirework. A brawl in an English restaurant, followed several minutes later by a fight with local thugs in which Jet uses a simple umbrella as his only weapon are showcases for Jet, not Tsui. By the time the film reaches its mid-point—an assassination attempt on Wong's life during a Peking Opera performance—Tsui's stylistic signature is more evident, becoming increasingly so until the final face-off. Remarkably, the embellishment never seems to detract from Jet's skills, director and star so perfectly complimenting each other that, by the end, there seems little point in trying to discern their respective contributions.

A noteworthy footnote to the collaboration pertains to the respective foreign origins of both Jet and Tsui. A Beijing native and a American-educated Vietnamese immigrant coming together on a Hong Kong production about a legendary Chinese hero—ironic if not for the

Part Deux: *Once Upon A Time In China 2.*

pervasive message of tolerance qualifying the patriotic theme. "Everything is changing. What will we change into?", Wong asks early in the film. The answer comes by way of his relationship with "Aunt" Yee (Rosamund Kwan) for whom he has obvious feelings, despite the problems that her love of things Western creates for him. It is a relationship that directly reflects Hong Kong's own love/hate relationship with the West, suggesting that cultural conflicts can and must be resolved to the benefit of all parties.

The sequel

If *OUATIC* made Jet a star, the sequel turned him into a household name. It was, in almost every conceivable way, the perfect follow-up—no small achievement in an industry known for sequelizing its franchises to death. On the one hand, *Once Upon A Time In China* 2, released in 1992, delivered all the requisite elements that had made the first film so successful—dazzling action, historical insight, pristine production values and a complex storyline that once again dropped Wong Fei-hong into the center of a tangled, multi-factional fight for China's future. But at the same time, the new film managed to expand upon the themes and concerns of its predecessor, adding dimensionality to Wong's character and giving Jet a chance to showcase acting abilities barely touched upon in the previous film.

With two interlocking storylines and two distinct adversaries, Tsui's follow-up script maintained the original's feel for the chaos that dominated the politics of late 19th century China, but with a more accessible story-line. On the one hand there is the mystical White Lotus Sect, an idol-worshipping, xenophobic cult with the bizarre dual aims of killing all foreigners and liberating the poor. On the other, there is the future president of the Chinese Republic, Dr Sun Yat-sen, whom the government has labeled a dangerous revolutionary, entrusting his arrest to Regional Commander Lan (Donnie Yen). It is into this uncertain and volatile environment that Wong Fei-hong arrives for a Canton medical convention, accompanied by Aunt Yee and his student Fu (Max Mok replacing Yuen Biao). Ever the moral barometer, Wong wastes no time taking sides against the White Lotus Sect and befriending the charismatic Dr Sun, putting himself on a direct collision course with both Commander Lan and the White Lotus Sect's secretive leader, Priest Kung.

That Wong's enemies in the sequel are Chinese, rather than foreign, is easily its most fundamental departure from the original, a thematic shift that enables Tsui to recast Wong as a more vulnerable, compassionate, compromising and romantic hero. Because audiences had already responded so strongly to Jet's softer portrait of heroism, pushing Wong even further in the same direction was a logical progression. He had already proven himself a hero and an unbeatable fighter. Now, Tsui and Jet would have the chance to prove him a human being.

Early in the film, when Aunt Yee reveals her true feelings to Wong, the confession stirs an almost adolescent awkwardness beneath the heroic veneer. Later scenes become irresistibly cute, with Jet evoking the embarrassment, uncertainty and wide-eyed bliss of first love, at one point even succumbing to a mild bout of jealousy. Elsewhere, a more fatherly Wong emerges to care for and protect a group of children whose instructors have been killed by the White Lotus.

A more elemental softening of Wong Fei-hong's character stems from his brief, yet memorable encounter with Sun Yat-sen. When wounded Westerners are brought into the English consulate, Wong and Sun work together to relieve the suffering, bringing the best of two medical systems together: while Wong anesthetizes the patients with acupuncture, Dr Sun performs Western-style invasive surgery. What makes the scene so remarkable is less the awestruck reception that Wong's medicinal skills receive from the English than Wong's own awe at the wonders of Western surgery (watch for Hong Kong author Paul Fonoroff as a bearded doctor—he's the one getting his neck broken by Donnie Yen).

If one is to view the White Lotus Sect—with its empty populist rhetoric, mindless patriotism and worship of a Mao-like idol—as a thinly-veiled representation of the Red Guard, it becomes easier to read the Sun Yat-sen subplot as a comment on mainland Chinese intolerance of dissidence, democracy and détente, embodied in the person of Donnie Yen's obsessive, single-minded Commander Lan. In the aftermath of the Tiananmen crackdown, a number of veiled, cautionary attacks on the Chinese regime had appeared in Hong Kong films, led by John Woo's 1990 opus *Bullet in the Head*. But now the *OUATIC* themes of pride and tolerance, which had been preached to Hong Kong's onetime colonial scavengers, were now being delivered to its future rulers by a mainland-born actor.

Elsewhere, the messages are even more direct. The pre-climax confrontation between Wong and Priest Kung that exposes Kung's "powers" as a deception, ends with Kung being symbolically impaled on the finger of the Goddess. Regarding the Sect's Stalinist idolatry, Brother Luke, an associate of Dr Sun's, remarks, "Look at those fools. Giving up their lives for that idol. If all of us are as rotten as them, how can our country be saved?" Then, as if the message were not yet clear enough, Jet's Wong observes, "Gods are useless. You must rely on yourself."

Enter the Yuens

OUATIC 2 added the talent of Yuen Woo-ping—a well known Hong Kong director since Jackie Chan's 1978 *Drunken Master*, and a member of the "Seven Little Fortunes". Yuen's contribution is evident from *OUATIC 2*'s opening sequence—a strange White Lotus ritual highlighted by Peking Opera-style acrobatics and choreography. Yuen's touch is again evident in the stunning Wong/Kung battle which places the combatants atop an "altar" of precariously balanced tables (and later a ceiling beam), requiring them to find increasingly creative ways of not touching the ground (elaborate contests and exotic set pieces are as much a staple of Hong Kong cinema as high-noon gunfights are in American Westerns). But also pay attention to the symbiosis between Jet's wushu and Yuen's Peking Opera-inspired fight choreography, the first of many subsequent collaborations with the major "Yuens" of the industry. Jet had already worked with action directors Yuen Cheung-yan and Yuen Sun-yi on *OUATIC* but it wasn't until *OUATIC 2* and Yuen Woo-ping that the artful blend of techniques from supernatural films and straightforward kung fu films began to acquire the defining characteristics now considered a hallmark of Jet's work.

Today, the success of the *OUATIC* franchise ranks among Hong Kong film's proudest achievements—a triumph transcending both Tsui and Jet's personalities. Countless spin-offs and spoofs, a television series and four more sequels all testify to an enduring legacy.

OUATIC 3 was released in February 1993. Though promising in concept, the story (detailing the Dowager Empress' efforts to turn foreign interests against one another) did little to build on the successful elements of the first two films. It also marked Jet's last appearance as WFH for a while, and a split with Tsui. It is likely, though, that a greater influence on Jet's decision to further his career with other directors was *Swordsman 2*, an "interlude" film made between *OUATIC 2* and *3*.

Though Tsui Hark was still a guiding force as co-screenwriter and producer, the film—a sequel to the 1990 King Hu-directed adaptation of the popular Jin Yong novel—bore the unmistakable stamp of director Ching Siu-tung. Like Ching's *A Chinese Ghost Story*, *Swordsman 2* was an unabashed mythical hero film, featuring an all-star cast and a wild story about a quest for magical scrolls. It was everything that *OUATIC* and

That famous Jet smile, from *Swordsman 2*.

OK it's the back of Jet's head, but any excuse for a pic of Gigi Lai: *Kung Fu Cult Master*.

its sequel were not, proving that Jet's success was independent of Tsui Hark and Wong Fei-hong.

Swordsman 2 is not as Jet-specific as the OUATIC movies. Brigitte Lin as the sorceress Invincible Asia owns the film's best moments, foreshadowing her future triumphs in *Swordsman 3: East is Red* and *The Bride with White Hair*. Jet, despite his lead billing, often seems to be on hand largely for weapons expertise. Still, for the first time since becoming a bona fide star, he was working with another major director, playing a less-than-heroic character, and holding his own with an all-star ensemble; sharing screen time with such co-stars as Lin, his faithful OUATIC companion Waise Lee, Rosamund Kwan, and his future *Fong Sai Yuk* companion Michelle Reis.

The legend of Corey Yuen

1993 was an unusually prolific year for Jet Li—he made his first foray into producing his own films, forging new alliances with directors Corey Yuen and Wong Jing. Together, the pair directed eight of Jet's next ten projects. The five 1993 films that followed OUATIC 3 are also noteworthy for what they do and do not share with the OUATIC series. All are costume action films, of which four are OUATIC-style kung fu films centering on factual heroes from Chinese and martial arts history (Wong Jing's film *Kung Fu Cult Master*, a loopy remake of Shaw Brothers' *Holy Flame of the Martial World*, being the one exception).

Unlike the OUATIC films, however, most are surprisingly light and comic—as befits their directors—a conscious effort on Jet's part to forge a new persona closer to his own personality, while simultaneously distancing himself from Wong Fei-hong.

Wong Jing's *Last Hero in China* is easily the most obvious of these, a quasi-parody of the OUATIC films in which Jet plays a zany Wong Fei-hong as skilled in "chicken dancing" as drunken boxing. On a more serious note is Yuen Woo-ping's *Tai*

OK now it's Jet in battle: *Kung Fu Cult Master*.

Chi Master, a flashy tale loosely based on the life of the alleged originator of Tai Chi. But in the end it was Jet's first foray into producing—the Corey Yuen-directed *Fong Sai Yuk* and its sequel—that would have the greatest impact.

Fong supplants Wong

Fong Sai Yuk is based on the adventures of a real-life, Ching Dynasty-era hero—a kindred legend to that of Wong Fei-hong, yet without Wong's imposing cinematic legacy. Jet was free to fashion *Fong Sai Yuk* in his own image...with a little help from Corey Yuen, who inaugurated the careers of Cynthia Rothrock and Michelle Yeoh with such films as *Blonde Fury*, *Magic Crystal*, *Yes, Madam!* and *Royal Warriors*.

At the same time, as an action director on films like Tsui's *Zu: Warriors from the Magic Mountain* and director of the famed *Saviour of the Soul*, he had proven his skill at directing films with supernatural and mythical themes, earning a reputation as one of the most diverse directing talents in the business. Like most Peking Opera-trained directors, he's expert at constructing elaborate, theatrical set pieces, highlighted by back-breaking stunt-work and a particular fondness for integrating props and exotic locales into action sequences. Like his friends Jackie and Sammo, he also viewed genre conventions with skepticism, injecting his films with a mischievous irreverence ideally suited to helping Jet swap the unflappable Wong Fei-hong for the prankish *Fong Sai Yuk*.

Fong Sai Yuk owes as much to Hollywood as to Hong Kong, mixing traditional elements with those of farce and screwball comedy to produce one of the most utterly original Hong Kong films ever made, an entertainment that owes as much to Billy Wilder as to Tsui Hark. It's irresistibly clever.

The ingeniously constructed story finds the Ching emperor Ch'ien Lung so haunted by fear of assassination at the hands of the Red Flower Society, that he sends Governor Oryeetor (Zhao Wen Zhou) to seize the Society's list of members and hunt them down one by one. Meanwhile, in Canton, a former bandit-turned-landowner named Tiger Lu (Chen Sung-yung) looks to legitimize himself with the locals by offering the hand of his daughter, Ting Ting (*Swordsman 2*'s Michelle Reis), to whomever can defeat his wife Siu Wan (Sibelle Hu) in a kung fu competition. Mischief-making young *Fong Sai Yuk*—not realizing he has already met the real Ting Ting—almost wins, but intentionally loses when he mistakes a homely servant girl for the would-be bride. To salvage family pride, Sai Yuk's mother (played by the delightful Josephine Siao) enters the contest, masquerading as Sai Yuk's brother "Tai Yuk" and winning not only the hand of Ting Ting...but the heart of Ting Ting's mother. Sai Yuk and his mother then cook up a story about Tai Yuk's death, hoping the whole thing will blow over. But Tiger Lu demands a substitute groom, and Sai Yuk finds himself right back where he started.

As if things weren't yet complicated enough, Oryeetor shows up to enlist the help of Tiger Lu in tracking down the keeper of the elusive list... Sai Yuk's father (Paul Chu-kong). As both families suddenly feel the repercussions of being on the bad side of the Emperor, the film's jovial tone becomes somber, multiplying tragedy and misfortune until the carefree Sai Yuk is forced to rise to the occasion and become both a hero and a man.

Convincingly adopting a trajectory that was the diametric opposite of Wong Fei-hong's—a boy who becomes a man as opposed to a man coming to grips with his boyish predilections—was an impressive feat, as was Corey Yuen's deft juggling of so many diverse comedic and dramatic elements. Funny, touching, thrilling and romantic—*Fong Sai Yuk* was a cinematic potpourri that Hong Kong audiences wouldn't soon forget.

Key to the tricky execution was exploiting Jet's own charisma and personality, giving audiences enough campy action and self-referential wit to insure that everyone was in on the joke. After an early run-in with police, Sai Yuk assuages his two friends' fears that their parents might find out, confessing that he gave false names to the police. When his friends ask what name he gave for himself, he strikes the familiar pose of Wong Fei-hong and declares, "Wong...Jing!" It's a ferociously funny double-joke that endears a new hero at the expense of an old one while paving the way for Jet's future transition to contemporary action films. The setting of *Fong Sai Yuk* may have been period, but its spirit was inescapably modern.

Though stylistically campier than anything in the *OUATIC* series, Corey Yuen's approach was essentially the same as Tsui Hark's, using the elegance and versatility of Jet's wushu to seamlessly fuse techniques from both traditional kung fu films and supernatural films. Many of the resulting set pieces testify to a chemistry between actor and director that surpasses even that between Jet and Tsui Hark, with the tower-top challenge a must-see. The contest has one simple rule—whoever touches the ground, loses. Every imaginable possibility and combination is exploited. At one point, the furious combat shifts from the tower onto the heads and shoulders of the spectators!

Although most of the scene is wirework-aided, there is still ample opportunity for Jet to showcase the range of his martial talents. Bodies run, jump, hurl, fall, fly, kick and spin so quickly and so elegantly that technique almost disappears. Subsequent scenes adhere to the same stylistic recipe, although with less complexity and, oftentimes, even more humor. In one such scene, Sai Yuk and his mother furiously trade blows with Oryeetor, eventually backing off and simply staring as Oryeetor embarrasses himself by continuing to fight opponents that are no longer there. The joke proved so popular that it was repeated in the sequel.

And yet, it is neither action nor humor for which *Fong Sai Yuk* and its sequel—released an amazing four months later—are best remembered, but the chemistry between Jet and Josephine Siao, a one-time superstar herself during the 1960s. Together, Sai Yuk and Mama Fong are more like a kung fu Laurel & Hardy—partners and co-conspirators in mischief with a familial knack for kicking butt... and mucking up just about everything else (Jackie Chan echoed the schtick in *Drunken Master 2* with Anita Yuen as Jackie's stepmother). Again, it was a dynamic for which Jet was uniquely suited—he played both the impulsive son and the fearless fighter with equal aplomb.

Picking up where the first film left off, *Fong Sai Yuk*'s one great strength is that it expands upon the relationship, further developing the character of *Fong Sai Yuk* in much the same way that *OUATIC 2* helped evolve Wong Fei-hong through his relationship with Aunt Yee. As an internal political struggle threatens to tear the Red Flower Society apart, even threatening his marriage to Ting Ting, only Sai Yuk's relationship with his mother remains constant. In the awe-inspiring climax—reminiscent of a similar scene in the first film—Sai Yuk must balance a column of chairs to save his mother from a hangman's noose, while fending off an army of attackers. It's a magnificent tour-de-force for Jet, Josephine and Corey Yuen that proves the formidability of their collaboration and the "*Fong Sai Yuk*" formula.

Even if *Fong Sai Yuk* had failed to redirect Jet's career, it's certain that *Tai Chi Master* would have done the job. Jet's only collaboration with Yuen Woo-ping as a director (who has thrice served as action director on Jet Li films) bears a sharp resemblance to the style, substance and formula of the *Fong Sai Yuk* and *OUATIC* films while adding enough of Woo-ping's own patented artistry to keep the recipe fresh.

The story is a fictionalized telling of the alleged creator of the martial art Tai Chi wrapped around a more conventional "friends-turned-enemies" morality tale. Raised from childhood to be monks at the *Shaolin Temple*, Tianbao (Chin Siu-ho) and elder brother Junbao (Jet Li) are the most unlikely of friends. Though technically the senior, Junbao is compassionate and forgiving to the point of naiveté, while egotistical Tianbao resents all authority and longs only for power and privilege—appetites that eventually get them both expelled from the Temple and cast into the harsh world of the Ching Dynasty. As the political realities of the era magnify their respective differences and ambitions, the friends part ways—Tianbao joining ranks with the powerful Eunuch Liu Jin, and Junbao falling in with a group of anti-government Taoist rebels, including a ferocious fighter/jilted wife named Qiuxue (Michelle Yeoh).

Ruthlessly determined to work his way up the imperial ladder at any and all costs, Tianbao uses his friendship with Junbao to lure the rebels into an ambush from which only Junbao, Qiuxue and the redoubtable Reverend Ling manage to survive. The betrayal pushes Junbao into a catatonic stupor from which he emerges only after being struck by an epiphanic realization regarding such fundamental Taoist principles as man's harmonious relationship with nature and the redeeming qualities within oneself. Dragsville.

The realization, however, does more than simply lift his spiritual burden—it prompts him to a deeper understanding of the martial arts whereby he evolves a powerful, revolutionary new style of fighting in which less becomes more as the aggressive force of one's opponent is turned against them. Or, as it were, against Tianbao during the ensuing and obligatory finale. When Tianbao finally demands to know the name of this invincible new form of boxing, Junbao proudly proclaims, "Tai Chi."

Given Jet's stature as the foremost interpreter of heroes and historical figures—not to mention his broad skills with all forms of martial arts—it's hard to imagine anyone else in the lead. Indeed, his riveting demonstrations of Tai Chi boxing are among the film's great joys. The end-battle is a logical extension of the *OUATIC* finale, with Jet once again the victorious vessel of inner peace.

Like *Fong Sai Yuk*, Junbao is a carefree youth dragged kicking, screaming, and ultimately triumphantly into adulthood through personal tragedy. Several key scenes closely parallel set pieces in the *Fong Sai Yuk* films. Junbao's rescue of Qiuxue from Tianbao is a case in point—a near-perfect duplicate of the two previous "rescue" scenes in the *Fong Sai Yuk* films, with additional throwbacks to the infamous tower challenge. While Qiuxue hangs from a cross atop a log scaffold, Tianbao and Junbao do battle first on the ground and then with the logs—Tianbao working to destabilize the tower and topple Junbao while Junbao struggles to free Qiuxue and keep the tower from collapsing.

By early 1994, another career shift was in the offing. But this time Jet would not have to abandon his director—he had found in Corey Yuen a talent that perfectly complemented his own—a director forceful enough to bring out his best, yet versatile enough to change and grow with him.

With Corey Yuen as action director, they next worked together on Wong Jing's 1994 *New Legend of Shaolin*, another effective exploitation of Jet's successful "gentle warrior" persona. Borrowing from the popular Japanese "Lone Wolf & Cub" films (better known as the "Babycart" series), Wong's screenplay refashioned the story as a mix of "Ming Rebel" and "Shaolin Temple" genre elements, spiced with his own unique brand of haphazard outlandishness. The saving grace was the magical pairing of Jet and Tze Miu—a seven-year-old scene-stealing martial arts prodigy—as a devoted father and son kung fu team. The pairing proved so popular that they re-teamed on Corey Yuen's far-better *My Father is a Hero* the next year.

New Legend of Shaolin, is fun but it's not a unique contribution to Jet's body of work. In contrast to his best work with Tsui Hark and Corey Yuen, there is a sense that he is no longer an equal participant in the action. Outside of some impressive spear and staff fighting, the film is so dominated by wirework and Wong Jing's signature weirdness, that any discernible technique on Jet's part is lost in the shuffle. Even the humor seems oddly uninspired, highlighted by only a handful of memorable deadpan moments between Jet and Tze Miu and a closing cameo by Wong that takes a friendly swipe at *Fong Sai Yuk*.

Ordinarily, it would be easy to dismiss the film as an anomaly in the Jet Li corpus. But the coalescence of so many familiar elements—and cast-members—from previous films, with so little additional innovation, is a sobering reminder that since his *OUATIC* breakthrough, Jet had made nothing but period hero films—a total of ten in four years. If the sheer novelty of finally placing him in a contemporary setting weren't enough to justify the transition now, nothing would.

My director is a hero

The twelve-month period between summer 1994 and summer 1995 would see the release of four (mostly) contemporary films with which Jet would further refine and redefine his image. Ironically, the new career phase followed roughly the same beat as the previous one, with Jet's grittier new persona once again shepherded by the intuitive talents of Corey Yuen and capped by a blast of Wong Jing excess (the action satire *High Risk*) to force yet another career makeover. But by that time, Jet's transition to full-fledged action hero would be complete, leaving nothing unapproached but the path to Hollywood stardom.

Though the move to tougher, more realistic contemporary films (hereafter referred to as "toughies") was the riskiest step of Jet's career to date, at least three of the four films from the period—two directed by Corey Yuen—seem consciously designed to minimize potential pitfalls. Both Corey Yuen projects—*The Bodyguard from Beijing* and *My Father is a Hero*—cast Jet as a fish-out-of-water Mainlander, while the third film—*Fist of Legend*—refashions Bruce Lee's fact-based *Fist of Fury* character as a Wong Fei-hong-style patriot, fighting for Chinese honor against Japanese aggression. All three films also feature a retreat from the high-stylization that had constrained his freedom to showcase unaided wushu techniques in his last few period films. *Fist of Legend* and *My Father is a Hero* in particular contain some of the best examples of straight combat found in any Jet Li film. Best of all, the films belonged to a more "generic action" genre with which Corey Yuen was both familiar and comfortable.

MORE SEX, BETTER ZEN, FASTER BULLETS

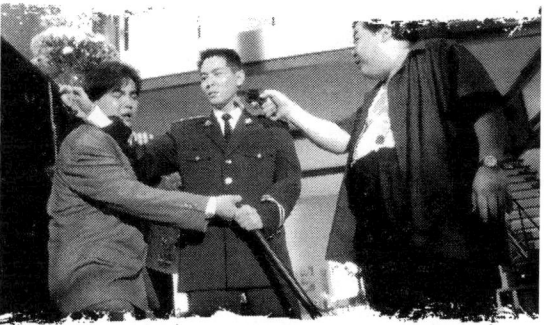

Kent Cheng gets the drop on Jet: *The Bodyguard from Beijing*.

Korean poster for *My Father is a Hero*.

As the first of the four toughies to be released, the success of *The Bodyguard from Beijing* was pivotal—not unlike *Fong Sai Yuk*, their last collaboration on which Jet also served as producer. An amusingly shameless rip-off of the Kevin Costner/Whitney Houston smash *The Bodyguard*, it featured Jet as a stone-faced, hotshot member of an elite Beijing Police bodyguard unit who lands the inauspicious job of protecting a murder witness named Michelle Yeung (Christy Chung), the spoiled girlfriend of a wealthy Hong Kong businessman.

Anyone familiar with *The Bodyguard* can easily fill in the rest, although in this variation, an outright romantic consummation between Jet and Chung is not to be had. The real surprise is that the film contains so little actual fighting. *The Bodyguard from Beijing* doesn't lack action—abundant gunplay and several excellent "lurking assassins" set-pieces give it plenty of juice. But Jet had never so much as touched a gun before—and now he was executing attackers by the dozens. Audiences, fortunately, didn't seem to care. Jet Li the Personality had finally superseded Jet Li the Martial Artist.

Amusingly, the most memorable scene in the film is the climactic showdown—a housebound fight between Jet and Ngai Sing as a revenge-crazed assassin. The sequence is vintage Corey Yuen. As natural gas fills the room, Jet and Ngai are forced to abandon their guns and fight hand-to-hand. But the thinning air and risk of suffocation raises the stakes, turning an ordinary kitchen faucet into a life-saving grail. Props play a part, too—countertops, table legs, venetian blinds and even a wet towel. In visible contrast to the fantastical spectacles of the previous years, the action was rough and realistic—a first-rate showcase for the versatility of Jet's wushu and the sadism of Corey Yuen's rib-cracking stunts.

More and better was the mantra of the duo's next film—*My Father is a Hero*—their last such collaboration to date and viewed by some as the definitive example of their ability to bring out the best in each other. In some ways more reminiscent of a forties-era Hollywood melodrama than a traditional Hong Kong action film, *My Father is a Hero* relates to *Bodyguard* in much the same way that the *OUATIC* and *FSY* sequels relate to their predecessors, broadening the emotional tapestry of Jet's character while adhering to the same narrative and character parameters established in the previous films.

The story re-teams Jet and Tze Miu as another devoted father/son duo—Kung Wei and Kung Siu-ku—who, with their ailing wife and mother, Kung Li Ha, form a seemingly average Chinese family—except for one nagging detail. Unbeknownst to his loved ones, Kung-wei is an undercover police officer. "Just three more months," promise his superiors, and he'll be able to return to a normal, open life. In the meantime, one more assignment awaits—infiltrating a Hong Kong-based smuggling ring run by the psychopathic Po Kwong (Yu Rong Guang).

Shortly after he penetrates the smuggler's inner circle, however, things go disastrously awry, beginning with a semi-botched heist during which Wei is identified by Hong Kong police inspector Fong (Anita Mui). Believing him to be a mainland criminal, Fong travels to China to insinuate herself into the friendship of his family. But her heart is softened upon meeting Siu-ku and Li Ha—now severely ill—who dubs her "Auntie Fong" and, on her death bed, entrusts her with returning the boy to his father after she has died. Suspecting that Wei may be an undercover police officer after all, Fong returns to Hong Kong with Siu-ku and works to fulfill her promise to Li Ha by reuniting the boy with his father and helping extricate Wei from an increasingly dangerous predicament. Wei, meanwhile, fights a complicated battle of wits with the crafty Po Kwong, struggling to maintain his cover while protecting his son from escalating jeopardy. The film culminates in a gripping clash of titans as father and son fight side-by-side against Po and his henchmen.

Despite a higher action quotient than *Bodyguard*, *My Father is a Hero* is actually the dramatically riskier of the two, a mix of sentimental melodrama and action that relies heavily on the abilities of Jet and Corey Yuen to work within the confines of more serious material. Thanks to their versatility—and the smart casting of Anita Mui—many of the film's most memorable scenes involve neither action nor comedy.

When Siu-ku sends an emergency page to his father, alerting him to Li Ha's death, it is Jet Li the actor—not the fighter—who rises to the occasion, wrestling with his emotions, trying to contain his grief for fear of revealing himself to Po Kwong and his gangsters. Corey Yuen then pushes the emotional envelope even further, plunging the audience inside Wei's mind and heart by intercutting his memories of a happier time with the present, and muting the soundtrack so as to create a surreal sense of immediacy. More harrowing still is a later scene in which Wei and Siu-ku must feign ignorance of one another to keep from disclosing Wei's identity to Po Kwong, even as he resorts to beating Siu-ku to within an inch of his life.

The same strain of immediacy runs through the film's many impressive action scenes, most of which place a stronger emphasis on character and relationship than traditional thrills. In the first major set piece, in which Wei battles a pair of assailants on the catwalks of a sports arena while Siu-ku participates in a martial arts competition below, the sophisticated intercutting between Wei and Siu-ku delivers a stern announcement to the audience that there is more at stake than

MORE SEX, BETTER ZEN, FASTER BULLETS

Wei's life—if he loses, Siu-ku may be deprived of a father before his very eyes. It is the beginning of an unabashedly sentimental undertow that governs virtually every scene in the film. It is not simply the triumph of good over evil for which audiences are being prompted to root, but the reunion of a fractured family's two remaining members.

Only during the finale—a shipboard auction of rare artifacts which Po Kwong hopes to hijack—does a recognizable Corey Yuen emerge to indulge more playful instincts with his star of choice. And what indulgence it is. The thunderous clack and clatter of colliding clubs jump-starts the finale as Jet disposes of the first wave of henchmen before moving on to Po Kwong and his lieutenants (*Bodyguard*'s Ngai Sing and Jackie Chan regular Ken Lo). Several bone-crushing minutes later, after Tze Miu joins the fray, the action shifts to Corey Yuen's beloved props—auction artifacts and the ropes suspending them suddenly transformed into weapons of destruction. By the time Wei finally ties Siu-ku to a rope and uses him as a kind of human bola/yo-yo, the audience is having too much fun to object to the shift in tone.

In a sense, it could be argued that the scene is a throwback to the Iron Fist Yim finale of *OUATIC*, a sudden burst of mythical hero film madness purchased with the preceding 90 minutes of relative realism. But by the end, the scene proves to be substantially more daring than derivative. After five years of defining the quintessential gentle hero for Hong Kong audiences, one aspect of Jet's heroism had remained unimpeachable—none of his characters had ever had to rely on luck, good fortune or the good will of others to disentangle themselves from a dilemma. Not so with Wei, who, despite his better efforts, is unable to finish off Po Kwong until the "nick of time" arrival of Inspector Fong. Throughout the film,

Fist of Legend

Wei's fate is more often out of his hands than in, marking an ironic counterpoint to Jet's own career at the time—an actor finally gaining control of his own destiny, opting instead to portray a character so loosely in control of his.

Surprisingly, the most interesting of the toughies for many fans—and martial artists in particular—is the only one of the four with which Corey Yuen was not involved: 1994's *Fist of Legend*, released during the period between *Bodyguard* and *My Father is a Hero*. But *Fist of Legend* featured more than enough Yuen-power to compensate for the absence of Jet's most trusted confidant and director. Written and directed by *Bodyguard* co-screenwriter Gordon Chan, the picture's action team represented a virtual Yuen family reunion from the first two *OUATIC* films—Yuen Woo-ping heading a team that also that included two of the original *OUATIC* action directors, Yuen Cheung-yan and Yuen Sun-yi.

The result—a loose remake of Bruce Lee's *Fist of Fury* and Jet's last effort as a producer to date—was nothing if not spectacular—a rough-and-tumble fight film that plugged his realistic new "contemporary" persona into a more traditional *OUATIC* template.

Based on factual events that transpired in Japanese-occupied 1921 Tsingtao, *Fist of Legend* details the quest of a renowned martial artist named Chen Zhen to expose his master's killers and seek appropriate vengeance. Beginning with the Japanese karate master alleged to have defeated his master in a challenge, Chen follows a conspiratorial trail that finally leads to an epic confrontation with the (seemingly) invincible General Fujita (Billy Chow), a hulking wall of a man hell-bent on humiliating the Chinese into submission by any means necessary.

The obvious hurdles were not unfamiliar—Jet was again playing a revered historical hero with cinematic baggage, a character that most movie fans would forever identify with Bruce. And *Fist of Fury* was anything but obvious source material for a Jet Li film. Bruce's smoldering sexuality and bad-boy arrogance ran counter to everything that audiences had ever responded to in Jet Li. Worse was the film's vicious anti-Japanese rhetoric, anything but reflective of the *OUATIC* message of patriotic tolerance. In the end, however, the contrasts worked in Jet's favor, for they were precisely what gave *Fist of Legend* a revisionist identity all its own.

Not surprisingly, the new and improved Chen Zhen emerged as a slightly more modernistic reflection of Wong Fei-hong—a wise and true patriot who opposes the Japanese aggression against China, yet refuses to project indiscriminate hatred against all Japanese. By no coincidence, the point on which *Fist of Legend* differs most dramatically from *Fist of Fury* is also its most revealing point of commonality with *OUATIC*, namely the decision to give Chen a problematic girlfriend. The girl, a fellow student from the University of Kyoto named Mitsuko, plays a role similar to an Aunt Yee, helping soften Jet's heroic edge, while calling attention to the need for cultural détente between the warring factions. She is, after all, Japanese.

Such considerations, however, played a small role in earning the film its current cult status. For fans, *Fist of Legend* is most revered as a virtual clinic on the martial arts, with Jet demonstrating a mastery of nearly every imaginable fighting style in the world. This is why the Yuen Woo-ping team was assembled, less for the theatricality of their staging than for their encyclopedic knowledge of the varied fighting styles that Jet would be required to master and convincingly execute.

Mere minutes into the film, when Chen is attacked by anti-foreign demonstrators while still a student in Kyoto, he defends himself with Japanese style locks, traps and throws such as one might expect to see in a Jiu-jitsu or Aikido demonstration. Then, half-way through a challenge with his deceased master's son (*Tai Chi Master*'s Chin Siu-ho) for the head-mastership of their school, he abandons traditional kung fu for a cocktail of tactics borrowed from western boxing, Thai kick-boxing and Korean Taekwando. A later challenge with Mitsuko's karate expert uncle, Master Funakoshi—played by real-life karate master Shoji Kurata—goes a step further, with each man fluidly adopting the style of the other.

Finales, of course, are what Jet's movies are made for, and here's where *Fist of Legend* attains the status of legend. The towering, knock-down/drag-out brawl between Chen and General Fujita is marked by nearly fifteen minutes of combative physical abuse so relentless that, at times, it almost doesn't seem to belong in a Hong Kong movie. The contrast of styles so prevalent in previous fights literally disappears in the heat of the anything-goes free-for-all. For once, there are no fancy props, no clever visual gimmicks, no furniture gags. Just two outstanding martial

MORE SEX, BETTER ZEN, FASTER BULLETS

artists (and a team of expert choreographers) working at the peak of their abilities to create what still stands as one of the most blisteringly visceral hand-to-hand confrontations ever recorded.

Jet's farewell to the toughies was also his final Hong Kong collaboration with Corey Yuen and Wong Jing—the Wong-directed 1995 action film satire *High Risk*, in which he played an unsung and under-appreciated movie stuntman who emerges from the shadow of a fading action star (Jackie Cheung) to become the hero of a *Die Hard*-style hostage situation. It was a strange—if predictable—case of history repeating itself, with both Jet and Corey Yuen (as action director) again overshadowed by the excesses of Wong Jing's style—excesses which, as before, capped an era and helped launch a new one.

Identity crisis

In five years, Jet had made fifteen films, reinvented his image (twice), incarnated some of the most cherished figures in Chinese history, and worked with a host of prestigious filmmakers, adapting to and excelling under a diversity of directorial styles. As far as his audience was concerned, he had proven that he had nothing left to prove.

Ironically, Jet's final four Hong Kong films—made between 1996 and his 1998 departure for the financially greener pastures of Hollywood—speak less of a star entering his prime than a creeping identity crisis; a celebrity seemingly more at ease with himself than his image. Now in his early thirties, he still possessed the innocent, youthful demeanor needed to power the dichotomous characters that had defined his place in the movies. But something had begun to change. Characters once deceptively easy to underestimate were giving way to characters that were simply deceptive.

1996's *Dr Wai in 'The Scriptures with No Words'* is the story of a newspaper serialist who guards an imaginary secret life, fancying himself the hero of his own wild 1930s era adventures. A cross between *Raiders of the Lost Ark* and *The Secret Life of Walter Mitty*, the Ching Siu-tung-directed film also reunited Jet with Rosamund Kwan for the first time since *Swordsman 2*.

Later that same year, a re-teaming with producer/writer Tsui Hark and action director Yuen Woo-ping on the Daniel Lee-directed *Black Mask* took the premise a commercial step further. This time Jet's secret superhero alter-ego was real, not imagined, taking its cues from comic book and science fiction influences in America and Asia. In the tradition of *The Heroic Trio* and Corey Yuen's *Saviour of the Soul*, it featured Jet as a seemingly mild-mannered librarian by day, chemically-engineered super-soldier by night. Like *Dr Wai*, it was high-concept and big-budget, long on effects and short on kung fu. High style, however, seemed to make up the difference, with many content to simply soak in Jet's cool new look, complete with trenchcoat, black hat, corrugated steel mask and accompanying James Bond-like guitar theme.

Five months later, it was back to the past as—at long last—Jet rejoined the series that made

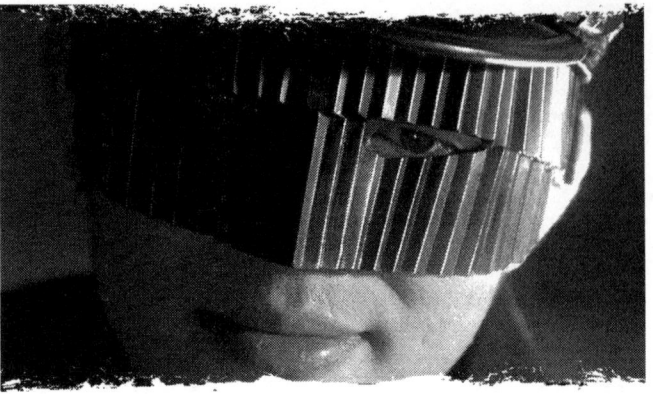
Black Mask

him a star, playing an amnesiac Wong Fei-hong stranded in the American West in the Sammo Hung-directed *Once Upon A Time In China* and *America*. Unlike his characters in the previous four films, Wong wasn't just pretending to be someone he wasn't—he truly believed he was someone he wasn't. This time, there was no missing the obvious real-life parallels, which mirrored Jet's own efforts to escape from and "forget" the character of Wong.

Just months before his Hollywood debut, the most telling portrayal of all unspooled in director Stephen Tung's *Hitman*, in which Jet played a kindly would-be killer-for-hire who had actually never killed anyone. Once again, he was pretending to be something he was not, only this time Jet was flirting with the line separating bad guys from good guys. Unlike the undercover policeman in *My Father is a Hero*, his *Hitman* character—Tai Feng—really does intend to be a killer-for-hire. While both endeavor to conceal an underlying goodness from their criminal cohorts, Tai Feng's moral barometer is more ambiguous. And though the character is never less than endearing—thanks to the contributions of comedian Eric Tsang as Tai Feng's bumbling "agent"—there is no escaping the fact that for the better part of the film, Jet is playing a character on the verge of doing the wrong thing.

Unlike Jackie Chan, whose most popular characters are nearly all variations on himself, Jet had built a career playing individuals whose personalities often contrasted sharply with his own, characters frequently at odds with their own natures. It's clear that as the struggle became an increasingly redundant part of his roles, it spoke to something more personal in his career.

Taken as a group, Jet's last four Hong Kong films cast valuable insight into what may have been transpiring for him professionally and personally. In a seeming attempt to counter the influx of Hollywood product that had begun crippling homegrown product in the late 1990s, the emphasis is on special effects and stylization at the expense of inspired action choreography. Also a factor was the absence of Corey Yuen's guiding influence to help Jet transition once more to a new level in his career, a career built as much on his versatility as an actor as a martial artist. By 1998, it was obvious to many that he was no longer being challenged as either.

But these films are not lacking in entertainment value. *Black Mask* remains a popular favorite, particularly among non-Hong Kong audiences more likely to be seduced by

Hitman

the cyberpunk style than the handful of Yuen Woo-ping designed fight scenes. *Hitman* too has its share of impressive moments, including a nail-biting battle with a gunman in an elevator shaft and an explosive fists-and-bullets climax that keeps audiences guessing to the very end. But the singular attributes of Jet's wushu—his capacity to adapt to any style, to do anything asked of him, to fluidly and artfully accommodate the most demanding action directors, to give the camera precisely the dynamism it needs at any time and from any angle—were no longer being maximized. It was, by all counts, the right time to move to Hollywood. And, more importantly, Hollywood wanted him.

Lethal Hollywood

Given the experience of making his final quartet of Hong Kong films without Corey Yuen, it's not surprising that Jet would make his involvement in *Lethal Weapon 4* contingent upon Corey Yuen's participation, ensuring that he and his favorite collaborator would have as much control as possible over the choreography and staging of his action scenes. The fact that he was playing a villain opposite a superstar like Mel Gibson meant that he would need all the help he could muster in making a positive impression with American audiences. Ironically, it wasn't Corey Yuen's choreography that won audiences over, but the magnetism of Jet's presence, the same fearless intensity behind the youthful, innocent face that Asian audiences had known and loved for a decade. Critical response was fast to embrace Jet as well, with most citing him as the film's sole redeeming element.

What the film did not provide was a clear-cut indication of where Jet's Hollywood career might lead. That he was able to rise above *Lethal Weapon 4*'s preponderance of offensive stereotypes and Asian clichés—at times appearing so dignified as to almost redeem them—was an undeniable positive.

China and the West

The two decades of Jet Li's post-New Wave career have proven as turbulent as the previous two were ascendant. Much of that turbulence, of course, has been beyond Li's control: Hong Kong's 1997 handover to China precipitated an exodus of talent—initially to Hollywood, but more recently to the mainland—that forever altered the kinds of films on which Jet could once rely to bolster his persona. After paying his dues as a cartoon villain in *Lethal Weapon 4*, his initial Hollywood forays were largely in keeping with that persona. The loosely Shakespearean overtones of *Romeo Must Die* (2000), co-starring the late pop star Aaliyah, were evocative of many of Jet's previous hero characters, while his collaborations with French action mega-auteur Luc Besson in *Kiss of the Dragon* (2001) and the spectacularly entertaining *Unleashed* (2005) afforded him a chance to showcase both his action chops and his growing skills as an actor.

As with any Hollywood career, there were also missteps—2001's misbegotten science fiction film *The One* and 2008's desperate attempt to sustain a waning franchise, *The Mummy: Tomb of the Dragon Emperor*, noteworthy only for its wasted re-teaming of Jet Li and Michelle Yeoh. The changing face of Chinese cinema, however, offered new opportunities at home as well. No stranger to legendary figures, Jet's casting in Zhang Yimou's historic 2002 blockbuster *Hero*, alongside *Crouching Tiger, Hidden Dragon* alum Zhang Ziyi and an all-star roundup of fellow Hong Kong emigres including Maggie Cheung, Donnie Yen and Tony Leung Chiu-wai, shattered records across the

THE AFTERBURNER

Jet Li: *Hero*.

nation, earning him his biggest hit to date.

Ronny Yu's *Fearless* (2006) and Peter Chan's *Warlords* (2007) further exploited his resurgent popularity with familiar variations on previous characters, splashily repackaged in the kinds of glossy, big-budget spectacles that only a massive infusion of mainland cash could have facilitated.

Still, despite such successes, it was fast becoming clear that Jet was aging—and increasingly doing little more than offering fans a "greatest hits" assemblage of previous performances. By the time of his pairing with Jackie Chan in 2008's *The Forbidden Kingdom*—an entertaining but overblown wuxia epic aimed at American teenagers—it was a "too little, too late" harbinger of things to come: two aging stars, past their prime, looking to borrow just enough of each other's bygone glory for one last cinematic fling. No surprise that two years later Jet would join Sylvester Stallone's equally shameless aging action star mashup *The Expendables*, effectively conceding the passing of his era.

Between *Expendables* sequels, Jet's screen presence in recent years has been consistent, but unremarkable—like the name directors with whom he continues to work (Tsui Hark on *Flying Swords of Dragon Gate* and Tony Ching Siu-tung on *The Sorcerer and the White Snake*, both in 2011), he now seems to live largely off the nostalgia for an era when films made for a fraction of the cost and resources felt tenfold more original and spirited. None of which is to suggest that Jet is in the twilight of his career, nor that yet another resurgence is out of the question, however unlikely it may seem. If Jet Li has learned anything from his on-screen counterparts, it is that champions are forever.

John Woo on the set of A Better Tomorrow.

CHAPTER FIFTEEN

BETWEEN THE BULLETS: THE SPIRITUAL CINEMA OF JOHN WOO

by Michael Bliss

John Woo is the man of a thousand faces. He's the romantic Christian idealist who loves guns and explosions. He's the man of peace who choreographs death and destruction better than anyone working in movies today. He's the action director who numbers among his favorite films *Citizen Kane*. He's the Hong Kong auteur who made the Hollywood system listen to a truly ethical voice for the first time since the heyday of Griffith and Stroheim.

John Woo is the most important director to emerge from Hong Kong cinema. Like Akira Kurosawa, Woo is a difficult fit because he blends Western humanism with Asian attitudes. And like Kurosawa, he's a man who knows that often, violence and peace are inextricably linked.

Just about everybody has seen or heard about *The Killer* and *Hard-Boiled*, and most agree that nobody since Sam Peckinpah has stylized violence the way that Woo does. But unlike Peckinpah, whom Woo greatly admires, Woo isn't a pessimist. Peckinpah was a disgruntled man who thought that most people were a disappointment. Woo believes in people, and feels that faith, redemption, and friendship aren't just ideals but realities.

There's a classic moment in Peckinpah's *The Wild Bunch* to which Woo often refers (he even resurrects it in the last minutes of *A Better Tomorrow 2*). Tired of running from bounty hunters and the law, The Bunch risk their lives by going back into the middle of a small Mexican town to rescue their friend. Woo would have shaped Peckinpah's film a bit differently, though. In Woo's films, characters don't just do the right thing when their backs are to the wall—their morals are always on display.

Most likely this is because in Woo's universe, everyone is always close to the end of the line. Woo probably wouldn't admit it, but he's apocalyptic. For him, life is short and unpredictable so we have to act conscientiously always, not just when we're forced to do so. In addition to all of the delirious gunfire in Woo's films, there's always a powerful morality operating. Where did this philosophy come from, and how did it get into the films? To answer that question, we have to go back to Woo's childhood.

Genesis

John Woo was born in 1946 in China's Guangdong Province, which is only 70 miles upriver from Hong Kong. Woo's father didn't like living under Communist rule, so in 1951 he moved the family to Hong Kong. But in 1953, after a terrible fire, the family found itself homeless. They lived in the streets for a year, then in a slum. His father contracted tuberculosis and was unable to work; the family was too poor to send John to school. Fortunately, an American family's donation through a church was used to send John to a Lutheran school. Woo never forgot this generosity. He planned to become a minister so that he could in some way repay it.

After his father's death, Woo became interested in film, but he had to be self-taught because there were no film schools in Hong Kong. In 1969, he became a production assistant at Cathay Studios. In 1971, he began work at the Shaw Brothers studio as an assistant to the studio's most prolific director, Chang Cheh. One of the major things that Woo learned from Chang was to be honest in films. Woo says that Chang was like Peckinpah, especially "in his unrestrained way of writing emotions and chivalry."

Fists, kicks, laughs, and a redemptive return

As a Shaw employee, Woo realized that he would have to make films in line with the studio's emphasis on formulaic martial arts dramas. Woo directed his first film, *The Young Dragons*, in 1975. *Dragon Tamers* was next, followed by *Hand of Death*, in which Woo directed a young Sammo Hung and an even younger Jackie Chan. He then turned to comedies with *Money Crazy* (a big hit) and *Follow the Star*. He tried to branch out with the heroic *Last Hurrah for Chivalry*, but the studio wasn't pleased with the film's serious tone, so Woo, who had been dubbed the "new king of comedy," was encouraged to make the lighthearted *From Rags to Riches*, which was followed by 1981's *To Hell with the Devil*. Unfortunately, *THWTD*'s mix of comic and serious elements didn't please the studio either. Nor did a film called *Sunset Warriors* (1983), a story about modern-day mercenaries trying to topple a drug lord. (The film was shelved, although it re-emerged in 1987, re-cut and retitled as *Heroes Shed No Tears*.)

The following years, 1984-85, were the worst in Woo's career. Dubbed by the studio as old-fashioned, he was sent to Taiwan, where he was able to direct only two films, *Run, Tiger, Run* and *Time You Need A Friend*. It was a time when Woo really needed a friend, and one came through for him: Tsui Hark, a young director whom he'd helped years before. Tsui had started his own studio, Film Workshop, and offered Woo the chance to direct something he really believed in. The result was the astounding *A Better Tomorrow* (1986).

If you want to find the starting point for *ABT*'s excitement, you don't have to go back much further than *To Hell With the Devil*, which is the first real John Woo film. It's a story about an aspiring pop singer (played by comic actor Ricky Hui) who sells his soul in exchange for fame. Two men fight for the singer's soul: a newly-made devil and a bumbling priest (Paul Chun Pui), who will get into heaven only if he wins the battle. *THWTD* is a Hong Kong Faust story with touches of Brian De Palma's *The Phantom of the Paradise*. The task for Woo seems to have been: how do I tell people how easy it is to hazard one's soul without boring everyone to death? A comedy was the answer. Woo had made plenty of them before. Now, he realized that he could use low comedy to serve a high purpose. There are silly bits involving video games, lasers shooting out of the priest's eyeballs, and the devil getting his head knocked off and running around looking for it, but eventually, the singer is saved.

Just like Woo was saved by Tsui Hark. When Tsui gave Woo the chance to direct something with heart, something he really believed in, how else do you suppose Woo saw it if not as a miraculous rebirth? When Woo returned to Hong Kong to make *A Better Tomorrow*, he must have felt like *THWTD*'s pop singer: back from damnation. Woo put everything he had into his comeback film, bringing with him a slew of ideas born out of his personal, difficult experiences. He took stories from his childhood, blended them with his notion that the triads were morally eating away at Hong Kong society, and wrote a scenario. Then he called up a television actor who'd had a bit part in *THWTD*, Chow Yun-fat. The result was the most influential Hong Kong film of the 80s.

Trenchcoat icon

A Better Tomorrow revolutionized Hong Kong filmmaking, not only by taking sword fighting and

martial arts interplay and updating them to men with guns, but by blending together high moral codes, chivalry, Chinese Opera, and the notion of the knight errant. As you might expect, this is no mean trick. Woo didn't flinch from violence or humor and he wasn't afraid to be sentimental. Reaching deep down inside himself, he gave his film history, soul, and an unabashedly romantic story. The characters in this film shed tears from the very beginning They sweat out their anxieties about family and friends. Although there are nods to earlier Woo films (the slapstick comic business with Leslie Cheung's Kit and Kit's girlfriend, Jackie), *ABT* is mostly a story about a man and his brother, on opposite sides of the law, who come to a painful reconciliation thanks to the intercession of a triad figure of epic proportions: Chow Yun-fat's Mark Lee.

Use the term "heroic bloodshed" to describe the film if you like, but make sure you understand that Woo means it literally: that's a hero shedding his blood. Mythologist Joseph Campbell says that the hero is a man who undertakes a dangerous mission for the sake of his race; that he must go through a perilous night journey to bring back a message that will heal us. In Woo's opinion, Hong Kong society, torn by the actions of gun-running gangsters, needed a healing.

ABT brought it to them in fictive form. Its central character is a man you feel compelled to admire. Suave, debonair, spirited, Mark enjoys himself, but we know that his type of playful insouciance can't last. Schmoozing with street vendors and cops, and lighting cigarettes with bogus hundred dollar bills, are actions that signal a high lifestyle bound to be toppled.

Mark's friend Ho is headed for a similar fall. His secret grief and fear is for his brother Kit, who doesn't know that Ho is a triad. After a shootout, Mark is crippled, reduced to wiping off the windshields of triads' cars for money thrown onto the sidewalk. Kit is passed over for promotion. Ho is betrayed by a typical Woo villain—an amoral triad-aspiring punk—and is jailed.

When he emerges, he's greeted by a cop (played by Woo) who tells him that redemption won't come easy. But it does come, thanks not only to the help of some ex-cons but to Mark reconciling Kit and Ho and then shooting his way into myth. *ABT* uses the typical Woo film plot: harmony to destruction to restoration. Perhaps not coincidentally, it borrows elements from the classic story of the resurrected god, from Adonis to Jesus.

Look for Woo in the film and you don't have far to go. He's more than just the cop in the scene outside the prison: he's Mark at the beginning, loving life; he's Mark midway, down and out, crippled, in decline but never despairing. When Mark is given a chance by an old friend to redeem himself, that's Woo in Taiwan getting the call from Tsui to come back into real filmmaking. And when Mark goes out in a fiery gun battle, that's Woo devoting himself totally to this film.

Much of Woo's attitude toward the characters in this and his other films is based on the traditional Chinese emphasis on loyalty and family. At the beginning of the Chinese epic novel The Three Kingdoms, which takes place in the 3rd century during a time of political chaos, three men meet secretly in a peach garden, swearing to come to their war-torn nation's aid. Here's their oath:

We three, Liu Pei, Kuan Yu, and Chang Fei
Though of separate birth,
Now bind ourselves in brotherhood,
Combining our strength and purpose

MORE SEX, BETTER ZEN, FASTER BULLETS

To relieve the present crisis.
Thus we may fulfill our duty to home and country
And defend the common folk of the land.
We could not help our separate births,
But on the self-same day we mean to die!
Shining imperial Heaven, fruitful Queen Earth,
Witness our determination,
And may God and man
Jointly scourge whichever of us
Fails his duty or forgets his obligation.

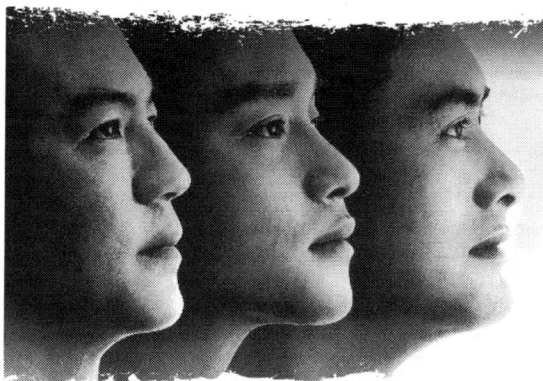

That's Woo's creed in a nutshell. His heroes are devoted to doing the right thing, to restoring order and balance to a troubled world. They are determined to fight to the death, and allegiance to the oath is more important than anything else.

Unfortunately, Woo comes dangerously close to enshrining *ABT*'s Mark as a figure to be emulated. In fact, youths all over Hong Kong started imitating the way that he talked and dressed. Woo tried to make amends for this reaction, not only in the 1990 film *Just Heroes* (in which a young man's glorification of triad life is repeatedly debunked) but also in *ABT 2* (1987).

The film is not only about redemption but resurrection, most notably via the appearance of Mark Lee's twin brother Ken (also played by Chow), whose character leaves us with ambivalent

feelings. Apparently, Woo felt that given Mark's popularity, he couldn't completely kill him off, yet he was obviously reluctant to bring Mark back and once again risk glorifying him. There's an interesting scene in the film in which we meet a sketch artist who has turned Ho and Mark's exploits into illustrated adventures. Talking to Ho, with the movie-like storyboards all around them, the artist says, "Many things are memorable. I put down all the incidents of your life into many stories." When Ho protests that his life is "nothing much worth writing about," the artist replies in just the way that Woo might. "It's not true," he says. "The world nowadays no longer has people who are friends like you are."

It's to Woo's credit that when Ken dons Mark's sunglasses and duster, and puts a toothpick in his mouth, thereby reviving his brother's character,

Woo underplays the moment's drama. Like *ABT*, though, *ABT 2* still manages in spite of itself to add a dangerously compelling sheen to its shootouts.

Often, Woo seems to be a victim of his cinematic talent. But maybe Woo's gun battles can be understood better if they're seen them as the director wants them to be.

The person of whom Woo is most reminiscent is American southern writer Flannery O'Connor, an avowed Catholic whose stories are filled with violent characters. O'Connor once used a quote from St. Cyril of Jerusalem that works to highlight Woo's use of violence as a cinematic motif. "The dragon sits by the side of the road, watching those who pass. Beware lest he devour you. We go to the Father of Souls, but it is necessary to pass by the dragon." Woo may be trying to direct people toward the Father of Souls, or God if you will, but he knows that you can't talk about Heaven without talking about the dragon's province, Hell;

that you can't talk about peace without talking about violence.

Woo would probably say that it's not only important to do so, it's necessary. O'Connor adapted one of her books' titles from Matthew 11:12: "from the days of John the Baptist until now the kingdom of heaven suffereth violence, and the violent bear it away." For Woo, part of the kingdom of heaven is the real world, and it always suffers violence. Will the violent bear the world away? Not if Woo and his tarnished heroes can help it.

Predominantly, Woo is a religious filmmaker. Remember, it was religion that got Woo off the streets, and he's never forgotten it. As Woo notes, "I still think a person's faith will transcend over everything at all times. As long as you have confidence and faith, you will overcome all kinds of difficulties and can have a breakthrough."

For Woo, religion is much more than sermons and rituals. It's also the important things that happen between family members and friends and lovers. In Martin Scorsese's *Mean Streets*, the main character, Charlie, says it best. "You don't make up for your sins in church. You do it in the street. You do it at home. The rest is bullshit, and you know it." Woo admires Scorsese (to whom he dedicated *The Killer*), doubtless because Scorsese puts his religious attitudes and his upbringing (with all of its conflicts and problems) into his films. Woo does the same thing. What are movies for, Woo would ask, if not to entertain, educate, and improve people?

It's a shame that Woo has been saddled with the term "action director" since it lumps him in with men like Hal Needham and Don Siegel. Woo may direct films in which there's action, but he's hardly an "action director." If Woo is like anyone in American films, it's Paul Schrader. A Methodist like Woo, Schrader makes films in which violence is always religious violence. It was Schrader who gave us *Taxi Driver*'s Travis Bickle, the prototypical urban demented loner: self-inspired, agonized, a man nailed to a cross of madness and pain. And it was Schrader who at the end of *American Gigolo* turned a meeting between a lady and a hustler into a scene of confession and absolution.

St Augustine said, "that which is not of the city of God is of the city of the Devil," which is where Woo's unrepentant triads live, men whose only concern is their self-aggrandizement. Splitting the world into two camps is a pretty harsh and exaggerated view, yet to a great extent, that's the way Woo sees things, perhaps because those years when he was living in the streets taught him a simple lesson: live or die. Just look at the exaggerated way that he opposes characters in his films. On the one side are his all-too-human heroes: *ABT*'s Mark, *Bullet in the Head*'s Ben, *The Killer*'s John, *Hard-Boiled*'s Tequila. On the other, there are street scum elevated to the level of high-living thugs: *ABT*'s Shing, *Hard-Boiled*'s Johnny Wong, *Hard Target*'s Fouchon. Woo knows that there's great entertainment value in bad characters, and he's smart enough to exploit them for this quality. But he never commits the mistake of making these characters attractive: they're all unctuous son-of-a-bitches who deserve to die and, usually, they do. The meting out of a rude form of justice is what makes the deaths of Paul

Chow chats with "Mr Woo": *Hard-Boiled*.

and Johnny Wong so appealing. These men never showed mercy to anyone, and their righteous executioners, Ben and Tequila, show them no mercy. Paul isn't killed; he's executed—just as are Shing from *ABT* and Johnny Wong from *The Killer*, both of whom flaunt the fact that they're going to get away with murder. The latter two are slain by a silver bullet of righteousness fired from a cop's gun, which means that for Woo, the cops are doing God's work on earth.

As an artist working in a popular medium, Woo sees himself as something of a messenger. That's why he occasionally appears in his films in the role of a spiritual and moral adviser, as in his bit part in *ABT*. In *Hard-Boiled*, he plays ex-cop Mr Woo, the owner of the Jazz Club where Tequila plays clarinet. When Tequila isn't sure if he should risk his already precarious position for Tony's sake, he goes to Mr Woo for advice. "Mr Woo, he's a true friend," Tequila says. "He and I are both in serious danger right now. In my position, what would you do?" Woo makes his answer simple. "If he was a really a friend, I wouldn't hesitate, whether he was right or wrong. Even if I was still a cop, yes, I'd help him." "Such character," Tequila says. "Not me, old buddy," Woo says, pointing upwards. "It's the guy

up there." In the hands of any other director aside from Kurosawa (who—with the exception of *Ran*—was never this explicit about religion), this scene would be preachy or embarrassing at best. Woo makes it work because he delivers the lines sincerely; and as we know from watching his other films, Woo not only means what he says about trusting oneself to a higher power, he proves it through the convincing actions of his characters.

Woo is also a master choreographer. Woo's choreography is based either on the music of violence or counterpoint music that connotes peace. Of all of Woo's films, *Bullet in the Head* is the one that is most like a piece of music. It starts out with a dance in a Christian school gymnasium that is cued to the tune of the Monkees' "I'm A Believer."

Prominent among the dancers is Tony Leung Chiu-wai's Ben. What's appealing about dance is its innocent depiction of a wedding between grace and passion. Dance scenes also have power because often, they're without words. Woo's dance sequences link up with his action scenes, which draw heavily on Chinese Opera's insistence that all actions be stylish enough to be dance-like. Not surprisingly, at *Bullet*'s beginning, Woo cuts from the gymnasium dance sequence to a gang fight in which Ben and his friend Frank participate, making us draw a connection between the two scenes. Essentially, we're in Martin Scorsese's mean streets, places where if you don't have courage and integrity you're not only a fool, you're a dead man. Remember, though: Scorsese got his idea of mean streets from Raymond Chandler, who wrote, "But down these mean streets a man must walk who is not himself mean." That sums up the type of person that Woo elevates to the status of a modern-day knight: the one who fights for justice and isn't afraid to get bruised in the process.

Throughout *Bullet*, we see various kinds of battles: the one in Saigon; the one at Frank's house; the one between Frank and Ringo, the street punk who tries to steal his money; the ones among the friends over the gold that the third friend, Paul, covets. Mostly, though, these external wars reflect each character's warring passions. Paul puts it best when the trio, with a café singer in tow, are trying to escape from

MORE SEX, BETTER ZEN, FASTER BULLETS

Vietnam. He wants to take along his cask of gold leaves, even though it weighs him down. Paul says, "All I want in this life is simple: just this box of gold. Is that too much to ask?", which tells us what a pathetic state he's been reduced to. *Bullet* does something that Woo has never since attempted. It shows us how one becomes a triad: by abandoning not only your friends but your better instincts, opting instead for money as the measure of self-worth. The fact that Paul comes from a family whose father is a self-described failure, and who tells his son that in this world, only money counts, demonstrates that Woo knows how family can mold your attitudes. Paul's counterpart is Ben, who Woo says is based on himself. An admirer of Elvis and The Beatles, Ben has a loving mother, and is the only one of the three friends who seems to have a girlfriend (he envisions her, in slow motion, walking to the strains of a tune stolen from George Harrison's "Do You Want To Know A Secret"). What alienates the trio is greed and war (for Woo, the two are the same).

Skull communions

The Tiananmen crackdown of June 4, 1989 upset Woo greatly. He recalled this event not only in *Bullet*'s riots (which mirror the violence of Hong Kong's 1967 riots, which left an impression on the young Woo) but also by replaying the famous image of a lone protester facing down a tank, and he dramatized the exaggerated emotions associated with high-tension confrontations by reworking the Russian roulette sequence from *The Deer Hunter*. *Bullet*'s Saigon section, which features a café that has a suave tough guy with a yard-wide sentimental streak (the wonderful Simon Yam), seems to take on elements from *Casablanca*. Ultimately, though, like so many Woo films, *Bullet* is about loss: loss of friends to crime or drugs, near-loss of family. More devastatingly than gunfire, political chaos and selfishness tear *Bullet*'s people apart (Frank says to Paul at one point, "Are you putting this gold before your friends? You're pointing your gun at a buddy of over ten years. Do you measure your friendship in gold?"). It's a bittersweet film about devotion and abandonment, and it ends on a bloody, flaming wharf in a showdown between Ben and Paul, with the dead Frank's skull bearing witness to a final retribution that could only occur in hell.

Stealing a laugh

It's understandable that after *A Better Tomorrow 1* and *2*, *The Killer*, and *Bullet in the Head*, Woo would want a change of pace; he found one with *Once A Thief*. With its Mediterranean setting and sunny atmosphere, the film gives off a glow that provides a nice contrast to these previous films' predominantly gloomy atmosphere. Yet things are never unmixed in Woo's universe; even the brightest sunlight casts dark shadows somewhere, and Woo was careful to balance this film's frothiness with a grim back story about good and bad parenting.

Borrowing elements from Hitchcock's *To Catch A Thief*, Woo makes Chow a high-class robber à la Cary Grant's John Robie. Chow's partners, Jim and Cherie, are played by Leslie Cheung and Cherie Chung. All three characters were originally street kids raised by a Fagin-like manipulator (Kenneth Tsang) who had them steal for him. This sinister father has his counterpart in a local street cop who tries to reform them. Again we see Woo splitting the world into diametrically opposed camps. Naturally, this set of conflicting allegiances influences the kids, doubtless much as Woo was in his own life faced with a similar choice: a life of crime in the streets or the more difficult road, moral behavior. Because *Thief* is a comedy in the classic sense, Woo is able to blend both worlds. The kids grow up to be professional thieves, but they're good-hearted ones.

The emphasis in the film's first half is on fun; the thefts are carried out skillfully, with great humor. Yet midway, the film takes a dark turn. As he did with *ABT*'s Mark and *The Killer*'s Sally and John, Woo invokes handicap as a cinematic element. In *ABT*, Mark's response to his debilitating leg injury was to refuse any sympathy regarding his affliction. Sitting with Ho and Shing in a nightclub, Mark at one point hoists his bad leg onto the table, pours whisky over it, and says, "To Shing and my leg. Happy?" As Joe in *Thief*, Chow seems to be even further away from self-pity. Injured and then (presumably) confined to a wheelchair, Joe at one point goes to a ball and has a lovely pas de deux with Cherie. He's so adept at using the chair—spinning, turning, at one point leaning as far back in the chair as you think is possible—that you forget he's in a wheelchair and tend to see the chair as merely a small part of the dance's greater mechanism.

The film holds out many surprises, not least that Joe's crippling is a ruse to draw out the returned bad father so that the trio can have their revenge on him. The scene in which the bad father shoots at Joe's legs, after which Joe lifts himself up out of the hollow casts his legs have been hidden behind, is more than just a great moment in cinema: it's also another of Woo's thinly veiled resurrection references, meant to show us once again that well-intentioned people will always triumph over the world's debilitating effects. What we have here is serious business in the midst of comedy, a lesson Woo learned from classic literature.

For a while toward the film's end, it looks as though this lovely trio is going to be dissolved. Jim and Cherie have gotten married. Where can Joe fit in? Instead, in a wonderful final scene, we see Jim and Cherie at home. Jim is in slacks, his wife's hair is in curlers, and Joe, in an apron, is tending to the housekeeping and babysitting chores. While the parents look on, Joe gets so involved in dusting objects and then tossing them aside that after picking up various stuffed animals, he picks up the baby, dusts it, and then tosses him aside, while the parents look on stunned. The film closes on one of those classic Hong Kong comedy freeze frames, but its exuberance flows on long after it's over. More than a film, *Once A Thief* is like a prayer: John Woo's hope that everything will turn out all right.

Ninety-seven reasons

Even if they do span a period of three years, Woo's two most stylish films work as companion pieces.

MORE SEX, BETTER ZEN, FASTER BULLETS

The Killer: Thai poster.

In *The Killer* (1989) and *Hard-Boiled* (1992), Woo not only made two of the most important films in world cinema, he also upped the stakes. Why had the stakes been upped? In a simple phrase: 1997. Remember, Woo views things from an apocalyptic point of view. Woo also sees the world as divided into two opposed camps: good and evil (although Woo is keen enough to know that many of his characters have both traits). When Woo saw reunification looming, he saw it in terms of the destruction of the colony he'd grown to love. These feelings came out in *The Killer*, which reflects Woo's political anxiety, and *Hard-Boiled*, his metaphor about Hong Kong threatened by the takeover.

The Killer uses blindness as a figure for various kinds of vision: seeing the world, seeing what one's values are, seeing what you mean to other people. More so than the film on which it's based, Jean-Pierre Melville's *Le Samourai*, *The Killer* is a film whose world is spiritually played out. This quality of Woo's films can't be over-emphasized. The exhilaration that comes from watching Woo's action scenes is counterbalanced by the sense of letdown experienced when you start to recover from the rush of excitement that the shootouts cause.

The same thing happens to the characters involved in the action. After all of the excitement, one begins to think about the implications of what's been done. This is precisely what happens in *The Killer* to Chow Yun-fat's John: he comes to see that all of his rationalizations for his assassin-for-hire lifestyle don't change the fact that he's murdered a great many people, most of whom he didn't even know. Yet Woo is also aware that you can take this response too far. In *Hard-Boiled*'s hospital shootout, Tony (as Tequila had done earlier in the teahouse) accidentally kills a cop. Both men feel a sense of terrible regret, but unlike Tequila, Tony is stunned by his guilt. Tequila snaps him out of this response with some very practical advice: Tony must continue to function because mistakes happen. What we see here is Tequila acting as priest to Tony's penitent parishioner, cautioning him not to overindulge his grief. In *ABT 2*, Chow's Ken doles out the same advice to Lung (Dean Shek), who also collapses because of the slaughter around him. In each case, Woo tells us that indulging our grief is not only selfish but, especially if one has heroic qualities, a waste of time.

One wonders, though, if audiences actually react to Woo's violence as many of his characters do. Sam Peckinpah thought that audiences would be able to see that his exaggerated action scenes were meant as a condemnation of violence. Martin Scorsese hoped that people would regard *Taxi Driver*'s final shootout the same way. But as Peckinpah and Scorsese came to understand, and as Woo doubtless realizes, people don't always recoil from violence. Sometimes, they get caught up in a film's excitement, and morality seems to get left behind. That's why Woo puts so many

Danny Lee and Chow back-to back: screengrab from *The Killer*.

scenes involving healing between his shootouts: to give the audience a chance to reflect, and perhaps realize that we need to resist the pleasure that violence can create.

The Killer seems to have been prompted by Woo's thoughts along these lines. The film's beginning and end take place in a church because that's where Woo's heroes go for refuge, as does the director. "I never feel as completely at peace as I do after I go to confession," Woo has said. You can read *The Killer* as Woo's extended confession about his obsession with violence. The film tells us a story about a man who tries to free himself from a fate that's self-woven. And it's full of irony. John takes an assignment for a mob hit while staring at a giant cross. He comes to see himself only after blinding a cabaret singer. The singer realizes who John really is only after she loses her sight. John's friend Sidney regains his dexterity with a gun shortly before he is killed. The cop on John's trail (Danny Lee's Inspector Li) becomes aware that rather than hating his prey, he admires him. "He's different from other murderers," Li says at one point. "He doesn't look like a killer. He comes across so calm. It's like he has a dream... eyes filled with passion." In fact, the whole film is drenched in passionate feeling, much of it having to do with the pain of loss, physical damage, and the consolation that having true friends can bring. In the midst of a world dominated by triads who only believe in materialism and money ("I don't trust anyone, including you" gang boss Johnny Wong says to Sidney), *The Killer* gives us many examples of strong friendship: Sidney and John, John and Jenny, Li and his partner, Chang.

Unfortunately, most of the time in *The Killer*, good intentions come too late: John intends to donate his corneas to Jenny so that she can see again, but in the film's concluding shootout, he's blinded. One of the film's final images shows us Jenny and John, both now blind, crawling toward each other—but they can't see, and miss each other completely. Does this mean that the film has a despairing point of view? Only if you think that the slippage between intention and action is inevitable. Woo doesn't believe this. That's clear from *The Killer*'s counterpart, *Hard-Boiled*.

Hard-Boiled is John Woo's farewell to Hong Kong filmmaking. By the time he began production on *Hard-Boiled*, Woo and his producer Terence Chang had already decided to leave Hong

Chow Yun-fat with co-star: screengrab from *Hard-Boiled*.

MORE SEX, BETTER ZEN, FASTER BULLETS

Supervisor Pang counsels Tequila: screengrab from *Hard-Boiled*.

Kong so Woo made *Hard-Boiled* his magnum opus. It's the most apocalyptic, violent, and emotional of all of his Hong Kong films. Chow's character, Tequila, is a maverick cop on the trail of triad boss and gun-runner Johnny Wong (Anthony Wong, at his smoothest and creepiest). Tequila is professionally impassioned but emotionally flawed. He's on the outs with his girlfriend (Teresa Mo) and at odds with his superior, Pang (played by ex-RHKP officer Philip Chan).

The opening shootout takes place at a teahouse where triads come to sell guns that are stashed in the false bottoms of bird cages. This metaphor of corruption underlying innocence and things of the spirit appears many times in the film, especially in the form of a hospital (like churches, for Woo symbols of spiritual succor) in whose basement Johnny Wong has his arms cache. For Woo, this is a symbol of Hong Kong society—a whited sepulchre: on the surface, clean, attractive, promising peace and succor; underneath, riddled with moral depravity.

The film is a series of enormous set pieces best described, in Woo's words, as "operatic." What he means, of course, is Chinese opera, whose stories are well known, and in which performers have to be adept not only at acting but at gesture, singing, and, perhaps most significantly for the film linkage, dance. Sergeant Yuen doesn't just shoot people: he's as graceful as a dancer when he does so, as though he were Fred Astaire with a .38. Many of Tequila's movements also involve moving down into a scene, as when he half-leans on and slides down a banister while firing his guns during the teahouse shootout, or when he rappels into an arms warehouse fracas like an angel of fiery retribution.

Tequila's problem is that he's too passionate in his hatred of evil. Pang cautions him to act with restraint, but he can't. Tequila's impulsiveness is counterbalanced by the cool veneer of undercover cop Tony (Tony Leung Chiu-wai), who's as conflicted an individual as Tequila, but hides it, partly by necessity. Conflicted characters are nothing new in Woo's films, but no one approaches the level of conflict that Tony must undergo; he's a nowhere man, trapped between the world of the cops and the world of the triads. As a result, he's more of a ghostly figure than anything else, living in a universe of cloudy uncertainty, only at peace when on his boat, which is moored in the aptly named Clearwater Bay.

If Tequila's fault is that he too strongly believes in everything, his nemesis, Johnny Wong, believes in nothing. Like *Bullet*'s Paul and *ABT*'s Shing (both played by Waise Lee), Johnny is an unrepentant bastard with no values or allegiances. Johnny gets into an argument with his right-hand man, Mad Dog, during the hospital shootout that concludes the film. Mad Dog says that Johnny is wrong to endanger the patients, that he's out of line. "What's this about out of line?" Johnny asks. Like a textbook sociopath, he knows what this morality business is all about, but he doesn't give a damn. Johnny's also a bit of a drama addict. On the way to raiding a rival gang leader's warehouse, Johnny, attempting to hand Tony his gun, says, "either we conquer the world or you kill me tonight with this."

Johnny (Anthony Wong) is not a nice man: screengrab from *Hard-Boiled*.

You have to wonder what men like Johnny Wong, Shing, or Johnny Weng do for fun, since they never seem to enjoy themselves. Perhaps they're all a bit like *Hard Target*'s Fouchon and *Broken Arrow*'s Deakins, taking pleasure in destruction and attempting to profit from it. Essentially, they're angels of death feeding on negation. They're also a lot like John Milton's Satan, who says with both pride and regret, "myself am Hell."

Opposing these forces are the ones oriented toward life and regeneration. That's where Woo's use of Chow Yun-fat comes in. A reviewer once said about Jackie Chan that Chan made sweeping his change off a dresser look graceful. Chow is the same way, except that Chow commands more integrity than Jackie can muster because he's not only graceful, he's more beautifully chiseled. Chow's leaps in *The Killer* and *Hard-Boiled* are more than examples of operatic choreography: they also show his joy in living. As a consequence, in *Hard-Boiled* you can sympathize with Tequila's need to get along with Teresa and his desire to make Tony his friend.

Hard-Boiled's end is as melancholy as that of *The Killer*. The hospital, which Woo uses as a symbol of Hong Kong society, is destroyed, perhaps to make way for a new society (the same idea is in *The Killer*, whose church is in a symbolic state of disrepair). Woo seems to be saying that at least part of Hong Kong, the part that houses criminals, has to be destroyed in order to save the rest. It's a typical Christian conceit: something must die in order to be reborn. These are fairly weighty concepts for a popular art form to bear. Woo gets away with this kind of filmmaking because he entertains us so well. In a sense, he's like a medieval troubadour: his set pieces are his songs, and Christian ethics are his lyrics.

Woo traffics heavily in Christian symbols, among which are birds, representations for the spirit. In *Hard-Boiled*, the most recognizable bird forms are the paper cranes that Tony makes each time he kills someone. The film's most indelible image occurs when Tony is sitting in the boat's cabin. The smoke from his cigarette wafts up, billowing among the cranes, which seem to be swimming in an ethereal fog. It's an image that comes back to haunt us at the film's end, when Tony (who, like a true hero, has sacrificed himself so that Johnny Wong can be shot) sails off into the white mist of that cold region to which he's been headed all along. Death? Antarctica? You can't say for sure which. (Woo refuses to comment on this question.) What we do know is that the film's end recalls the mournfulness of much of *The Killer*. The echo of Tequila's saxophone playing wails in the

Teresa and Tequila: screengrab from *Hard-Boiled*.

distance. The boat silently cuts through the water. Tony, his head bandaged (why, if he's dead, would it need to be?) sails away into a white nothingness.

The sense of melancholy at *Hard-Boiled*'s end is central to Woo's filmmaking. Most of his films are steeped in a sense of loss: of innocence, purity, the feeling that you can be at peace with your world. Woo seems to be acutely aware of the distance we've come from Eden, where everything (supposedly) was right. We already know that he believes in a savior of souls, so this melancholy must come from the disappointments people sometimes subject us to, and also from the continual presence of evil, compromise, and deceit. Ideals in Woo's world make sense not only because they're the opposite of corruption, but because they just seem right. But even a life well-lived can be riddled with doubt, and Woo wouldn't be the complete filmmaker that he is if he didn't show us that at times, even people of great faith undergo empty moments when action's exhilaration gives way to a terrifying silence.

Exodus

Apocalypse may never be far from Woo's mind, but not even he could have foreseen the Armageddon

John Woo and Lance Henriksen on the set of *Hard Target*.

JCVD and Lance Henriksen: screengrab from *Hard Target*.

that he was getting himself into when he went to Hollywood to make 1993's *Hard Target*. Fearing that this Asian maverick might run amuck, Universal assigned eight producers to keep an eye on Woo. The studio wasn't as savvy as it thought it was, though. One of the producers was Chuck Pfarrer, the film's screenwriter, who was only too glad to see Woo bring his story to life. Two others were Robert Tapert and *Evil Dead* director Sam Raimi, admirers of Woo, who said that they felt lucky to be paid to sit back and watch Woo work. But things still didn't turn out smoothly. Woo was given quotas as to how many people could be shot. Try to picture the scenario: "Mr Woo, we're from the MPAA. You killed 27 people in the last scene, so by our calculations you can only kill 16 in this one."

Woo also had to deal with Jean-Claude Van Damme, who got the notion that he should be allowed to have a say in the film's final editing. Whether he did is doubtful. If you compare Woo's cut of *Hard Target* (available from sundry video sources) with the film's released version, you'll see that aside from a few lost pieces of business (Lance Henriksen's Fouchon saying that his men are "as dumb as a sack of hammers", Van Damme and Yancy Butler playing out a very restrained

BETWEEN THE BULLETS

Fouchon takes aim in this French lobby card for *Hard Target*.

love scene), the film is relatively intact.

Many Woo fans don't like *Hard Target*, but the film shouldn't be underestimated. Woo and Terence Chang recognized that it would be a wise move to make a film that blended American patriotism with a none-too-subtle critique of the way that America treated its Vietnam veterans. The film's focus on homeless vets, with Van Damme's Chance Boudreaux fighting on their behalf, is rousing. Better yet, because *Hard Target* is set in New Orleans, many of the hunts, and much of the action, take on the atmosphere of a homicidal carnival run amuck.

Woo makes Boudreaux a Bayou native (which neatly glosses over Van Damme's Belgian accent) and focuses on Jean-Claude's athletic ability. Woo repeatedly photographs Van Damme so that light haloes around him, and often features him in graceful slow-motion shots with steel guitar music in the background. The "muscles from Brussels" is turned into an avenging god.

Woo gives Van Damme a delicious set of gangster types to react against. Fouchon, who runs a Most Dangerous Game hunt-a-guy-for-dollars operation, is so smooth and sleek that you love to hate him. Henriksen cleaves to the role, gleefully wasting people with a big-bore, single-shot Thompson Contender pistol.

Fouchon's sidekick, Pic van Cleve (Arnold Vosloo), is decked out with a punk haircut. Woo has van Cleve scowl a lot, look at people through his eyebrows, and deliver monosyllabic dialogue (if you're trying to identify his accent, it's South African). In one scene, Fouchon and Van Cleve walk into the Mardi Gras graveyard warehouse where the film's final showdown is to take place. Van Cleve looks around, obviously doesn't like the set-up, and, ever so slowly, says, "This...is...not...good."

Much of *Hard Target* is a replay of bits from Woo's Hong Kong films (in fact, the whole film is like a John Woo primer for the uninitiated). Boudreaux gets to jump over and slide around pieces of Mardi Gras floats and use the Chow Yun-fat two-fisted, two-gun-salute on plenty of bad guys. In a wonderful variation on the scene in *Hard-Boiled* in which Tequila descends from the rafters into the fray, Boudreaux drops down into the midst of Fouchon's men while perched on the back of a gigantic sculpted crane. Woo has Yancy Butler reprise a Teresa Mo bit from *Hard-Boiled*: a thug calls her a "bitch" so she shoots him. Woo says that he was glad to have the opportunity to redo these pieces of business, like the one (again from *Hard-Boiled*) in which two opponents (this time van Cleve and Boudreaux) walk parallel to each other on either side of a wall, all the while firing their guns. Aside from an embarrassing performance by Wilford Brimley, *Hard Target* is a wonderful romp.

MORE SEX, BETTER ZEN, FASTER BULLETS

Cage, Woo and Travolta on set: *Face/Off*.

Unfortunately, after *Hard Target*, Woo was unable to get funding for some of his other pet projects, including *King's Ransom* (which he wanted Chow to star in) and *Tears of the Sun*. To keep Woo's hand in, Woo and Terence Chang took on *Broken Arrow*, which Chang refers to as "a popcorn movie." Written by *Speed*'s Graham Yost, *Broken Arrow* is little more than *Speed* with stolen nuclear weapons instead of a runaway bus. Since the film is driven by its special effects, Woo has little to do other than orchestrate the work of technicians. The film did accomplish two things, though: it demonstrated that Woo could helm a big-budget Hollywood production and it brought Woo together with John Travolta, which made *Face/Off* possible.

Mr Woo makes the A-list

To understand *Face/Off*, you have to go back to the notions of melancholy and loss in Woo's films. *ABT*'s Mark puts it best. Staring at the nighttime Hong Kong skyline, he says, "I never realized that Hong Kong was so beautiful at night. It'll vanish one day. That's for sure." True enough—material things never last. That's why Woo places his trust in a higher realm. The things that we take with us from Woo's films are qualities that we can treasure forever but which we can't touch: love, honor, devotion. We believe in them, we live our lives by them, not only because they matter but because, not being material, they can't be corrupted as long as we aren't. And for Woo, what protects us from that corruption is not only our resolve but our faith.

Face/Off's Sean Archer (John Travolta), an FBI agent, tries to compensate for the death of his son Michael by fixating on his work, not as a

Faces: *Face/Off*.

source of comfort but as a font for pain. Obsessed with revenge against the man who shot Michael, terrorist Castor Troy (Nicolas Cage), he's unable to feel pleasure, is incapable of relating emotionally or sexually to his wife, Eve (Joan Allen), and is unsuited to be a father to his daughter.

Castor, on the other hand, revels in the sensuous, and shows almost embarrassingly tender affection toward his brother and partner-in-havoc, Pollux. The face touch gesture that Sean uses with his son during the film's opening carousel ride disappears from Sean's life until the film's very end, but Castor has a form of this kind of intimate bonding, and he displays it all the time: he repeatedly bends down to tie Pollux's shoes. In a strangely perverse way, he's far more of a caregiver than Sean seems to be. Though the two characters are on opposite sides of the law, the situation is ripe for their bonding.

Of course, there's been bonding between characters in previous Woo films but not like this. The ads for *Face/Off* put it succinctly: "in order to trap him, he must become him." But not quite. Even after a high-tech operation during which the two literally trade faces, Sean is still Sean. He's just in a body that looks like Castor's. For Sean, this transformation is hellish, as we see when he wakes up from the operation and smashes the mirror that shows him that physically, he's now his evil twin.

Transformations have occurred in other films before, sometimes with comparably gruesome results. John Frankenheimer's *Seconds* is about a man who trades in his old body for a new one, only to discover that he liked the way he'd been before. The process in *Seconds* can't be reversed. For Sean, after he's trapped in Erewhon prison ("nowhere" spelled backwards), reversal also seems impossible. After he escapes, he must rely on Eve's believing that he's still himself in order to survive. With the strength that her faith gives him, he's able to defeat Castor.

Face/Off is a major triumph, not just because it's so entertaining, but because of what it represents. It's a film with the usual Woo pyrotechnic muscle, but it was made in the United States, in English, with American actors. Too many people fail to realize how difficult it is for foreign directors to work in another language, in a new country, and still retain their traditional themes. Great directors such as Jean Renoir and Wim Wenders were broken by Hollywood and returned to their home countries. Woo mastered the filmmaking process long ago; now it seems that he's mastered "the system" (meeting after meeting about what he intended to do, studio interference, market research pressures) too.

Woo got out of Hong Kong with his innocence intact yet he hasn't given up on violence. In *Face/Off*, though, the real violence isn't the shootings: it's the violence done to the idea of harmony, of heaven. It's Castor accidentally shooting Michael, or blaspheming to the tune of Handel's "Messiah." It's Sean doing himself violence by holding fast to the scar of his pain over his son's death instead of, as Castor suggests, getting some fun out of life. Aside from Sean and Castor (both before and after their operations), many of the people in the film wear false faces. Sean's daughter retreats behind a painted punk veneer meant to mask her grief over Michael's death (as Castor-as Sean tells her, "you haven't been the same since Mike died, hiding behind someone else's face, hoping you wouldn't feel the pain"). Eve adapts to a marriage without love by being cool and professional. Ironically, when Castor-as-Sean reads in Eve's diary that Sean and his wife haven't made love for months, he says of Sean, "what a loser," not realizing that he's correctly identified the source of Sean's sexual problem: loss. So Sean, like Tequila, becomes a wild avenger.

Face/Off isn't the seamless piece of work that The Killer is, but it's close enough to show us that even in the midst of all the Hollywood bullshit (Woo wanted to have the opening run without titles, but the studio nixed the idea), Woo was still able to make a sincere film about pain, suffering, and their antidote, love and devotion. Face/Off's theme of heavenly reunification seems to heal the wounds that Woo has been carrying ever since he lived in the slums of Hong Kong.

Music critics have said that the notes of fate sounded at the beginning of Beethoven's Fifth are offset by the "Ode to Joy" in his Ninth. At Face/Off's end, Woo takes the sense of doomed foreboding from The Killer and Hard-Boiled and turns it into its opposite, hope and wonder. The film's opening music returns, but in a lighter key. Sean emerges out of gauzy, bright light as though seen through ecstatic tears, comes to his house's door, and integrates Castor's orphaned son Adam into his family. The moment is touchingly beautiful and tremendously moving. The family unit—for Woo the repository of a peace that truly passes understanding—is restored. Having taken

Woo fans have seen this before: Face/Off.

you up with the film's exciting opening, Woo takes you even higher at its end.

It's rare to go to a film and feel uplifted. Sometimes, movies are so bad that they paralyze you with their stupidity, as though someone injected Novocaine into the old cerebral cortex. But Woo's films invigorate you. His films have the same effect as Kurosawa's Red Beard. A vain young doctor who's been assigned to a poor clinic run by a physician known as Red Beard (Toshiro Mifune) rebels at the clinic's crudeness and what he feels is his low position there. But by the end of the film, he's come to see in Red Beard a man of passion, tenderness, and wisdom. As a result, he vows to follow Red Beard for the rest of his life in order to give back to people what he's learned. This master/disciple tale gets to you, so much so that you feel that you, too, would sacrifice everything for even a little taste of the young doctor's discovery of existence's true meaning

Woo's films are like that. Not only by his stories but his powerful artistry, Woo makes you come away from his films energized and hopeful, trusting that somehow, what will win out over what Hard-Boiled's Tony refers to as "all this darkness" is a goodness that anyone can reach.

Wong Kar-wai in his iconic sunglasses.

CHAPTER SIXTEEN

CREATIVE CHAOS: THE DISORGANIZED WORLD OF WONG KAR-WAI

by Jeremy Hansen

Wong Kar-wai was keeping someone waiting. He was hunkered down in an editing room, frenetically cutting the thousands of feet of footage that made up *Happy Together*, his sixth movie as director and his entry to the Cannes film festival in 1997. In typical Wong Kar-wai fashion, the crucial editing was taking place later than the last minute—an executive from the festival's organizing committee who had come to take the print back to France had already extended his stay. Nobody should have been surprised that it was taking longer than expected. Perpetually laconic, Wong himself had said he didn't know what the film was about until he got into the

Flyer for *Happy Together*.

editing suite. Eventually, a three-hour version of the film was assembled from four months of footage shot in Argentina, before Wong made yet another last-minute decision to cut half the footage out, including some actors' entire appearances. Eventually, he handed over a 90-minute film to the Cannes agent, who immediately jetted back to France to show the Cannes jury the work.

Wong's working style is the directorial equivalent of walking a tightrope, an ad hoc approach which would petrify every test-screening obsessed Hollywood producer. Making a Wong Kar-wai film requires both cast and crew to battle through a haze of abrupt script changes and aimless days of filming, guided only by the flickering light of Wong's instinct. Wong's longtime cinematographer Chris Doyle, who has collaborated with him on every film since 1990's *Days of Being Wild*, kept a diary of his experience filming *Happy Together* and published it under the title "Don't Try for Me Argentina". The book beautifully illustrates the seat-of-the-pants nature of Wong's way of working:

"Wong as often says 'don't change a thing' as 'that angle's not interesting enough'," Doyle recalls in the book. "Today what he liked most was when my assistant laid the camera on Tony's bed in the break when I went to take a pee. We messed the bed up a bit more, half covered the lens with a dirty shirt and some underwear and the style for a whole sequence was born! I put the camera in a cupboard, underneath the sofa and bed, on a window ledge, anywhere casual, improbable, or where it hadn't been before.

"Sure, this style is a mirror for the discarded feeling Tony has now that he's broken up with Leslie for the umpteenth time. But it wasn't intellectualized into being, or even planned. It just seemed visually more interesting and unexpected, and solved the problem of how to shoot this minuscule space we've been in and out of for 30 days by now! Style is more about choice than concept. It should be organic, not imposed."

Tony's new dimension

Happy Together wasn't an easy shoot. One of the leading men, Tony Leung Chiu-wai, arrived on set in Argentina expecting to play a man searching for his gay father in Buenos Aires. He found the rough script he'd seen when he signed up for the role had changed into what Wong called a "sequel" to his original proposal, and he was now playing a gay character. This wouldn't necessarily have been a problem, except the revised script called

CREATIVE CHAOS

Leslie Cheung and Tony Leung Chiu-wai: *Happy Together*.

for a blunt, boisterous sex scene between Leung and Leslie Cheung, the other leading man, which later attracted an Category III rating from the Hong Kong censors. Doyle remembered shooting the scene in his diary:

"It's a beautiful and sensual scene. Tony and Leslie really look great in bed. But Tony is devastated when it's all done. 'Wong said all I had to do was kiss,' he confides to me, 'now look how far he's pushed me.' Leslie is in a spirited, bitchy mood. 'Now you know how bad I've felt all these years pretending I want to put my thing in that extra hole that women have!'"

Compared to much of Wong's other work, the end result of *Happy Together* is cohesive and straightforward. This is remarkable not only because Wong has a reputation for creating difficult movies, but because by all accounts the film was verging on the shambolic when Wong started to edit it. It was a production plagued by constant script changes, last-minute cast additions in the hope of re-igniting the plot and an almost overwhelming sense of lethargy and alienation. The plan was to have a six-week shoot; they ended up spending over three months in Argentina. "Wong is holed up somewhere reworking the script and schedule," says one of Doyle's diary entries, entitled "Director for a Day." "Leslie is leaving very soon. Thursday and Friday there's a general strike. As if boring us to death, delaying us to death and cheating us to death isn't enough...We've been here 40 days now, but we've only worked 10...The structure of a Wong Kar-wai film is like a fat man's feet. They more or less get him from place to place, but he can't see them until the end of the day."

"Wong Kar-wai is a very nice guy," actor Leslie Cheung told journalist Frederick Dannen in a rare interview. "But he changes his mind a lot, and it's very hard for an actor or actress to follow him."

Most of *Happy Together* is about how Yiu-fai (Tony Leung Chiu-wai) and Po-wing (Leslie Cheung) make each other miserable. They move to Buenos Aires hoping to "start over" and resurrect their floundering relationship. Po-wing is flighty, slutty and selfish—all characteristics that drive serious, sensible, mixed-up Yiu-fai up the wall. Their moments of togetherness are exquisite to watch—when they tango and kiss in the soft light of their apartment building's dingy shared kitchen, for example, or when Po-wing falls asleep like a child on Yiu-fai's shoulder in the back seat of a taxi. But they are fleeting glimpses of happiness in a flood of bitching and bitterness.

In rocky patches in their relationship, Po-wing

Yiu-fai is happiest when Po-wing is asleep: *Happy Together*.

takes other lovers. These flings usually end with Po-wing being beaten up and running back to Yiu-fai for comfort and a cheap place to stay. Yiu-fai, romantic fool that he is, can't help but take him back.

When they first arrive in Argentina, they buy a car and try to visit the Iguazu Falls. They get lost on the way there and don't see them after all, but still dream of trying again one day. They buy a tacky tourist lamp depicting the falls which sits beside the bed in their dingy apartment. They mean for it to represent their aspirations, but its twirling lights only mock their failure to reach the falls and, implicitly, their failure to make their relationship work.

Eventually Yiu-fai finds the strength to break free of Po-wing and Argentina. He visits the falls by himself then returns to Asia. The film ends with the movie's title track booming as he takes a train ride around Taiwan. In a sense, he's been freed from his relationship to embrace the future. But because this is a Wong Kar-wai production, he'll always be burdened by his past. "We end on a subway ride in the rain," Doyle says of the film's final scene in his diary. "'All that remorse,' is all Wong manages to say."

It's a sad but strangely uplifting movie. When it was complete, both Wong and Doyle thought it was their finest work. The jury at Cannes agreed, granting *Happy Together* the coveted for Best Director prize at the festival, the highest award any non-Hollywood director can receive. The only problem was, it was hard to tell if Wong was actually pleased with this triumph. Facing the press after the announcement, whatever delight he might have been feeling seemed to be overwhelmed by his frustration at misplacing his omnipresent sunglasses.

Local boy makes cool

Wong Kar-wai may not be Hong Kong's most commercially successful filmmaker, but he is one of the city's—and Asia's—most important. A darling of the international art-house film crowd, his baffling, charming, visually stunning films—a thoughtful contrast to the smack-'em-up flicks which normally dominate the Hong Kong box office—are loved and loathed in almost equal measure. Sometimes the adoration can get a bit much. In 1996, for example, Premiere magazine embarrassingly anointed Wong as the epitome of hipness. "Ask anyone in today's alt.culture crowd where the coolest movies are made and the answer will be 'Hong Kong,'" the magazine gushed. "But if you ask anyone in Hong Kong who the coolest filmmaker is, the answer is 'Wong Kar-wai.'"

Wong's terminal insecurity means such of compliments won't go to his head. He seems to see himself as a bit of a geek. "People have said 'You're the hippest director in the world,'" he says, "and I say 'I'm not hip.' I think I'm very old-fashioned."

Wong Kar-wai was five when he moved with his mother from Shanghai to Hong Kong. When he arrived in 1963, Hong Kong was regarded as a second-rate shipping port in comparison to the booming, bustling metropolis of Shanghai. Five-year-old Wong was the youngest of three children. He found settling into his new home far from easy. He didn't speak the language, for a start.

"When I got [to Hong Kong]," he says, "I spoke nothing but Shanghainese, whereas Cantonese was, and still is, the local dialect. For some time, I was totally alienated, and it was like the biggest nightmare of my life...I did not have a particularly happy childhood."

He was a lonely kid, but he spent his spare

Wah pops a cap in triad Tony's trousers: *As Tears Go By.*

time in ways that were to have an enormous influence on his future. His mother loved movies. Every day after school, when his father was still at work, she would take her young son to the cinema, where they would sometimes watch two or three films a day. This experience led to his teenage enthusiasm for the more adventurous filmmaking of Bertolucci, Godard, Bresson and the Japanese masters Ozu and Kurosawa.

Wong lived in Tsim Sha Tsui, a frenetic jostle of shops and apartment buildings on the southern tip of the Kowloon Peninsula, a ten-minute ride on the old Star Ferries from the center of the city on Hong Kong Island. Today, TST is the tourist and shopping heart of Hong Kong, where glamorous boutiques and hotels battle for space with Hello Kitty specialty stores and men hawking copy-watches. (It's also the home of Chungking Mansions, the seedy rabbit warren of brothels, cheap hotels and Indian restaurants that is the setting for much of Wong's 1994 film *Chungking Express*.) Wong remembers the Tsim Sha Tsui of his childhood being far more down-at-heel that its modern counterpart.

"[It was] an area frequented by girls who were generally known as 'Suzy Wong'—girls who worked in the bars entertaining sailors arriving on those battleships," he told journalist Jimmy Ngai in the book *Wong Kar-wai*. "There were lots of bars and clubs in the area which was my world at the time, and I was very much attracted to this sort of sleazy establishment."

Partway through a graphic design course at a local polytechnic, television channel TVB started offering classes in production. Wong quit his studies to join the program, which led to a job as production assistant on some of the channel's regular soap opera and drama series. He soon discovered his pent-up creativity needed an outlet. He started writing screenplays, and did well enough at it to be able to leave TVB and take a position as a full-time writer for Cinema City, a Hong Kong company modeling itself on the Hollywood studio system. He worked there for a year without having a single script put into production, and left soon afterwards. The next few years he spent on the fringes of the film industry as a freelance scriptwriter, writing comedies, action films, kung fu and porn scripts—contributing to or writing a total of about 50 screenplays between 1982 and 1987. His most notable (and personal favorite) was *Final Victory*, a tale about second-rate gangsters directed by Patrick Tam.

Wong was making his living as a writer, but he always felt he would eventually direct his own films. He got his chance when his screenwriting talent was noticed by Alan Tang, a well-known 1960s actor who had since turned his hand to producing. Tang liked to give would-be directors a break, and offered Wong the opportunity to direct *As Tears Go By* in 1988.

Gang banging

To a certain extent, Wong's directing debut

MORE SEX, BETTER ZEN, FASTER BULLETS

Fly chained in old-school toilet after a thrashing: *As Tears Go By*.

followed the established Hong Kong formula. *As Tears Go By* included the requisite number of well-choreographed gun battles and epic bloody beatings, but the action took a back seat to an emotional clash of love and loyalty. The film was about the difficulty Wah (Andy Lau), a well-respected gangster, was having keeping face because of the idiotic actions of Fly (Jacky Cheung), his *sai lo* (triad "little brother"). Wah's rough ways are moderated when he falls for the domesticated charm of a second cousin (Maggie Cheung) who comes to visit his flat to recover from an illness. She uncomplainingly washes the bloodstained clothes of his triad mates and buys new glassware to replace the stuff he angrily smashes after a bad night out. But Wah is forever leaping from the bed of his anxious lover to get Fly out of trouble, even though the only reason Fly gets in trouble is because his harebrained schemes to impress Wah usually end up with him lying on the pavement spitting blood.

The film ends miserably. To salvage his irredeemable reputation, Fly goes on a suicidal mission to kill a prominent gang leader. Wah follows him, and when Fly's bullets fail to kill the bad guy he steps in to finish the job and is gunned down himself. The locals loved the sad stuff, and the film scored big at the box office. Wong quickly became one of the territory's directors to watch.

Poster: *Days of Being Wild*.

He's lived up to the hype—but in ways nobody could have predicted. Each new Wong Kar-wai film, while retaining some thematic similarities, is a bold step in a new direction, as if Wong feels obliged to reinvent himself every time. Nowhere was this imperative more evident that in his second feature, *Days of Being Wild*, when he all but abandoned traditional narrative structure.

Days of Being Wild begins with a lengthy shot of lush tropical jungle—but a holiday-in-paradise movie it is certainly not. All the elements were in place—a star-studded cast list being the most important one for advance sales—but Wong screwed with them in ways the audience didn't appreciate. The film was set in the 1960s and featured up-and-coming actress Carina Lau, Maggie Cheung, and teen idol and Cantopop star Andy Lau. Leslie Cheung (a Cantopop star himself) played the beautiful, petulant heartbreaker Yuddy, a man with a fondness for whiling away the hours seductively cha-cha-ing in front of his mirror.

Women go crazy for him, but he can only break their hearts. Yuddy's vanity conceals a great insecurity—he is an adopted child who doesn't know who his real mother is. His weary

Leslie Cheung and Carina Lau: *Days of Being Wild*.

aunt who has raised him, dressed in elegant cheongsam dresses and entertaining a host of young toy boys, won't reveal his real mother's identity for fear of losing him. It seemed like a perfect recipe for a tale of redemption, but Wong obviously had other things on his mind. He sends Yuddy on a trip to the Philippines, where his real mother lives. Yuddy finds her house, but her servants won't allow him in. He leaves, gets in a fight with some hoods over a forged passport, and is shot and killed.

Mystery tour

Every character is miserable at the start of *Days of Being Wild*, and nobody is any happier at the end. *As Tears Go By* wasn't a happy movie either, but at least it was easy to follow. Wong's fans responded to *Days of Being Wild* with howls of outrage, but Wong didn't seem to care about this or the poor box office receipts. The critics had loved the film and more importantly, he had made a big discovery.

"My works tend to become 'character films' rather than 'story films'," Wong says. "[When we made *Days of Being Wild*] I was concerned that a film with some clear characters in it, told in simple narrative form, could be very predictable, thus unappealing. I tried to get around it. One day, I discovered I could chop those happenings into small pieces, and rearrange them with numerous possibilities. It was like I saw the light."

Since Wong cut himself loose from the strictures of linear plot structure, his character experiments have followed an increasingly unplanned path. His unpredictable working style has its fans—not least the Hong Kong superstars who line up to play havoc with their clean cut teenybopper images. In a town where the leading actors are usually the biggest-selling crooners of cheesy Cantopop records, a Wong Kar-wai movie is a rare opportunity to temporarily cut themselves loose from their slavishly planned careers.

As an actor in a Wong Kar-wai film, you never know what you might end up doing—or where you'll end up doing it. Takeshi Kaneshiro had to massage a pig's carcass in 1995's *Fallen Angels* (Wong says the porcine massage was Kaneshiro's idea), but at least he got to stay in Hong Kong. The actors in the 1994 martial arts epic *Ashes of Time* spent several arduous months filming in the deserts of northwest China. (Asked about the experience on the set of *Ashes of Time*, Leslie Cheung would only say "I spent too much time on that.") The cast and crew of *Days of Being Wild* spent just as long in the steamy jungles of the Philippines where Wong, in an inadvertent homage to Francis Ford Coppola's erratic behavior during the making of *Apocalypse Now* in the same country, found the tropical heat made him go slightly crazy. ("After [making *Days of Being Wild*]," he says, "I learned to control myself. I would never again forget that I am just making a film.")

Wong's approach sometimes seems as haphazard and random as the lives of the characters he depicts. His disorganization has led some to suggest that other members of his team are the real brains behind his productions. Wong is part of a creative trio which includes Australian-born, Chinese-speaking director of photography Chris Doyle, and art director and editor William Chang. They have worked together ever since making *Days of Being Wild* together in 1991. Doyle started working in film while studying Chinese in Taiwan and got work for Wong after participating in a couple of attention-getting Taiwanese movies.

In the vacuum created by the absence of linear plot lines in Wong's films, the arresting visuals have become a trademark, an exhilarating mix of techniques that intoxicates some and alienates others. Some say the story should take center stage, but Doyle disagrees.

"The sixties and seventies line was that the best cinematography is seamless, you didn't notice it," Doyle says. "I don't think so any more. The younger audience is so used to being visually excited by an image. It's a vehicle for emotional impact and the energy of the film. It's much more obvious to the audience, and they think 'Wow, this looks good!'"

The prominence of his distinctive visuals is what has led some critics to suggest it is Doyle, not Wong, who is the real cinematic genius in their creative partnership. Doyle has obviously become accustomed to fending off such speculation.

"They are visual films, so of course people are going to remark on the visuals," he says. "What you see on the screen is 60 percent [art director] William Chang. I don't think you can separate one from the other. Without being falsely modest, it's very much the collaboration that makes the film, but the idea is Wong's and the way it evolves is his. He usually says things like 'That all you can do, Chris?' which is a very refreshing approach

Poster: *Chungking Express*.

and it pushes you further. He's so cool and I'm so involved. It's just like a love relationship or a football team—you start to know each other's weaknesses and you work from there."

Very unhappy, definitely not together

Most Wong Kar-wai films won't pick you up when you're feeling down. Not even the 1994 hit film *Chungking Express*, which is often praised for its lighthearted sense of fun. It is undoubtedly humorous, but the humor is only a weapon the characters use to stave off the great loneliness that surrounds them. The film's slapdash charm is partly a result of the way it was filmed; thrown together during a three-month post-production break in the making of *Ashes of Time* (which by that point had been over two years in the making and was several million Hong Kong dollars over budget). Wong produced, directed and wrote the film himself, scribbling out the script by day and filming at night.

The narrative has two overlapping but separate parts, both focusing on the hard-luck love lives of two policemen named only by their numbers: #223 and #663. Both are pining for ex-lovers who have abandoned them, a lamentation of lost love which is undeniably funny but also terribly sad. They live in one of the world's most crowded cities, but are utterly alone. It's as if Hong Kong's bustling, vibrant, neon-slicked streets are conspiring against them, teasing them with chance encounters and fleeting love affairs which are doomed to fail. The city taunts characters in other films in just the same way.

"We rub shoulders every day," says He Zhiwu (Takeshi Kaneshiro) in *Fallen Angels*. "We may never know each other, but we could become good friends someday." In a Wong Kar-wai film? Not likely. As the cook at the takeaway counter Midnight Express says to #223 in *Chungking Express*, trying to explain that his ex-girlfriend is never coming back: "You wait, time goes. Time goes, heart freezes."

Wong offers no way out of this trap, because any attempt to break out of the tight cocoon of everyday life is an invitation for greater unhappiness. *Happy Together*'s main characters go all the way to Argentina to rekindle their love, only to encounter an even greater sorrow, as bleak and cold as the wintry streets of Buenos Aires. Most of Wong's characters aren't even afforded the dramatic dignity of a downward spiral. Instead, they're on a flat, featureless life trajectory where the infrequent glimmers of hope and inspiration are illusory.

Cuz I'm cooool: Leon Lau in *Fallen Angels*.

People like the hitman Wong Chi-ming (Leon Lai) in *Fallen Angels* have relinquished all hope of shaping their destiny. Chi-ming even pretends he likes it that way. "The best thing about my profession," he says, "is there's no need to make any decision." Considering his profession is the high-risk business of killing people he's never met, the decision-making thing doesn't seem like much of a perk.

Yet it's not as if modern urban living is the problem: the mythic characters who populate the vast empty deserts of *Ashes of Time* are also slaves to an apparently eternal melancholy, and worse still, they're unequipped with the wryness their city counterparts use to deflect it. "I don't care how others think of me," Ouyang Feng (Leslie Cheung) says at the beginning of *Ashes of Time*. "I just don't want others to be happier than I." Luckily for him, Wong seems prepared to grant him this wish—the rest of the characters are a laughably unhappy bunch. Huang Yaoshi (Tony Leung Kar-fai) is so miserable he drinks wine of amnesia so he can forget everything. The grief of Murong (Brigitte Lin) is so great she has developed a split personality, becoming not one, but two bitter, off-the-edge characters, Murong Yin and Murong Yang—each of them trying to kill the other. Tony Leung Chiu-wai's

Leslie Cheung and Jacky Cheung: *Ashes of Time*.

character is a swordsman whose sadness is so great it has turned him blind. At one point, Hong Qi (Jacky Cheung) asks Ouyang Feng what could lie beyond the desert in which they live. "Another desert," is Ouyang's grim reply.

Love really hurts

It's not as if the characters in Wong's films don't need love. Rather, they're obsessed with it. In *Chungking Express*, #223 (Takeshi Kaneshiro) munches through 30 cans of just-expired pineapple (his ex-lover's favorite fruit) in a bout of self-flagellation for losing her. #663 (Tony Leung Chiu-wai) talks to bars of soap and his dishcloth about his foolishness at letting his ex, a flight attendant, get away. Yet #223 is stricken when he gets a chance to make a romantic connection with the mysterious blond-wigged assassin (Brigitte Lin) he meets in a bar after vomiting up all the pineapple. He goes back to her hotel room and eats salad and watches TV while she sleeps, leaving early in the morning without establishing a way to contact her later. He hopes the memory of their fleeting encounter, heartbreaking in its insignificance, will last "10,000 years." (The whole thing would never have worked anyway, since she was a criminal and he a cop.)

Similarly, Ouyang Feng in *Ashes of Time* is

Faye Wong and Brigitte Lin: *Chungking Express*.

crippled with remorse about the woman he let get away, just as she, at the end of the film, is weeping for the love that might have added meaning to her empty life. There's a great big gaping hole in the middle of many of Wong's characters, but most of them are so paralyzed with regret that they're unable to do anything to fill it. The best he'll grant them is another chance at an unspecified future—Ouyang Feng making a move to see what's beyond the desert at the end of *Ashes of Time*, for example. The characters may be allowed to try and make a new start, but Wong will never let them break free of the regrets of their past.

"I guess I find this 'loss of innocence' thing deeply intriguing," Wong says, attempting to explain the misery he puts his characters through. "Time, to me, forever brings a loss of innocence. As you go through time, you are bound to look back with hindsight, you begin to reminisce about things that you dreamed about doing but didn't get to do, you begin to wonder what would have happened on that particular day if you had taken a different turn in the road. You have no answer for sure, but you are distressed by the possible

The Agent (Michelle Reis) spending quality time on hitman Chi-ming's bed while he's otherwise occupied: *Fallen Angels*.

outcome of things you didn't do. You cannot help but regret." And so regret runs like a swollen river through Wong's work.

You could get frustrated at Wong's characters for not trying harder to find a way out, but inertia is actually the best option, because he often punishes the people who try to make a change. Wong's message? Life without love may be lonely, but attempting to take control of your own destiny can have fatal consequences. A historical analogy is irresistible here: That the heart of this sense of powerlessness lies in the tension, the hype and the frustration which surrounded Hong Kong's handover from Britain to China in 1997.

"You know, every time we visit other countries," said Wong, "we people from Hong Kong have been forced to answer the question of 1997 for many, many years. It got pretty boring, repeating your opinion every 10 minutes. One of the reasons I chose Argentina [as the location for *Happy Together*] was that it is on the other side of the world, and I thought by going there, I would be able to stay away from 1997. But then, as you must understand, once you conscientiously try to stay away from something or to forget something, you will never succeed. That something is bound to be hanging in the air, haunting you."

This sense of powerlessness, of suspension, of having no choice but to deal with what fate hands out, is a fundamental part of Wong's movies. Although he has shown signs of mellowing in his later films—in *Happy Together*, Yiu-fai breaks free from his disastrous relationship and returns to Asia, for example—anything other than dull resignation is generally frowned upon in a Wong Kar-wai movie. The punishment for transgressing this code of inactivity is usually death. It's dished out to Wah, the gangster in *As Tears Go By*, who is gunned down just as he's finally falling for the domesticated charm of his cousin and about to break free of his triad life. Yuddy, the heart-breaking drifter of *Days of Being Wild*, is also killed for the transgression of attempting to resolve his rootlessness by finding his real mother. Similarly, Chi-ming, the hitman in *Fallen Angels*, gets shot almost immediately after he decides to throw in his career for the love of the Agent (Michelle Reis). They've spent three years in a business relationship which rarely involves them seeing each other. The Agent arranges his killing missions, and faxes him details of where to carry out the shooting. She also cleans his flat when he's out and masturbates on his bed while fantasizing about him.

When he finally makes the rather surprising step of deciding to be with her, he's killed off after taking one last job. In the stunningly filmed death sequence, Chi-ming asks, "Who's to die? When? Where?" in a voice-over, as gracefully spinning neon lights herald his slide into oblivion. "It's all been planned by others. I'm a lazy person. I like people to arrange things for me. I've been a bit different lately. I want to change my habit. Be it right or wrong, I must make a decision myself."

Defying malaise

The heart of Wong Kar-wai's films lies in the ways his characters combat this sadness that blocks out the sun from their lives. The only way they can deflect the misery that bears down upon them is with humor, which Wong has grown increasingly comfortable with using. The ultra-serious *Ashes of Time* represented rock-bottom in his bleak way of looking at the world, but since then he has allowed the smallest hint of devil-may-care defiance to creep into his movies. The hurried production of *Chungking Express* was when Wong first wised up to the power of a laugh, or at least a rueful grin—the perfect antidote to the self-indulgent seriousness of *Ashes of Time*.

Aside from the scripted humor in *Chungking Express*, there's high-wire pleasure to be had in watching Tony Leung Chiu-wai battle to hold back a smile when filming an obviously improvised scene with the real-life owner of takeaway counter Midnight Express, or Takeshi Kaneshiro berating a worker at a late-night convenience store for not considering the feelings of the cans of pineapple he just discarded. Both cops are indulging in a self-aware sort of madness to add some interest to the routine banality of their daily lives and their unpredictable riffs have an infectious charm.

Wong was obviously exhilarated by the humor injection in *Chungking Express* too, as he allowed Takeshi Kaneshiro an almost slapstick performance in 1995's *Fallen Angels*. In it, Kaneshiro plays He Zhiwu, a character so desperate for work that he takes over other people's businesses after hours, forcing passersby to buy things from him. There's a surreal, farcical scene in which he drives an entire mystified family around in an ice-cream van he's hijacked, forcing them to eat flaming ice cream while he drives

The Agent (Michelle Reis) on Zhiwu's bike: *Fallen Angels*.

nowhere in particular. It's hilarious stuff, but there's still sadness lurking beneath the surface of this escapism. Zhiwu is mute and lives with his father. His mother was killed after being hit by an ice cream van. Is he driving away from, or trying to confront something about his mother's death? We never find out, but the humor of the moment defuses the tragedy, making Zhiwu's boisterous, brutal optimism into something uplifting.

The best parts of Wong Kar-wai's films are the irresistible moments when the characters are allowed a rest from the daily battle of their lives. In *Fallen Angels* the Agent meets Zhiwu one day in a noodle shop, some time after his father has died and Chi-ming the hitman has been killed. Before they meet, Zhiwu gets into a fight with some other diners, trashing the noodle shop in the process. While mayhem reigns just behind her, the Agent sits oblivious, eating noodles and staring vacantly into space. Soon afterwards, in the film's last scene, we cut to another shot of the Agent with the same vacant expression on her face, only this time she's sitting on the back of Zhiwu's motorbike, her head slumped on his shoulder as they speed through a tunnel. The Agent speaks in a voice-over: "When I am about to leave, I ask him to take me home. I haven't ridden on a motorbike for a long time. Actually, I haven't been so close to a man for a while. The road is not that long, and I know I will be getting off soon. But I feel such warmth this very moment."

The misery that Wong heaps on his characters only makes these moments more powerful. When they find comfort despite the tragedy of their lives, they amplify the light from these seductive glimmers of happiness, and shine it full-beam back at the audience. It's a poignant, bittersweet onslaught that few can resist.

Home is where the heat is

If Wong Kar-wai's ego ever starts to swell, the close-to-home comments would quickly cut him down to size. Local critics have called his work overrated, pretentious and (a strange insult, this), "European". There is jealousy at the way his films, none of which has been a runaway success, seem to easily attract willing investors.

It often seems that Wong hears these voices of criticism the loudest. In every interview he seems embarrassed at any attempt at flattery and rebuffs it as if it were being directed at someone else. He seems to prefer discussing his mistakes than his successes. He even seems to read his victory at Cannes as the placing of a greater burden of expectation on his subsequent work, rather than something that has opened up new opportunities.

"From day one, it has been like striving to survive," he has said. "I have no idea how I entered into this, but ever since I have been striving to survive. After *Days of Being Wild*, my feeling has always been like a single pair of hands facing an entire army—you don't know when you're going to perish."

Wong has yet to combine praise from the critics with honest-to-goodness financial success, but he keeps finding backers for his films nonetheless. "The whole thing has gone against what our industry collectively believes in," Wong says of the controversy. "Making a film that doesn't sell is already bad enough; a commercially failed filmmaker getting more work is even worse. And on top of that, a whole bunch of people are telling everyone that this filmmaker has made some very, very good films. This is about as controversial as you can get."

Love him or hate him, Wong's profound influence on the Hong Kong film industry in the nineties cannot be understated. In the boom times of the eighties, producers could make money from a film without sweating the details. Having enough big stars on the cast list was enough to guarantee overseas sales, as nobody ever asked to see a script. Conventional wisdom suggested that with the right actors, stuntmen and action choreographers, a healthy profit was a sure thing.

In Hong Kong, where many films were slapped together literally days before they reach the screen, Wong's style was constantly imitated (and parodied, on occasion: Tony Leung Chiu-wai and Jacky Cheung took the hilariously disrespectful step of playing triad brothers not dissimilar to the pair in *As Tears Go By* in the madcap *Days of Being Dumb*). As jump-cuts, hand-held camera and other visual trademarks were rapidly incorporated into the Hong Kong cinematic lingo, Wong has no choice but to stay one step ahead of the competition.

"If something sells like a hotcake [in Hong Kong]," he says, "everybody tries to make a copy as soon as possible, hoping they are not too late. The situation doesn't allow you to sit and write about something you really want to write about, and then carry it around trying to sell it. Tarantino could have been sitting inside the video shop for many years before he came up with [his] scripts. But the [Hong Kong] industry wouldn't allow that."

Much of Wong's visual brilliance comes from this need to stay ahead of the pack. The results are obvious in every film but particularly so in the unorthodox cinematography of *Fallen Angels*, where the colors are so vivid they threaten to burst the frame, and the languorous slow-motion and artful freeze-frames of *Happy Together*.

"People are always very curious about the visual effects in my works," he says. "The not-so-romantic truth is that lots of those effects are in reality results of circumstantial consideration: if there is not enough space for camera maneuvering, replace the regular lens with a wide-angle lens; when candid camera shooting in the streets does not allow lighting, adjust the speed of the camera according to the amount of light available; if the continuity of different shots does not link up right for a sequence, try jump cuts; to solve the problem of color incontinuity, cover it up by developing the film in black and white...tricks like that go on forever."

"Our styles come from the way we work. Like in *Fallen Angels* we started working in a very small teahouse, and the only way we could shoot the scene was with a wide angle lens. But I thought the wide angle lens was too normal, so instead I preferred an extreme wide angle. And the effect is stunning because it draws the characters very close to the camera, but twists the perspective of the space so they seem far away. It became a contrast to *Chungking Express*, in which people are very far away from the camera but seem so close. Also, we work with very limited budgets and we don't have permits, so we have to work

Japanese poster for *Ashes of Time* (1994).

like CNN, just breaking into some place and taking some shots. We often don't have time for setups, and sometimes when neighbors walk into the frames we have to cut them out, and that becomes a jump cut.

"I think 10 or 15 percent is preconceived," Wong says. "Most of it just happens."

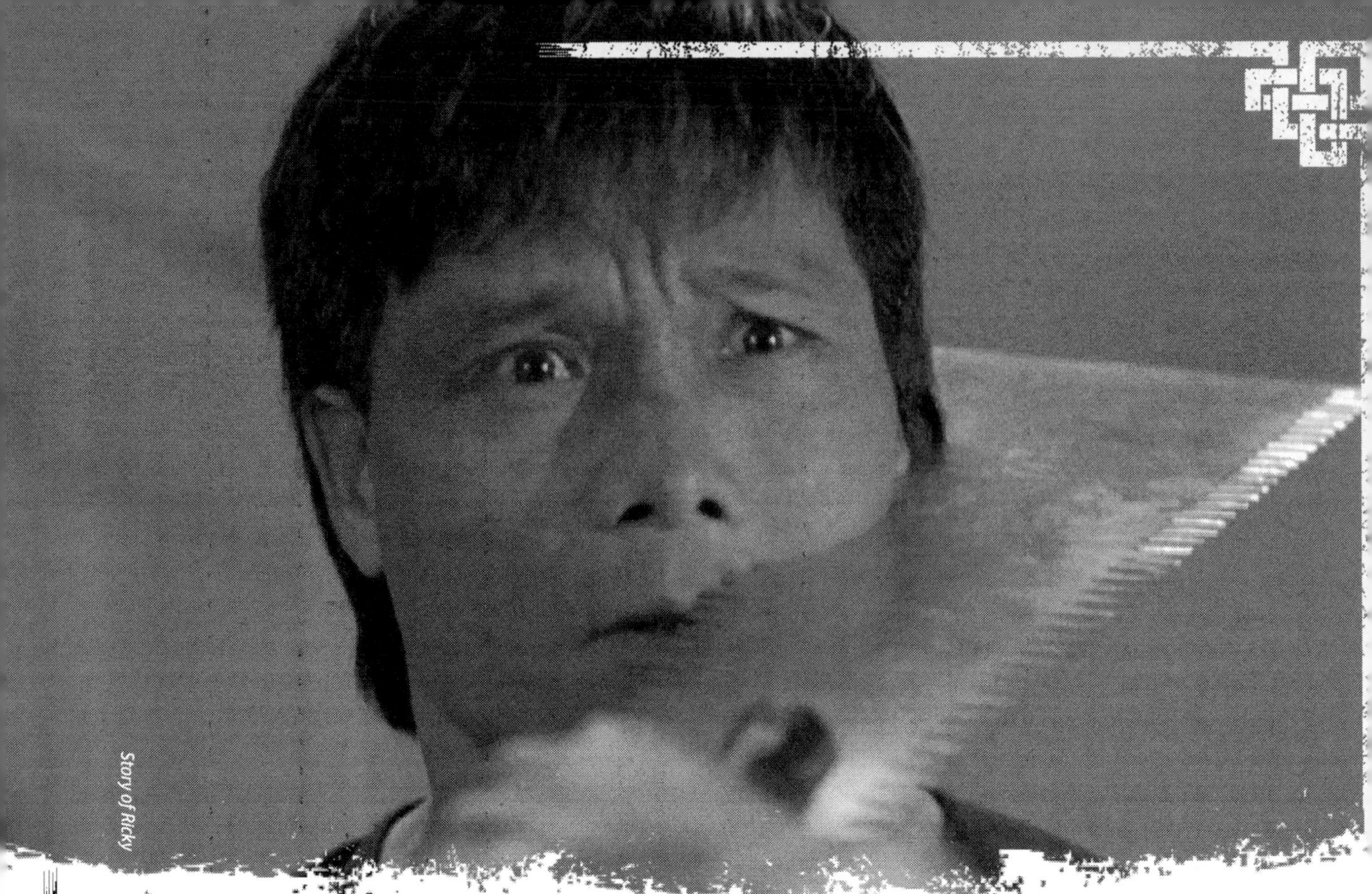

Story of Ricky

CHAPTER SEVENTEEN
HEWN AND SCATTERED

"The only film that an independent can make and survive with is a film that the major producers cannot or will not make...if you cannot titillate them with production value, you titillate them with something else."
—Director Herschel Gordon Lewis

xtreme cinema used to be the province of farsighted fringies like Lewis, whose *Blood Feast* (1964) established precedence for Grand Guignol cinema. Lewis made movies where people died with their eyes open, and pioneered non-toxic stage blood that actors could ingest.

Hong Kong film never had such inhibitions. With a population of over seven million souls living on top of each other, the real-life struggles which spring from the pages of Hong Kong's *Apple Daily* provide plenty of raw material for grind-'em-up plots.

Many notorious tales of grue are taken from actual cases. One true story was filmed by Clarence (*Naked Killer*) Fok as *Remains of A*

Woman (1993). The plot's simple: boy meets girl, boy meets other girl, boy gets original girl to help dismember the other girl, boy pretends to find salvation in jail because of pious third girl and gets sprung, leaving surviving original girl to take the murder rap.

Many Hong Kong actors have a laudable appreciation for the ghoulie/roughie/kinkie tradition and know that the villainous roles are the plum assignments. Ben Ng shudders and strips. Lily Chung screams and strips. Anthony Wong does everything short of grinding his murder victims up, baking them into pastries and serving them to the investigating cops.

Wait a minute, he does that too. Many Hong Kong actors will do whatever is necessary to vibrate that taut metal wire in the collective belly of their quivering audience. Hong Kong film filmmakers don't shrink from a juicy story—even if the juices don't run clear when pricked with something sharp.

These films are sometimes referred to as "guilty pleasures", but that's a cop-out. Many filmgoers vicariously enjoy depictions of nastiness, and Hong Kong has dished out (and dished up) some of the nastiest.

Nothing wrong with escapist entertainment. But there is something wrong about wasting ninety minutes on a film which tries to cover up laziness of plot and characters by dumping buckets of red corn syrup over everything, which is why *Horrible High Heels* (1997) and *Bloody Mary Killer* (1994) aren't here.

These films don't exist in a vacuum. Try explaining the plot of *The Silence of The Lambs* to someone who hasn't seen the film. Then explain why you liked it, then why it won a truckload of Oscars. Hannibal Lecter's necrophagic shenanigans may have been novel

for mainstream US audiences, but not to the Kowloon grindhouse faithful.

Hong Kong filmmakers aren't the sort to shy away from a meaty story. Unlike *Silence*, many of these films are based on fact. HK's cramped environs have created more than a few corpse-disposal problems for the colony's murderers, and the acid-bath beckons. The wartime atrocities depicted in the tough-to-take *Man Behind the Sun* actually occurred. On the flip-side, nothing in *Story of Ricky* has ever happened, or ever could.

If you lean toward the extreme, you'll enjoy these recommendations. Load up on too much caffeine and peek through your trembling fingers. Go ahead.

Dr Lamb (羔羊醫生)
1992 | Starring Danny Lee Sau-yin, Simon Yam Tat-wah, Kent Cheng Jut-si, Lau Siu-ming,

Parkman Wong Pak-man, Emily Kwan Bo-wai, Chung Bik-wing, Wong Wing-fong, Julie Lee
Directed by Danny Lee Sau-yin

Dr Lamb owes its notoriety as one of the most lurid of Hong Kong Category III films in part both to its censorship baiting subject matter and the over-the-top performance of Simon Yam as taxi driver Lam Gor-yu, who murders lone female passengers before raping and dismembering their corpses. The widely banned film features explicit footage of necrophiliac intercourse and graphic (if fake looking) images of dismemberment sessions. The film's gleeful depravity is amply evidenced in one sequence of investigating officers stumbling across a victim's dismembered breast and tossing it among one another in horror, or another of a circular saw spraying a victim's gore over a living room goldfish tank. Dr Lamb offers not only moments of such fiendishly jet-black humor, but also intermittent flourishes of a neo-noir visual style, with explicit nods to *Taxi Driver* (1976), as Lam prowls the rainy, neon-flooded, prostitute-thronged streets of Hong Kong in search of the rare object of feminine virtue and purity.

But beyond the film's abject sleaze, there also seems something peculiarly resonant about the *Dr Lamb* narrative, based in fact upon the true story of serial killer Lam Kor-wan—Hong Kong's answer to the notorious American serial killer Ed Gein—who like his Wisconsin counterpart has been the inspiration for several films, sometimes acknowledged, sometimes implicit. While the film's anti-protagonist does not elicit much in the way of sympathy owing to the shocking nature of his crimes and the seemingly irrational and mercurial cast of his behavior as portrayed by Yam, the film nevertheless goes out of its way to project a modest level of social critique throughout, suggesting that while the killer might embody evil, he is also to a large extent symptomatic of a warped social environment. The film offers the suggestion that the killer has developed the way he has in part because of a lack of proper guidance as a child—having had an overly permissive father and an uncaring step-mother. Perhaps an even greater blame is attributed to his adult circumstances, in particular his home life with an utterly dysfunctional extended family, his co-residing relatives so alienated and inattentive that they fail to catch clues of the carnage of taxi passengers taking place within their shared Hong Kong apartment. But this dysfunction is linked in turn with the material difficulty of the family's circumstances, the need to work long hours even to maintain their meager living arrangements, and thus offers a measure of class critique; indeed, even the moniker of "Dr Lamb," which most overtly alludes to the driver's home-grown surgical skills, also implicitly references the impossibility of someone in the cab driver's Hong Kong social circumstances ever having the opportunity to become a genuine medical doctor.

Nor are Hong Kong's guardians of law and order spared the film's social criticism. The killer may indeed be cruel and repugnant, but this does not discount the fact that the police are represented as being consistently and habitually brutal in their investigation of the murders, beating their suspect (and various family members) savagely; the overall impression is that the apparatus of Hong Kong's legal system is simply another manifestation of overall social illness. Among further ironies is the fact that the team investigating this case of murderous abuse of women consistently treats its one female member poorly, and the fact that one of the murders occurs right at a police kiosk which at that moment happens to be unmanned.

Indeed, one can ultimately read the film as an intentionally sick and savage parody of the Hong Kong police detective film. Danny Lee here plays as in numerous other films the highly committed senior member of a police investigative team (appropriately, an eponymous Inspector Lee), and we have the typical conventions of the key criminal feeling connected (if not obsessed with) his main police pursuer, and a focus on the dynamics of the police team. But here such conventions are undermined, not only because the grotesque dimensions of the crimes make the mechanics of police procedure seem inconsequential by comparison, but also because the bullying and bumbling team itself has questionable moral authority (for the reasons noted) to begin with, and the linkage between detective and criminal ends up precipitating no higher understanding or redemption for either: In a final gesture aimed to bring Lam back within the realm of the civilized world, Lee accedes to Lam's request to pay him a visit in jail, only to be summarily sent on his way when the criminal hears that no, Lee cannot give him back the lurid photographs he has taken of his murder victims and niece, photographs he still ardently longs for.

—Adam Knee

Ebola Syndrome (伊波拉病毒)
1996 | Starring Anthony Wong Chau-sang, Lo Mang, Cheung Lau, Marianne Chan Miu-ying, Angel Wong Chui-ling, Vincent Wan Yeung-ming, Shing Fui-on, Baat Leung-gum, Cindy Yip, Lori Shannon
Directed by Herman Yau Lai-to

Watching this oozing chunk of splurted-out Hong Kong splatter is like being trapped in a 4D

Kai, Ebola Patient Zero in Hong Kong, chops a biohazard-suited peace officer while holding a child hostage in *Ebola Syndrome*.

IMAX rendition of a repulsive traffic accident in hyperslow agony-vision—a violent split-second impact expanded to ninety poignant, torturous minutes—a free-form charnelfunhouse thumbing its nose at its meager budget and leaving no avenue unexplored in its relentless quest to assault sensibilities, insult everything and everyone, and send the stomach contents of every viewer whooshing out in a collective geyser. *Ebola Syndrome*'s bratty anarchic vileness trumps the bilious efforts of notorious filmmakers like Jorg Buttgereist, Gaspar Noë, or Tom Six.

By the five-minute mark, *Syndrome*'s protagonist Kai (Anthony Wong) has performed a lifetime's worth of evil. He's caught *in flagrante delicto* with his boss' wife, then grovels before the furious cuckold (Boss Kwan, played by Shing Fui-on, who heaps vile Category III-level Cantonese on him). Kai then offers to castrate himself with a pair of those curved-blade scissor-like tools used to amputate small branches.

Instead, he stabs Kwan's bodyguard in the crotch, assaults Kwan and strangles him with the folding legs of a mahjong table. He grabs the terrified wife and slices off her tongue with the shears, then turns his homicidal attentions to Lily,

Kai doesn't like condoms but working girls Cindy Yip and Lori Shannon like his stolen C-notes—alas, to their detriment: *Ebola Syndrome*.

the cute daughter of the freshly splattered couple.

The girl cowers. Kai douses her with gasoline and starts fumbling with his Zippo. He comforts the weeping girl by telling her: "Don't worry, it won't hurt." But before he can torch the lass, a neighbor comes knocking on the door wondering what in the heck is going on. Kai's line, delivered as he saunters out, sets the tone for his character throughout the film: "I'm killing them, what's wrong?"

If you've figured out by now that *Ebola Syndrome* is a black comedy, bonus points for you. But there ain't no brakes—hop on this toboggan and you're going all the way. Next stop is South Africa, where Kai the exile is working in a Chinese restaurant, hacking up live frogs with a cleaver. Kai is under no vegan delusion that "meat is murder"—he knows that meat is meat, and murder is murder.

Kai's being exploited by his employers, a Taiwanese couple (Lo Mang and Cheung Lau) engaged in the time-honored trade of the overseas Chinese: running a Chinese restaurant. They pay him a pittance and hurl abuse at him.

There's little sympathy for Kai though—he's disgusting. For starters, he refuses to bathe lest it wash away the aroma of the slaughtered pigs he carries into the restaurant. Pork is his metaphor—Kai gets his kicks by listening to his employers have weird wild sex while masturbating with a puce-translucent piece of purloined pork loin from the larder (UK extreme horror flick *Mum and Dad* (2010) paid homage to Yau's film by recreating this nasty bit of business).

The "marinated" pork is later served to an obnoxious gwailo customer. Kai is plagued by lust, but the local hookers won't touch his custom.

An opportunity occurs when he and the restaurant owner drive to a rural village to buy a couple of pigs at discount rates. The natives are infected with the Ebola virus, but our heroes escape with the precious carcasses and start driving back across the veldt. When the truck breaks down, and Kai spots a native girl collapsing by a nearby riverbank, of course he's gotta run over and take advantage.

She explodes mouthwise in a milky geyser, drenching Kai in body fluids and, you guessed it, she's got the dreaded bug. And though it's fatal and there's no cure, one person in 10,000 is immune and survives, only to become a carrier of the most hideous make-ya-bleed virus ever. And what are the chances that Kai, miserable chunk of humanity that he is, just happens to be a carrier, spreading horrible convulsive death by contact with any of his bodily fluids?

But before he even figures out that he's got this perverse Midas touch, there he goes again: slaughtering his employers and stealing their cash. Then it's back to Hong Kong to look up his ex-girlfriend Har (Marianne "*Sexy and Dangerous*" Chan).

Wong and Yau's demented comedy picks relentless at the viewer's fevered brain. If a taxi pulls up to a curb in *Ebola Syndrome*, it runs over a rat. Wong misses no opportunity to sneer, wear pompous hats, grab his crotch or taunt hookers (Cindy Yip and Lori Shannon) into condom-free deathtrips with stolen US$100 bills. There's even "Mouthcam" shots like some mutant dental hygiene industrial film. Seldom does an audience laugh, moan, and scream so ardently for biohazard-suited cops to open fire. No sequel to this one—as Yau lamented: "I like this kind of movie. But it didn't make money. Too bad!".

Lost Souls (打蛇)
1980 | Starring Chan Shen, Moo Yuk-Fan, Stephen Chan Yung, Wan Seung-Lam, Hung San-Nam, Hung Fung, Jenny Leung Jan-lei, Shum Lo, Chow Kin-ping
Directed by Mou Tun-fei (as T.F. Mous)

Lost Souls is the work of director Mou Tin-fei—working under the name "T F Mous" and also director of Man Behind the Sun (reviewed in this chapter). Both films are about men in power abusing that power against innocents, but while MBTS addresses the horrors of Imperial Japan's biological warfare experiments in the 1930s and 1940s, LS is set near the Hong Kong/China border, and the souls in limbo here are mainlanders seeking to illegally immigrate to Hong Kong, while their tormentors are "snakeheads": criminals who provide entry to the-then Crown Colony in exchange for cash.

Lost Souls is about aspiration's descent into desperation, and the cast are primarily non-professionals as few actors would accept such roles: they're career-squashers. Mou seems to have drawn inspiration from Pier Paolo Pasolini's Salò (1975), and the film is not for those with faint hearts or fluttery stomachs. Even by today's standards, it's a shocker. The late Shaws regular Chan Shen garners bonus screen-villain points here for his portrayal of a crippled, amoral, and deeply perverse human smuggler here.

Man Behind the Sun
aka Men Behind the Sun
(黑太陽731)
1990 | Starring Wu Dai-yao, Wang Gang, Wang Run-shen
Directed by Mou Tun-fei (as T.F. Mous)

Occasionally, something comes along to challenge the acceptable limits of cinema verité. Mondo Cane, Medium Cool and Faces of Death all generated controversy for their increasingly graphic portrayals of misery and bloodshed. Add to this tradition Man Behind the Sun. Even viewers used to the hack-and-bleed, head-exploding effects of George Romero and David Cronenberg

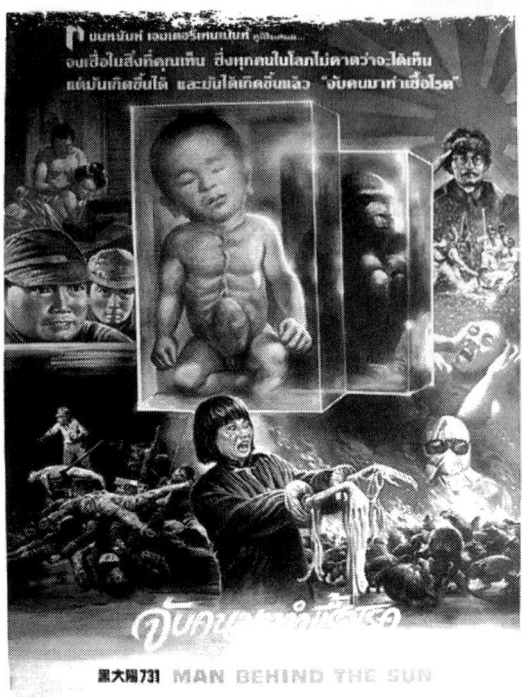

Yeesh...Thai poster for *Man Behind the Sun*.

find *Man Behind the Sun* shocking.

Japan-occupied Manchuria, 1930s: a cat is thrown into a room full of rats. We see it bound around, trying to defend itself against the horde of rodents, eventually collapsing as the rats chew at the head and neck of the dying feline. In the film's most spectacular scene, we see hundreds of flaming rats leaping and writhing in agony, trying to escape immolation.

Killing stunt animals is gratuitous and uncool, but *Man Behind the Sun* is not a cheap attempt at exploitation. it's based on the true story of Unit 731 (731部隊), the brainchild of Japanese militarist Lt General Shiro Ishii. Starting in the 1930s, Ishii (played by Wang Gang) built fortified installations in occupied Manchuria for the purposes of developing new biological weapons and for experimenting on the effects of extreme conditions on human subjects.

Ishii, the camp's commander, was a cruel and twisted man, using Chinese and Russian peasants for his test subjects. Ishii's main goal was to develop a plague-dispersing bomb (that explains all the rats). *MBTS* suggests that Ishii achieved his goal, but not in time to help the war effort.

The film does not try to hide its fury over the Japanese behavior. Chinese prisoners are called "maruta" (the Japanese word for "wooden logs"), and members of the Japanese youth corps stationed at the camp are slapped when they refer to the prisoners as human beings.

Still, the Japanese aren't portrayed as plain old evil. Takamura, the camp's security chief, is portrayed as passionate but misguided, believing in his heart that the camp's work is worthwhile. Doctor Ishii is sick and cruel, but the film portrays him as mentally ill—a victim of chemical unbalance.

Man Behind the Sun is well made, which makes it all the harder to take. Scenes of the camp's destruction seamlessly blend stock footage with staged shots, and the autopsy of a living boy looks disturbingly real. In one scene, the last remaining survivor among the prisoners—a boy who has hidden among the corpses—is killed while a Japanese woman gives birth. The movie flits back and forth between the two events with a disquieting rhythm. The symbolism is obvious, but effective. The brutality may prove too realistic for many viewers, but the subject matter demands it.

— Jim Morton

Naked Poison (獸性新人類)

2000 | Starring Samuel Leung Cheuk-moon, Gwennie Tam Kwan-yee, Sophie Ngan Chin-man, Co Co Chow Ka-yu
Directed by Cash Chin Man-kei

MORE SEX, BETTER ZEN, FASTER BULLETS

Naked starlets accessorized with spiders and snakes: movie-painting adorning the President Theatre, Causeway Bay, Hong Kong (Photo: Stefan Hammond, 2000).

Pathetic nerd Ng Chi-min (Samuel Leung) is a perennial loser. Lacking in social skills and plug-ugly, Min works in an office and creeps around in a constant state of sexually frustration—fueled by co-workers Chan Mei-ling (Gwennie Tam) and Winnie Wong (the boss's mistress, played by pneumatic Sophie Ngan).

Min lives with his grandparents in their traditional Chinese medicine shop. He pervs on the next-door neighbors, is caught, and thrashed.

But suddenly Grandpa dies and Grandma moves back to China, leaving the shop to Min. He proceeds to concoct a potent herbal aphrodisiac and just guess who he's gonna use it on.

Naked Poison has its moments—like when Sophie and the boss's horrid wife catfight in front of a huge TV screen erupting with a distorted color-bar pattern. But it's pure sleaze. The only reason to watch this thing is to see Sophie Ngan naked.

Red To Kill (弱殺)
1994 | Starring Lily Chung Suk-wai, Ben Ng Ngai-cheung, Money Lo Man-yee, Baat Leung-gum
Directed by Billy Tang Hin-shing
How exactly to best describe Billy Tang's *Red To Kill*...hmmm...phrases like "scurrilous, pot-boiling mayhem" and "obscenely twisted squirtin' excess" aren't strong enough. Let's say that if the Romans had had film as a device to wean their citizens from bloody spectacles pitting humans against wild beasts, they would have loved *Red To Kill*.

This film is wild at heart and guaranteed to offend. It hurls itself headlong at Hong Kong's dirty secrets—the stigma of mental illness, the desperate cramped quarters of public housing estates and the mob mentality of their residents. Stacked on top of these serious social issues are unforgettable portrayals of predator and prey by Ben Ng and Lily Chung, respectively.

Ng plays a Jekyll/Hyde rape-murderer, and his depiction of tortured humanity is gobstopping. Ng's hands and muscular forearms lurch into frames like vengeful snakes. Low-angle shots of his distended mouth quivering in the grip of reptilian-brain lustmord are spookier than any writhing data-drawn beastie.

Lily plays innocent in her simplistic portrayal of a woman described as having the "mentality of a ten-year old". People suffering from mental or emotional problems are stigmatized in Hong Kong society, and although strides have been made in recent years, many of the old prejudices remain. By presenting such a character as a victim in a violent film, Tang twists the knife in these outmoded beliefs. Like Stravinsky's Rite of Spring, *RTK* delights in stepping on everyone's toes.

A human beast is stalking a Hong Kong housing estate, which includes a hostel for emotionally scarred people. The hostel inmates are a cheery bunch, yet the bickering and vengeful residents of the estate are convinced that they are responsible for a series of recent crimes: women wearing red are ending up as violated corpses. The residents are

Miss Cheung dresses in red to bring out the beast: *Red To Kill.*

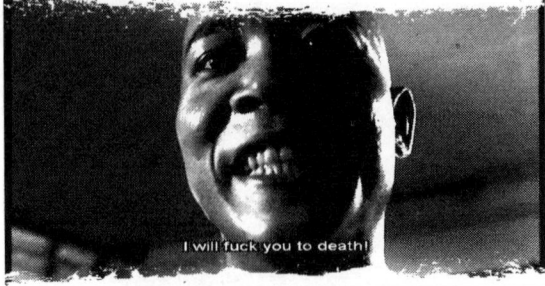

And it works: Chan the monster in *Red To Kill.*

convinced they've nabbed the "sex lupine" when hapless Brother Chubby trips drunkenly down the stairs late one night, but he's a red herring.

Real red rage continues to surge as Chan Chi-wai (Ng) relieves and recreates bloody childhood trauma. Eventually the violations reach the door of Ming Ming (Chung), who was moved into the hostel by social worker Miss Cheung (Money Lo) after Ming Ming's father was killed in a car crash. The Beast corners Ming Ming and does his vile thing. He's attracted by her mental disability, lunatically declaring it a match for his own and (delusions of matrimony raging through his festering skull) spares her.

Mistake? Ming Ming 'fesses up with the help of Cheung and the authorities clap him in irons. Justice? Chan's scumbag lawyer viciously cross-examines Ming Ming in the courtroom, painting her as a demented slut. She freaks out, the judge dismisses the case, and the perp walks. But in Hong Kong, the color of revenge is red.

Chan has developed a monster crush on Ming Ming and is heading over the edge (for a guy whose hobby is psychotic rape and murder, this is remarkable). Cheung, enraged by Chan's carefree homicidal tendencies, dolls up in a lipstick-red dress and taunts him sexually.

Chan rushes around like a dog coated with raw meat, dumps a pail of ice down the front of his jockstrap, then shaves his head and dons a pair of skin-tight biker shorts for the final confrontation with the vengeful social worker and her charge. The floor slick with blood and broken glass by film's end, it's thumbs-down for Ng's sociopathic lust-killer, but despite the Grand Guignol red-daubed finale, no one is particularly happy by film's end.

When *RTK* hit Hong Kong screens, the first two weeks brought plenty of box office action, but revenues started to sag during Week Three. Martini Films' quick-thinking boss Kimmy Shuen came up with a strategy straight out of the AIP/Nicholson-Arkoff playbook. Shuen replaced the film's newspaper ads with plain red text on a black background—a message from Lily Chung claiming that a certain scene would be trimmed

Fortunately, though tough, he's not invincible.

from the video release, and if the audience was interested, they were best advised to see it while they had the chance. Cha-ching!

Remains of a Woman (郎心如鐵)
1993 | Starring Carrie Ng Kar-lai, James Pak, Loretta Lee Lai-chun, Jacqueline Law Wei-kun, Money Lo Man-yee, Melvin Wong, Dennis Chan, Kenneth Tsang
Directed by Clarence Ford (Fok Yiu-leung)

Remains of a Woman is based on a murder case which rocked Hong Kong in the early 90s. The story unfolds in herky-jerky flashbacks as Billy Chan (James Pak) prepares for his retrial on the charge of dissolving the body of air hostess Lisa (Jacqueline Law) in an acid bath. When Billy meets Judy (Carrie Ng), he recognizes her as an easy mark. Judy's addictions fire on all cylinders—love, sex, cocaine, co-dependence—and soon she's embezzling from work and turning over the cash.

When Billy adds Lisa to his stringer, the women fight over him with coke-fueled-inner-child intensity. It's a hard day's night for the creep—if he's not busy betting on the ponies or sticking stuff up his nose, he's indulging in fluff-porn with Lisa or S&M with Judy.

When the flashback-clock arrives at the air

Carrie Ng and James Pak get primal in *Remains of a Woman*.

Carrie sheds her bondage collar and gets ready to rumble in *Remains of a Woman*.

hostess death scene, it's presented as a Sid & Nancy-type screwup followed by Grand Guignol mayhem. Billy is too freaked and shivery to dispose of the body, so Judy must do it herself. She shoots cocaine in her tongue, then screams "Don't look at me!" into dead Lisa's wide-open eyes before commencing hacksaw corpse-disassembly.

Once arrested and jailed, Billy hooks virginal, Bible-toting prisoner-visitor Annie Cheung (Loretta Lee). Annie helps authorities see that new-leaf Billy deserves to get another trial. What he really deserves, though, is a short dance on the end of a rope.

The spine and soul of *ROAW* is Carrie Ng's performance as a woman manipulated over the edge. Her sans-makeup closeups in the courtroom (as Billy is let off the hook) scream of twisted romantic obsession. Ng's sensual creepiness won her the 1993's Best Actress award at Taiwan's Golden Horse Film Awards (see note at end of this review).

The scariest thing about the movie is not its gore, but the way Billy turns women into putty by feeding them cocaine, rough sex, or religious beatitudes. Good-looking and soulless, Chan is the sort of heartless bastard that otherwise

Carrie Ng as Judy Yu gets zorched before corpse-disassembly in *Remains of a Woman*.

rational women crawl over broken glass for, while nice guys like us shrug our shoulders in resigned disbelief. In *Remains of a Woman*, they crawl over a lot worse.

NOTE: *ROAW* bombed in Hong Kong, but Taiwanese audiences loved it and box office went boffo.

When Carrie Ng learned she'd earned a Best Actress nomination at Taiwan's upcoming Golden Horse Awards, it was unprecedented. No Cat III film had ever received any sort of nomination, but on the night, Ng was named Best Actress of 1993 for her performance.

She came onstage to accept her award, but was completely overwhelmed and was unable to deliver her acceptance speech. The gracious Golden Horse organizers allowed her to return later in the show to do so. Later she told reporters: "This award means different things to different people, but for me it is one of the most important things to ever happen in my life. It represents 12 years of my undying effort."

Ng was also nominated for Best Actress at the 13th Hong Kong Film Awards but lost to Anita Yuen—who starred in 1993's runaway hit *C'est La Vie Mon Cherie*, a film in which Ng also appeared.

Story of Ricky (力王)
1992 | Starring Louis Fan Siu-wong, Yukari Oshima, Frankie Chin, Gloria Yip, Koichi Sugisaki, Fan Mei-sheng, William Ho Ka-kui, Wong Kwok-leung, Tetsuro Tamba, Philip Kwok Tsui
Directed by Nam Nai-choi

Over-the-top gore offerings oft end up tedious voyeuristic voyages, trying to top their predecessors by having more reddened corn syrup spraypainting the walls, and more stuff chopped off and wiggled. But this isn't the case with The *Story of Ricky*, which instead resembles some sort of deranged Japanese comic book. There's good reason: this twisted tale of incarceration is based on a deranged Japanese comic book (a *manga* called Rikki Oh). Its chops have been ground and pounded here into one mighty stew of grue.

It's the near future and prisons have been privatized, presumably to provide even scummier administrative personnel. Our hero, Ricky Ho, is a lithe muscledude (played with blockheaded

Can Ricky defeat this arrogant snot-nosed monster?

Does this answer your question?

insouciance by Louis Fan) jailed for killing the drug kingpin responsible for his girlfriend's suicide. His fellow inmates are a heinous lot—they like drug kingpins—and threaten him with bodily injury.

Body-shredding, however, does not seem to faze Ricky, who doesn't seem to mind sharp metal objects rammed into his body. He can certainly dish it out as well. A feeble-minded, sumo-sized sadist is sent to squash Ricky in the shower, but our boy plunges his bare hand into the goon's ample abdomen and rips out his intestines.

This stunt earns Ricky an audience with the assistant warden (Fan Mei-sheng, Louis Fan's father in real life): a loathsome, carnivorous churl who stores breath mints in his glass eye and whose bookshelves are stocked solely with dozens of luridly boxed porno videos. Unimpressed by prison authority, Ricky duels with the wicked boss of the North wing, Hai—covered in muscles and tattoos—in the prison courtyard.

A hard slap to the back of Hai's head pops out an eyeball, which is immediately eaten by predatory birds. The brute hastily attempts *seppuku*, but only so he can attempt to strangle Ricky with his outpouring innards.

Hai's demise forces the other three prison bosses to deal with Ricky. This unlikely trio of inmates—a creepy simian needle-hurler, a huge galoot with Elvis sideburns (Koichi Sugisaki), and a very butch Yukari Oshima—start to make life difficult, but a touch of comic relief is provided by the arrival of the head warden (William Ho) and his pudgy spoiled-brat of a son (Wong Kwok-leung).

This terrible kid is the movie's worst monster—until the warden works voodoo to transform himself into a hulking rubber-bladder beast. In a final-reel battle which recollects Ted V Mikels' *The Corpse Grinders*, the warden-beast is fed directly into an enormous...you get the picture.

The comic-book viscera is impossible to take seriously; at one point, a skullcrusher punch is revealed as precisely that by X-ray. This isn't a movie one bumps into; this is a movie one seeks out and devours...if you like this sort of thing.

The Untold Story: Human Meat Roast Pork Buns
(八仙飯店之人肉叉燒飽)
1993 | Starring Anthony Wong Chau-sang, Danny Lee Sau-yin, Emily Kwan Bo-wai, Julie Lee
Directed by Herman Yau Lai-to

Some things are lost in translation. Take, for example, the title of this movie. The English title—*The Untold Story*—is innocuous enough.

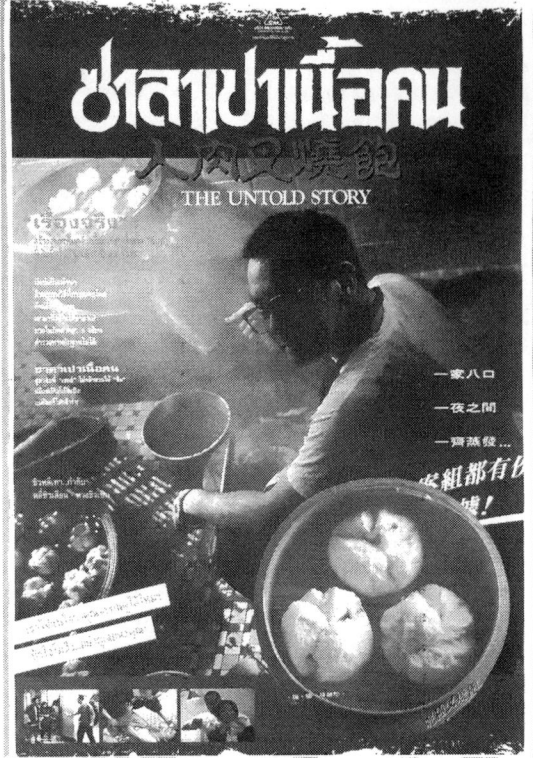

But the Chinese title translates as *Eight Immortals Restaurant: Human Meat Roast Pork Buns*. Frankly, that's a far more enlightening title for this picture, which is guaranteed to make you look twice at the next pork bun you purchase.

Chan Chi Leung (Anthony Wong) after a fight with a man who accused him of cheating at mahjong (he was cheating, but that doesn't seem to matter). Chan moves from Hong Kong to Macau, adopts a different name, and gets a job working in the kitchen of the Eight Immortals Restaurant in Macau, cutting up pigs and making buns. When the restaurant owner also accuses him of being a mahjong cheat, Chan slices and dices the man and his family, grinds them up for pork bun filling, then takes over the restaurant.

The Untold Story combines low humor and high gag without blinking. The Chief of Homicide (Danny Lee) always shows up with a different call girl on his arm, and a love-struck but ignored female detective finally dresses as one to get his attention. Chan originally earns police benevolence by being extra-generous when filling squad orders for pork buns. Long, lingering shots of policemen gorging themselves on free human meat roast pork buns—they have no idea, but the audience knows—elicts "Eeewww's" in unison.

As soon as the jokes stop, it's right back to rape, mutilation, torture, beating, and murder. When bags of human remains wash up on the beach, the police follow the trail back to Chan. he's arrested, but it's only after days of constant psychological and physical torture that Chan finally tells the story of what really happened that night at the Eight Immortals restaurant.

The Untold Story is a pretty good character study, evoking sympathy for the murderer (at least at first) without ever asking you to like him. Anthony Wong's killer is repugnant and insane, but he still comes across as a human being. Wong's impressive performance won him 1993's Hong Kong Film Award for Best Actor.

— Jim Morton

ADDENDUM: The REAL Untold Story

Sometimes a legend folds itself like a Moebius Strip. When Herman Yau's provocative version of the Sweeney Todd legend hit cinema screens in 1993, it horrified viewers, caused controversy over its use of child actors in the local press, earned Anthony Wong his first Best Actor Award, and—most importantly—did well at the box office.

It's a unique film and a must for fans of the genre. And it's based on a story that everyone believed was true at the time, and has since become a Hong Kong urban legend.

There's only one problem: the real "*Untold Story*" has never been fully told. Until now.

Like many revealing stories, the truth is more intricate and funnier than the tale. The events that created this urban legend took place in Macau, then a Portuguese colony, before the era of instant news and mobile phones. Veteran Macau journalist Harald Bruning is the only person who was first-person privy to the real events and able to recount the story in English.

According to Bruning, the story started as a prank between rival Chinese-language newspapers in Macau. "One had a large staff of about 20 reporters," recalls Bruning, "while the other had only a few." Macau during the late 80s was far different from the faux Vegas moneypit it is now. Bruning says were no formal border controls and it was common for people, even whole families, to simply relocate within the Pearl River Delta region of China, just north of the Macau border.

"Northern Macau at that time was relatively rural, with squatter-huts," said Bruning. "A family-owned eatery, the Eight Immortals restaurant, hired a worker named Wong Chi Hang, and then the family disappeared—no one knows where. Rumors circulated and Macau's police force (known by the Portuguese name Policía Judiciara or PJ for short) detained Wong for questioning."

Here's how the prank started. According to Bruning, the larger newspaper had a low-ranking employee who eavesdropped on reporter conversations, scavenging for tips. If she heard something promising, she would rush to a payphone on the ground floor of the newspaper building and call her boyfriend, who worked for the smaller paper—which fed a newswire in Hong Kong. If her boyfriend sold a juicy story, he got a commission, so she kept a sharp ear while in the office.

Knowing this subterfuge, the reporter who had just spoken to the police loudly spun a horrific-and-false tale to his colleagues. He told them emphatically that the restaurant worker had confessed not only to killing the entire family, but butchering them and using their flesh in the restaurant's dishes—including their famous *pat sin tong* ("Eight Immortals soup"). Of course, the woman listened carefully to this made-up story, then ran down to use the payphone, while the reporters chortled over their prank.

Bruning says that no trace of human butchery was uncovered by the police at the restaurant (which he visited as a reporter after the case broke). Also, he says, the refrigeration equipment there was inadequate to store more than a small amount of perishables.

The missing family members were never found. However, some human bones were later found at Hac Sa Beach and a forensics expert from the mainland speculated that they could belong to some of the missing family members. But at that time, mainlanders who could to swim to Macau would be granted Macau citizenship. Some made the arduous journey, but more than a few unlucky souls drowned. As genetic forensics was still in its infancy, it was impossible to determine the origin of the bones...which of course added to the legend.

Suspect Wong Chi Hang committed suicide in jail, after sending a letter to a local newspaper director (Chiu Iu Nang, director of Macau's Va Kio Pou newspaper) protesting his innocence.

Bruning says that the local police quickly adopted the human-meat angle because, while they couldn't solve the case, no one cared about the investigation after hearing lurid tales of body parts used for soup. The horrific fable gained

DVD cover for the US release of *The Untold Story* (courtesy Tai Seng Video).

traction after Hong Kong newspapers splashed it on their front pages.

It was much like the type of stories the National Enquirer and dodgy UK tabloids used to peddle. The story was repeated so often that it became urban legend, like the blind albino alligators living in New York City sewers. Without an official debunking, the myth stands.

While *The Untold Story* became tabloid-fodder and later served as film-template (there are two sequels) and Herman Yau's film showcasing Anthony Wong's award-winning talents is well made and suspenseful, were human beings really ground up into *char siu bao* filling??

Nope. You read it here first.

The Untold Story 2
(人肉叉燒包2天誅地滅)

1998 | Starring Anthony Wong Chau-sang, Emotion Cheung Kam-ching, Yeung Fan, Pauline Suen Kai-kwan, Helena Law Lan
Directed by Andy Ng Yiu-kuen

The original *Untold Story* was a salty tale of meat and murder. Five years later, the sequel (produced by Danny Lee) thudded into the grindhouses of Mongkok like a sodden pork bun from Beelzebub's own steamer. This film's Chinese title translates roughly as "Human Roast Pork Buns 2: Suffer In Hell", and it has little in common with its "prequel" save carnal revels and Anthony Wong. It's a tightly wrapped tale of sexual jealousy, murderous intent—walls of flesh and wanton lust for more sex, more money, and more freshly roasted meat.

Cheung (the actor's name is Emotion Cheung) is a nice-guy proprietor of a Hong Kong barbecue restaurant. Both Officer Lazyboots (Wong) and the local triad boss (played by *Robotrix* director Jamie Luk) hang out chatting over plates of crisply roasted pork and "4 Treasures rice". The shop employs a few locals like Third Aunt (Helena Law), who pushes a mop and chides the customers, and the cash drawer is full of greasy red banknotes at the end of each long workday.

Cheung has problems. Number One is his wife Kuen (Yeung Fan), who's young, gorgeous, abusive, spiteful, avaricious, narcissistic, and insatiable. Her incessant sexual demands and wanton demeanor have embarrassed him throughout the neighborhood and rendered him impotent. She physically kicks him out of bed when he fails to perform, then spends the shop's earnings on lingerie to entice her goldbricking supercreep girl-toy—a callow studpuppy named

Methinks Kuen (Yeung Fan) doth complain too much: *The Untold Story 2*.

Fai. Kuen enjoys hard-drinking sessions, and returns to her husband only to spew vomit and moan for more of Fai's ghastly caresses.

Henpecked Cheung retreats into a pathetic shell of a man and functions mostly as a cash register and beer disposal unit. Greasy, impotent and apathetic, he numbly chops up slabs of flesh as his wife flaunts her ripe cleavage in customers' faces and scoops up the cash to finance her trysts. "You are thirst in sex," observes the leering triad boss. "I'm not free now," she responds.

A savior arrives suddenly: Fung (Paulyn Sun), Kuen's visiting cousin from Guangzhou. She's a bit of a plain Jane, but Cheung is attracted by Fung's shy and sweet manner. When he spies her lathering up in the shower, he "experiences priapism." But she's no artless bumpkin, as we learn when she walks in on Cheung's bath to seduce him.

The lead returns to Cheung's pencil. Of course, this sets off his wife's alarms—she rapidly figures out the new arrangement and hell hath no fury. Fung deals with the situation by skewering her screaming cousin repeatedly with a long sharp metal rod. Cheung dissolves into a quivering jelly as his ex-wife's body slides to the floor, but Fung softly reminds him of her promise: "I will be the last woman in your life."

She fills the bath, deposits Kuen's wide-eyed,

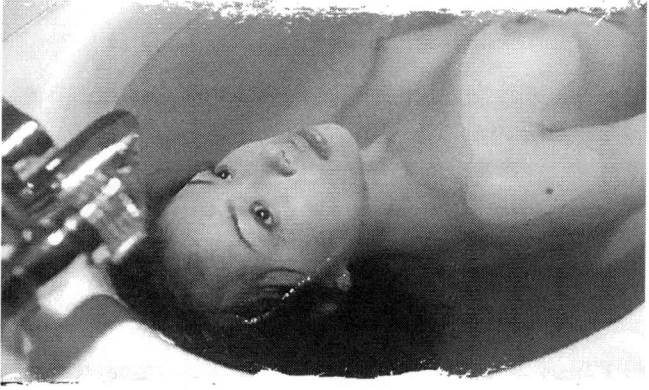

Kuen's post-mortem bath.

stark naked corpse in the tub and nonchalantly disassembles it with a heavy-duty electric knife as Cheung cowers feckless, reddening from the spray as the murderous mainlander's vorpal blade goes snicker-snack.

Resigned, he fires up the barbecue. Closeups of Fung's delighted face are intercut with closeups of sizzling grease and flesh, eliciting groans from the audience. When the red, succulent barbecued rib-slab is hoisted onto Cheung's retail rack, round holes punched by the killing rod clearly visible between bones, the audience begins their collective in-their-seats squirm-tango. When Officer Lazyboots and his triad buddy start gleefully sucking the barbecued flesh off the

Kuen's severed head in the frigidaire.

The local triad boss compliments the chef.

bones, audience-members jettison their snack bags of pork floss.

Things spiral downwards from there, as Fung indulges her homicidal urges. *US2* refuses to get sidetracked, defining its characters and snapping right along. The gore is kept to a minimum of screen time, making it far more effective. Extra credit for Taiwanese bomblet Yeung Fan as the amoral spitfire Kuen, who's as scary as she is sexy—living, dead, or as a head.

Mondo Documentaries

The word "mondo" gets its modern meaning from a 1963 Italian documentary, *Mondo Cane* (literally "Dog's World," but translated as "Cruel World"). The film depicted unusual vignettes from all over the world: religious flagellation in Europe, shark-bitten fishermen in the South Seas, insect-based haute cuisine served in American restaurants. Some of the scenes were faked, but the film was a huge hit, and the theme song—"More"—wormed its way into the pre-Beatles pop-instrumental lexicon. *Mondo Cane*'s success inspired many imitators, including *Mondo Bizarro*, *Mondo Pazzo*, *Mondo Balordo* (narrated by Boris Karloff), *Mondo Mod* etc etc.

Hong Kong uses its proximity to many of the leading mondo-exporting nations to fashion modern documentaries along these lines. Most HK mondo concentrates on mainland China, exploring the eccentric habits of the various tribes inhabiting the Middle Kingdom. Narration is conducted in jabbering hyper-Cantonese, punctuated with the drawn-out exclamation WAAHHHH! whenever the live monkey main course's head gets cut off, or the wedding veil parts to reveal a toothless old crone.

Amazing Marriage Customs

Fascinating look at courtship rituals among the Chinese tribes who haven't yet been dragged into the modern world. Bright costumes, mating dances, tee-heeing young brides. A maiden reclines on her bed—potential suitors announce themselves outside the house, then poke a straw through a hole in the wall. She grabs the straw of her favorite.

AMC features plenty of this sort of diversity, including the public trial of a couple accused of adultery. They're convicted by the headmaster, and the punishment is administered in full view of the assembled village: they must walk three times around the fire holding freshly hacked water-buffalo parts above their heads. The woman gets the head and the man gets the hind part, but we've no idea if this is significant.

Yes that thing on his tongue is ON FIRE: screengrab from *Shocking Asia*.

Shocking Asia

1984 | This monstrous shockumentary is difficult to top. *Shocking Asia* got its stateside press in the seminal New York fanzine *Sleazoid Express* when it first hit 42nd Street grindhouses in 1984: "Phrases like 'shock value' or 'extreme' tire when describing [this film]," wrote editor Bill Landis.

Shocking Asia kicks off with the festival of Thaipusam, where devotees skewer their cheeks with metal spears and put burning Sterno lozenges on their tongues. Japanese dwarf-wrestling, Nazi-drag S&M spectaculars, and "stamina" restaurants where bespectacled salarymen chow down on animal testes and penises to (theoretically) boost their sexual prowess are presented in 16mm Technicolor. Chinese restaurants dish up so-fresh-it's-still-alive snake, bat, and turtle, and the gory Hell-statues of Tiger Balm Gardens are showcased.

A look at back-alley transvestites in Singapore culminates in the sex-change operation of one: five nonstop minutes of lunch-losing surgical footage. As Sleazoid put it: "By this point, the audience is one long groan." *Shocking Asia* is a masterpiece of sorts, and will either enthrall your friends or drive them screaming from the room.

Shocking Asia 2

More of the same, but not as memorable as the original. A visit to a Thai monastery shows their emetic cure for heroin addiction. Filipina go-go dancers shake their tailfeathers. A Japanese salaryman is shown visiting various sex establishments: a "no-pan" coffeeshop, a dominatrix who dresses him in diapers and tucks him into a crib, and a "Lucky Hole" emporium best left undescribed.

The Scene of the Crime

Some of these horrific films aren't defensible as a whole. Yet, knowing how much you rubberneckers want to know just what was hewn off and where it went flying, here's a listing of some especially ripe scenes.

Skin Striperess

1992 | Poor Chi (Chan Wing-chi) is a pale lovely from mainland China who's forced to entertain a corrupt official named Yung (Stuart Ong). When she's accidentally disfigured, her "pimp" (Billy Lau) hires a rogue wizard to make her lovely once again, a process that requires a busted snake's head, the chewing of a live frog and the entire peeled skin of a female victim. Of course, it works like a charm, and Yung gets his jollies.

But just then, a group of teenagers accidentally dig up the victim's body, removing the protective Sacred Salt. Chi morphs demonoid and turns the tables on the terrified Yung, ravaging him impolitely as the walls and ceiling manifest dripping blood. She tosses him through a glass wall and goes to find the wizard, who beats a big drum and shakes his jowls. This Larry-Moe-Curly defense fails him as the monster he created reaches right out with her claws and peels his bark off.

OCTB CASE: The Floating Body

1995 | Li Chien-wan (Ben Ng) finds himself with an unexpected corpse (Lily Chung) to deal with. After meditating over it, he arranges a number of totems on the living room table: a bottle of XO cognac, a couple of reefers and a Makita electric chainsaw. Ng fires up one of the joints and starts smoking it though his nose in a fit of pre-dismemberment whimsy. Amplified heartbeats mix with elephant trumpetings as he crunches a

Little Cabbage (Yvonne Yung) wonders how bad things might get in this screengrab from *A Chinese Torture Chamber Story*.

A kindly judge explains the legal situation in *A Chinese Torture Chamber Story*.

few potato chips, rips the cork out of the XO and guzzles. By the time he tenderly deposits the corpse in the bathtub and starts the blade whirling on the Makita, most viewers will be sufficiently creeped out enough to mash the eject button, but it's only fifteen minutes into the movie!

A Chinese Torture Chamber Story

1994 | Poor Little Cabbage. Humble and righteous Little Cabbage (Yvonne Yung) is the daughter of a Ming Dynasty-era silk-maker. Her bound feet attract concubine-minded scholar Yang Ni-mu (Lawrence "*Sex & Zen*" Ng), who's also righteous. Not so Mrs Yang, whose licentious bent drives her into the arms of her lover Hoi-ning, but lessens not her jealousy for hubby's petit chou.

While Yang's away on a business trip, his wife marries Little Cabbage off to tofu-maker Got Siu-tai (Tommy Wong), whose member is described by elephant impersonations. Wedding night: shy and retiring Little Cabbage, tofu-lad with his big swinging trunk, and one tael (a goddam tael—that's five times the usual dose) of aphrodisiac...we're set.

As the aphro courses through Got's veins, he levitates the dining room table with his trunk, turns crimson and weird, then hoists flustered Cabbage from the ceiling with red silk. Temporarily regaining his senses, he insists she tie him up for her own protection. Coitus an impossible dream, she attempts to provide hand relief, as the anthem of their forlorn affection (a muzaked-up instrumental version of the Drifters' "Unchained Melody", you know: "ohhhhhh, mah daaaarlin', I hunger, for, your touch"...) drenches the scene in unexpected pathos. The principals involved (flat-faced Tommy Wong as the supine victim, and luscious Yvonne Yung as the star-crossed cutie) deserve special acting awards for their straight-arrow, sweat-crunged performance in this harrowing handjob scene. Regrettably, as Got achieves orgasm, his gargantuan penis detonates in a slo-motion room-filling red mist.

Category III

Hong Kong films are divided into three rating categories. Each category is denoted by a roman numeral set in a simple geometric symbol, which grow increasingly angular as they become more restrictive. Nobody much cares about the difference between Category I (a single stick in a cute round circle) or Category II (two sticks in a less-friendly square). But the Category III rating (three sticks in a sharp-edged triangle) means under-18 types are *verboten*.

Category III was invented in 1988. Public service announcements in HK depicted born-too-late youths unceremoniously ejected from theaters showing such fare. Some cinemas displayed a life-sized cardboard cutout of a stern-faced police constable emphasizing the punitive possibilities.

Most Category III films are cheap, rapidly-made softcore ninety-minute-wonders, usually featuring instantly-forgettable starlets. These are manufactured and consumed with the fanfare of a bowl of instant noodles: boil water and scarf 'em down. Sometimes gore is added to the mix to spice things up. Much as we salute the exploitative spirit—the "ghoulie, roughie, kinkie" mantra—most of these films are a waste of time.

The catch-all category also serves as an "NC-17" category, and some worthwhile films do end up with the stigma of the Triangular Triple-I, like Jacob Cheung's award-winning *Cageman*—a sensitive look at life in Kowloon's infamous Walled City. The film featured no sex, violence or nudity, but was rated Category III solely due to its inventive use of Cantonese slang. Knowing in advance that a film will earn a Cat III rating means filmmakers are free to let their characters rip with authentic vulgarities scraped from the grimy underside of Cantoslang. A prime example is Shing Fui-on's primal cursing in Herman Yau's *Ebola Syndrome*—that's street-real lingo that would earn you a beating in Mongkok if you spewed it at the wrong guys.

We could compile of a list of all Category III films, but someone at Wikipedia already did it.

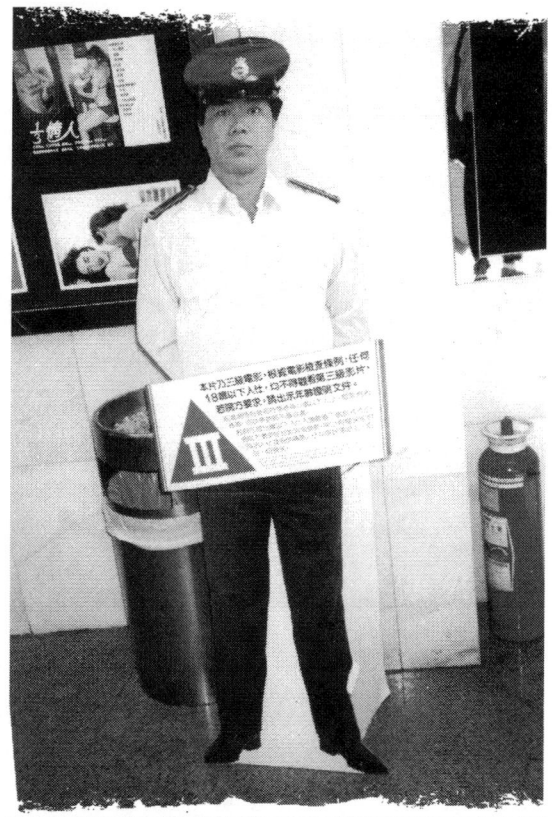

Photo by Stefan Hammond, Hong Kong, 1993.

Hex Errors: Chaos Theory

"No underwear! Penis disappear! No underwear!"
The Fortune Code

"Pits off! Pits off! Pits off!"
Brother of Darkness

"What, what? You filthy good!"
First Shot

"My asses!"
Sex & Zen 3

"I kneak again..."
Temegotchi

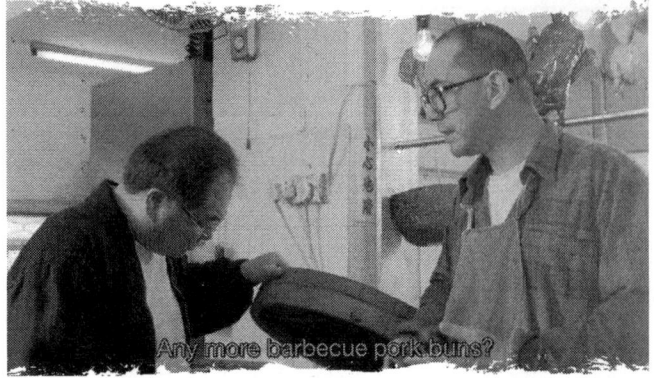

Hot fresh barbecue pork buns: *The Untold Story* (1993).

"Eat, eat, eat you hell!"
Give and Take...Oh! Shit!

"Don't bother the wringles."
The Eternal Evil of Asia

"Bite my fresh."
Devil's Woman

"I've down the sea!"
Blood Reincarnation

"my eeg"
Witch Edited

"Being fat it's not it, shit!"
Women's Prison

"Each pheces now, go ahead"
Circus Kids

"You are like caecum."
Casino

"our dog is lout enoug"
Witch Edited

"See, you are hot! But Milky is under aetas legitima."
Our Neighbor Detective

"Booshit!"
The Eagle Shooting Heroes

"Give my boss a Big Bust Tea, I want a Mingle."
Raped By An Angel 2: The Uniform Fan

CHAPTER EIGHTEEN
THE TEMPLE OF SHAW

No single volume, let alone a chapter, can give more than a brief intro to the output of Shaw Brothers Studios. Fortunately, Celestial Pictures acquired the entire Shaws library in 2000 and began the painstaking task of restoring these films for reissue (over 770 complete feature films). Hundreds are now available on DVD, Blu-ray, and via streaming video with the work of Shaws directors like Chu Yuan, Sun Chung, Ho Meng-hua and Kuei Chih-hung now available for home consumption.

The Shaws dream factory created far more than martial arts films: drama, musicals, horror, erotica, crime films and other genres lit up screens across Hong Kong, Southeast Asia, and Chinatowns worldwide. They imported talent from Japan and had brief tie-ups with Japan's Nikkatsu Studios and England's Hammer Productions. A complete account of the Shaw Brothers story would run several volumes at least.

Founded by Sir Run Run Shaw—the son of a wealthy Shanghai textile factory owner—and his three brothers, Shaw Brothers Studios built a post-war celluloid empire that included production, distribution and exhibition across Asia. Despite competition from Golden Harvest (whose boss Raymond Chow signed both Bruce Lee and Jackie Chan), the name Shaw Brothers was synonymous with Hong Kong films for decades.

Run Run was knighted by the British Government, while his brother Runme supervised

Five fingers of steel: *One-Armed Swordsman*.

their Singapore operations. In the mid-80s, SB scaled back film production drastically and founded TVB, now Hong Kong's major supplier of televised dramas and serials.

The Shaw movie-factory in Clearwater Bay had twelve sound stages and their stable included such actors as Gordon Lau (*Tiger on Beat*, *Peacock King*), Ti Lung (*A Better Tomorrow 1 & 2*), David Chiang (*Once Upon A Time In China 2*), Lo Lieh (*Sex & Zen*, *Police Story 3: Supercop*) and Philip Kwok

Chui (*Hard-Boiled*), along with many others.

On the action side, Shaws most famed directors diverged. Former screenwriter Chang Cheh became one of Shaws' pivotal directors. Chang's blood-soaked *One-Armed Swordsman* (1967) featured Jimmy Wang Yu as a differently-abled death machine, and the box-office receipts piled up higher than the bodies. Like most Shaws releases, Chang's films were in Mandarin (the most common Chinese dialect, but not the vernacular dialect of Hong Kong: Cantonese). The film's success had a knock-on effect—as fellow Shaws director Chu Yuan put it: "Chang Cheh came out with *One-Armed Swordsman* and wiped Cantonese films clean off the face of the earth."

Chang created another goldmine with *Five Venoms* (1978), and the "Venoms Team" went on to appear in several other Shaws films. Thanks to Celestial, fans can now enjoy *Heaven and Hell* (1980), Chang's only supernatural film, featuring members of the Venoms team fighting both on Earth and in Hell.

Actor/director Liu Chia-liang (Lau Kar-leung is the Cantonese version of his name) often served as fight director for Chang. Lau re-invigorated the Cantonese martial arts films at Shaws—he was an old-school martial artist whose kung fu lineage stretched back to the real Wong Fei-hong (see "Wong Fei-hong," page 105). Lau made his directorial debut in 1975, but hit paydirt with *The 36th Chamber of Shaolin* (1978). Liu injected new life into tired kung fu plots, starred in many of his films, lensed an unforgettable cameo in Sammo Hung's excellent *Pedicab Driver* (see page 21) and directed Jackie Chan's *Drunken Master 2* (1994).

These two directors were but part of the Shaw dream factory that made so many great films. Here are a few of the good ones.

Heroes of the East (中華丈夫) aka Shaolin Challenges Ninja

1979 | Starring Gordon Lau, Yuko Mizuno, Yasuaki Kurata, Cheng Kang-yeh, Cheng Miu, Naozo Kato, Riki Harada, Tetsu Sumi, Manabu Shirai, Nobuo Yana, Yasutaka Nakazaki, Hitoshi Omae, Lau Kar-leung, Norman Chu Siu-keung
Directed by Lau Kar-leung

Director Lau Kar-leung built his Shaw Brothers career with ground-breaking, creative kung fu films, revitalizing a genre that many people thought moribund. The underlying philosophy of *HOTE* is quite different from the usual Shaw mayhem. For starters, it's an action-packed kung fu film

Heroes of the East: East meets East, common sense prevails.

in which no one dies. Compared to Chang Cheh's bloodbaths like *Super Ninjas* and *One-Armed Swordsman*—where a combatant will lay waste to a hundred men in a single scene—Lau's *Heroes* is a radical change of pace.

The film challenges ethnic and national stereotypes. The Chinese and Japanese have always been at odds, and the Japanese occupation of parts of China during WWII didn't help matters. Japanese are the staple villains in dozens of kung fu films, and they are—predictably enough—ruthless, bloodthirsty killers.

In *HOTE* we get something starkly different. Gordon Lau plays a Chinese man who weds a Japanese woman. Even during the wedding there are signs of cultural clashes, but it's not until the honeymoon that the fried rice hits the fan. The couple spend their waking hours fighting and arguing over which martial arts styles are superior: Japanese or Chinese. Never have hurled chopsticks and rice bowls carried such deadly intent.

Lau triumphs in every match, until his wife uses the elliptical art of ninjitsu to best him. Lau, however, is far from impressed by what he calls the "art of dirty tricks." Sensing irreconcilable martial differences, his wife leaves him and returns to Japan.

Lau tries to win her back by writing a personal "challenge-letter": if she beats him in any duel, he'll acquiesce (and presumably, take up kendo). The letter is interpreted by her brothers—all skilled Japanese martial artists, played by Japanese actors—as a collective challenge. Needless to say, they accept and travel to Hong Kong intent on kicking ass.

The ensuing skirmishes prove that neither nationality proves more valiant than the other. When one of the Japanese offers his sword handle-first to Lau, as a sign of respect, he slaps it away, ignorant of what the gesture means. In *HOTE*, the real villains are ignorance of another culture, a lack of understanding, and an unwillingness to learn or accept new ideas or part with old traditions.

Fortunately, this message is delivered amid a flurry of exquisitely staged martial arts duels. By the film's close, the former adversaries have come to respect and admire one another, and the couple reunites with enhanced understanding.

— Keith W Allison

Crippled Avengers (殘缺) aka *Return of the Five Deadly Venoms*
1978 | Starring Chiang Sheng, Lo Mang, Sun Chien, Lu Feng, Philip Kwok Chui, Chen Kuan-tai
Directed by Chang Cheh

Chang Cheh's *Five Venoms* is based on a simple premise: five guys with virulent martial arts skills rip the bejesus out of their opponents and one another. The film proved popular, and Cheh used the Venoms cast in an even weirder sequel: *Crippled Avengers*. The five actors (leader Philip Kwok Chui, Chiang "Cutie Pie" Sheng, block-faced Lo Mang, high-kicking Sun Chien, and sneaky Lu Feng) are horribly crippled at the outset. But rather than demanding wheelchair ramps or Braille versions of *Dream of the Red Chamber*, our heroes develop crackerjack kung fu based on their physical challenges.

A nobleman (Chen Kuan-tai) is driven mad when his family is butchered and his son's arms are chopped off by ruthless enemies. After outfitting his son with mechanical arms that can elongate and fire darts, the nobleman becomes a vengeful thug. But rather than developing a thoughtful, comprehensive plan of revenge, he simply goes around mutilating anyone who

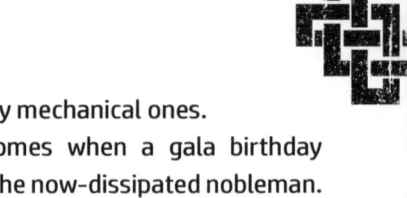

outfitted with deadly mechanical ones.

Their chance comes when a gala birthday party is thrown for the now-dissipated nobleman. Security is assured by the presence of every evil kung fu master in the kingdom. Undaunted, the gang of cripples head off to avenge the loss of their cherished parts. The furious endbattle sees the band's mentally challenged leader skewered by a volley of darts from the evil son's metal arms. But the remaining crippled avengers complete their bloody task with acrobatic aplomb.

Fans of the underdog will love this drenched-in-scarlet eccentricity. Clearly, having essential body parts hewn off is no disqualification for martial arts hero status and eventual victory. Although *FDV* is the classic Venoms films, *Crippled Avengers* is a great (mechanical) kick.

The "Venoms Team" strut their stuff in *Crippled Avengers*.

displeases him. A trinket salesman (Philip Kwok Chui) makes the mistake of pointing out his son's armless condition: "He has no arms." "But you have no eyes." "What do you mean? I have eyes. I have...AAAH! AAAAAHH!"

The mad nobleman also chops off the feet of a passerby (Sun Chien) and deafens a hapless blacksmith (Lo Mang). But the most horrible torment is reserved for a martial arts hero Chiang Sheng who arrives to rid the village of this outta-control blue-blood. He's turned into a mental midget by having a metal band slowly tightened around his skull.

The four afflicted ones join forces and seek out the last victim's sifu. They learn to communicate despite their disabilities and develop special kung fu skills. For example, the guy with no feet is

Descendant of the Sun (日劫)

1983 | Starring Cherie Chung Chor-hung, Derek Yee Tung-shing, Ku Kun-chung, Lung Tin-hsiang, Yeung Ching-ching, Yau Chui-ling, Louis Fan Siu-wong
Directed by Chu Yuan

Another beautifully photographed efforts from Shaw Brothers studios, *Descendant of the Sun* imbues an electric life to scenes from classic Chinese scroll paintings. Fans of beauty Cherie Chung (*Peking Opera Blues*, *Once A Thief*, *Wild Search*) will want to seek it out—this was one of her earlier films.

Descendant is a fairytale revolving around a pair of supernatural babies from "fairyland." Naturally, one is righteous and the other is evil. The good baby is discovered embedded inside a huge glowing obelisk and extracted by a kindly woodcutter, who raises it as his own. When the kid—Shih Sheng, played by Louis Fan Siu-wong, who starred in *The Story of Ricky* as

MORE SEX, BETTER ZEN, FASTER BULLETS

Superheroes and supervillains spar in *Descendant of the Sun*.

a grown-up—turns eight, he displays some remarkable talents: causing peaches to sprout from dead branches, fires to start, and people to levitate. His foster parents wisely counsel him to keep his powers under wraps, and he grows into a strapping young man (Derek Yee) without incident.

When corrupt government officials start conscripting villagers for labor, Shih Sheng thrashes them using his super powers and takes refuge in a nearby palace. He's hassled by cheeky handmaidens Pao and Pei (Yeung Ching-ching and Yau Chui-ling, respectively) for inadvertently freeing their caged birds, but is rescued from a threat of beheading by the Princess (Cherie Chung). He magically recalls the coop-flown birdies, then charms the palace parrot into reciting the steamy folktale *Dream of the Red Chamber*.

This amusing stunt earns him a job at the palace as houseboy. Before beginning his new job, however, he visits the glowing obelisk for advice. The spirit therein tells him of the Evil Infant haunting the globe with a chip on his evil shoulder.

Meanwhile, the regent of the province (Lung Tin-hsiang) decides to embark on a eugenics program, rounding up babies and eliminating the weak ones. Realizing that the Princess will never stand for such evil, he decides to terminate her, and sends a band of killers to the palace. Shih Sheng does a quick-change into a gold-and-white tunic to stomp the brigands, while preserving his Clark Kent identity as palace go-fer. The Princess goes ga-ga over the mystery superman.

Unfortunately, before love blooms, the evil regent releases Evil Infant Mo Ying from its green-glowing sarcophagus, and it instantly becomes a full-grown evil guy (Ku Kun-chung). Trouble.

The unleashed Mo Ying does battle with Super Shih, with each transforming themselves into giant feuding objects: shears versus carpet, axe versus tree. Finally the evil one turns into a scuttling crab and Shih becomes a monolithic rock column and falls over, cracking the malevolent crustacean. It looks bad for Mo Ying, but leaps atop a giant feng shui mirror and summons the forces of darkness: "Come, every evil, to my aid." Earth and walls split as gleeful ghouls come pouring out to attack Shih. Finally, Mo Ying explodes and virtue reigns again.

Five Venoms (五毒)

1978 | Starring Chiang Sheng, Sun Chien, Philip Kwok Chui, Lo Mang, Lu Feng, Wei Pai, Ku Feng,

THE TEMPLE OF SHAW

Seminal, venomous tale from the fertile oeuvre of Chang Cheh.

Wai Pak, Qi Dong, Johnny Wang Lung-wei, Dick Wei
Directed by Chang Cheh

Five Venoms (aka Five Deadly Venoms) was the first of a successful series of Shaw Brothers movies, all starring some or all of the original male leads. A Kung Fu Theater favorite, it was seen on late night American TV by millions of kids, and many made Venom masks out of grocery sacks, then ran around trying to Lizard and Toad each other. It's a wild story of greed, betrayal, and friendship.

The venerated sifu of the Poison Clan (Dick Wei) is dying, his last student at his side. Over the course of his life, he trained five other students, each in one of the five deadly forms—Snake, Centipede, Scorpion, Lizard and Toad. Student #6—Yan Tieh (Chiang Sheng), a righteous man— is trained in all five Poison styles. Sifu makes Yan Tieh promise to seek out the others and kill those who are doing evil.

The catch is, he can't do it alone. Having learned a part of each style, he's master of none. To eliminate any of the other five, he must pair up with another Venom.

Yan Tieh has one clue to help him find the other Venoms. Sifu's old partner has amassed a fortune with Poison skills and is now retired under an assumed name. Sifu rightfully believes that the other *Five Venoms* will come out to claim the treasure.

All the Venoms converge, but they don't know who the sifu's partner is. They don't even know each other, because each was trained separately, wearing masks. Toad, the nice-guy beefcake with an iron skin (Lo Mang), finds Lizard (Philip Kwok), an honest cop, and they decide to "redeem" the clan by getting the treasure.

Centipede (Lu Feng) and Snake (Wei Pai) find sifu's partner first and slaughter his whole family. No treasure is found and a local boy spots Centipede leaving the scene. But Snake is well connected, and fixes it so that a bribed witness helps Centipede get acquitted, while Toad is falsely accused, then drugged, tortured, and smothered. The judge is so crooked you're sure he's the Scorpion.

Lizard and Yan Tieh team up to find and kill Centipede and Snake. But when they rendezvous for revenge, they run into the virtuous Captain Ma (Sun Chien), who has quit the police force and agrees to help them destroy the astray Venoms.

Snake knows he's doomed and waits for them stretched out on a chaise lounge in white satin and pearls. Lizard and Yan Tieh fight him and his partner, Centipede, while Captain Ma stands off to one side and refuses to fight. Snake finally confronts him, saying "I know who you are, you're the Scorpion."

Ol' Ma gives an evil laugh, then rips out Centipede's guts. Yan Tieh and Lizard are invincible, though, and after deposing of Snake and the unmasked Scorpion, take the treasure map from Scorpion's and march off to do right. Yan Tieh wants revenge on the crooked judge, but Lizard says, "All judges are crooked and the next one might be worse. You can't kill them all." Some things never change.

—K A Tarapata

Five Fingers of Death
aka King Boxer (天下第一拳)

1972 | Starring Lo Lieh, Tien Feng, Gu Man-chung, James Nam, Wang Ping, Tung Lam, Bolo Yeung Sze
Directed by Cheng Chang Ho

Five Fingers of Death (also known as *King Boxer*) was the first kung fu movie to hit the American crossover market. Without the success of *FFOD* paving the way, even a Bruce Lee might not have received his overseas due.

Five Fingers of Death features eye-gouging, disemboweling and hands being pushed into burning sand; it's a carnival of carnage that's truly not over till it's over. No character is too minor to avoid getting nailed in some nasty way.

Lo Lieh plays Chow Chi-hao, a nice orphan kid who lives with his kung-fu teacher, Sung Wu-yang (Gu Man-chung). Sifu says that if Chow wins the upcoming kung-fu tournament, he can marry his cute daughter Ying Ying (Wang Ping).

The sifu of a rival school, Meng San-yeh

Trilingual poster for a showing of Karato (*FFOD*) at a Belgian cinema, back in the day.

(Tien Feng) wants to bag the tournament's title himself. The problem is that his son is a no-talent gangster with a cigarette holder permanently attached to his sneering mouth (Tung Lam). The solution? Hire some hoods and kill all your opponents before the contest. The gangster son meets a head-butting heavy named Chan in the marketplace and brings him home. Dad hires a band of "Japanese" fighters (Chinese guys in black fright wigs), just in case.

Old Sung sends Chow to study with an old friend to sharpen up his skills. The current favorite at the new gym, Han Lung (James Nam), gets jealous and crosses over to the evil team. They use him for awhile, then poke out his eyes and throw him in the street. They kill Chow's old teacher, and then they flatten Chow's hands so he can't learn the Iron Palm technique (he does anyway). Some folks are just plain bad.

Evil Meng sends the Japanese assassins to ambush Chow on the way to the tournament, but wild man Chan has seen enough Japanese savagery, so he tips Chow off and ends up paying

THE TEMPLE OF SHAW

HFOTMW: A whirling rampage of revenge, slinging steel, and Ghostly Cries.

arrives, carrying the head of Chan for effect. Chow has to throw him through a brick wall twice before he dies. Only then can Chow walk off with his girl and his one remaining living friend.

—K A Tarapata

Holy Flame of the Martial World
(武林聖火令)
1983 | Starring Max Mok Siu-chung, Mary Jane Yung, Philip Kwok Chui, Lau Siu-gwan, Leanne Lau Suet-wa, Jason Pai-piao, Yeung Ching-ching, Candy Wen, Chang Tao
Directed by Lu Chin Ku

A movie this much fun oughta be shown big, to a packed house of families on an afternoon outing, kids screaming with delight until their shredded squid snack comes shooting out of their tiny nostrils.

Flame's mile-a-second pace may bruise the viewer's skull. Combatants spend more time in the air than on the ground, somersaulting repeatedly over one another, clinking swords or shooting energy gobs. Martial energies turn people bright blue, gold, or red, and can peel flesh, producing instantaneous skeletons. Despite evil entities like the Snake King and the Blood-Sucking Clan, the film is more goofy than scary—a Méliès matinee melee, if you will.

The Seven Clans—led by the evil lady sifu Yi Tsing-yin (Leanne Lau)—waylay and kill an innocent couple who refuse to reveal the location of a potent kung fu weapon. Madam Yi and her evil cohort, Ku Pan-kuai (Jason Pai), are about to do away the couple's infant children when they are beset by sifu Yama Elder (Philip Kwok Chui), who rocks the scene with his special martial arts skill: Ghostly Cries. The children are spared and the boy, Yin Tien-chu, is reared by Yama Elder,

with his life. Chow makes it to the tournament just in time and wins. Sound like the end of the movie? No! Meng stabs Chow's new teacher out of spite and heads for home.

The blinded Han Lung, meanwhile, is hiding in Meng's school. When Meng and his son enter the darkened building, Han Lung blinds the son and, using a girl singer for stage directions ("Aim high!" "Straight ahead!"), manages to fight the older Meng and get him to accidentally kill his own son. Enraged, Meng kills them both. Chow arrives too late to save them. He corners Meng, who commits suicide. Sound like the end of the movie now? WRONG! The leader of the Japanese while the girl, Yi Tan-fang (Yeung Ching-ching), is raised as a member of Madam Yi's O-Mei School of Virgin Swordplay.

Eighteen years later, Yin has grown into a strapping young man (Max Mok), and is sent by Yama to retrieve the Holy Flame—a peculiar edged weapon which his unfortunate parents had secreted in a cave. Yin must solve a strenuous physical riddle based on an enormous feng shui mirror and torso-sized Chinese ideograms which spin and fly noisily about the chamber. A huge drum splits, revealing a skeleton with a book in one claw and the Holy Flame in the other.

The weapon comes in handy when Tu Chuan-erh (Mary Jane Yung), the comely daughter of the local snakecatcher, is kidnapped by Lin (Chang Tao)—the evil leader of the Blood-Sucking Clan, which uses virgin's blood to resurrect a weird pet monster. The sorcerer unfurls demons on painted scrolls, which come to life and fight furiously with Yin and his friend, Tuan (Lau Siu-gwan), who torch the adversarial mutations. Lin then animates the monster, who is masked like a Mexican wrestler, speaks in English, and fights with superhuman strength. Only the Holy Flame can pierce and dissolve him.

Meanwhile, a lucky snake encounter gives the snakecatcher's daughter's right index finger the power to knock people senseless with energy bolts. It turns out there's another Holy Flame (the blue yin version of Yin's red yang one) which Yin and Yi eventually unite to blast the baddies into skeletal oblivion, leaving the theater aisles littered with little giggled-out bits of squid.

NOTE: The DVD, from Well Go USA, is well mastered and has an English dub as well as the original soundtrack and English subs. *HFOTMW* moves so fast that watching it dubbed allows you to pick

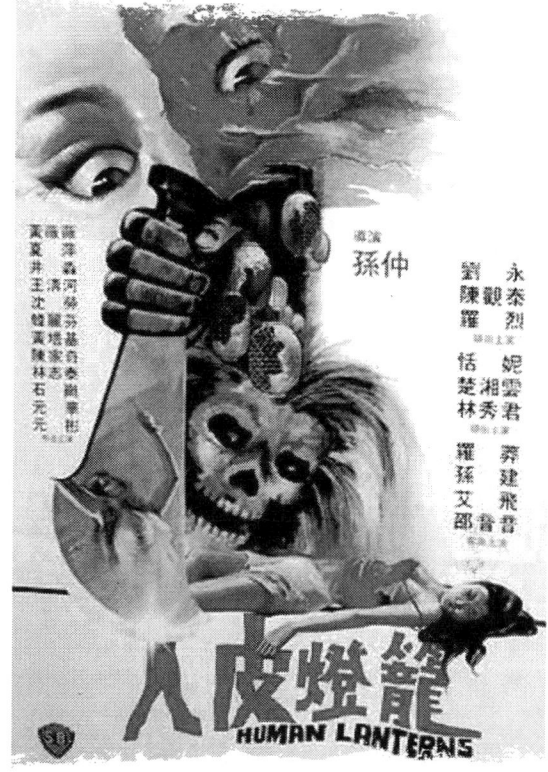

"Money and fame are hollow"—and so are *Human Lanterns*.

up split-seconds of action you might miss reading subs. Even if you prefer subs, try the dub on second (or seventh) viewing.

Human Lanterns (人皮燈籠)
1982 | Starring Lo Lieh, Chen Kuan-tai, Lau Wing, Sun Chien, Tanny Tien Ni, Lo Mang, Lu Feng
Directed by Sun Chung

A wonderfully gruesome tale of the mighty brought low by pride. Lo Lieh stars as Chao Chun Fang, lantern maker by day, gibbering madman by night. When the spirit strikes him, he leaps around in a monkey suit and a skull mask, kidnapping beautiful women and stripping the bark off of them for lantern material. Pride, jealousy, misunderstandings and violence. Lives ruined, beautiful women flayed alive.

Chun Fang's clients are Lung Shuai (Lau Wing), and Tan Fu (Chen Kuan-tai). These two local big shots are insanely jealous of each other. They both want to rule the town, and each thinks that their end justifies all possible means.

Lung is introduced to Chun Fang, the maker of Tan's beautiful lanterns, and recognizes him as an old rival in love, whose face he once cut and scarred in a duel. Lung suggests that Chun Fang "forget the past, get rich and famous," and contracts for the most beautiful lamps possible, no matter what it takes. What it takes is the hides off Lung's favorite courtesan, his wife, and Tan's sister.

When Tan's sister Yen Chu—the town beauty—disappears, Constable Pan (Sun Chien) thinks Lung has kidnapped her out of jealousy. But she's actually in a basement being peeled by Chun Fang.

Tan suspects that it's Lung's doing, and hires a killer to take him out. But the killer, Kuei (Lu Feng), is an old friend of the wacko lantern maker, and while Kuei is fighting Lung, Chun Fang kidnaps his wife. When Kuei fails to kill Lung, Tan kills him, using a fan with knives hidden inside.

Tan begins to see that this is getting out of control.

Tan's men take the dead Kuei out of town to dump the body. Chun Fang kills them just for fun, though, and hangs their heads in the town square. He then makes sure that Lung knows who hired Kuei in the first place. Tan realizes they're both being set up.

Rumors start circulating about lamps made from human hides. Lung's suspicions lead him back to Chun Fang. Breaking into the old mill where Chun Fang works, he finds his flayed wife and sees three lovely lanterns. One has his wife's beauty mark prominently displayed on it. Tan arrives to ask Chun Fang, "Why me?" Chun Fang says, "You're his rival. Now you both know that money and fame are hollow."

Fists and swords are put to work to end this madman's mayhem, but in the struggle, the mill catches fire and collapses, leaving Chun Fang and Tan dead and Lung horribly burned. In the final scene, Lung realizes he's lost his wife, his health and his looks. Constable Pan says: "It's over. Forget it." Lung does just that, moving to a monastery to atone for his stupid pride.

—K A Tarapata

Legendary Weapons of China
(十八般武藝)
1982 | Starring Lau Kar-leung, Liu Chia-yung, Gordon Lau, Alexander Fu Sheng, Hsiao Ho, Kara Hui Ying-hung
Directed by Lau Kar-leung

During the 1890s—with big chunks of China under foreign control—some kung fu societies tried to find a "spiritual" kung fu strong enough to stop bullets. In *LWOC*'s opening sequence, four martial arts students stand before four marksmen, rifles aimed at their bared chests. Bang! They're still standing as a chanting Shaolin monk pastes yellow paper spells over the bullet holes.

Those watching the demonstration smile and nod; invulnerability to bullets has been attained! Then the quartet drops dead. The sifus sigh. Sooner or later they'll get it right, if they don't run out of disciples first.

Clearly, this is no way to treat one's students, and sifu Lei Kung (Lau Kar-leung) recognizes the futility of the situation. He disbands his school and drops out of sight, assuming a new existence as a woodcutter. The other sifus don't want the

Hoodoo gimmicks no match for the *Legendary Weapons of China.*

foreigners to learn of his skepticism, therefore, he must die.

Assassins are dispatched in the form of Shaolin monk Ti Tan (Gordon Liu) and Tieh Hou (Hsiao Ho). As they head off in search of Lei Kung, they're shadowed by the monk's niece (Kara Hui Ying-hung, disguised as a man). They converge in Kwantung, where narrow alleyways form a maze as the assassins angle for info.

Because they all expect to find a bragging, swaggering Lei Kung (convincing the townspeople with a bewildering array of kung fu stunts), that's who they find. But it's not really Lei Kung, it's a con man (Alexander Fu Sheng) who's been hired to impersonate Lei Kung by his brother Lei Yung (Liu Chia-yung). Lei Yung is a shadowy hypnotist who uses voodoo to transform Fu Sheng into a kung fu kook. He hopes to draw out his brother and show him who's really the boss.

The monk's niece tracks down the real Lei Kung. She's become convinced that Lei Kung is right and the society must be disbanded. Lei Kung also befriends Tieh Hou, and when Tieh gets sick (from fighting Fu Sheng in a cesspool, no less), he and the niece nurse him back to health.

Poor Tieh Hou. Every time he tries to get out of bed to kill Lei Kung, all he gets is hot soup and sympathy. Eventually, he's converted, but then there's Kung's duplicitous brother Yung to deal with. The last third of the film is combat (using all eighteen of your favorite weapons) between monk and magician.

In the end, "spiritual" kung-fu is no match for actual martial arts skill. When the magician finally limps off, a shattered wreck, Lei Kung tells him, "Just say you killed me." Lei Kung couldn't care less about fame in the martial world, and this self-effacing sifu is a true martial arts hero.

—K A Tarapata

Mad Monkey Kung Fu (瘋猴)
1979 | Starring Lau Kar-leung, Liu Chia-yung, Gordon Lau, Kara Hui Ying-hung, Alexander Fu Sheng, Hsiao Ho, Lo Lieh
Directed by Lau Kar-leung

Mad Monkey Kung Fu is squatting, screeching, rocket-fast madness. The heroes don't pose in robes, they dangle from the rafters, scratching, and laughing like maniacs. *MMKF* is a typical Shaw tale of remorse and revenge, but director Lau Kar-leung (who also stars) bends the brittle master/student/revenge storyline into something with humor and even dignity.

Liu plays Chen Po, a traveling Peking Opera performer. After a successful stage performance

THE TEMPLE OF SHAW

Styles makes fights: *Mad Monkey Kung Fu.*

as the Monkey King, he accepts an invitation from smirking local boss Tuan (Lo Lieh). Chen has such a high opinion of himself that he doesn't even notice Tuan leering at his sister (Kara Hui). Proving that "the higher the monkey climb, the more he expose," Chen gets so drunk he passes out. Tuan's evil wife, in exchange for her very own brothel, frames Chen for an imaginary rape. Adding injury to insult, Chen's sister is delivered to Tuan as a love-slave and Chen's hands are smashed flat with bamboo poles.

The broken Chen gets a monkey and sells candy on the street, his crippled hands wrapped in black bandages. He befriends a street kid, nicknamed Monkey (Hsiao Ho, one of director Liu's real-life students), who uses tricks to steal from the local extortionist dandies.

But when Chen can't ante up enough protection money, the evil grifters slam his monkey's head into a tree. Human Monkey replaces simian monkey, and the kids love it.

Monkey convinces Chen to train him in monkey-style fighting, and incorporates his own antics into the style. Half-trained and half-cocked, Monkey takes on the cigarette-holder mob. With wild-style Monkey boxing, he literally ties them in knots. When one hood squats with his palms forward and starts projecting his "chi energy," Monkey says, "That's old fashioned. No one wants to see that anymore," then slaps him silly with his own shoes.

Monkey finds out that the man behind the protection racket is Tuan, but Tuan grabs him, then punches his head through the center of a table. Tuan's going to serve him up as "live monkey brains, a good winter dish." Chen's sister—still Tuan's concubine—not being a big fan of brains, "accidentally" rips the skirt off the boss's wife, creating havoc so Monkey can flee. Monkey escapes, but the girl is thrown off the balcony to her death.

Chen and Monkey go to the brothel for revenge. Chen can fight but can't win with his mangled mitts. Monkey forces Tuan's hands into a glass lamp. Looking at the bloody results, Monkey says "eye for an eye, right, master?"

Chen's not so sure. Restraint was the code he broke that started this tragedy. But before he can stop it, Tuan's lying dead and Monkey's ready to finish off everyone else in the brothel. Chen just shakes his head. Together they walk away, Monkey still the disciple, Chen still the master.

—K A Tarapata

Seeding of a Ghost (種鬼)
1983 | Starring Philip Ko Fei, Norman Tsui Siu-

keung, Maria Yuen Chi-wai
Directed by Yang Chuan

Barmy Shaw sorcery 'n' revenge flick which draws inspiration from slasher films, Z-grade Yankee sexplo, and John Carpenter's *The Thing*. The film's plot recalls Dada's "Exquisite Corpse," where one person starts a story, then the next person continues it with only the last line to go on. It will find favor with the grindhouse/drive-in set whose idea of heaven is a dusk-to-dawn beastfest.

Chou (Philip Ko), a Hong Kong taxi driver, accidentally runs over a wandering sorcerer. Even though the sorcerer appears to have come through the accident unscathed, he puts a hex on Chou and his family. The taxi driver scoffs at the curse...until things start going hideously wrong.

First his wife, Irene (Maria Yuen), runs off with a married man named Fang Ming (Norman Tsui). When Fang Ming refuses to marry her, she storms out of his car on a desolate road in the middle of the night, is assaulted by a pair of teenage criminals, then accidentally plunges to her death.

The bereaved husband, remembering the curse, goes back to the sorcerer and asks for his help in avenging his wife's death. The sorcerer performs an ancient ritual known as the "seeding of a ghost," warning the husband of the grave consequences of this ritual. Irene's body is dug up (already looking as if it had been entombed for eighty years), and Chou's life energy is supernaturally drained into the corpse, fertilizing a killer-zombie baby ready to rock.

Up until this point, *Seeding of a Ghost* looks like a Category III film from Hong Kong. We saw Irene in the shower, while the cool jazz saxophone obligatto played in the background, the camera zooming in on her breasts. We saw Irene frolicking with her lover; running topless through the surf in slo-mo. And, of course, we saw Irene and Fang Ming making love to more saxophone jazz. Then the film turns nasty with a brutal rape scene reminiscent of a some mid-sixties American sexploitation film.

Suddenly we are watching a different movie. Now *Seeding of a Ghost* becomes a crime drama, with police investigating the woman's death. A few scenes later the film veers into the realm of the supernatural, with Buddhist priests battling the sorcerer for possession of another woman's body. Before the film is over, it has mutated into a low-budget monster movie when a mahjong game gets interrupted by a murderous placenta-like thingie with teeth.

Seeding of a Ghost is a carnival ride that heads in one direction, then suddenly careens off at a right angle. Although Yang Chuan is billed as the director, the changes in the tone and plot are so sudden that it seems as if every fifteen minutes someone else takes over the production. Reasoning is useless, give up and enjoy it.

—Jim Morton

The Bamboo House Of Dolls
(女集中營)

1973 | Directed by Kuei Chih-hung (*Killer Snakes, Hex, Corpse Mania*), this is Shaws' only women-in-prison film. Naturally, it's set in Hong Kong during the Sino-Japanese conflict and the evil prison-keepers are Japanese. Needless to say, a prominent guard is a sadistic lesbian (Terry Liu). Of course there are European women in Hong Kong who get thrown right into the prison showers along with the other inmates. No WIP trope is left unturned—the planned mass-escape complete with guess-the-traitor, the prison cafeteria food fight, and perilous punishments. But Lo Lieh gets the girl (lovely blue-eyed Danish actress Birte

Kuei Chih-hung channels Roger Corman: *TBHOD*.

All sorts of moral messages about greed, drugs, and violence, as well as lots of scenes of drugs, greed, and violence.

Dirty Ho (爛頭何)

1979 | A kung fu Melvin and Howard, *DH* features a wise-ass street kid protecting a prince in disguise, who then gets left in the dust. Gordon Lau plays the wine-tasting prince who has slipped out of the palace for some R&R, and Jimmy Wang Yu plays Dirty Ho, a jewel thief he picks up on the way. The prince must fight his way back into the palace in time for the naming of the new emperor. One of the first kung fu movies to feature introspection and character

Tove) so you know that justice triumphs in the end.

The film has achieved cult status over the years. Author Richard Kadrey, an avowed Shaw Brothers fan, named a fictitious Los Angeles tiki bar after the film—it serves as a hub for characters to interact with other characters populating Kadrey's "Sandman Slim" universe.

The Chinatown Kid (唐人街小子)

1977 | After getting in trouble with local gangs in Hong Kong, a young man (Alexander Fu Sheng) flees to San Francisco, where the same gangs are still causing problems. He becomes a part of one gang, and eventually decides to play them against each other in order to clean up the town.

HKFOGs from San Francisco fondly recall Sacramento Street— poster for *The Chinatown Kid*.

development along with the requisite collisions of fists and skulls.

Eight Diagram Pole Fighter (五郎八卦棍)

1984 | Savage tale of bloodlust and double-crosses. The mood is bleak, angry, and depressing. It didn't help that one of Shaw's favorite sons, Alexander Fu Sheng, was killed in a car accident during filming. The spectacular final battle has Gordon Lau and Kara Hui taking on a gang of villains, in a room filled with a pyramid made of coffins. A battalion of monks show up to "defang the wolves;" a painful sequence in which the monks use poles or their bare hands to rip out entire sets of villain teeth.

Eight Diagram Pole Fighter is on the Hong Kong Film Archive's list of "Best 100 Chinese Motion Pictures".

The Flying Guillotine (血滴子)

1975 | The emperor is getting paranoid, and orders a loyal subject to invent an undefeatable weapon. The result is the infamous flying guillotine, a sort of a hatbox attached to a rope. Thrown like a frisbee, it settles on a person's head then swiftly slices it off! The device is yanked back and the newly-shorn corpse drops to the earth. The infernal Flying G also appeared in *The Flying Guillotine 2* and Taiwanese homage *Master of the Flying Guillotine*.

One-Armed Swordsman (獨臂刀)

1967 | A supreme swordsman gets attacked, but is saved by his servant who dies in his master's place. The swordsman takes the servant's son, Fong Kong (Jimmy Wang Yu) as his own, teaching him everything that he knows. But the swordsman's daughter grows jealous of Fong, and in an attack she orchestrates, Fong's arm is lopped off. He retreats, studies diligently and learns the one-armed sword technique, then returns and slaughters everyone. The first sword-hero film to feature extreme violence and brutality, which became a trope in many subsequent martial arts films.

The Legend of the Seven Golden Vampires aka The Seven Brothers Meet Dracula (七金屍)

1974 | Britain's Hammer Studios brought their brand of gothic horror to HK in this co-production with Shaw Brothers, directed by Roy Ward Baker. Dracula (John Forbes-Robertson) assumes the identity of a Taoist priest and flees to China, where

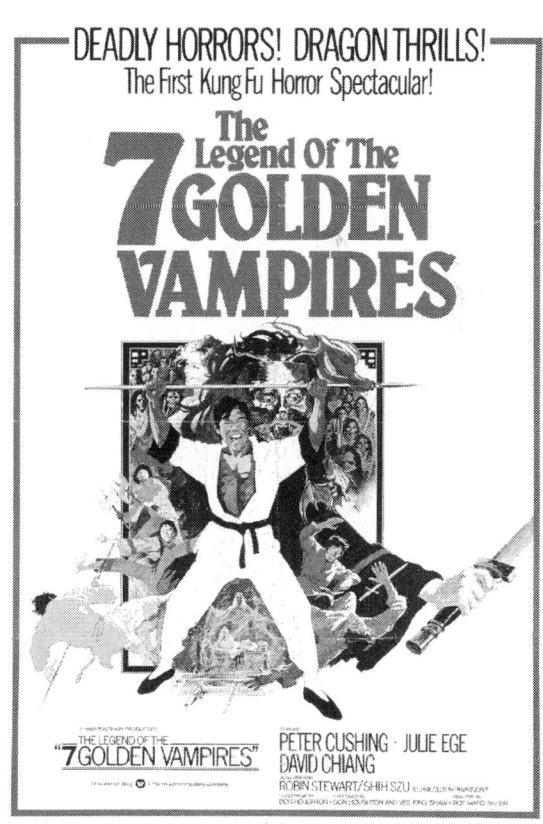

he resurrects an army of Chinese zombies. The fiend is pursued by Dr Van Helsing (Peter Cushing) who's aided by Shaw stalwart David Chiang. The East meets West schism reaches its absurd zenith when Cushing explains to Chiang that crucifixes are useless in China, and they must use statues of Buddha to repel the ghouls!

Five Element Ninjas
aka Super Ninjas (五遁忍術)

1982 | Another Chang Cheh dismemberer. A kung fu clan is decimated by a band of ninjas imported from Japan. The ninjas then destroy the people who imported them and set themselves up as rulers of the martial world. One sequence features baddie Michael Chan Wai-man stabbed through the abdomen, and as he keeps on fighting, his intestines slowly seep out of his belly. He's killed when he accidentally steps on his own innards and trips. In the end, the heroes pull apart the lead villain with their bare hands.

Black Magic (降頭)

1975 | Shot in Malaysia and directed by Shaw's go-to-guy for supernatural weirdness Ho Meng-Hua, *Black Magic* seethes with sexual jealousy and lust for pricey love-curses. The former is served up by lovely Luo Yin (Tanny Tien Ni) who's determined to snatch hunky Xu Nuo (Ti Lung) from his fiancée Wang Chu Ying (Lily Li). Tanny oozes avarice and other sins with her posh house/servants/car/outfits, all supplied by her now-deceased husband.

The curses are courtesy of sorcerer Shan Chien Mi (Ku Feng) who charges hefty fees for his black magic. The witchery involves purloined hair and blood, dismembered body parts, and human breast milk, but they work, as local lothario Liang Chia Chieh (Lo Lieh) discovers to his eternal regret.

Can Master Fu Yong (Ku Wen-chung) defeat the evil sorcerer and his fiendish worm-curses?

Thai poster for *Black Magic*.

RESOURCES

MORE SEX, BETTER ZEN, FASTER BULLETS

2020 UPDATE:

In 1996, we were sending people either to cinemas, or to video rental shops. Tech advances have shredded that paradigm, but all HKFOGs remember those days, and so do we...

FILM

The 1990s cinema experience was rich: you'd see these films on the big screen and meet fellow Hong Kong fanatics. And you could take newbies. They'd expect creaky chopsocky and they'd get ultracool Chow Yun-fat with matchstick and Berettas, or freaky-deaky blue-lit supernatural epics. You could sit there and watch them go rigid in their seats—silent, staring, mind racing...then out in the lobby they'd grab you by the collar and bombard you with questions.

The Landmark chain got prints from an LA-based company called Rim Films and would run "Hong Kong movie nights" one night a week—always double-features. San Diego, Seattle...but the best was the thousand-seat UC Theater in Berkeley. If a Jackie Chan or Chow Yun-fat film was playing, you'd show up 45 minutes early and stand in line to be sure you got in. The fans would go NUTS. It was more like a rock concert than a film—and of course, the lobby was bedlam.

Nowadays, Asian films are found at most film festivals. But several outlets are worth special mention:

Europe
Udine Far East Film Festival (Italy)

This film fest in northern Italy started showing Asian films exclusively about twenty years ago, and is now an internationally recognized showcase. Altogether there are about 60 films at the festival each year, including retrospectives, with around ten new Hong Kong films each year.

www.fareastfilm.com/EasyNe2/eng/homepage.aspx

North America

The Fantasia International Film Festival is a genre film festival that has been based in Montreal since its founding in 1996. Regularly held in July of each year, the festival isn't exclusively Asian, but regularly features films from Hong Kong and Asia, including premieres.

www.fantasiafestival.com/festival/en

The big festival in the States is the New York Asian Film Festival (aka Subway Cinema).

Subway Cinema is a nonprofit organization dedicated to the exhibition and appreciation of Asian popular film culture in all its forms, with year-round festivals and programs. In 2002, Subway Cinema launched its flagship event, the annual New York Asian Film Festival (NYAFF), which has been presented in collaboration with the Film Society of Lincoln Center since 2010.

www.subwaycinema.com

Cinemas have enjoyed a revival Stateside thanks to Alamo Drafthouse Cinema: cinema chain founded in 1997 in Austin, Texas. They now run about 30 cinemas and the chain is famous for its strict policy of requiring its audiences to maintain proper cinemagoing etiquette. They will throw you out of one of their cinemas for yapping on your cellphone or gawking at illuminated devices, and good for them.

They also revamped the fabulous New Mission Cinema in San Francisco's Mission District. We like Alamo Drafthouse, and we like their motto: "Birth. Movies. Death: It means you are born, you die and in between you go to the movies. It's a name that reflects the centrality of movies in our experience, in our lives. And it reflects the fact that the movies contain and comment on everything about life itself." (it's also the URL for their web magazine: www.birthmoviesdeath.com

However, the Drafthouse doesn't focus on Asian films exclusively, let alone Hong Kong films. Still, if there's one in your town, check it out.

Asia

Having participated in international film festivals, Sir Run Run Shaw was a firm believer in the importance of film festivals in showcasing the best a region had to offer. He also believed that film festivals provided good opportunity for those in the industry to renew fraternal ties. When Masaichi Nagata, President of Daiei, Japan, mooted the idea of forming a federation of Motion Picture Producers in Asia to hold annual film festivals in Asia, Sir Run Run was one of his closest supporters.

As a result, the South East Asian Film Producers Federation was inaugurated in Manila in 1953, with Japan, Taiwan, Hong Kong, Indonesia, Malaya, Philippines and Thailand as members.

The first Asian Film Festival was held in Tokyo on May 1954. It attracted 11 feature films and 10 non-dramatic films. The Golden Award was won by a Japanese film, *Konjiki Yasha*, and the Silver Award by a Thai film, *Sante Venus*.

In its production heyday, Shaw films from both Singapore and Hong Kong dominated the festival, winning scores of awards for acting and production value. The closest rivalry to Shaw came from the MP & GI Productions of Cathay's Yung Hwa studio in Hong Kong.

The Federation was renamed Asian Film Producers' Federation in 1957 when membership was enlarged to include South Korea. From 1982, the federation changed its constitution and name to include the Pacific. Today, The Federation of Motion Picture Producers in Asia Pacific (FPA) is the organizing body for the Asia-Pacific Film Festival. Each year, the Board of Directors selects a different member as the festival's host city. Participating member cities are Bangkok, Bombay, Hanoi, Hong Kong, Jakarta, Kuala Lumpur, Kuwait, Manila, Moscow, Seoul, Singapore, Sydney, Taipei, Tashkent, Tbilissi, Tehran, Tokyo and Wellington.

The APFF seems to have dissolved after its 2013 incarnation, but is the earliest example of an Asian film festival we've been able to find.

In Japan, the Focus on Asia Fukuoka International Film Festival is more Hong Kong-centric than the annual Tokyo fest. Organized by the Focus on Asia Fukuoka International Film Festival Executive Committee and the City of Fukuoka, it aims:

- To promote an understanding of Asia and Asian cultural exchange through motion pictures.

- To introduce excellent Asian motion pictures to the world and discover and foster new cinematic talent.

- To contribute to the creation of a "creative city of entertainment" by putting together new functions and features to promote city activity, business matching events and human resource development.
www.focus-on-asia.com/en/

The Hong Kong Asian Film Festival is run by the Broadway chain, has occasional local film premieres and adds small retrospectives:
www.hkaff.asia

And of course, cinemas in Hong Kong and

Macau show first-run Hong Kong films. Of special note are the Dynasty Theater in Mongkok, and the Teatro Allegria in Macau—both have the classic lighted-letters-in-metal signage at the box office.

The Festival

In Hong Kong, the annual Hong Kong International Film Festival deserves special mention. Established by the Hong Kong Urban Council, the first HKIFF was held in the summer of 1977 with a focus on world cinema, while the second HKIFF included its pioneering Hong Kong cinema retrospective on Cantonese films of the 1950s. In 1978, the HKIFF began publishing its acclaimed bi-lingual publications that have since been a notable hallmark of the HKIFF Society. The HKIFF was the first film festival in East Asia, and the first festival to focus on Asian films.

Many "film festival circuit" films are included, and since most will not be playing other local venues, it's a great opportunity for Hong Kongers to catch up. But the dedicated festival programmers aren't content to simply replicate the Rotterdam or Vancouver program in Asia. Each HKIFF presents a themed retrospective dedicated to Hong Kong films and filmmakers—this "Hong Kong Cinema Retrospective" section started with the second festival in 1978.

According to HKIFF Director TS Lo, many print-owners are loathe to lend them outside of Hong Kong. This means that these films often show only at the HKIFF—thanks in no small part to the efforts of programmer Law Kar, one of the best known and trusted names in Hong Kong film circles. The prospect of seeing long-buried Shaw Brothers films like Chang Cheh's *The Singing Thief* (1969) or *Hong Kong Nocturne* (1967) on the big screen draw film-lovers to the HKIFF. Other high points for Hong Kong fans are the catalogs, featuring interviews with local filmmakers and invaluable contributions from writers like Stephen Teo, Tony Rayns, Sek Kei and Li Cheuk-to. For years, these catalogs were virtually the only source of English-language information on Hong Kong films.

How worthwhile are these Hong Kong Cinema Retrospective sections? The "Mandarin Musicals" retro of 1993 presented the transcendent Grace Chang in a series of films from the fifties and sixties. A sold-out showing of *Mambo Girl* (1957) caused a phenomenon I've not seen before or since: as the opening scene faded up from black, the audience broke into a spontaneous ovation. The shot (any description makes it sound prosaic, but let's say it involves Chang's shod feet on a checkerboard-tiled floor) was so perfect that you simply couldn't NOT applaud. The film also included her hit "Jajambo", a catchy Mandarin-dialect ditty that instantly relaunched itself into the Pop Culture matrix of Hong Kong 1993. In tune with the nostalgia movement evident in the territory that year, celebs cut new versions of the Shanghai-goes-Caribbean tune and it blared from TV/radio airwaves.

The Hong Kong Film Archive has a symbiotic relationship with the HKIFF, and has staged mini-festivals and exhibits of film-related artifacts concurrent with the festival. This relationship means that the Archive has restored prints for exhibition at the HKIFF, which greatly enhanced retrospectives like "Transcending the Times: King Hu and Eileen Chang".

The festival's measure of support for the local industry has increased in recent years. The HKIFF's opening film for 1998 was Gordon Chan's *Beast Cops*. A sold-out crowd at the Hong Kong Cultural Centre was treated to a pre-film presentation with Chan, Kathy Chow and Anthony Wong, the latter garbed in ostentatious sunglasses and white shoes. Only in Hong Kong!

The 1999 HKIFF went even further in lauding local films. A "Director-in-Focus" section was added to the Hong Kong Panorama and the first director covered was Johnnie To Kei-fung (see the chapter "The Unexpected").

During the festival, films are shown at a number of venues around town, including Hong Kong City Hall in Central, the Hong Kong Cultural Centre in Tsim Sha Tsui, the Science Museum in TST East and other venues. The exact dates for the HKIFF fluctuate from year-to-year, but hover around Easter. Schedules are available online early in the year.

Hong Kong International Film Festival:
Tel: (852) 2970-3300
E-mail: info@hkiff.org.hk
www.hkiff.org.hk

The Archive

The term "archive" conjures up images of dusty shelving crammed with crumbling treasures, tended by desiccated denizens bowed double by the weight of history. In the case of the Hong Kong Film Archive, however, this brittle model shatters.

The archive was created in 1993, decades after it was needed to preserve now-lost fragments. The attitude of many Hong Kong film studios towards their product has traditionally been one of disposability: crank out the films, wring out the box office, then bin 'em. The perennial focus of Hong Kong filmmakers is financial return, and during the gravy years (which ended around 1993 as the apocalyptic footfalls of Spielberg's dinosaurs sent the local industry into a tailspin), preservation of the product seemed absurd.

Perhaps it was the burgeoning interest among English-speaking fans that helped serve as a catalyst for collation. Perhaps it was the looming handover that tweaked the nostalgia gland and helped spur a fascination with bygone days and teenage idol Josephine Siao's white plastic go-go boots. Perhaps the headlong rush onto the mobile com/data superhighway spawned the longing for scratchy monochromatic light projecting the electric shadow of Kwan Tak-hing. Whatever the genesis, the creation of the Hong Kong Film Archive is one of the defining events of Hong Kong film history. Its support will ensure that generations to come will remain aware of Hong Kong's celluloid triumphs.

That support has not been slow in coming. The archive has already collected over 2,800 film prints and 38,000 items of film-related material. Siao donated a fistful of her awards dating back to the sixties. Chow Yun-fat donated sixteen of his Best Actor awards. The late Chua Boon-hean donated hundreds of the screenplays he used to approve during his forty years as Shaw Brothers' Singapore distribution manager. And Kwan Tak-hing donated a trunkful of mementos, including props and costumes from his dozens of appearances as Wong Fei-hong.

The concept of film preservation is hardly new. At the advent of sound in the late 1920s, both the Museum of Modern Art in New York and the Academy of Motion Picture Arts and Sciences in Beverly Hills realized that the films of the silent era would be lost if steps were not taken to preserve them. These organizations began to selectively acquire films for study and appreciation. Throughout the 1930s, the film archive movement picked up momentum, leading to the founding of the International Federation of Film Archives in 1938. In the 1950s, the Academy laboriously re-photographed 3,300 paper prints from the 1893-1918 period, creating the single greatest resource for the study of early American cinema.

But Hong Kong lagged far behind the USA. As author Paul Fonoroff tells it in *Silver Light: A Pictorial History of Hong Kong Cinema 1920-1970* (1997): "I realized some time ago that in order to research Hong Kong film history, I would have to amass the primary source materials myself." 90% of the photos in Fonoroff's unique book are from his private collection.

Why aren't there more prints of old Hong Kong films? The main culprit is the region's heat and humidity. Unless prints are stored in properly controlled conditions, the forces of entropy make quick work of the raw material. Films shrink due to loss of moisture, solvents, and plasticizer—when some parts shrink more than others, the film buckles. Sprocket holes widen or tear, colors fade, and scratches are so common that their patterns are defined as "tramlines" or "rain." Worst of all is the dreaded "Vinegar Syndrome," in which the acetate emulsion experiences chemical release and separates from the film base, causing irreversible damage. The only sure prevention for this witches brew of decay is restoration by trained technicians followed by storage under controlled conditions.

Which is precisely what the Archive offers. The prints restored by HKFA technicians are placed in storage in the Archive's warehouse, and donating prints for storage does not represent abdication of copyright: Film companies without their own storage facilities can donate prints (subject to HKFA approval) and access them for duplication or video transfer as they see fit. The Archive works in concert with commercial interests—they understand that donors want their business interests safeguarded.

Preservation contributes more than good citizenry. The release of films on video is a golden opportunity to include outtakes, additional footage, trailers, or allow the director to create a "director's cut" which spurs interest in the video release. But without the raw material, in presentable shape, the opportunity for a re-release to pump up viewer interest and squeeze more revenue out of pre-existing material is lost.

The Archive's temporary office was housed in an Urban Council complex in the heart of Mongkok—a locale more suited to live-goldfish shops than limelight grandeur. Altogether, a staff of twenty (including Yu Mo-wan, who has spent 30 years chronicling Hong Kong film and compiling a multi-volume filmography of all Hong Kong films) labors to overturn the throwaway mentality which has decimated film-related collections in Hong Kong.

The Archive's most crucial project is their ongoing Oral History Project. This pressing task involves conducting interviews with Hong Kong film personalities, with the immediate goal of recording their memories before they either pass away or retire into oblivion. In an industry lacking a systematic documentation of materials and events, oral histories are critical. The Archive has interviewed over 150 industry kingpins (including Shaw Brothers' Chang Cheh and Golden Harvest's Raymond Chow) and publications are ongoing.

The Archive is dedicated to screening their treasures where possible. They have organized screenings in conjunction with the Hong Kong International Film Festival and each year, the Hong Kong Film Archive presents two mini-retrospective film programs, usually in February and September.

However, the full potential of a living, growing archive reached full expression when its permanent home opened in January 2001. The structure's primary purpose is to serve as a controlled environment for preservation of film prints from the Hong Kong film industry. In many cases, the copies being stored are the only ones in existence.

Apart from collecting and restoring prints and other related film materials, the archive staff will also catalogue its materials into data to be stored in its library system for access by scholars and researchers. The new building also houses a 128-seat cinema, an exhibition hall, film laboratories, and a library of film books. The Archive sponsors film shows and exhibitions, holds educational seminars and discussions, and publishes study materials, including a complete Hong Kong filmography.

The Archive started operation in 1993, when its Planning Office was established by the then Urban Council. Besides conducting campaigns to secure and preserve films and related materials, it also launched a series of publications and presented film programs and exhibitions. The Archive joined the International Federation of Film Archives (FIAF) in 1996. Upon the dissolution of the Urban Council, the Archive became a part of the Leisure and Cultural Services Department in 2000.

The Archive building, opened in January 2001, houses a cinema, an exhibition hall and a resource center. Thanks to the support of filmmakers, film companies and movie lovers, the Archive has been able to put together a vast collection of treasures. It is their mission to open the Archive's collection to the public and to facilitate researchers and filmmakers in using the materials we have accumulated, so that the heritage of Hong Kong cinema can be shared. The building is open to the public and admission is free.

How to donate material to the Archive

The Archive collects a wide range of materials that illuminate the development of local film culture. They also collect materials that facilitates research on local cinema history, as well as independent films and artifacts that illustrate the development of the local film industry. Most donations come in mixed categories including film elements, prints and trailers; audiovisual materials in different formats; documents and graphics that come about in both pre- and post-production such as production files, agreements and financial records, correspondence, scripts, house programs, posters, stills, photographs, press books, interviews, previews and reviews, manuscripts and personal papers; props, costumes and other artifacts. The Archive welcomes you to join them in preserving the rich film culture of Hong Kong by donating your cherished memorabilia. Please feel free to contact them with any questions.

Hong Kong Film Archive
50 Lei King Road, Sai Wan Ho, Hong Kong
Tel: (852) 2739 2139
E-mail: hkfa@lcsd.gov.hk
Website:
https://www.filmarchive.gov.hk/en_US/web/hkfa/aboutus/openhl.html

VIDEO

We mentioned it in the beginning but we'll do it again: most of these films are available subtitled on DVD or Blu-ray. There are different region-codes for different parts of the world for both formats, and it's up to you to make sure your player supports the product's region (we recommend multi-region players).

The Hong Kong Film Archive
香港电影资料馆

This world-class facility houses Hong Kong's impressive film history. Complete with both an ultra-modern film storage facility and public areas for screening films, the facility has the most comprehensive collection in Hong Kong.

保存了珍贵的电影拷贝、相关的影音资料及电影书刊等，让旅客及市民有机会分享及重温昔日珍贵的电影片段，也希望使香港的电影文化事业得以延续。

game. VHS versions with burned-on Chinese/English subs provided great Hex Errors (cracked subtitles), but expository scenes when characters wear white shirts or sit in front of a white tablecloth were maddening.

Audio is an increasingly important part of home-video setups, but realize that most Hong Kong films were shot with little or no attention paid to audio quality. Sound was usually added in post-production as films were released in Mandarin or Cantonese versions, depending on the market.

And of course, some are dubbed in English and other languages. The speed with which these films were produced (the highest annual total for Hong Kong films is about 230: that's over four films a week) precluded close attention to soundtrack-detail. We prefer the original language—generally Cantonese, with bits of other languages mixed in.

If your presentation offers a 2-channel or mono soundtrack, with readable English subs and a decent picture, you're ahead of the

GLOSSARY

MORE SEX, BETTER ZEN, FASTER BULLETS

Anime Animated version of manga, a Japanese comic book form known for its stylized presentation of often violent and explicit subject matter. Some HK films (*Story of Ricky*, *Wicked City*, Jacky Chan's *City Hunter*, *Saviour of the Soul*) are based on or styled after on existing anime or manga works.

Cantopop Formulaic pop music sung in Cantonese. Film stars often have Cantopop careers on the side, and may be more famous for their music than their acting. But Cantonese, with its multiple tones, is tough to sing. Reproducing the tones for meaning—while sticking to the melody—motivated Cantopop superstar Sally Yeh to say that "singing in Cantonese is like singing in prison."

Category III This is the "adults-only" category, reserved for films with nasty sex and/or violence. A few films have been slapped with a Cat III tag solely for inventive abuses of Cantonese, which is pretty impressive (see page 304).

Char siu bao Steamed buns filled with roast pork. A favorite with Hong Kongers and impecunious writers working a VCR remote control to capture that sublimely cracked subtitle.

Chi The breath of nature. Chi symbolizes a cosmic force that created the universe, whose duality (yin/yang) is expressed in many ways, like inhalation/exhalation. Martial arts teach how to concentrate one's chi energy and apply it (often with a loud yell).

To chop In addition to its traditional meanings, this verb means to attack someone violently with a machete-like weapon referred to as a "chopper" (cleavers are also used, although they're more common and thus become impromptu weapons). Premeditated chopping attacks are rare and bloody, and the most skilled attackers aim to cripple their victims permanently rather than kill them.

Durian A football-sized fruit with a hard, spiked exterior. If you wanted to grab a tropical fruit to bash in the head of a bad guy, you'd pick a durian. Hack one open and a durian yields a unique combination of delectable flesh and rotting garbage stink: "the taste from heaven with the smell from hell." Many Asians love the fruit, but most Asian hotels and public conveyances ban durians from their premises.

Eunuch In Imperial China, males who voluntarily subjected themselves to castration became eligible for tops political posts which were denied the betesticled. Known as eunuchs, they wielded considerable power within their areas of influence. Voluntarily ceding male "essence" often leads to an increase in supernatural power in HK movies, and older eunuchs are fearsome adversaries.

Face You can view this as "respect" and it's important in all societies. It's just a bit more complex in Chinese society, especially in films featuring gangsters, molls and cash. Debates over a lack of face given by one to another often lead to cinematic free-for-alls between various factions.

Fatty anyone not as thin as a straw can be referred to as "Fatty" in Hong Kong movies. Peter Coe and his friend Dave, Thirteenth and Fourteenth Sifus of Dumpling Thunder Fist, insists that the "Gang of Fatty" referred to by Michelle Yeoh in *Butterfly and Sword* must be an elite cabal of HKers. They swear that being down with the Gang of Fatty attests to one's Hong Kong film savvy, or proves that you were at a banquet with portly Hong Kong actor Kent Cheng.

Feng shui Literally "wind and water", feng shui is the ancient science of arranging architectural elements, furniture and other objects to ensure that cosmic elements remain undisturbed by earthlings. It requires a geomancer to scope out the surroundings, often with the help of a divining wheel. When Bruce Lee moved into Kowloon Tong (a place notorious for bad feng shui), he had an enormous feng shui mirror put on the roof of his house to deflect the evil energy. A typhoon blew the charm off his roof and Lee died soon thereafter.

Feng shui mirror Octagonal mirror whose round reflective center often has a Yin/Yang symbol. Rectangular block diagrams around the edge represent the I-Ching. Can be used as a weapon against ghosts.

Fist game This noisy guessing game is played in hostess bars or at banquets or other gatherings. Opponents throw out a number of fingers as they chant in ritualized fashion. Basically, they are guessing the number of fingers their opponent will display. Loser has to slug down a glass of something alcoholic, which is the point of this rather silly game. If you see characters in an Hong Kong movie shouting and gesticulating with their fingers, then drinking, now you know what they're doing. Amazingly, a brief English-language version of this game appears on the English soundtrack on the *Beast Cops* DVD.

Gai Literally, "chicken", but also slang for "callgirl". The punning possibilities are myriad and obvious. The word for "duck" is used to refer to working boys rather than working girls. Some people like chicken, some people like duck.

Grand Guignol Established in 1897, Paris's *Théâtre du Grand-Guignol* was notorious for their repertoire of horror plays, plays so horrific that a doctor was stationed in the lobby to revive fainting spectators. The theatre's fame was so great that Parisian guidebooks used to list it among the city's most popular attractions along with the Louvre, the Eiffel Tower, and legalized brothels. The phrase "Grand Guignol" became synonymous with bloodletting and gore.

Grindhouse An inner-city theater—often a faded Golden Age movie palace—which for many years was the only US venue for HK fare. Your feet would stick to the floor and lycanthropic drunks howled in the seats behind you. Today they've been supplanted by mallplex corporatia. However, directors Quentin Tarantino and Robert Rodriguez created a three-hour montage of features, trailers and addenda in 2007 simply called "Grindhouse" which conjured the grindhouse experience and lent it hipster-legitimacy that endures.

Gwailo A foreigner of American, British or European extraction. Literally: "foreign ghost" or "foreign devil." Some controversy over whether gwailo is a derogatory term or not. Depends on how you say it, but basically, nah.

Gyonsi A Chinese vampire. These "hopping ghosts" hop up in many a spooker.

HKFOGs Hong Kong Film Original Gangstas. Acronym made up because it sounds cool. If you contributed to alt.asian-movies, you know what we're talking about.

Horsehair wigs "As a common law jurisdiction, court dress in Hong Kong is practically the same as court dress in England and Wales," notes Wikipedia. This means that, in courtroom scenes in Hong Kong movies, lawyers and judges wear black robes and ornate white wigs originally made of dyed horsehair. This oh-so-British tradition was, surprisingly, not scrapped after the handover. So now you know why Zhang Jingchu wears that wig during her court scene in *Beast Stalker*.

ICAC The Independent Commission Against Corruption, founded in the mid seventies. A watchdog organization that keeps high-level corruption to a dull roar in the SAR. The ICAC story was made into a 1993 film, *First Shot*, starring Ti Leung, Maggie Cheung and Charles Heung.

Macau The tiny Pearl River Delta community is sixty kilometers from Hong Kong and its successful gaming industry made it a known haven for goodfellas. Its fascinating blend of European roots and Chinese soul (Macau was a Portuguese colony for four centuries) has given it a character far different from nearby Hong Kong. On December 20 1999, Macau returned to Chinese rule for the first time since the sixteenth century, becoming (like Hong Kong) a Special Administrative Region. Technically, it's not an SAR though—but rather an RAEM, as the acronym is taken from the Portuguese term.

Madam A policewoman, not a hooker. In some HK films, though, policewomen comically portray hookers in order to catch criminals.

Mahjong The Hong Kong equivalent of bridge, this four-player table game is a noisy and fun way to lose money. Rather than flimsy playing cards, plastic tiles are used, which are slapped on the table as players blister their way through a four- or five-hour mahjong session. The combatants noisily criticize their fellow players' gutless, sure-to-lose strategies as the tiles flip belly-up. Characters in supernatural films sometimes end up in a ghost mahjong game, which is not a pleasant sort of contest.

Méliès, Georges Early 20th century French director who single-handedly invented every special effect in film's pre-digital past. Méliès created nothing but flights of fancy, and is best known for *A Trip to the Moon* (1902), a film which depicts an Earthly rocket which flies directly into the eye of the Man in the Moon. Although the Frenchman never traveled to the East, we can't help but think that the unheralded Father of Special FX is sitting on a cloud somewhere, his wings shaking with laughter over *Mr Vampire* or *Zu*.

Mongkok Famed area of central Kowloon favored by HK filmmakers seeking that cluttered urban look.

NG A "no-good" take. These used to end up on the cutting-room floor until Jackie Chan started including montages of NGs under the closing credits of his films.

Ninja Japanese assassins. Not part of the Chinese warrior tradition, but in the pan-Asian glare they turn up in HK films, often as heinous villains.

PRC The People's Republic of China, often simply referred to as the mainland.

PTU Police Tactical Unit, one tier up from typical Hong Kong cops. PTU officers wear berets and snappier uniforms. They're also more highly trained, and walk street beats on a regular basis.

RHKP Royal Hong Kong Police (pre-1997). Hong Kong's police force functioned under the auspices of the Queen of England, and some of the officers were (and are) British. Even when beat cops talk to Chinese supervisors in Cantonese, the conversation ends with "Yes, sir!" said at attention. Post-1997, the force is known as the Hong Kong Police and the crown atop their logo was replaced by the bauhinia flower which is the emblem of the HKSAR.

SDU Special Duties Unit, the equivalent of SWAT teams elsewhere. Black tactical gear, body armor, helmets, Heckler & Koch 9mm submachine guns—these troops are highly trained and only deployed during crisis situations.

Seppuku Ritualistic Japanese suicide by self-evisceration. Also known as *hara-kiri*.

Sifu A respected teacher of martial arts or Taoist technique. Sifus can be either male or female, but are usually portrayed as older men with eyebrows out to here.

Swastika A four-armed symbol with right-angled endpieces. A Buddhist symbol in use for over eight centuries, swastikas still denote vegetarian restaurants and food products in Asia. Misappropriated several decades ago by a frustrated Austrian artist.

Tael Ancient unit of measurement, still used for gold. Also still in use: the catty, another eccentric measuring unit used for foodstuffs.

Triads Chinese gangster societies. More than 40 are reported to have operations in Hong Kong, though there are only two or three main market share leaders and influence has waned over the years. Triad societies participate in traditional criminal enterprises like gambling, loansharking and prostitution, and have also branched out into legitimate businesses. The triad lifestyle—money, guns and girls—is prime film fodder.

Wai gor Literally "Brother Wai", this is the Cantonese term for Viagra. It's a homonym but also a pun—just as "*sai lo*" means "little brother" but is also slang for, well, it applies only to men and you can probably guess now can't you.

Walled City of Kowloon When the Chinese ceded HK to the Brits in the 19th century, they walled off a small portion of the territory and declared it part of China, a face-saving gesture. Since HK laws did not extend to this enclave, it became a haven for criminals, who turned it into a rabbit warren of illegal businesses and overcrowded residences for undesirables. The Walled City was demolished in the early 1990s but has since acquired cult status. It's the subject of books and documentaries, and both the 1982 Shaw Brothers film *Brothers from the Walled City* and 1984's *Long Arm of the Law* have sequences shot *in situ*. It's been reproduced in video games and a partial recreation of the Kowloon Walled City exists in the Kawasaki Warehouse, an amusement arcade in Japan between Tokyo and Yokohama. The design's atmosphere includes narrow corridors, electrical wires, pipes, postboxes, sign boards, neon lights, and frayed posters.

Wire-work A technique in which actors are suspended from wires, giving the illusion of defiance of gravity or outright flight. A staple in supernatural films of the 80s and 90s, when Hong Kong stunt performers were suspended by metal wires the thickness of a pencil. Nowadays, they use stronger cables and digitally remove them—allowing Hollywood heavyweights to "fly" or perform other stunts.

Wushu The organized-sport version of martial arts—you won't see it at the Olympics, but you will at the Asian Games. Like gymnastics, it's performed in costume either with or without apparatus, and judged by a panel of experts.

Wuxia Even a cursory explanation of wuxia is beyond the scope of any glossary. It's a genre of Chinese fiction that revolves around martial heroes who fight for righteousness, often against organized villains. Wuxia features protagonists and antagonists that exist in the "martial world"—an alternate universe populated with martial artists capable of mythic kung fu feats. This fertile fictional canon informs the plots of many Hong Kong films.

XO Expensive cognac packed in ornate bottles. In Hong Kong films, it's usually consumed in large snifters by underworld characters anxious to show off how tough they are.

Yakuza Pronounced "YAH-ku-zah" not "yah-COO-za": this Japanese wiseguy syndicate has been the source of countless films and film characters in Japan. They also appear, usually in cartoony fashion, as villains in Hong Kong gangster flicks.

Stefan Hammond finds himself in a predicament.

AUTHOR BIOS

**AMMOND** is co-author (with Mike Wilkins) of *Sex and Zen & A Bullet in The Head: The Essential Guide to Hong Kong's Mind-bending Films* and author of *Hollywood East: Hong Kong Films and the People who Make Them*. He lives in Hong Kong.

WADE MAJOR is editor-in-chief of entertainment site CineGods.com and appears regularly on NPR affiliate KPCC's *FilmWeek* program—he is also producer/host of the longstanding *DigiGods* podcast, as well as a regular guest on KABC radio and KNBC television. Major's work has been featured in the *Los Angeles Times*, the *New York Daily News*, People.com and ABCNews.com.

The author and/or editor of a baker's dozen of film criticism books, **MICHAEL BLISS** teaches writing, literature, and film at Virginia Tech. His latest book is *A Uniquely American Epic*, a collection of essays on Sam Peckinpah's *The Wild Bunch*.

JEREMY HANSEN is a writer and journalist based in Auckland, New Zealand. From 1997 to 2002, he lived and worked in Hong Kong, covering the city's film scene for LA-based *Variety*. He still thinks Wong Kar-wai's *Happy Together* is one

Jude Poyer

of the saddest and most bewitching films ever made.

From 1996-2004, **JUDE POYER** lived in Hong Kong, where he worked as a stuntman & "evil gwailo" actor. When not getting beaten up or killed by the likes of Jet Li, Jackie Chan & Jean Claude Van Damme, he was RTHK Radio 3's Hong Kong film reviewer. Now based in his native London, Jude puts what he learned in the East to use in the West. More info at: www.reelpowerstunts.com

DAVID CHUTE is a freelance journalist and film critic based in Los Angeles. He writes as often as possible for Film Comment, the LA Weekly, the Los Angeles Times and the video server at amazon.com. His favorite movie varies on a daily basis, but Seven Samurai, *The Killer*, Kiss Me Deadly, Sword of Doom, and Two Tars are never far from the top of the list.

DAVE KEHR is a New York-based film critic whose work has appeared in many anthologies and publications, including the *New York Times*, *Film Comment* and *Entertainment Weekly*. He worships at the shrine of Maggie Cheung.

ANDY KLEIN is a Los Angeles-based film critic who went bananas over Tsui Hark's *Peking Opera Blues* in the summer of 1989. He has subsequently written extensively about Hong Kong cinema for Variety, the Hollywood Reporter, the Los Angeles Reader, Bikini, New Times Los Angeles, and Martial Arts Movies.

ADAM KNEE is Dean of the Faculty of Fine Arts, Media & Creative Industries at Lasalle College of the Arts, Singapore. He has also held academic appointments elsewhere in Asia and in Australia and the US, and has written extensively on Asian and US popular film.

JIM MORTON is a film historian who writes about films that are either overlooked or forgotten. In the early eighties, he wrote and published *Trashola*, devoted to exploitation and horror movies. He was the guest editor for RE/Search's *Incredibly Strange Films*, the first book to take a critical look at exploitation and low-budget movies. He is currently working on a history of East German films, and is the author of The East German Cinema Blog: www.eastgermancinema.com

KAREN TARAPATA grew up in Detroit during the Golden Age of Kung Fu movies, first seeing dubbed classics in downtown grindhouses, then developing an addiction to everything Shaw Brothers at weekend triple features (martial arts/police, comedy/sentimental, softcore/horror) in suburban theaters catering to extended Chinese families. Karen currently works in Midtown New York, where she can eat pork bao and congee for breakfast. She proved her HKFOG cred by donating her collection of Southern Screen film magazines from the early 80s to the Hong Kong Film Archive.

MORE SEX, BETTER ZEN, FASTER BULLETS

FILM REVIEW INDEX

Symbols

9413 129

A

Above The Law. *See* Righting Wrongs
Ah Kam 98
Aloha Little Vampire Story 48
Angel 166
Angel 2 166
Angel Enforcers 28
Armour of God 186
Armour of God 2: Operation Condor 187
The Avenging Quartet 122

B

The Bamboo House Of Dolls 319
Battle Creek Brawl. *See* The Big Brawl
Beast Cops 130
Beast Stalker 16
A Better Tomorrow 3: Love and Death in Saigon 178
Beyond Hypothermia 144
The Big Brawl 204
Big Bullet 131
The Big Heat 71
Bio Zombie 37
Black Cat 157
Black Cat 2: Assassination of President Yeltsin 166
Black Magic 322
Black Magic With Buddha 124
The Blade 171
Blonde Fury 166
Breaking News 151
The Bride with White Hair 38
Burning Paradise 222
Bury Me High 73

C

Call Girl 92 73
The Cannonball Run 204
Centipede Horror 49
The Chinatown Kid 320
A Chinese Ghost Story 2 35
A Chinese Ghost Story 3 36
A Chinese Ghost Story 15
The Chinese Stuntman 97
A Chinese Torture Chamber Story 304
City Hunter 188
City on Fire 223
Crime Story 204
Crippled Avengers 309
Crocodile Evil 123

D

Deadful Melody 39
Death Triangle. *See* A Serious Shock: Yes Madam '92
Descendant of the Sun 310
Devil Fetus 40

Dirty Ho 320
Doctor Vampire 49
Dog Bite Dog 59
Dragon Inn 172
Dragons Forever 207
Dream Home 60
Dreaming the Reality 166
Dr Lamb 287
Drunken Master 204
Drunken Master 2 189

E

Eastern Condors 209
The East is Red 179
Ebola Syndrome 289
Eight Diagram Pole Fighter 321
Encounter of the Spooky Kind 2 210
Erotic Ghost Story 49
Erotic Ghost Story 2 115
Escape From Brothel 29
The Eternal Evil of Asia 41
Evil Cat 50
Exiled 145
Expect The Unexpected 146
Extreme Crisis 97

F

Fantasy Mission Force 191
First Mission 204
The First Time is the Last Time 63
Five Element Ninjas 322
Five Fingers of Death 313
Five Venoms 311
Flirting 73
The Flying Guillotine 321
Full Alert 224
Full Contact 17

G

Gangs 64
Ghostly Vixen 51
The Ghost Snatchers 50
The Golden Swallow 52
Green Snake 173
Gunmen 65

H

Hard-Boiled 19
Haunted Jail House. *See* Jail House Eros
Heart of the Dragon. *See* First Mission
Her Name is Cat 112
Heroes of the East 308
The Heroic Trio 158
Her Vengeance 73
Holy Flame of the Martial World 314
Holy Weapon 30
Hong Kong Showgirls 124
Hong Kong X File 124
Horoscope 2: the Woman From Hell 52
Human Lanterns 315

I

I Love Maria 179
The Incorruptible 74
Infernal Affairs 62
In the Line of Duty. *See* Royal Warriors
In the Line of Duty 3 159
In the Line of Duty 4 161
Intruder 147

J

Jackie Chan: My Stunts 98
Jail House Eros 53

K

Kickboxer's Tears 167
A Kid from Tibet 212
King Boxer. *See* Five Fingers of Death

L

Laboratory of the Devil 122
Legacy of Rage 132
Legendary Weapons of China 316
The Legend of the Seven Golden Vampires 321
The Log 133
Long Arm of the Law 65
The Longest Nite 148
Lost Souls 291

M

Mad Monkey Kung Fu 317
Magnificent Warriors 162
Malevolent Mate 123
Man Behind the Sun 291
Men Behind the Sun. *See* Man Behind the Sun
Miracles. *See* Mr Canton and Lady Rose
The Mission 152
Mission of Justice 167
Mr Canton and Lady Rose 192
Mr Vampire 20
Mr Vampire 3 43
My Lucky Stars 194
My Neighbours Are Phantoms 53

N

Naked Killer 110
Naked Poison 292
Naked Soldier 119
Naked Weapon 120
New Police Story. *See* Crime Story
Nightlife Hero 98
No Regret No Return 97

O

OCTB CASE: The Floating Body 303
The Odd One Dies 152
Once Upon a Time in China 174
Once Upon A Time In China 2 180
Once Upon a Time in China 3 180
One-Armed Swordsman 321
On the Run 66
Operation Pink Squad 2 54

P

Painted Faces 97, 213
Peacock King 214
Pedicab Driver 21
Peking Opera Blues 175
Pituitary Hunter 29
Police Story 195
Police Story 3: Supercop 23, 197
Possessed 2 54
PR Girls 123
Princess Madam 167
Prison on Fire 225
Prison on Fire 2 226
Project A 198
Project A, Part 2 200
The Protector 205
PTU 24

Q

Queen of Temple Street 67
Queen's High 30

R

Red Spell Spells Red 44
Red To Kill 293

Remains of a Woman 295
Return of the Five Deadly Venoms. *See* Crippled Avengers
Righting Wrongs 215
Rigor Mortis 46
Roboforce. *See* I Love Maria
Robotrix 118
Rouge 72
Royal Warriors 162
Runaway Blues 97

S

Satin Steel 163
Saviour of the Soul 54
School on Fire 227
Seeding of a Ghost 318
A Serious Shock: Yes Madam '92 156
Seven Brothers Meet Dracula, The. *See* The Legend of the Seven Golden Vampires
The Seventh Curse 47
Sex and the Emperor 117
Sex & Zen 25
Sex & Zen 3 113
Shaolin Challenges Ninja. *See* Heroes of the East
She Shoots Straight 164
Shocking Asia 303
Shocking Asia 2 303
Skin Striperess 303
Spiritual Love 55
Stone Age Warriors 168
The Stool Pigeon 69
Story of a Gun 168
Story of Ricky 296
Super Ninjas. *See* Five Element Ninjas
Swordsman 2 176
Swordsman 3. *See* The East is Red

T

Taxi Hunter 70
The Dragon Attack!. *See* Fantasy Mission Force
Tiger Cage 74
Tiger on Beat 134
To Live and Die in Tsimshatsui 135
Too Many Ways To Be No. 1 149
Trivisa 136
Trust Me U Die 123
Twin Dragons 201

U

The Ultimate Vampire 55
The Untold Story 2 300
The Untold Story: Human Meat Roast Pork Buns 297

V

Vengeance 150

W

Wheels on Meals 216
The Wicked City 177
Widow Warriors 168
Wild Search 229
Women's Prison 74

Y

Yes Madam! 168

Z

Zu: Warriors from the Magic Mountain 27

A HEADPRESS BOOK
First published by Headpress in 2020
headoffice@headpress.com

MORE SEX, BETTER ZEN, FASTER BULLETS
The Encyclopedia of Hong Kong Film

Text copyright © STEFAN HAMMOND
This volume copyright © HEADPRESS 2020
Cover & book design : MARK CRITCHELL : mark.critchell@googlemail.com
Cover model photographer : JEFF MEIN SMITH
Cover model hair & makeup : PEGGY WONG

10 9 8 7 6 5 4 3 2 1

The moral rights of the author have been asserted.

The views expressed in this publication do not
necessarily reflect the views of the Publisher.

Images are from the collection of the author unless noted
otherwise and are used here for the purpose of historical
review. Grateful acknowledgement is given to the respective
owners, suppliers, artists, studios and publishers.

All Rights Reserved. No part of this book may be reproduced,
stored in a retrieval system, or transmitted, in any form or by
any means, electronic, mechanical, photocopying, recording or
otherwise, without prior permission in writing from the publisher.

A CIP catalogue record for this book is
available from the British Library

```
ISBN     978-1-909394-64-3 (paperback)
ISBN     978-1-909394-65-0 (ebook)
NO-ISBN  (hardback)
```

>>HEADPRESS. POP AND UNPOP CULTURE.<<

Exclusive NO-ISBN special edition hardbacks and
other items of interest are available at

HEADPRESS.COM